TAKEN ON TRUST

TERRY WAITE
Taken on Trust

Hodder & Stoughton
LONDON SYDNEY AUCKLAND

British Library Cataloguing in Publication Data

Waite, Terry
Taken on Trust: Recollections from
Captivity
1. Title
283.092

ISBN 0-340-58196-4

The publishers and author wish to thank the Society of Authors, as the literary representative of the Estate of John Masefield, for granting permission to use four lines from 'The Seekers', a poem by John Masefield from *Collected Poems* (1938), and Faber and Faber Ltd for granting permission to use a poem by Saturno Montanari from *The Translations of Ezra Pound* with an introduction by Hugh Kenner.

Published by Hodder and Stoughton,
a division of Hodder and Stoughton Ltd,
Mill Road, Dunton Green, Sevenoaks, Kent TN13 2YA.
Editorial Office: 47 Bedford Square, London WC1B 3DP.

Photoset by Rowland Phototypesetting Ltd,
Bury St Edmunds, Suffolk

Printed in Great Britain by
Butler and Tanner Ltd, Frome, Somerset

To Frances, Ruth, Clare, Gillian and Mark

CONTENTS

ILLUSTRATIONS

(Between pages 114 and 115)

My father as a police cadet
My parents' wedding, 1937
First photograph, 1939
A school holiday in 1951
In uniform
A student in the early sixties
Commissioned into the Church Army, 26 July 1960
Marriage to Frances Watters, 1964
The twins, 1965
The family in Blackheath, 1981 *(Press Association)*
At Lambeth during the Runcie years *(Judah Passow)*
With Richard Chartres in 1981
Meeting Chinese leaders, Beijing, 1983
The Archbishop's meeting with Forbes Burnham, Guyana, April 1984
With Archbishop Runcie
Father Lawrence Jenco at the Vatican, July 1986
    (Arturo Mari/L'Osservatore Romano Città Del Vaticano)
With Archbishop Desmond Tutu, 1985 *(Popperfoto)*

(Between pages 274 and 275)

A cartoon which appeared in the London *Times*, 1985 *(Barry Fantoni)*
With Jean Waddell, John and Audrey Coleman and Iranian hostages,
    Tehran, February 1981 *(Amit Roy/Daily Telegraph)*
Meeting Colonel Gaddafi, Tripoli, 1984
At Gatwick with the Libyan hostages, 1985 *(Popperfoto)*
The hostages' letter to the Archbishop of Canterbury, 8 November 1985,
    and the Polaroids of the hostages
With Vice-President George Bush at the White House, 1985
    (David Valdez, The White House)
Jacobsen, Weir and Jenco, Lambeth Palace, November 1986 *(Popperfoto)*
In Beirut, January 1987 *(Associated Press)*
Outside the Commodore Hotel, Beirut, January 1987
With Samir Habiby, Christmas 1985 *(Press Association)*
Last picture before captivity, January 1987 *(Associated Press)*
Blindfold and magnifying glass
John Bunyan in Bedford jail, from a window in the Bunyan Meeting
    Free Church, Bedford *(Fidelity Lithographic Company Ltd)*
First photograph after release, 18 November 1991 *(Press Association)*
Blackheath, 1992 *(David Secombe)*

ACKNOWLEDGEMENTS

THERE ARE SO MANY PEOPLE to whom I am indebted for my release and recovery that it is impossible to name them all, but I want them to know how grateful I am for their care and support. To everyone who took the trouble to write to me and my family and to everyone who kept the names of the hostages alive – thank you.

The late John Lyttle worked tirelessly from Lambeth Palace to secure the release of hostages and his premature death meant that we never met. I think of him with gratitude. My mother, my brother and sister, and my cousin John also did everything they could for us. They experienced many difficulties, but they never faltered.

Soon after my release in November 1991 I flew to New York to thank the Secretary-General of the United Nations, Pérez de Cuéllar, and his envoy, Giandomenico Picco, for all they did on our behalf. Señor Picco is a brave and modest man to whom we owe much, and I am grateful to them both. Dr Gordon Turnbull and his colleagues at RAF Lyneham and at Headley Court were marvellous. What more can I say?

Otherwise I have restricted my acknowledgements to those who directly aided me in the writing of this book. First, the title: in the final months of captivity I was kept together with John McCarthy, Terry Anderson and Tom Sutherland. We discussed whether or not we would each write a book, should we ever be released. We suggested titles. 'Yours is easy, TW,' said John, '"Taken on Trust".' I have been unable to think of a better title than that and readily thank John McCarthy for his inspiration.

Samir Habiby and Kamal Khoury know more about the Middle East than I ever shall. They were always ready to respond to my questions, and I thank them.

In the past I had heard dismal stories about literary agents, but Mark Lucas in London and Sterling Lord in New York not only gave me sound professional advice, they also gave me a great deal of personal support. They have both become good friends and without them life would have been much harder.

Recently I read a review in which John Curtis was described as 'the prince of editors'. Both John in London and Anne Freedgood in the US well deserve such an accolade. I could not have wished for better advisers. Jane Birkett introduced me to the mysteries of copy editing and her help was invaluable.

Every word of this book has been written in my room at Trinity Hall, Cambridge. Soon after my release I was elected Fellow Commoner of the college and decided to spend the middle part of each week there. The Master and his wife, the Fellows, students and staff have given me more than they can ever know. In particular I would like to thank Graham Howes and also my friends at the Wednesday Club.

I decided to write this book by hand and filled several Cambridge refill pads. Wyn Kirkman in London worked long and hard to produce the typescript and without her expert help I would have been quite lost. My special thanks also to Russ and Posy Ewald and Virginia Binger in the USA, and to my friends in the Presbyterian Church.

It was Francis Bacon who said, 'The worst solitude is to be destitute of sincere friendship.' Fortunately I have not experienced that, and although many of my friends would not wish to be mentioned by name, I would like to record how much I value them, particularly those who supported me during the difficult year of 1986. I can't resist mentioning two: Beryl Bainbridge, who encouraged me in my writing, and Francis Witts for his constant help.

Finally, gratitude to my family for all they have endured over the years.

July 1993

FOREWORD

DURING MY LONG YEARS of solitary confinement in Beirut when I had no pen or paper, no books and no news of the outside world, I 'wrote' in my imagination. I travelled back to my earliest memories and recalled the sensations of childhood. As I lay chained, fearfully awaiting interrogation, I examined the events which had led to my capture. At times, when I thought of my family and friends, the process became too painful and I had to retreat for a while into fantasy or mental arithmetic. I always managed to return to my story and thus was enabled to preserve my sanity and identity.

On my release I took a pen and started to write. In Beirut I relived my past, and in Cambridge, where this book has been written, I have relived it yet again. There have been days when I have been gripped by fear and days of pure joy when I have experienced the beauty of solitude and the harmony of family and friendships. Living for years deprived of natural light, freedom of movement and companionship, I found that time took on a new meaning. Now I can see that past, present and future are carried in the experience of the moment, and the exhortation of Christ to live for the day has assumed a new depth and resonance for me. We all suffer. Many individuals have suffered so much more than I have. I am truly happy to have discovered that suffering need not destroy; it can be creative. I would wish that for my captors and for all the communities in the Lebanon, as I would for all who feel oppressed and without hope.

This is the story I wrote when I was totally alone. It concludes when, after four years, I was moved to be with other hostages. If you read this book as a captive, take heart. Your spirit can never be chained.

PROLOGUE

WHEN I AWOKE, it was dusk. For a moment I lay still, slowly, reluctantly returning to the conscious world. It was unusually quiet. A gentle breeze stirred the faded hotel curtains, bringing with it a hint of the sea. Somewhere in the building a tap was turned on, sending the pipes in my bathroom into spasm. I swung my legs over the edge of the bed and walked to the window. On the pavement below, the street vendors had gone for the day. The only people left were the journalists. They sat on the seawall, smoking, chatting, waiting like pilgrims for a miracle. I closed the window and drew the curtains, shutting out the last of the dying light. I had already packed to depart for London, and now I checked my pockets: one blank memo pad, one ballpoint pen. Nothing more. I debated with myself whether to wear my wedding ring or lock it in my briefcase. I decided to wear it and my watch. I tuned my small radio in to the World Service of the BBC. World News would be broadcast on the hour; it was a link with home. While I balanced the radio on my briefcase and waited for the familiar strains of 'Lily Bolero' there was a knock at the door. I opened it just enough to see who was there. As I had expected, it was one of my Druze bodyguards.

'Are you ready, sir?'

I invited him in, switched off the radio and made a final check. Everything was packed. It would be a matter of minutes to collect my bags and leave for the airport. I picked up a black leather jacket from the back of a chair. My bodyguards had spent several days searching Beirut before they found one large enough to fit me. Again I checked my pockets – nothing but a pen and a notepad. My guard pointed to a bullet-proof vest lying on the bed.

'Aren't you going to wear that?'

I shook my head. If one of the kidnappers wanted to kill me, he would be near enough to shoot me in the head; a bullet-proof vest would be useless. I took a last look around the room and moved towards the door. Several more guards were standing in the corridor, each with an automatic weapon. We walked towards the lift. A guard with a chest like a beer barrel propped open the door.

'We leave by the basement.'

The antiquated lift descended slowly through the faded glory of the Riviera Hotel. With a gentle groan it touched down, and the gates were cranked open. Two men went before me, two behind. We threaded our way through the subterranean maze, emerging in a side street. I turned up my collar and hunched down into my jacket. The road was full of potholes and strewn with bricks and slabs of broken concrete. It was raining when we reached the car. I squeezed into the back, totally surrounded by protective Druze. As we drove away from the hotel, I saw the journalists still watching and waiting and hoping. In a few minutes we were in a street close to the American University of Beirut (AUB). The car stopped, and I shook hands with the guards.

'Thanks for your help. Whatever happens, don't try to follow me.'

They smiled, large, friendly, roguish smiles. 'Be careful.'

I slipped out of the car and watched them drive away. It was dark, and apart from a few parked cars, the street was deserted. In the distance I could hear the sound of shellfire as Beirut warmed up to yet another night of carnage. By now a steady rain was falling. I walked briskly up the street, looking neither left nor right, past the petrol station, past the apartments, straight to my rendezvous. As agreed, the main door was left ajar. I pushed it open and went in. In the shadows, a pair of eyes peered at me from behind the barely open door of the porter's room. I looked straight back at them, and slowly, as if by remote control, the door closed. I stepped inside the lift and ascended to the apartment of my intermediary, Dr Mroueh. He occupied two apartments in the block. One he used as his consulting rooms, the other as his residence. He opened the door as soon as I rang the bell and invited me into his study.

'Hello, Terry, good to see you again.'

He smiled nervously and lit his pipe while I looked around. Nothing had changed. The same chromium-and-glass desk, leather chairs, framed certificates on the walls. He gestured to me to sit. We chatted inconsequentially until the telephone rang. He spoke softly in Arabic for a few moments and then stood.

'I am so sorry, but I have to leave.'

'Why?'

'A patient is in labour. I am needed urgently.'

'Can't you wait a little longer?'

'That is not possible – I am sorry.'

Somewhere in the back of my head a bell, which had been ringing gently for days, increased in volume.

'I have to go to the hospital. I'll leave the door on the latch. When you leave, please lock it behind you.'

We shook hands, and he left. I crossed to the window and stared down at the empty street. It was not too late to walk away. Within a few minutes I could be back at the hotel. I turned and looked at the bookcase. Nothing but medical tomes. I walked down the corridor to the surgery, slipped off my shoes and stood on the scales: 236 pounds – almost seventeen stone. Too heavy; I ought to be fifteen stone, probably less. I returned to the other room and paced up and down, trying to quell my mounting anxiety. I thought of Terry Anderson and Tom Sutherland and for a moment wondered what it was like to be imprisoned for month after month. I had been alone in this room for less than an hour, and already I felt the walls and ceiling pressing in on me. I sat in one of the leather chairs and tried to regain my composure. Then I heard it: the gentle hum of an electric motor. Someone was coming up in the lift. I stood and crossed the room. There was a faint thud as the lift came to an abrupt halt. I heard the lift door open, and a second later the doorbell rang. A small stocky man wearing a single-breasted suit stood on the landing. He was my principal contact with the kidnappers, and we had met previously. I could feel his nervousness.

'Are you alone?'

'Yes.'

He stepped into the apartment. 'Are you armed?'

'No.'

'Please, I shall have to search you.' He patted my body and turned towards the door. 'We must leave right now.'

We got into the lift and silently descended. In the lobby the porter's door was firmly closed. We walked into the empty street and found it was still raining. After a few paces, the man halted beside a large car.

'You sit in the back. If we are stopped, you must say I am responsible for driving you around Beirut.'

I climbed into the back seat, and we drove out into the night. As we went through the battered streets I remembered a similar journey I had made years ago in Tehran. Then, as now, there were no reliable guarantees. I got into a car totally at the mercy of kidnappers and was driven to a secret location. The Iranian Revolutionary Guards had kept their word; they took me to the hostages they were holding and returned me to Tehran a few hours later. Now, I had been given a promise that I would be allowed to see Terry Anderson and Tom Sutherland, who, according to their captors, were depressed and ill. The kidnappers knew it was an invitation I could not refuse. It was because my contact gave me his word 'as a Muslim' that I had decided to trust him. I peered through the side windows of the car. Every minute or two a brilliant flash of light illuminated the surrealistic landscape. Only an El Greco could have captured the stark drama of the scene. The pain, the horror, the light, the shadows, the beauty, and behind it all a people suffering, weeping, dying. Suddenly, without warning, the driver pulled the car to the side of the road.

'Why do we stop here?'

'You must get out – we have a puncture.'

I knew he was lying. It was obvious that we would change cars at some point. Why tell such a stupid and pointless lie? There was another car in front of us now, with two men in police uniforms sitting inside.

'Get into the back quickly.'

The man in the suit sat beside me. 'Now, I am sorry, I must blindfold you.'

He produced a strip of curtain material and covered my eyes. It wasn't the change of car that worried me or the blindfold. I had expected both. It was the lie. From that point on I began to prepare myself for capture. We drove for half an hour or so. My companions exchanged words in Arabic. I said nothing. It was as though I had walked on to a track and all I could do now was to follow it wherever it led. I have no memory at all of my thoughts and feelings during that half-hour of darkness.

Suddenly the car slowed. We turned into a side road, lurched through water-filled potholes and stopped. The door opened. 'Get out please.'

I stepped out of the car, guided by one of the party. From under my blindfold I could see an old apartment block. The southern suburbs? We walked a few paces towards the building and began to climb a flight of stairs. At the second floor, we stopped. A door was unlocked, and I was led through. I was conscious of other people in the room into which I was taken. As we crossed the floor and entered a side room, I could see several pairs of feet in the rough homemade sandals worn by the poorer members of the Muslim community.

'Mr Waite, I must ask you to change your clothes.'

Again, I had expected this. It would probably be followed by another body search – even an examination of each of my teeth. They were looking for locator devices, minute electronic instruments which, I am told, can be implanted in the body to enable an individual to be tracked. I removed my clothes and subjected myself to a search. A long Islamic gown and a pair of slippers were then handed to me.

'You must now wait some time. You can sleep.'

They guided me back to the main room.

'Some people will stay with you tonight. You must not speak.'

I sat down on the couch. Someone brought me a blanket. I swung my legs up, turned to face the wall and loosened my blindfold. Within a few moments I was asleep. I slept fitfully. Throughout the night I was conscious of people coming and going. Other people were sleeping in the room. Someone was always awake. I spent the whole of the next day blindfolded, sitting or lying on the couch. In the evening the man in the suit returned.

'Mr Waite, how are you?'

'I am well. When will you take me to see the hostages?'

'Later.'

'How much later?'

'Not long now.'

He handed me a sandwich bought from a street trader.

'Eat, Mr Waite. It's good.'

It was good. Pieces of chicken wrapped in unleavened bread. I ate it all.

'Now, Mr Waite, we must go. Please stand up.'

I stood.

'You must do exactly what I tell you. You must not speak – understand?'

'Yes.'

Several people surrounded me, and someone tightened my blindfold and pulled it down over my nose. People on either side of me took hold of my arms and led me across the room. The apartment door was opened. I felt a cool draught of night air. It was very still – so still that I could hear the breathing of the people around me. We waited – one minute, two, longer. Someone whispered. I was guided forward, at first slowly and then faster as we crossed a corridor. Within a moment we had entered another apartment. I was led to a couch and told to sit.

'You can sleep, Mr Waite.'

'How long do I wait here?'

'Not long.'

I heard some of the party leave the room. Others settled in a far corner. I put up my feet and slept.

During the whole of the next day I dozed. More sandwiches were brought. Once I was given some hot tea. I tried to assess my position. When I had agreed to visit the hostages I knew that I was taking a very high risk. I took it because I felt I must do everything within my power to help them and their families. If anything went wrong, I would have to carry the full responsibility. Up to now everyone had been polite. I had suffered no violence. I had been blindfolded for a couple of days but had not been chained or secured in any other way. However, something was amiss. The whole 'feel' of the situation told me so.

'You sleep a lot.'

Someone was standing behind me.

'I am very tired.'

'It is good to sleep.'

'When will you take me to see the hostages?'

'I don't know.'

'Who does know?'

'I speak little English – sorry.'

It was late evening of the second day. I sat blindfolded, waiting, wondering, hoping. The door opened.

'Stand up, Mr Waite.'

I rose.

'We are now going to take you.'

I made no reply.

'You must do as you are told. No speak.'

Once again I was surrounded by guards. No one spoke.

A voice whispered behind me, 'I am going to take the cover off your eyes. You must keep your eyes closed. Understand?'

'Yes.'

A door opened. Again a wait. A hand pushed me gently from behind. 'Walk.'

I moved gingerly down two flights of stairs. Someone guided me into a large van. A sliding door clicked shut and was locked.

'Sit down, Mr Waite. You can open your eyes.'

It was the man in the single-breasted suit. He stood by the door, holding a two-way radio in one hand and an automatic pistol in the other.

The van was littered with building materials, and the front compartment was completely sealed off from the back so that I could not see the driver or see out of the window.

'Are you taking me to the hostages?'

'Do not speak.'

I sat on a sack of cement. The van lurched forward, crashing through potholes like a drunken elephant. The radio telephone crackled into life. To my surprise it was a woman's voice. The man in the suit replied. Finally, we came to an unsteady halt, and I could hear voices. A roadblock? The driver was conversing with someone outside the van. The man in the suit looked anxious. Suddenly, the conversation ceased, a door slammed, we moved forward.

Again we must have driven for about half an hour. The road surface improved and deteriorated again.

'Close your eyes. Do not speak.'

We stopped. The van's engine was switched off, and it was deathly quiet. I climbed out, squinting through half-closed eyes. We were in a garage. I was guided to a far corner, where a trapdoor in the floor had been lifted.

'Step down.'

I looked down. There was a drop of about nine feet to an underground room.

'It's too far to step down.'

Someone below, wearing a scarf to conceal his face, pushed a cupboard towards the opening. 'Step on to that and jump.'

I stepped warily on to the cupboard and jumped down to the earthen floor. Both my arms were taken by other masked men.

'Close your eyes.'

They led me across the floor: twelve paces in all. We stopped, someone turned a key, a door opened and I was pushed forward. The door closed behind me, and the key turned again. When I opened my eyes, I was in an empty cell lined with white tiles. I sat down on the floor and looked around. The room was almost seven feet across and about ten feet long. The height varied between six feet and six feet nine. I could be certain about that because I am six feet seven inches tall and in places it was impossible for me to stand upright. A heavy steel door with several thick iron bars on top secured the entrance. Cautiously, I looked through. There were a number of cells in this underground prison, in which dim lights burned. I assumed they were occupied. I had heard of the underground prisons of Beirut: 'the Lebanese gulag' as Terry Anderson had described them. There were stories of prisoners being incarcerated for years in such places. I sat down again and began to prepare myself for an ordeal. First, I would strengthen my will by fasting; I would refuse all food for at least a week. Second, I would make three resolutions to support me through whatever was to come: no regrets, no sentimentality, no self-pity. Then I did what generations of prisoners have done before me. I stood up and, bending my head, I began to walk round and round and round and round . . .

« I »

A SMALL BOY sits on a garden chair under a clear blue sky. The day is part of that eternal summer which belongs to all who journey back through memory to the best of childhood. The boy sits at a table. A black box stands on it. Someone appears, turns a handle, and for the first time in his short life the boy hears music from a gramophone:

> Run rabbit, run rabbit, run, run, run.
> Here comes the farmer with his gun, gun, gun.
> He'll get by without his rabbit pie, so
> Run rabbit, run rabbit, run, run, run.

The reedy tones of the singer, the uncertain strains of the orchestra echo across the years, across the generations, across a lifetime.

Someone approaches the boy and takes his hand. Reluctantly he is led away, across a lawn, down a corridor, into a room chilled by the shadows of a fading afternoon. Before him is a window, the largest window he has ever seen. On the other side of the glass stand a man and a woman. They smile and wave at him. Someone tells the boy to wave back. He waves impatiently, anxious to return to the land of sunshine and rabbits. The lady has a handkerchief. She is crying. The boy tugs at the arm of his companion. He is told to wave once more. He waves and turns away quickly.

The boy is in another place. This time no window separates him from the man and the woman. The woman tries to embrace him, but the boy is afraid. Who are these people? Why do they want to capture him? He frees himself from the woman and hides behind a settee. Again the woman cries.

I sit on the floor of my underground prison remembering the dawning of conscious life. I have walked until I can walk no more. My feet are sore; my neck and shoulders ache from constant bending. I have measured and counted my paces. A quick calculation produces a total of seven miles walked today. Now, physically exhausted, I sit and explore my memory. The man and the woman were my father and mother. I had been taken away from them at the age of three because I had contracted scarlet fever. My mother was due to give birth, so I was put into an isolation hospital for some weeks. When I returned home, I had a new sister, Diana. My sister and I were never particularly close as children, largely because she spent a great deal of time with my younger brother who had problems with walking. In later life we became much closer. Could my early isolation in hospital be one of the reasons why my relationship with my parents was so ambivalent? Does it help to explain why relationships with other people have been so important to me all my life, and yet frequently so difficult? Wanting, even craving affection, and yet being afraid of it.

Someone bangs on the door of my cell. I quickly cover my eyes with the curtain material as I have been instructed. The door opens, and someone enters. I hear something being thrown on the floor. The door closes. After a moment I uncover my eyes. There is a piece of foam rubber and a blanket in front of me. I make my bed away from the door and lie down, turn towards the wall and tap gently on the tiles. Nothing. No reply. I tap again . . . silence. There are certainly other prisoners here with me. I have heard them being guided to the toilet. There is definitely someone next door. I tap once more. Nothing. Outside the shelling begins. I suppose I ought to feel safe deep underground, but I am afraid. Fears flash through my head. What if a shell hits the building above, and we are buried beneath the rubble? Perhaps we would never be found. Another knock on the door.

'You want sandwich?'

'No, thank you.'

'You want tea?'

'Yes, please.'

I hear liquid being poured into the small plastic beaker I have been given, and it heats up in my hand. The door closes. I sip the hot tea; it gives me meagre comfort. I lie down again and allow my mind the freedom my body is denied. The shelling outside sends me back to the years when soldiers marched past our house, singing, whistling, onwards to a war of indescribable horror. Slipping out of the front gate, I march alongside them in my four-year-old pride, until my confidence wavers. They stride on, down a road that leads through the Cheshire countryside directly to the trenches of France, the camps of Germany, the deserts of North Africa. On they go, singing their way towards a living hell and adding 'Tipperary' and 'Pack up your troubles' to my repertoire of wartime songs.

I return to the present, to my cell, and pray. I think of those who tonight are afraid. Of those who will die during the night. I pray for peace. I think of my family and friends. One by one I call them to mind, and in my solitude I hold on to them. Again I leave my cell and go back to the 1940s, to my first memory of church. The smell of pine, polish and old hymnbooks. I sit in the pew and hear my name called. Sliding out of my seat, I step into the aisle and march towards the altar, swinging my arms like the soldiers who passed our house. Why do the people in church laugh? The Vicar hands me a prize – for what, I can't remember: *The Three Little Kittens* published by Blackie – Wartime Economy Edition. The book is still on my shelves.

When I was four, I was sent to the village school at Henbury, across the road from the church. My mother gave me strict instructions never to cross the road without her. One afternoon, she was late collecting me. I looked right, left, and right again, as I had been instructed. I remember being blinded by a strong sun. I stepped into the road, and the next moment I was bouncing along the tarmac. Within a few seconds I was in front of a jeep, repeating my name, address and telephone number to a man in uniform. This was my first, painful contact with the American military forces. Some time later, while I was playing in the front garden, a jeep pulled up, and an American serviceman got out and came up the path with an enormous box in his arms. It was one of the famous American food parcels. I remember it distinctly because it was the first time in my life that I had seen a banana.

I lie on my makeshift bed trying to collect the fragments that remain in my conscious memory. The sights, sounds and smells of the forties. The warplane which crash-landed in a side road by the church. The scream of its engine as it passed within a few feet of our house. The smell of freshly baked bread in Pimlotts' bakery in Macclesfield. I must have slept for some hours. My watch has been taken from me, so I have no idea of the time. I find that disturbing, very disturbing. Perhaps it is early morning. I get up and walk towards the door. Looking through the bars, I can see the cell to my left, which is set at a slight angle. The guards have hung a blanket from the ceiling to make it impossible to see the occupant.

Immediately opposite is a shower and a toilet – obviously the place was constructed for long-term use. This underground prison must extend a considerable distance, I decide, since after the guards had left, they disappeared down a passage, and it was impossible to hear their conversation.

I return to my bed, fold my blanket and sit cross-legged on the floor. I want to pray. The words of the Communion service from the Book of Common Prayer come to mind. I find that I remember most of the service. When I come to the consecration of the bread and wine, as I have neither, I use my imagination and go back to a church I have known in the past – St Bartholomew's, Wilmslow, the church in which I was confirmed. I am sitting with people I love. Tomorrow I will imagine myself among friends at the Russian Orthodox Church in Kensington.

There are so many places to visit. I swear to myself that whatever is done to my body, I will fight to the end to keep my inner freedom. When the Communion service is over I meditate on why I am fasting. If I am strictly honest, I have to admit that I am refusing food partly because I am angry at my captors. I am also angry at myself. Angry at being such a fool that I could be duped so easily. Is anger really the main reason I fast? I decide it isn't. I want to be – need to be – very strong within. I know only too well how weak and vulnerable I am. Fasting will strengthen me. I will not eat for several days.

I remind myself of my vows: no regrets, no self-pity, no sentimentality. My only chance of surviving what is to come will be to develop an inner strength. This I tell myself I will do.

I have spent about four days in the underground prison – at least I think it's four days. The guards won't tell me the time, and I can only guess the hour from when they come to take me to the toilet and bring me food. I am allowed one visit a day to the toilet. They have given me a bottle in which to urinate. When they come to my cell, if I need to speak to them they instruct me to whisper. Whenever they knock on my door I must put on my blindfold and keep it on until I am alone and secured behind the locked door. They offer me food two or three times a day, and I refuse each time. To my surprise I don't feel at all hungry. At the moment hot tea, without milk or sugar, seems quite sufficient. The thing I find most worrying is not being able to measure the passing of time. If I am to keep myself together I must find some means of doing this. The first problem is to divide day from night. If I could hear the call to prayer from a mosque, that would be as good as a watch, but below-ground it cannot be heard. There is, however, a sound from somewhere above-ground that puzzles me. A curious thumping noise. I sit on the floor with my back against the tiles and listen. Thump-thump-thump. Of course, someone is beating a carpet. I remember standing on the flat roof of the Riviera Hotel and watching housewives hang their carpets over the balcony railings and beat the daylights out of them with a cane beater. That could mean it's mid-morning.

I start to walk again. As I begin, I have to decide whether I am going to measure how far I walk or not. If I keep track of the distance, it's difficult to be accurate and think at the same time. Each pace has to be counted and remembered. I decide to save my thinking until I have walked a mile or two, and off I go. Round and round. After some miles I lapse into a trance-like state. My body has settled into its own rhythm. At the front of my mind I count, and behind it I drift into extended dreams. How long can I survive down here? How long can I tolerate being alone? I stop, sit down and consider these questions. I have heard of priests in China surviving twenty years or more in solitary. If I can keep mentally and spiritually healthy, I can survive anything. Perhaps I will be free shortly. I lie on my mattress and return to my childhood . . .

I don't remember much about our move to Styal, eleven miles south of Manchester. We went there from Henbury to occupy a rural police station. It was then that I became fully conscious of the fact that my father was a policeman – Constable No. 556 of the Cheshire Constabulary. The house was large with a huge garden. The one room designated as the police office was furnished with a filing cabinet, some chairs, and a desk on which stood a candlestick telephone. To ring a number we had to pick up the receiver and wait for the operator in Wilmslow, some three miles distant, to answer. In the front garden by the gate stood a noticeboard. One regular poster advised locals to keep a sharp eye open for the Colorado beetle. Another gave advance warning of sheep-dipping, which my father had to supervise. Pictures of wanted criminals never appeared.

Almost as soon as we moved in, my father set to work on the garden. It was a wilderness, which he slowly and painfully transformed into a means of supplementing his limited income. Potatoes were planted to clear the ground. They were followed by all manner of fruits and vegetables: raspberries, blackcurrant bushes, cabbages and Brussels sprouts. In season my parents made pounds of jam and sold fresh fruit to visitors to the village. Sometimes the garden gave up unusual treasures: a George III penny, a silver fourpenny piece, numerous Victorian coins and one I later learnt was a token used to pay industrial workers in the previous century. I kept this collection of coins in a wooden box and cherished it for years.

My father was a man of great integrity and unusual sensitivity. He was born just over the Cheshire border in Kidsgrove, Staffordshire. His father had run his own painting and decorating business until he fell victim of the Depression following the First World War. During these difficult years my grandmother, an accomplished pianist and teacher, augmented the family income by playing the piano at the silent films. If I was able to persuade her, she would run through her entire repertoire for me.

My father did not have a happy childhood. Although he showed promise at school and won a scholarship that opened the way to higher education, he was forced to leave early to help provide for the family. On the few occasions when he spoke to me of his father, it was with sadness. For reasons unknown to me, their relationship was so poor that my father ran away from home in his early teens and settled in Chester where, after suffering considerable hardship, he joined the police force. The insecurities he experienced as a child marked him for life and affected my relationship with him.

When I first knew Greg's Mill at Styal it was in a sorry state. A handful of workers was employed to keep the machinery turning over. I remember seeing a small group of women walking along a country lane towards their cottages and being told that the mill had finally closed down that day. To me, it was a place of mystery – a place where my imagination could run free. The Bollin, normally a placid and quiet-flowing river, suddenly changed character when it approached the mill, seeming to throw itself into a frenzy as though it resented the industrial intrusion into its rural life. Ghost stories circulated among the children of the village. The mill manager's house, an imposing building on the banks of the Bollin, went into private hands. It was said that one night the daughter of the new owner saw the ghost of a former servant who was supposed to have thrown a child from a bedroom window into the river below. That was why there were bars on the window. The windows in the Apprentices' House were also barred. To me, the mill in its semi-derelict state was an eerie place. I couldn't imagine how my father could be so brave as to patrol there in the dead of night. Harry Greg, a direct descendant of the founder, lived in the village and occasionally opened his garden to the locals. He had the most wonderful model steam train which he would drive proudly round a track on the lawn. Although he was regarded with deference and respect by the villagers, he no longer had any real power in the community.

The farmers of Styal were hard-working and only moderately prosperous. Dick Watson drove through the village every morning with his horse and cart, which carried two or three milk churns, and he would measure out the milk directly into the jugs of his customers. John Hope ran the farm behind our house. Grenville Gardiner was the tenant of Oak Farm which was made famous when the old farmhouse was pulled down in 1875 and a crock full of money was found in the rafters. As the coins came from Charles I's reign, it was assumed that they had been hidden during the Civil War and then forgotten. I knew Oak Farm the best because Alan Gardiner, the son of Grenville, and I played on the farm together. The most exciting time of year for us was when the steam engine lumbered into the farmyard, pulling behind it a threshing machine and a baler. The engine did the rounds, visiting all the farms in turn. Extra helpers were recruited, and Mrs Gardiner would be kept busy in the kitchen preparing 'baggin', the local slang for refreshments: tea, cake and sandwiches.

Alan and I once shared a disastrous camping expedition on the farm. I had read of exhausted travellers finding a barn and sinking into the hay to enjoy a night of blissful sleep, so we pitched our small tent in a field close to the farmhouse, filled our sacks with straw and climbed in. Alas, the straw pricked our skin, insects bit furiously, and at midnight we declared the expedition over and made for home.

Next door to the police station was the old police house, which had been taken over by a building contractor named Tom Renshaw. Tom had been in partnership with his brother Jim, but they quarrelled, and Tom started his own business just a few hundred yards away from his brother's. After the quarrel they never spoke to each other again. Tom Renshaw was also the local funeral director. Many times I watched as he made the most superb coffins out of solid oak. A few yards down the road was the grocer's shop run by Harry Earlam. I can still see his dismal post-war window display: boxes of national dried egg and blocks of special margarine – nothing more. Harry Earlam also ran the post office and newsagent, and when I was old enough I delivered the morning papers and the *Manchester Evening News* to save money to buy my first bicycle.

When we moved to Styal, certain foods were still rationed. I remember my mother despairing at the inadequacy of the cheese ration. 'How will that feed a family?' she would say. We needed our plentiful garden.

Jim Mottram, the shoe repairer, had the shop next to the grocer's. His hands were blackened and cracked and as tough as the leather he worked with. Old Mr Slater ran a cycle repair shop across the road from the post office. Years before, he had had a car-hire business and his one magnificent limousine stood gently disintegrating in a garage behind the shop. Next to him was the Ship Inn run by Mrs Middleton. She made her upstairs sitting room available to the Rector of Wilmslow, Canon Reeman, who conducted my Confirmation classes there. I remember little of the instruction he gave, but I can still see in my mind's eye a most curious item of furniture: part of an elephant's leg, which was used to store walking sticks and umbrellas. Every week I gazed at this bizarre object as the Rector took his small class through the articles of faith.

The village was well if not over supplied with church buildings. All Saints Anglican church stood at the top of Hollin Lane. It was a simple, unpretentious building known locally as 'the tin tabernacle' because it had a corrugated-iron roof. I joined the church choir soon after we moved to Styal and sang in it all the years we were in the village. Since I had to deliver the newspapers, I rarely went to Sunday morning services, but I hardly ever missed Evensong.

It was in this building that the rudiments of the Christian faith were communicated to me, almost as if by osmosis. I became totally familiar with the Book of Common Prayer and without realising it at the time, developed a love of the English language. All Saints also gave me the basis of a musical education as I worked through hymns, chants and anthems. Once a year we joined the Methodists and the Unitarians, the other two churches in the village, usually for an evening of community hymn-singing.

The Unitarians were brought to the village by the Gregs who were apprehensive of the trade-union activities of the Methodists. They occupied an attractive little church situated at the entrance to Styal Woods. My dominant memory of the Methodists is their annual Christmas party and concert, which I attended on several occasions. I couldn't believe my eyes when Eric Newton, several years older than I and a demon bowler with the local cricket team, appeared on stage and gave a very creditable rendering of 'O for the wings of a dove'. At the end of the concert a large basket which had been suspended from the ceiling was lowered, and gifts donated by parents, aunts and uncles were distributed to the Methodist children. I always vaguely hoped that someone might have put a gift for me in the basket, but not surprisingly my name was never called.

It was difficult to be the son of the village policeman. I was known by everyone and had to be especially careful in my behaviour. This meant that I frequently spent time by myself. Every November the fifth an enormous bonfire was lit on the village green to celebrate Guy Fawkes Day, and after the fire had burned low a few boys would stay behind and bake potatoes in the embers. On one such evening I was alone, prodding a potato with a stick, when a group of boys came running past me. Without thinking, I left the dying fire and ran after them towards the village. As we were racing along, I happened to catch the leg of the boy in front of me, and he went sprawling on the cobblestones. There was a yell as he was seized by someone from behind and hauled away. At that point I left the group and made my way home.

I was lying in bed when my father returned. He called to me to come downstairs. 'Where were you this evening?' I felt a dreadful mixture of irrational panic, guilt and fear.

'At the bonfire.'

'How long were you there?'

'All evening.'

'Did you leave the bonfire?'

'No.'

'But you were running with some boys up the village.'

'Yes.'

'Why?'

'I was just running.'

'What do you mean – just running? You must have had a reason.'

Why was I running with them? I couldn't think. I ran because they ran.

'Did you know John Francis was caught?'

'No.'

'He says you were with them this evening.'

Was I? By now I was so afraid I couldn't think straight.

'What did you do?'

'I don't know.'

'You don't know, but you were running up the village?'

'Yes.'

I was now virtually paralysed with fear. The whole evening dis-
solved into a confused blur. I certainly couldn't explain why I had
been running with the others.

'I don't think you are telling me the truth.'

I was too bewildered to know. What was the truth?

He placed me over his knee and gave me a beating. I went to bed
in a state of miserable confusion. Perhaps I had done wrong. I didn't
know. Later I learnt that someone had put a firework through the
letter-box of a villager named John Snowball. As Mr Snowball lived
in a thatched cottage, this was a particularly dangerous prank. He
had given chase to the group, and the boy whom he had caught had
told my father that I was with the culprits. On this occasion W. S.
Gilbert's dictum about a policeman's lot not being a happy one
applied equally to Thomas Waite's offspring.

I don't know how long I have been lying on my mattress. Two
hours? Three? Possibly longer. It's hot down here. The tiles drip
condensation, and the air smells of disinfectant, petrol fumes and
sweat. The guards must be away in their own quarters along the
passage. I wonder who the previous occupants of this cell were?
Perhaps the very hostages for whom I was searching. There is not
a mark, not a clue in the cell to suggest the identity of any earlier
inhabitant.

The fasting has done me good. I feel well – even strong. I know
that can change quickly, but I will resist sinking into despair. I get
up and begin to examine each tile in turn. Perhaps one is loose –
someone may have left a message behind it. I crawl across the floor,
examine the walls – nothing. In every book about prisoners I have
ever read there have always been graffiti in the cell, or at least the
initials of a previous occupant. Here there is nothing but a blank
white waste. I return to my corner and sit down. Surely they will
release me soon. They know perfectly well who I am – they know
about my contacts. But perhaps I have seriously underestimated their
paranoia. They might keep me for years – or kill me.

Even worse, they might torture me. A sudden thought: Isn't that why underground cells are tiled? They are easier to clean up after torture.

Suddenly my stomach tenses. Torture terrifies me. The thought of deliberately mutilating a human being is utterly repulsive. Of course, they want me to be afraid. They want to 'soften me up', to get me to create my own fears and fantasies. I make a deliberate attempt to stop this train of thought. Just think of the people you have known, I tell myself, in Africa – in China. Jailed, persecuted, tortured, but still alive and wholesome, lovely people. Join them. Today you have entered a new community of the imprisoned. Become one with them. Hold on to light and hope, hope, hope. I am so alone. Only a few days, and I feel so alone.

I was alone in childhood. Not all the time, but at heart I was a solitary individual. Content to be alone with books. If only I had a book. Remember the bring-and-buy sales at Styal? Remember how you used to haunt the bookstalls and come home with armfuls? Dickens' *Sketches by Boz*, *Out with Romany by Meadow and Stream*, Stevenson, Ballantyne. Remember how you journeyed across the centuries, across the continents? Remember how you used to stand by the A34 in Wilmslow and trace its route on a map through Birmingham, Stratford-upon-Avon and beyond? Remember Arthur Mee wandering romantically through the British Isles? Oh God, memories of a lonely, romantic childhood. Now it is part of your strength. You know how to be alone. There is plenty to draw on – over forty years of memories, dreams, reflections. Remember everything you have said to others about the importance of the inner journey? Now you must take that journey without any external supports. Off you go – up with the sail and out across the sea of the unconscious. You may be shipwrecked, you may drown, but at least you have the chance to explore. Remember your first bicycle? Remember delivering newspapers and bread and vegetables from the garden, all to save money for the chance to explore the world beyond Styal? Remember your feelings – impatience that the local garage took so long to respray the second-hand frame, excitement when your father came home with a box of new parts?

'What kind of handlebars do you want?'

'Racing.'

'Butterfly would be better. Not so tiring.'

Racing handlebars had caught my imagination. Racing handlebars it had to be. Remember the disappointment when you didn't get a

Derailleur gear – only a Sturmey Archer three-speed? No matter, it looked like a new racing bicycle. At last ready and away – past the cricket ground, along by Ringway Airport, down into Ashley and a stop by Rostherne Mere. Home seems a thousand miles away. Cheese and tomato sandwiches. How well the bike looks – light blue frame, gleaming chrome handlebars. Back aboard it and on towards Chester. What a lovely city Chester is. I walk, pushing the bike around the Roman walls. A small restaurant advertises lunch. The aroma is over-whelming. Steak and kidney pudding – shepherd's pie – why did I eat my sandwiches so early in the morning? I rummage in my pockets: a couple of shillings. Certainly not enough for lunch in a restaurant. Even if I had enough money, I would be too shy to enter and order a meal. I go on round the wall, leaving the restaurant to be recalled and savoured forty years later. I return home as the light ebbs away after a magical day.

There are great variations of temperature down here. At times it is stiflingly hot, later it becomes so cold that I shiver like a wounded animal. How I wish it were possible to communicate with my fellow prisoners. Further gentle tapping on the wall brings no response. Perhaps they can't hear or are too afraid to answer. Fragments of an Italian poem pass across my mind:

> *When the light*
> *goes, men shut behind blinds*
> *their life, to die for a night.*
>
> *And yet*
> *through glass and bars*
> *some dream a wild sunset,*
> *waiting the stars.*
>
> *Call these few, at least*
> *the singers, in whom*
> *hope's voice is yeast.*

My fists are tightly clenched; my whole body is tense. Relax, relax, breathe deeply. God, I'm tired. What am I afraid of? Again torture – that scares me. I am bound to be interrogated. Perhaps that's the only reason they have taken me, simply to find out what I know. Well, do your worst. I have nothing to regret, nothing. Thank God I can stand on the truth. I must reconstruct, as best I can, all I can

remember about this whole business. Either that or I allow myself
to sink into amnesia, and why do that? Already anxiety is attacking
me to such an extent that I forget the most elementary things –
names, places, events. A deliberate act of reconstruction might help
keep my mind alive and prevent me from deteriorating into a frightened, cowed specimen of humanity. When I first entered this cell I
said, 'No regrets.' Do I regret? I regret causing my family and friends
suffering, but that's different. With hindsight I might have taken
other decisions, but given the information I possessed, I have no
regrets at all – none. Then there is no problem. The real struggle,
the long-term fight against injustice, lies in the moral and spiritual
realm. I stood by what I believed and knew. If I did that, I can face
anything: torture, solitary confinement, even death. Steel yourself,
man. Grow up.

Someone is moving outside my cell. I hear voices. My door
opens.

'You want eat?'

'No, thank you.'

'Why not eat?'

'I don't want to eat.'

'OK.'

The door closes, and I am alone again. A small victory but a
pathetic one. Eventually I will eat; I have no intention of committing
suicide. First I will clear my mind, I will be strong. I repeat these
trite sentences to myself to build up a reservoir of inner courage.
I repeat one-line prayers: 'God give me strength', 'God help
me'. I am divided within. Why should I ask for God's help? What
am I really asking for? Simply grace and strength to pass with dignity
through whatever comes. I chose to enter this ring. No one told me
to. My choice, my responsibility.

My mind goes back to 1984. A September afternoon. I sat behind
my cluttered desk in Lambeth Palace, the Archbishop of Canterbury's official London residence. Outside in the courtyard a small
party of visitors gazed at an ancient fig tree while their guide repeated
some improbable story. The sun shone so brightly that I half drew
one of the heavy wooden shutters to give myself some shade. Before
me lay several thick files: details of journeys made, or about to be
made, by the Archbishop, Robert Runcie, to China, Australia, New
Zealand, Singapore. They represented the background work done
by the Lambeth staff. I picked up another folder labelled 'Libya'. In

that country four British citizens were being held, and for months I had been striving for their release. I was tired, tired of so much travel, of struggling with the bewildering political situation in Libya, of trying to do my work for the Archbishop and working for the release of hostages as well. Someone tapped on my door, and Stella Taylor, my assistant, crossed the room with an armful of documents.

'Not much peace, I'm afraid.' She smiled and placed the papers on the overcrowded desk. 'You must sign these so that they can be posted tonight. These people,' she handed me a sheet of paper, 'must be phoned before six. The Archbishop wants to see the final programme for his next overseas visit at ten in the morning. Here are the tickets and papers for your visit to China next week. This folder,' she placed another thick bundle before me, 'is from people who want help.'

Every day letters arrived from individuals facing some personal crisis: bereavement, imprisonment, illness. I attempted to reply personally to each and to help where I could.

'Finally,' Stella said, 'Mrs Russell has been on the phone. She wants to see you, if only for a few moments.'

Carol Russell was the wife of one of the Libyan hostages. I had assured the families that I would make every effort on their behalf, but I simply did not have the time or the emotional energy to meet them frequently and offer them the support they so needed and deserved.

'Should I see her, Stella?'

She was silent for a moment.

'It would help. She is desperately worried.'

'OK, try and find some time tomorrow. Otherwise it will be a couple of weeks before we can meet.'

Without Stella's competent administration, my life at Lambeth would have been quite impossible. I felt a twinge of guilt at how much I was asking of her. Often she arrived early and left late simply to keep abreast of the volume of papers facing us.

I took one of the files and began to work my way through it. The telephone rang. It was Stella.

'A call from the USA. A Reverend Fred Wilson asking to speak personally to Father Terry Waite.'

I smiled. I was often taken for a clergyman by those who assumed that only ordained men worked for the Archbishop.

'Do I know him?'

'No, he says he has never met you, but he would like a personal word.'

A soft-spoken American voice came on the line. 'This is Fred Wilson of the Presbyterian Church in America. We would like to come over and see you to discuss the case of Ben Weir.'

Ben, a Presbyterian minister in the Lebanon, had disappeared in May 1984.

'We know of your work with hostages and wondered if you could help us with Ben?'

My heart sank. I wanted to say no. There was already too much to do, far too much.

'It's really very difficult, Mr Wilson. I am totally caught up with the Libyan hostages at the moment. The Church should be involved in these matters on a humanitarian basis, but we have very slender resources.'

We continued to talk. Finally, I agreed that if someone from his Church came to London, I would discuss the case. I put the phone down and returned to my papers, not realising the path I had opened for myself.

'When we come into room, you cover eyes quick. Understand?'

The curtain material still serves as a blindfold. I use it whenever anyone comes into the cell.

'Quick, understand?'

This constant nagging to be quick with the blindfold irritates me but the threat is real enough. Released hostages had told me that failure to comply quickly could lead to a beating, or even to being shot.

'I am quick. Why are you so afraid? What are you ashamed of?'

Stupid questions, I know, but I want to fight back, not meekly obey.

'No speak.'

The usual reply. No speak – keep quiet – obey everything. Sit in this place day in and day out.

'Stand.'

I stand. Someone takes my arm. We walk across the earthen floor. I am pushed into the makeshift bathroom. Electric cables hang dangerously near the primitive shower. In the distance I can hear the steady hum of a generator supplying the underground prison with power. Outside the faint sound of car engines indicates that I may be near a main highway. The airport is not too far away – from time to time I hear the sound of aircraft engines.

'Quick.' A voice from the other side of the curtain sends a familiar message.

I use the bathroom, adjust my blindfold and am taken back to my cell for another twenty-four hours of reflection.

It's so hard to remember. Anxiety must be blocking my memory. Strangely, I can recall details of my childhood with greater clarity than I can the events leading up to my capture. Perhaps in returning to childhood I am looking for a security and protection that I now don't have. Did I ever have it? Am I playing the game of searching for a Golden Age, to calm my growing unease? I wander in my mind along the lanes of my childhood village and stop by the pond covered with algae. As children, we called it 'granny greenteeth'. We believed that there was a pike in the water with teeth so sharp it could snap off a finger or even a hand. We disturbed the green covering with a stick and stared into the blackness hoping for a sight of the terrible monster.

Did Fred Wilson come to London after he telephoned, or a representative from his office? I think someone called Lodewick came. Bob Lodewick. We discussed Ben Weir's situation. I don't believe I was too hopeful. In fact, I wasn't hopeful at all. Did the situation lend itself to a face-saving formula? I doubted it. It seemed to me to be full of the most obscure political complexities.

We also discussed the seventeen Shia Muslims who had been imprisoned in Kuwait on a variety of charges. My knowledge of the Middle East was limited to say the least, but it was clear that the Presbyterian Church was well briefed on the situation. I learnt that the prisoners belonged to a radical Shiite group known as the Da'was (al da'wa al-Islamiyya, the Dawn or the Call). They had planted six bombs in Kuwait in what was believed to be a reprisal for that country's support of Iraq in the Iran–Iraq war, two of which were car bombs outside the US and French Embassies. Several people died and many were wounded. Kuwait, possibly fearing reprisals from Iran, did not try the suspects for acts of terrorism but for lesser charges of societal and criminal activity. Of the suspects identified at the trial in 1984, three were Shiite Lebanese from Islamic Jihad, the radical Islamic fundamentalist movement. Two of these – Mustapha Bader-Edden and Hussain Youseff Musawi – had been sentenced to death, along with others. Bader-Edden was said to be a cousin of Imad Mugniyah, a leader of Islamic Jihad; Musawi was a first cousin of the Commander of Amal forces in the Bekaa Valley, forces which later identified themselves with the pro-Iranian Shiite group, Hezbollah.

Given this bloody and complicated history, I thought it very unlikely that the prisoners would be released in exchange for Western hostages. The most we could hope for was to try to get Kuwait not to execute those who had received the death sentence. I would have no difficulty making an appeal on humanitarian grounds.

I cautioned Bob Lodewick about going public with too many statements. This, I felt, could only cause more problems for Ben. I promised to do what I could behind the scenes, but I explained that I was fully occupied with the Libyan affair and overloaded with my regular work. In my heart I had no desire to enter into yet another hostage situation.

When Bob left my office, I thought about our meeting. I hadn't given a flat 'no' to his request for help, but I hadn't been over-enthusiastic either. I felt strongly that the Church should be able to help people in trouble, particularly those in acute distress. The appeal from the Presbyterian Church was a direct appeal from a sister church, and on those grounds alone could hardly be ignored. My most important consideration was whether Lambeth could make a contribution that could not be made by others. That contribution might be simply to keep the hostages alive and see if the situation could be eased later. With a heavy heart I turned to the other work which faced me, but the names of Ben Weir and his wife Carol had been imprinted on my memory for ever.

I wonder if Ben ever sat in this cell? I'm sure he told me he was kept underground for periods, but there are many underground prisons throughout the Lebanon. It's hard to imagine men working in secret, day after day, building this sort of place. It obviously cost a great deal. The door is at least four inches thick and made of solid iron. I must think of other things for a while. I don't want to think about my family – not yet. It's too painful, and I can't bear more pain now. Go back to the main story. At least get the principal points clear.

What happened after Lodewick left? I continued with Libya; Fred Wilson continued to keep in touch by phone, and I urged him to seek other intermediaries. Jesse Jackson was involved for a time, but

that came to nothing. I contacted friends in the Middle East to see
if they could advise me about Ben, and carried on with my work
for Dr Runcie and, when I could manage it, for the Libyan hostages. It's easy to rattle off my activities like that, but when I remember the pressures I shudder. Every waking hour was occupied.
How my wife, Frances, managed during those days I simply can't
imagine.

I find it hard to think clearly for any length of time. I follow one
line of thought, then my mind goes back to Frances and the children.
I feel a sudden chill as I remember where I am – the white tiles, the
ever-burning dim light, the mysterious comings and goings through
the trapdoor, my silent neighbours who never cry out, never seem
to stir. Perhaps they are ill and lie immobile day and night. Perhaps
they have been here for years. It's terribly hot now. I feel as though
I can hardly breathe. Someone is outside the door. Key in lock.
Blindfold on.

'You good?'

'It's very hot.'

'Nice – good.'

'Not good. Too hot.' I point to my body which is covered with
perspiration. 'Look, not good.'

'OK, no problem.'

The door closes.

Before I was taken captive, I visited many prisons in the British
Isles, often top-security establishments, to see Arab, Libyan or Iranian
prisoners. Once past the strict barriers to the secure central heart of
the prison, the inmates had a reasonable freedom of movement. They
were certainly better off than those who were kept alone on remand
and who were locked up for hours each day. This prison is hell.

The key is in the lock again.

'Keep eyes covered – OK?'

'OK.'

'Sit here.'

I sit with my back to the door.

'No move.'

'OK.'

What is happening? I hate not knowing. It makes my anxiety-level
leap upwards. Behind me I hear the sound of scraping and pushing.
Then I feel a draught of cool air.

'That good?'

'Yes, good – thank you.'

The guard, who speaks quite acceptable English, has somehow arranged an electric fan outside the bars so that the stale air is at least circulated. It cools the cell somewhat. Certainly it's better than nothing.

'It is a fearful thing to fall into the hands of the living God.' Where is that from? It sounds like the Old Testament, but it's not. How I wish for a better memory. Hebrews – the writer of Hebrews. That's it. Well, whatever he meant by it, I can understand it for myself now. My active life is over for a while, perhaps for ever. Maybe I will never leave this place. My life, such as it is, is in the hands of the living God. I don't feel that God is near. I don't feel comfort from my prayers. All I feel is a searching introspection, as though a light were shining into the deepest parts of my being. Everything will be called to face that light: positive gestures, foolish actions, deceptions great and small, self-importance and insecurity. In these days I must face myself without sham. No false pride, no dodging the questions. Remember, Waite, they want to use this experience to break you. They want your mind to be in such a turmoil that you will be glad to let them sort it out. I must know if I have compromised my integrity. Have I? Go on, remember. Look at the story. Tell it to yourself. If you've failed, admit it. Why this pathway, God – why?

≪ 2 ≫

I AM ALONE walking by the sea. It's dusk – I walk along the sand. The sea laps at my feet. Suddenly I am conscious of being alone. When I look up, I can no longer see land. The sea rolls in. I feel panic. I am going to be cut off. Unless I get off this beach quickly, I will drown. Why can't I find my way? I see in the distance two figures coming towards me across the sand. I recognise two of my children. They take me by the hand as they would a blind man and guide me off the beach to the shelter of a familiar town.

I wake up with a start. There is a sound outside my cell. Someone is being moved. In or out? I listen – someone is leaving. The trapdoor to the garage has been opened. Is a prisoner being taken away, or are the guards changing? Someone groans. A deep, primitive groan which carries with it the feelings of a lifetime of suffering. Are they going to move me? I lie still. The trapdoor is closed. Silence. I am breathing deeply – fear? Certainly fear. Fear of the unknown, the unexpected, sudden change.

What can my dream mean? I relive it in my mind and attempt to continue it beyond the point of entering the town. I want to speak to my children, and I desperately want them to speak to me. I call to them down the corridors of the unconscious. My voice echoes back to me. They remain silent.

'You want eat?'
'No.'
'Why?'
'I don't want to eat.'
'Why?'
'Tell me, why do you keep me here?'
'I don't know.'
'Why don't you know? You guard me. You lock my cell door.'
'You must ask Chef.'
'When will I see him?'
'I don't know.'
'What time is it?'
'I don't know. Speak little. You want anything?'

It's useless to question the guard. From behind my blindfold I guess he is probably in his mid-twenties. Almost certainly he knows little and will tell me nothing.

'Can I have some books, please?'

'You must ask Chef.'

'When will I see Chef?'

'I don't know.'

This conversation could continue for ever. I try one last question.

'How long will you keep me?'

'I don't know.'

Of course you don't know. Why should you know? In all probability you've been brought here from south Lebanon. Your home was destroyed, your family scattered, some members killed. Now you have a security of sorts and the opportunity to fight in a war of liberation. Why should you know anything except that the West is to be considered your enemy?

The door closes, and I am alone once more. First, some exercise. My feet are blistered from walking, but although it's painful I keep going. It is almost as if I am afraid that my body will fail me if I don't exercise. After what I assume is two or three hours, I stop and lie on my mattress. My limbs ache. I stretch and try to relax. Soon I am back in my home village. My father is shaking me gently by the shoulder.

'Wake up.'

I stir from the depths of sleep. 'What time is it?'

'Very early. It will soon be light.'

I sit up in bed.

'I want you to get dressed quickly and go and fetch Mrs Moss.'

Mrs Moss lived in a cottage by the Methodist church.

'Knock on her door. If she does not answer, take a small pebble from the garden and throw it gently at the bedroom window.'

In the early morning I dress and leave the house. The world is a different place. The air is still. The first fingers of dawn stretch gently across the sky, slowly warming the fields and the hedgerows. I stop to listen to a cow eating: chomp, chomp, chomp. She lifts her head, looks at me and, curiosity satisfied, continues with her solitary meal. Opposite the cricket ground I stop again to look in the holly hedge. The blackbird's nest is still there – beautifully made and quite secure. Onwards into Farm Fold. No one stirs. Past the Methodist church. Mrs Moss must be asleep as all the curtains in her house are drawn. I knock gently on the door, afraid that I might wake her neighbours. No reply. I knock again. Still no reply. I look for a pebble, and take aim at the bedroom window. It finds its mark and registers a satisfying 'ping'. The window opens, and an old lady appears.

'My father would like you to come please, Mrs Moss.'

'Right, I'll be along presently.'

She closes the window. I return home and go to bed. Later that day I learn that I have a baby brother, David John. Much later I discover that he was prematurely born, weighed only three pounds and that the birth was exceptionally difficult.

Music drifts through my head. *Chanson de Matin* – Elgar. When did I first hear that? Children's Hour, BBC North of England Home Service. It was the signature tune to a play for children. Somehow the emotions engendered by the music linked perfectly with the play. The play itself has long gone from my memory, but the melody remains. What was it that C. S. Lewis wrote on the emotional response to music? Something about inconsolable sorrows and well-fought fields rising within. My response to music must always have been predominantly emotional, I have so often been moved to tears by different works. Now, I have only memory to help me re-create the music I have known and loved. My mind jumps from music back to the wireless. The aunts and uncles I hardly knew in my own family were compensated for by the BBC presenters: Muriel and Doris in Manchester, Cicely in Northern Ireland, David in London. Every evening at five they visited my home and like the best aunts and uncles entertained and, incidentally, instructed me.

How many days have passed – five? – six? It's so easy to lose track. What will my wife, Frances, be thinking? My children, Ruth and Clare in France, and Mark and Gillian in London? They will expect me to disappear for a day or so – but six days! I wonder if the journalist Juan Carlos Gumucio has released the video tape I gave him. What did I say? We went to the flat roof of the Riviera Hotel to take advantage of the light. I told him that the tape was not to be made public unless I failed to return after several days. I remember saying that if I was captured no ransom was to be paid – no exchange made. Did I say why I had decided to accept the kidnappers' invitation to visit the hostages? No, I gave no reason on tape. Is my memory playing tricks? I have been thinking so much that it's difficult to distinguish between what I have said to others and what I have thought and kept to myself. If Juan Carlos has released the tape, will it anger my captors? Probably. My mind returns to 1985.

I let it be known that I was interested in doing what I could for the Beirut hostages and waited for a response. In what little free time I had I began to study the complexities of the Lebanese situation. I met contacts from the Middle East, some of whom I had known for years, and discussed the hostage problem with them. It was, to say the least, incredibly confusing. As I sit thinking about those days, a sudden chill grips me. If I am going to be interrogated, which I almost certainly am, I will be asked for the names of people who have contacted and helped me. I must be strong and not compromise anyone. Having lived with fear for a week, it's as though my memory is full of holes. It takes a hard, conscious effort to remember names. Whatever happens, those who have tried to help me will be safe with me. My thoughts take me back to my office in Lambeth Palace. To a day early in the year.

A small, well-dressed man sat opposite me. Dapper, intelligent, born in the Middle East, trained, so he said, as an international lawyer.

'It's fairly clear,' he declared, 'that the Lebanese kidnappers want the prisoners released from Kuwait in exchange for the hostages. That seems to be their principal demand.'

'It's impossible,' I replied. 'The best we can hope for is that the Emir will not execute them. We could certainly appeal to him on humanitarian grounds.'

He gave a wry smile.

'You could, and it might help. It certainly wouldn't be enough to free all the hostages, but it might bring the release of one or two.'

The situation in Lebanon was becoming increasingly tense. Bombings, further kidnappings; a depressing confusion of killing and gloom. Each day brought an event that made the task of achieving the release of the hostages seem even more impossible.

'Is there any way in which the Da'wa prisoners in Kuwait could be legally released?'

I was trying to explore every option, but so much was unclear. Was I facing one, or several, kidnapping gangs in Beirut? What was Iran's role? What was the relationship between the Lebanese kidnappers and their Iranian associates? Were the Libyans and Palestinians involved? I spent weeks meeting informants in an attempt to get a clearer picture. Most contacts had little to say, but occasionally one would appear with helpful information:

'The payment of "blood money" to the relatives of those who have been murdered could be sufficient, under Islamic law, to secure the release of the prisoners.'

I looked at my informant. 'Would that be morally acceptable?'

He nodded. 'To Islam, yes.'

The suggestion offered a glimmer of hope. If such an arrangement could be made, almost certainly some hostages in the Lebanon would be freed.

The Libyan hostage crisis came to an end in February 1985, didn't it? It did, because at the beginning of January there was another flurry of activity at Lambeth Palace when Father Lawrence Jenco, a Roman Catholic priest in Beirut, was captured. He was followed by the Associated Press correspondent, Terry Anderson, and the British journalist, Alec Collett. I remember Fred Wilson being in touch with me again, afraid that hostages might be killed if the US started military action in the Lebanon. The anxiety of the hostages' families increased. Fred Wilson called at Lambeth with Ben Weir's son, John. They were on their way to Damascus to see if they could get help from that quarter. Again, they urged me to do what I could for them. Without revealing sources, I told them of the contacts I had already made. I was beginning to get indications that the kidnappers knew I was involved, and I was hoping they would be prepared to talk to me directly. Fred and John departed, promising to visit Lambeth on their return.

The Archbishop of Canterbury lives in only a small part of Lambeth Palace: the remainder is used for meetings or office space for members of his private staff. My room was only a few doors away from the Archbishop's study. In the nineteenth century it had been a servant's room, but it provided me with quite adequate accommodation.

Robert Runcie rarely had formal meetings with his staff. He had a pleasant, relaxed way of working, trusted everyone to get on with their work, and preferred to meet with them individually, as and when necessary. If an urgent matter arose, it was always possible to see him immediately.

Shortly after Fred and John had left, the Archbishop and I discussed the Beirut hostages yet again. I told him that the demands of the kidnappers appeared to be linked to the Da'wa prisoners held in

Kuwait. I mentioned the meeting with Fred Wilson and said that the Presbyterian Church in America believed that we ought to be involved. The Archbishop raised sensible objections, which we both knew only too well: the volume of work, the Lambeth Conference which was only three years away, and the fact that the issue of the hostages could apparently run on and on. He also expressed his concern for the hostages and their families, however, and agreed that if we could make a contribution towards resolving the problem, we should do so. He pointed out that if Lambeth was to work for the release of American hostages, the approval of John Allin, the Presiding Bishop of the Episcopal Church in America, would be needed and said that he would contact him as soon as convenient.

Fred and John returned from Syria empty-handed. They had made useful contacts but gained no new information. It was an exceptionally busy time for me. Robert Runcie had set himself the task of visiting as many parts of the worldwide Anglican Communion as possible before the next Lambeth Conference. Several months earlier I had flown to Australia to prepare for a visit, and now, along with Chaplain John Witheridge, was about to depart on the Archbishop's official tour. I realised that as the Lambeth Conference approached, more and more of my time would be taken up with preparations for it. If I remained at Lambeth until the Conference in 1988, I would be obliged to stay until 1989 or 1990, by which time I would have served ten years in all. When I took the job, a senior clergyman advised me not to keep the position for longer than five years. From time to time, I discussed these issues with the Archbishop in a relaxed way, without coming to any conclusions. The Beirut affair simply increased the pressure on me to define priorities.

I need to break off for a moment. There is another hole in my memory. I count the white tiles which line my cell. When that simple task is over, I attempt mental arithmetic. My father was very good with numbers. When I was three or four, he would encourage me to add together the numbers on car licence-plates. Those were the days when all private cars were painted either black or white. No bright colours, just black or white, black and white ... My head spins. It must be lack of food. If I lie down for a while, perhaps I will sleep. I long for sleep. In sleep I can escape.

'Sweet deceiving sleep' ... Gurney? Yes, Ivor Gurney – poor tormented, creative soul.

> *And who loves joy as he*
>   *That dwells in shadows?*
> *Do not forget me quite,*
>   *O Severn meadows.*

Written while sheltering from battle in Flanders. Outside my cell a battle is raging. I lie on my mattress on the floor, eyes closed, mind wandering . . . Flanders, the Severn –

> *Only the wanderer*
>   *Knows England's graces,*
> *Or can anew see clear*
>   *Familiar faces.*

   My mother takes me by the hand. We walk along a country lane. She lifts me to look at a bird's nest in the hedge. The eggs are blue. A beautiful azure blue. I see my mother's face. She smiles. A smile tinged with sorrow. Her father died in the trenches in Flanders. She never knew how or where he was buried. She hardly knew him. Now she has a son whom she holds by the hand while they wander down a dusty lane, sit on the blue-green grass. Why is the sky so blue? We saunter home. Saunter – Santa Terra – Holy Land. The Holy Land is but a few miles distant. Flanders . . . Beirut . . . battle . . . memories . . . sleep . . .

There seems to be a lot going on outside my cell. Someone is entering through the trapdoor. Can I hear traffic noise? One day someone might ask me about this place: the exact dimensions of the cell, noises, anything. How much will I tell? As long as the kidnappers keep their word to me, I will not betray their trust. If they renege, then I am free of my obligations. It's as simple as that. Are they going to renege? Who knows? Take it easy, don't anticipate the worst. Someone is knocking gently on the cell door. Blindfold on. I hate this business: it's humiliating and intimidating; I am at a disadvantage. Someone enters, pulls my blindfold down and tightens it behind my head.
   'You must cover eyes, understand?'
   'My eyes are covered.'
   'You must cover eyes well. Understand?'
   I am too angry to reply.
   'Understand?' There is a hint of menace in his voice.

'Yes.'

'Take.'

Something is thrust into my hands. It might be clothing.

'Ten minute, understand?'

'Yes.'

I think I understand. He will be back in ten minutes. The door closes and I remove my blindfold. I have been given my clothes: my trousers, shirt, leather jacket. My shoes and socks are by the door. I feel a sudden surge of excitement. I am to be moved. Taken to see the hostages at last? Set free? I dress quickly. Although it's now a week since I have eaten, today I feel clear-headed and strong. I put on my shoes; my feet hurt because of blisters, but no matter.

There is further activity outside the cell. The trapdoor is again being lifted. A knock on the door. Blindfold on. People are standing on either side of me.

'You must do exactly as you are told.'

I make no reply.

'Understand?'

'Yes.'

I say a short prayer for my unknown silent companions whom I am leaving behind. Now I begin to feel anxious. My guards sound tense and nervous. We move out of the cell and across the floor to the cupboard.

'Up.'

I climb on to the cupboard and feel my way up the steps. Someone helps me through the trapdoor.

There is a strong smell of petrol in the garage.

'Get in the car.'

I stumble into the back of a vehicle.

'Lie on the floor.'

I lie flat.

'No speak.'

Several blankets are thrown over me. At least two people climb in and sit in the back seat. I hear the garage doors being opened. The engine starts, and the car moves slowly out of the garage. I am afraid. So afraid that my whole body is shaking. They might be taking me to be shot – taking me anywhere.

'Almighty God, unto whom all hearts be open, all desires known, and from whom no secrets are hid . . .'

I am repeating the opening words of the Communion service to myself. Why? Because I am afraid. Looking for comfort in the familiar? Oh God, you know me – my vanity, my stupidity.

'Cleanse the thoughts of our hearts by the inspiration of thy Holy Spirit . . .'

We bump along a road full of potholes. I can hear water splashing under the car. The car stops; the engine is switched off. Surely this is not our destination. We have travelled only a few hundred yards.

'. . . that we may perfectly love thee . . .' Tears come to my eyes. To love perfectly. What an impossible, crazy, wonderful goal. What must it be to love and be loved perfectly? The men in the car are whispering to each other. Someone gets out of the front seat. The engine is started, and we move off. Twenty minutes – half an hour? We stop again. I am cramped and uncomfortable. Someone lifts the blanket covering my head.

'No speak.'

Someone tugs at my arm. I crawl out of the car and stand. A blanket is thrown over my shoulders. Someone else takes my hand and guides me forward into the hallway of a building. A lift door opens. We enter. Up one, two, three, possibly four floors. We leave the lift and walk a few steps and enter what I assume is an apartment. We walk several more paces and turn left. I am pushed into a corner.

'Sit.'

I sit down on the floor. Someone removes my shoes and socks. What's that noise? My stomach lurches. Someone has a chain. I feel the cold metal as he fastens it around my ankle. Now the other ankle. Now my hands. Now he pulls and I am drawn into a foetal position. I lie on my side chained like the escape artist I saw on a Liverpool bomb site when I was a child. Someone tightens my blindfold.

'No speak – no move.'

I don't stand much chance of moving.

'Sleep.'

Sleep indeed. Sleep, dream, escape into the arms of those whom you love. Let them shelter you, hold you, comfort you. Sleep – the great mother. Sleep – the healer. Sleep – the lover.

> *Our birth is but a sleep and a forgetting . . .*
> *Shades of the prison-house begin to close*
> *Upon the growing Boy . . .*

Sleep.

*

I am looking into a pool of water. The sea? So clear it must be a tropical ocean. All manner of fish swim by. They are beautifully coloured. All the colours are vivid: the coral, the sand, the water. I watch the fish – so gentle, so graceful. I am not asleep. It's as though I am in a trance. I want the moment to continue. Am I asleep? No. The vision continues. Perhaps it's a result of fasting. Perhaps it's the tablet they insisted I swallow. No matter, let the gentleness of this submarine world calm and soothe and lead me to sleep . . .

There is a great deal of coming and going in the room. It seems as if there are two or three young men and an older man who appears from time to time. I know only because of the sound of their voices. From under my blindfold I can see that a large wardrobe has been pushed against the window to block the view either way. There is a bed for a guard at the opposite side of the room. I am never left alone. A television set is near the guard. Occasionally English programmes are broadcast, but as soon as news items are shown, the guard turns the sound down. Once or twice my name is mentioned, but it's impossible for me to hear more. I find this infuriating, but at least I can now order my day somewhat. Enough light comes from behind the wardrobe to indicate whether it's day or night. There are also noises outside. We seem to be located in a busy area. I can hear street traders calling their wares. A school must be near by; I can hear the laughter of children. There is also a mosque. Throughout the day the regular pattern of prayer continues. I am sleepy and doze a lot. Perhaps I have been drugged. Certainly they insist that I take tablets from time to time.

Why drug me? In preparation for interrogation? To keep me docile? Who knows? Who can understand the world in which these men live?

I miss my colleagues at Lambeth and wonder where Samir is now. The Rev. Canon Samir Habiby was appointed by the American Presiding Bishop to liaise with me on the hostage problem. I had known him for some years: affectionate, impulsive, generous, born in the Middle East, a naturalised American. Ever since I had been approached by the Presbyterians, Samir had helped me. He spoke Arabic and had a multitude of contacts. His boundless energy and aggressive approach irritated me at times, but my irritation probably had more to do with the pressures I was under than with Samir himself. I knew he was in touch with the American government, as any American citizen who became involved in matters affecting US foreign policy had to be. In my search for leads I had met several members of the American administration, both in England and overseas. I wanted to meet as many people as possible in order to gain as much information as I could. When I visited the US in May 1985, Samir suggested that I ought to establish contact with the administration and arranged for me to meet Donald Gregg, a National Security Adviser to President Reagan. Later the same day, Lieut.-Col. Douglas Menarchik appeared. I raised the suggestion of 'blood money', but I wondered how seriously White House officials regarded the hostage problem. I suspected they had agreed to meet me only out of courtesy. Samir strongly believed the 'blood money' suggestion was worth following up, as it involved only payment to the relatives of the Da'wa victims, all of whom we had identified. We had no idea how much money would be required, where it would come from, or if such a scheme would be acceptable to the various parties involved.

I had first met Jack Allin, the Presiding Bishop of the Episcopal Church, many years before and had got to know him well when I visited the US in the early eighties to prepare for the Archbishop's first official visit. I liked and trusted him. I took the elevator to his New York apartment at the top of the Episcopal Church headquarters. Ann Allin, Jack's wife, welcomed me and showed me to the guest room. Fred Wilson, Carol Weir and her son John were to meet with me the following day.

The next morning when they arrived Samir came up from his office in the building below. Fred began by bringing me up to date on his activities. For some time he had been trying to arrange a reliable contact with the American government so as to establish the administration's policy towards the hostages. Like me, he had found it difficult to get a clear view. Eventually former President Jimmy Carter had arranged for Fred, Carol and John to meet the National Security Adviser, Robert McFarlane. But first the party had been introduced to a military man, Lieut.-Col. Oliver North, for a preliminary discussion. He was, Fred said, the most concerned about the hostages of all the American officials they had met and displayed a knowledge of the situation which others seemed not to have. I told Fred it might be worth my seeing him. Fred agreed, telephoned Washington, and that afternoon North was on his way to New York to meet us.

Samir collected him from the airport. He was casually dressed and carried a small black briefcase. Bishop Allin, as host, greeted him and then excused himself, as he had work to do. The first thing I noticed, apart from Oliver North's quiet manner, was that he walked with a certain stiffness. Later, I learnt that he had suffered a back injury while on active service in Vietnam. We sat round a large polished dining table and began to talk. Carol Weir was angry with the Reagan administration and told North that she felt little or nothing was being done for the hostages. He listened politely and then explained that it was government policy not to negotiate directly with terrorists. At some point in the afternoon the 'blood money' proposal was discussed. Again, Colonel North listened. We spoke about the death sentence that had been passed on a number of prisoners in Kuwait, and I said that the Church would continue to appeal for a commutation of that sentence. At the end of our discussion I had to agree with Fred Wilson that Colonel North seemed to have a greater interest in doing something for the hostages than anyone else in the administration. At the time, however, I didn't regard the meeting as being of any particular importance.

It's about nine in the evening. For the last two days I have been chained and blindfolded for all but ten minutes a day. The guard comes and unlocks the padlocks on my hands and feet. Under my blindfold I can see two other guards standing at a distance. I suspect that they are armed. The man helps me to my feet, guides me across to the bathroom, ushers me in and locks the door. The bathroom is quite modern. The mirror has been removed from the wall, but otherwise it is fully equipped. Before I have finished washing, the guard is knocking on the door, urging me to be quick. Can't they allow me even ten minutes of limited freedom a day? I replace my blindfold and tap on the door. The key is turned, my arm is taken, and I return to my chains.

'You want eat?'

'No.'

'Chef says you must eat.'

I am hungry. Whatever point I was trying to make has been made, but still I am reluctant to eat. I make no reply. The guard leaves the room and returns a few moments later.

'Mr Waite.'

My heart goes cold. I recognise the voice of the man in the suit.

'Yes.'

'You must eat. We can make you eat.'

I don't want – don't need that. Without any further comment I agree to eat. The guard hands me a sandwich. Pitta bread with a few pieces of cheese inside.

I sit up, hold the sandwich in my chained hands and taste my first food for over a week. Part of me is sorry that the fast is over, part is glad of the comfort food brings.

'Lie down – face the wall.'

I obey. The guard turns on the TV. An English-language film is playing. I can hardly believe my ears. From the dialogue I understand that a Second World War film set in Germany is being shown. A woman agent has been captured and is facing torture. I begin to sweat.

'*We can break you, you know. You can only hold out for so long. Soon you will tell us everything.*'

I wish to God he would turn it off. I have the foolish notion that he might see something on the screen that he would then try out on me. Others enter the room. I hear them pouring a drink – tea, I suppose. They sit quietly. All foreign films are subtitled in Arabic, so they can follow this one without difficulty.

To my relief, the film comes to an end and is followed by an Arabic programme. My thoughts drift back to the first film I remember seeing: *The Lady Vanishes* starring Margaret Lockwood. It was shown one evening in the Styal Clubroom, and it terrified me. I saw very few films as a boy and, before 1953, virtually no television. Like so many people in the British Isles my father bought a set especially to watch the Coronation of Queen Elizabeth II.

'Watch this,' he said. 'I shall never see anything like this again in my lifetime, and you may not.'

The small black-and-white screen flickered in the corner of the living room. Outside the rain beat relentlessly against the window while my father sat by the fire, a pot of tea stewing in the hearth and a plentiful supply of Woodbines by his side. In the mid-afternoon the rain eased. Thankful for a break, I wandered to the cricket field where a sports afternoon had been planned. A few strips of coloured bunting fluttered from the pavilion. Large pools of water covered the pitch. Several gloomy-looking individuals squelched around the field. Altogether a desolate scene. I trudged home. The television was still flickering in the corner. My father was determined to miss nothing of the last such event he would ever see.

Ever since Fred Wilson first contacted me about Ben Weir in 1984, I had continued my inquiries, although I was careful to keep out of the public eye. At this stage I believed that publicity would not necessarily help the case. Letters were exchanged, and discussions took place with representatives of the governments of Syria, Iran, Kuwait, Lebanon and Saudi Arabia. It was my belief that if I could get into Kuwait to visit the prisoners, on humanitarian grounds, this might ease the situation and lead to further progress. Regrettably, approaches to the Kuwaiti authorities continued to be rebuffed. I developed my contacts outside diplomatic circles and was reasonably certain that the kidnappers were aware of my involvement and knew some of the action I was taking. In May, Alvin Puryear, a senior official of the American Presbyterian Church, wrote to the Archbishop asking him to allow me to spend more time dealing with the hostage crisis. He came in person to present his letter and discuss the matter with the Archbishop. Anxious to help, yet conscious of the pressures, Runcie finally agreed to his request.

One day as I was reading my mail, Stella Taylor handed me a slip of paper.

'Incredible,' I said. 'I can hardly believe it.'

News had just come through that there had been a bomb attack on the Emir of Kuwait's motorcade.

'Why, Stella, would anyone be so stupid as to think they could obtain the release of prisoners by trying to assassinate the Emir?'

She made no reply.

'That is,' I continued, 'if that's the object of the attempt. It could be a spoiling exercise, I suppose.'

The event worried me deeply, even though it was widely rumoured that the Emir kept the death sentences pending as a form of insurance against further terrorist attacks in his country. The execution of any of the prisoners in Kuwait would be very bad news indeed for the Western hostages. And my chances of getting into Kuwait would be further reduced.

Christine Weir, another of Ben's courageous children, visited London soon after this. All Ben's family were tireless in their attempts to attain their father's freedom.

*

The thought of Ben's children sends me back to the memory of my own. Here I sit, lost in the Lebanese gulag, without knowing whether I will ever see them again. I make a deliberate attempt to conjure up happier days and take myself back to Rome, our home for almost seven years. One night I stayed in a religious house beside the Tiber. I went to bed, fell asleep and was awakened by the sound of ghostly voices echoing across the night:

'Angelo, Angelo. Roberto, Roberto.'

I lay still. The voices seemed to be shouting down from the sky.

'Angelo, Roberto, Massimo.'

Finally they died away, and I slept. At breakfast I mentioned the experience. My hosts smiled.

'Friends and relatives of the prisoners,' they said. 'They stand on the hill and shout across at the Queen of Heaven prison. They often continue well into the night.'

'Roberto, Angelo, Massimo.'

Now I hear voices in my head. The voices of my children chattering in Italian. The gentle voice of Archbishop Achille Silvestrini as he greets me in the Vatican. He has an important diplomatic position in the Secretariat of State, and I have known him for many years.

'Welcome, Mr Waite, welcome.'

We walk together along the carpeted corridors. Archbishop Silvestrini is a man of great courtesy and charm. A natural diplomat with a warm, generous heart.

'How is Archbishop Runcie, Mr Waite?'

He opens a huge wooden door and guides me into a meeting room overlooking one of the Vatican courtyards. The only sound comes from an antique clock, which solemnly marks the passing of time against the background of eternity.

'Please sit down, Mr Waite.'

I sit in a gilded chair with a green velvet cushion. Two or three religious pictures adorn the walls. A highly polished table and sideboard gleam in the soft Roman light.

'This long episode is a cause of deep anguish to the Holy Father, Mr Waite.'

Archbishop Silvestrini is in his early fifties, slim and elegant in his plain black cassock. We discuss the problem of the hostages.

'We must be very careful, Mr Waite. The politics are very complicated.'

I tell him what I have done since we last met, of my continued desire to visit the prisoners in Kuwait.

'We have made many representations for you in Damascus and Beirut. It is very hard. We must have patience, Mr Waite. Patience.'

We talk on quietly, and the Archbishop promises to continue with his representations.

'Mr Waite, this afternoon there is a Mass in St Peter's. Would you wish to join us?'

I tell him I would. I long to sit in that great basilica and put my cares and responsibilities to one side.

We walk together through the corridors of the Vatican and enter an antique lift which might have operated in Fortnum & Mason's in Edwardian times. It creaks downwards. The Archbishop opens a door, and lo, we are in the basilica. The church is already full. To my embarrassment he leads me to the front and seats me on a red plush chair, hands me a printed order of service and says he will meet me afterwards. The organ is lovely, the choir dreadful. Pope John Paul II enters, surrounded by the principal performers. They take up their positions and the drama commences.

The service over, Archbishop Silvestrini appears as suddenly as he had earlier disappeared. He guides me into a room in the basilica. I wait for a moment, and the Holy Father comes in. He looks tired, but he smiles and greets me warmly. He asks for news of the hostages and assures me that the Roman Catholic Church will do everything to assist the Archbishop of Canterbury in his endeavours. He listens carefully as I explain the difficulties and tell him what action we are taking. Our conversation over, he turns and enters the ancient lift. The Vatican porter cranks a handle, and the Pope wings upward to his private apartment. Within a few moments the cage reappears, and Archbishop Silvestrini and I are similarly elevated for a final conversation with the Secretary of State.

Before I went to the Vatican, the newly appointed American Ambassador to the Holy See had been in touch with me. Reports had been received that the authorities in Kuwait were about to execute the Da'wa prisoners. I was asked to request the Vatican to intercede. I checked with a number of my Middle Eastern contacts and decided that while there was a certain threat, there was no immediate danger. If the US government felt there was such a danger, they could approach the Vatican through their own diplomatic channels. I phoned Fred Wilson and told him of the approaches being made to me and my decision not to raise the matter with the Secretariat. He replied that he trusted my judgement. Some weeks earlier, the Archbishop of Canterbury and the Presbyterian Church had written independently to the Emir of Kuwait requesting commutation of the death sentences. Commutation would, we believed, help to calm an already inflamed situation and enable us to continue our contacts with groups in the Lebanon. To my relief, the anxieties of the Ambassador were ill-founded, and the immediate threat passed.

Aventine, Palatine, Esquiline, Quirinal, Pincian. I stand on the Janiculum and look out over a city I have known and loved for years. The evening sky is tinged with red. The worn and broken stones of the Forum are silhouetted against a crimson curtain. Blood has coursed down the worn streets of this place; the blood of martyrs, vagabonds, innocents. In my mind I look across the city: Clemente, Prassede, Maggiore, Giovanni. Each day, within these churches, the mysterious sacrifice of thanksgiving is enacted.

'The Blood of our Lord Jesus Christ, which was given for thee, preserve thy body and soul unto everlasting life.'

My children chatter and laugh as they skip through the Piazza Navona. Hop – skip, across the silent stones. Hop – skip. The picture fades; my children disappear down the corridor of memory. I am back in captivity.

The sound of shelling outside continues to scare me. A hit on the building could mean that I would be buried alive – the whole apartment block could collapse. It must be a remote possibility, but a possibility nevertheless. A fierce battle is under way. My mind slips back over the years to Vietnam. The war was raging, and I had gone to assist the Church in the development of medical services for the civilian population in Qui Nhon. I arrived in Saigon one afternoon and went to the airline office, having been told that they would provide me with overnight accommodation. The airline clerk had no knowledge of such a promise. I insisted. The clerk refused. I insisted again. The clerk shrugged, wrote a few lines on a form and handed it to me.

Outside stood an antique bus of the kind used to transport American children to and from school. It was totally empty except for a driver who sat reading a newspaper. I climbed aboard, handed him the docket, and we set off. After half an hour of driving through potholed streets he stopped, turned round and spread his hands wide, indicating that he was lost. A few American dollars helped him regain his sense of direction, and we were off again. Finally we stopped outside what had once been a rather splendid hotel. Apart from one or two Vietnamese staff, it seemed deserted. My room was huge. The windows were shuttered, but when I opened them there was a marvellous view over the sea. The restaurant was on the top floor. Again, apart from a couple of elderly waiters, I was the only diner. I returned to my room and slept soundly. Next morning when I went down to the lobby, even the skeleton staff had vanished. There was no one at all in the building. I made my way to the airport and booked myself on a local flight to Qui Nhon. When I recounted my tale to the staff in the hospital there, they were incredulous.

'No one ever stays in that hotel,' they said. 'Every night that area is shelled. The hotel is bound to be hit one day.'

As I think about Vietnam, my thoughts return to Oliver North. Fred Wilson was uneasy about him and expressed this when he came to London with Alvin Puryear of the Presbyterian Church and Carol and John Weir. They had visited Colonel North at his office in Washington and had been disturbed by some of the aggressive slogans that adorned the walls. Later, I saw the posters for myself. I don't remember them in detail, but I recollect that they were directed against those perceived to be the enemies of America. To me, they seemed adolescent.

The posters were not the only reason for Fred's unease, but he found it impossible to be specific about this. Broadly speaking, he simply did not trust the Reagan administration. I argued that, as Colonel North was the person appointed by the administration to deal with the hostage problem, we had little option but to keep in touch with him. Fred agreed. I was able to tell the group of our activities at Lambeth. We had been in touch with President Assad of Syria to inquire what influence he could exercise. I told them of the efforts of the Vatican, and I also mentioned that I had a number of contacts whom I believed were able to get messages through to some of the kidnappers. At this stage I was still far from certain as to how many groups were engaged in kidnapping Western hostages. I had let it be known that we wanted a 'gesture' from the kidnappers which might help me make more significant progress in getting access to the prisoners in Kuwait.

A few days after returning to America, Fred Wilson wrote me a confidential letter. He, Alvin, Carol and John had again been to see Oliver North in Washington and found that his attention was shifting away from Syria towards Iran. Fred asked if I could explore ways in which I might establish direct contact with the Iranian politician, Hojatolislam Rafsanjani, making it clear that this request came from himself, Alvin, Carol and John, and not from Colonel North. After the group had departed I had been informed that President Assad could probably secure the release of some Western hostages if the US would be more 'forthcoming', whatever that might mean. I telephoned this information to Fred. In considering the whole problem, it seemed to me of vital importance that I somehow set up a face-to-face meeting with the kidnappers. I needed to hear from their own mouths what they were demanding and whether they were acting independently or being controlled by Iran. I didn't expect them to answer my second point, but I thought that a meeting might give me some clues.

I am exhausted. It's not only the exhaustion which comes from anxiety, although there is bound to be some of that. It's long-term exhaustion from living with high risk for years. When I think of the sheer complexity of the hostage situation, and the demands made on my time and energy, the uncertainty, the pressure, the loneliness, I am appalled. My poor family. I couldn't discuss my work at home. In fact, I was hardly ever at home. Thank God for Frances's strength. She maintained herself with dignity and gave everything she had to helping the children through their formative years.

There was also the pressure of surveillance. I had to be careful about becoming paranoid, but I was convinced that I was being watched, that my telephones were monitored. My assumption was that our own security service was keeping an eye on me, as well as agents from other countries. While I can, and do, say 'No regrets', I wouldn't want to live through the strain of those years again. I won't know for some time what they have done to me and to those I love, but I will try, try my utmost, to make this a creative experience. God, please help me.

Sitting here I could go on and on with fruitless introspection. Wishing my life had been different, regretting opportunities lost. Useless to think like that. I must go back to my story. A sign we had been waiting for was given. Ben Weir was released in Beirut in September 1985. He was immediately snapped up by US Intelligence

and flown to an aircraft carrier for debriefing before he was allowed
to see his family. Ben, circumspect as ever, was careful what he said
and insisted on being reunited with his family quickly.

I was in the Yukon at the time, accompanying the Archbishop on
a tour of Canada. The Archbishop, his Chaplain, John Witheridge,
and I had trekked across the country and finally arrived in the old
gold-rush town of Whitehorse. It was late in the evening when our
small plane touched down, but the local Vicar was on hand to greet
us and to drive us the sixty miles or so to Haines Junction where we
were to rest for a couple of days. We piled the luggage into the back
of a large station wagon and set off, with the Archbishop sitting in
the front next to the driver. We were soon driving along a remote
stretch of the Alaskan Highway. After about thirty miles, the headlights picked out a figure by the side of the road, hailing a lift. The
Vicar sailed past.

'Hold on a moment,' we shouted from the back. 'Wasn't that a
hitchhiker?'

He confirmed that it was.

'Isn't it dangerous at this time of night?' I asked.

'It can be,' he said. 'Bears sometimes come out of the woods and
have been known to attack travellers.'

We gleaned the information that it was very unlikely there would
be any further traffic on the highway that night, and all agreed that
we ought to stop and give the lone pilgrim the lift he had requested.
We reversed the vehicle and stopped. The young man told us he
was heading for Anchorage, where he was due to catch a plane back
to his home in the United States. He put his rucksack in the back
and squeezed into the front seat next to Dr Runcie. When we reached
Mother's Cosy Corner, the hotel where we were to spend a couple
of days, the Vicar told the hitchhiker it would be unsafe for him to
continue his journey that night. He invited him to have supper with
the Archbishop and his party and promised to find him a bed for
the night. At first the traveller could not believe what he was hearing.
Meeting the Archbishop of Canterbury on the Alaskan Highway on
a September evening? It seemed impossible.

Mother's Cosy Corner had served the last meal of the day several
hours earlier, so the ever-versatile Vicar phoned a member of the
church and asked if she could provide supper for the company. This
was yet another strange event. Our hostess turned out to be Libby
Dulac, a well-known painter of Yukon landscapes. John Witheridge

was convinced he had seen her before. Finally, he remembered. As a young boy in St Albans, he had seen a girl in the road where he lived weeping because her dog had been run over. That girl was Libby. During the evening the telephone rang. Libby, somewhat surprised, said the call was for me. It was Fred Wilson. Ben Weir had been set free.

When Ben was released, he provided interesting information. The captors had come into the room in which the hostages were held and told them that one person was to be released. They asked the hostages to decide who this person should be. Ben said that Terry Anderson ought to go because he was young and had family problems that needed his personal attention. When the captors returned, they refused to accept Terry and insisted that Ben be released instead.

Why did they do that? Were they sending a signal to the Church, the very signal I had been asking for? When the next hostage to be freed, in July 1986, was the other clergyman, Father Lawrence Jenco, it seemed certain that the captors were responding to our efforts. Once home, Ben gave a press conference at the National Presbyterian Church in Washington. He was unaware at the time of the efforts that had been made by Lambeth to secure his release, nor did he know of the close relationship between Fred Wilson and myself.

Fred contacted me again shortly after the press conference, and we discussed whether it would be a good idea to reveal my activities on behalf of the hostages. It would make known my desire to gain access to the Da'wa prisoners, and perhaps bring public pressure to bear to help me. It would also be an opportunity to acknowledge the kidnappers' gesture and give me an alternative route by which to reach them. While I knew I was communicating with the kidnappers, I wasn't at all certain that I was in touch with all of them. Were there several groups acting independently of each other, or one overall organisation? Messages purporting to come from the captors were variously reported as coming from Islamic Jihad, Islamic Jihad for the Liberation of Palestine, Islamic Holy War. It was deliberately confusing. I decided that going public might give me a small measure of protection if I could achieve a meeting with the kidnappers. The disadvantages were obvious.

'SIT UP.' A voice pierces the darkness of sleep and shatters my fragile peace.

I struggle to get into a sitting position. What time can it be? The television closed down hours ago. It must be two or three in the morning.

'Face the wall.'

I manoeuvre my body to obey the command.

'Be quick.'

I am tired, confused and frightened, but determined not to show fear. Someone strikes me on the back of the head and then on my back. I want to cry out – to ask how anyone can be such a bully as to strike a chained, blindfolded man. Instead I remain silent.

'You are going to tell us everything.'

Am I? What is there to tell? A year of trying to find a way to ease the plight of hostages. A year of exhaustion. A year that had left me feeling as though the very life was being drained from me.

I think there are three men in the room. One is the man in the suit, another has an older voice I don't recognise but he sounds as though he has a heavy cold. The third is my regular guard. A sharp blow catches me in the middle of my back.

'We have many questions for you.'

'I have a question for you also.'

'What?'

'Why do you keep me when you gave me your word you would not?'

There is a silence in the room. The man in the suit is close to the side of my head. Slowly, deliberately, he whispers in my ear,

'Never say that again. Understand?'

'I know what you said. You know what you said. God also knows. You must live with your own conscience.'

There is a further silence. I wait for another blow. Nothing. The door opens. Someone leaves the room. I am alone again with my guard.

'From swerve of shore to bend of bay.' This single line from the opening of *Finnegans Wake* runs round and round in my head. So simple, so elegant, so descriptive. As I go back in time, attempting to put events of the past years into some semblance of a chronology, my thoughts stray to poetry and literature. Already I long for books. I crave something to read. Now would be a marvellous opportunity to read James Joyce. Here, where time takes on a meaning totally different from the significance it had before, I might begin to understand Joyce's dream language. Remember 'The Dead'? A wonderful story full of the sights, sounds, smells and emotions of a Dublin household at Christmas. 'From swerve of shore to bend of bay.' A multitude of characters pass before me: Runcie, North, Wilson, Weir. They laugh, talk, plot and pray. Their images are here, where the only company is a solitary cockroach I can't bring myself to kill. In my mind I walk down a long passage. Step gently, step carefully, lest I kill a cockroach. One step, two steps. Day and night are no more. Time as I knew it has gone. Someone is outside the room. I hear a door opening. Whispering. The door closes. Silence, darkness.

The call to prayer heralds the start of yet another day in captivity. It echoes around the building, vibrates through the room and fills my soul with dread. These prayers are prerecorded on tape. I know this because some days ago the tape player had technical problems, thus giving the game away. This emphasises the impersonal nature of the whole proceedings. From the noises I hear I suspect the flat in which I am being kept overlooks a public square. The street vendors will soon make themselves heard, then the schoolchildren, chattering and laughing to each other as they make their way to the classroom.

Someone knocks on the apartment door. There are two voices – the old man with the cold, and a younger-sounding man. I hear them put down some packages – probably groceries. A guard makes coffee; I can smell the heavy, rich aroma. They are chatting together, totally ignoring me as I lie chained in the corner. Someone crosses the room and stands beside me.

'You want eat?'

'Yes, please.'

'Take.'

I struggle to sit up. A sandwich is put into my hand. Pitta bread with a filling of *lebne*, neither a cheese nor a yoghurt but something in between. Liquid – tea, I suppose – is poured into my small plastic beaker. As I bite into the sandwich, my teeth catch on something hard, and to my dismay I hear and feel one of my teeth crack. Damn. They have put whole olives in with the *lebne*. I sip the tea, rinse out my mouth, and probe the damage with my finger. One of my back teeth has split in two, and half is quite loose. As I prod and push, the pieces come away. I lift my blindfold slightly to examine what I can of the broken tooth.

'What you do?' The question is hurled across the room with the force of a well-aimed javelin. 'Cover eyes.'

I return my blindfold to its original position. Someone comes to stand by my side.

'What you do?'

'My tooth has broken.'

'Give me.' I hand over the piece. 'Why you look?'

'My tooth has broken.'

'No look – understand?'

'Yes.'

He tightens my blindfold and returns to his companions. I feel a despair out of all proportion to the damage done to my tooth. My body is breaking up, my limbs are stiff, I have skin problems from being chained for so long, my teeth are going. Hell. I make a deliberate attempt to stop this train of thought. I tell myself not to be pathetic. My problems are minor. I am strong within, and I will remain so. Gently I feel along the sandwich and discover several more olives. I remove them and continue my breakfast, finish my tea, try to make my chains more comfortable and lie down. Was it St Cyprian who said: 'These are not chains, they are ornaments'? I smile to myself and resolve yet again not to give way to self-pity. A new day has begun. From the mosque God has been honoured, children are being educated, people buy and sell, breakfast is served.

The minor dental problem has sent my mind back to the primary school in Styal village. It was little more than a dame school. Miss Bailey was in charge of children aged five to seven. Mrs Owen took the sevens to elevens. Once or twice a year a dentist would set up her equipment in the room where school dinners were served. The drill, so feared by generations of patients, was pedal-operated. The dentist pedalled furiously while the drill ground slowly. Thanks to this primitive but effective service, I managed to keep healthy teeth and gums.

The primary education given by the two teachers was basic. When I was seven, two of my best friends joined several other children and left for better, fee-paying schools. Those of us whose families had more limited finances stayed behind to prepare as best we could for the dreaded eleven-plus. This examination, which marked so many children as academic failures, was the subject of much discussion at home. My father, obviously frustrated by his own lack of educational opportunities, tried to encourage me to study harder. Unfortunately, he was no teacher. Learning by rote was the only method he knew, and he followed it with me. Time and time again he told me how very bad the secondary school in Wilmslow was, and how if I failed and had to go there, many opportunities in life would be lost to me for ever. The more these messages were drilled into me, the more anxious I became. Books and music enthralled me, but education, as I then understood it, was an ogre. The day of the examination finally arrived. We filed into the classroom where the inkwells had been freshly filled and new steel-nib pens were neatly placed on each desk. Mrs Owen distributed the examination papers and instructed us in the rules. At lunchtime our papers were collected, and I made my way home.

'How did it go?'

'OK.'

What else could I say? I hadn't a clue as to how it had gone. Few of the questions had interested me. When the results came through, only one member of the class had passed: Michael Bailey's mother had been a teacher, and she taught him every evening. But that single pass was one hundred per cent better than the school's record in the previous year.

I lie here thinking of my childhood. How is it that more than forty years later it's still so painful to consider my first public failure? It must be because I was made to feel that I had failed my father. Surely my childhood wasn't all sorrow and loneliness. Weren't there times of real happiness and companionship? Of course there were, but somehow I was made conscious from a very early age of an affinity between beauty and sadness. Sitting in the quiet of an evening, watching the changing colours of the sky, I would feel sad that I could not share my feelings. How could I? I can barely articulate them now.

Michael Bailey was one of my best friends at school. At weekends we would take our bicycles and set off through the countryside,

over the Derbyshire hills and down, down, down into Buxton –
free-wheeling for five miles or more. Sandwiches by the river, and
then the long haul back over the hills to the safety of our village.
Shortly before I was captured, I made this same journey, again with
a friend. But this time we drove. When we arrived in Buxton, it was
the time of the annual arts festival. We were drawn into a small
antique shop where an evening of Victorian music was being performed. I had lost touch with Michael many years before, but that
evening I remembered him with joy.

My guard appears to have been ordered not to over-communicate
with me. He is sitting on the opposite side of the room attempting
to read an instruction manual. In halting English he says: 'I am a
soldier. I must do as I am told at all times.' He shouts across at me,
'English good?'

I tell him his English is clear.

'Me soldier – catch.'

I hold out my chained hands. Something lands near me.

'Face wall – look.'

I turn towards the wall and peer beneath my blindfold. A hand
grenade lies on my blanket. I pick it up and throw it back to him.
He laughs.

'Not good – see?'

He has broken it open, and I realise it's a practice grenade. He
laughs again, and I laugh too at his simple humour. He is not so
bad really. He never hits me. Clearly he is under strict orders which
he does his best to follow, but his natural kindness shows through.

'You want eat?'

I do feel like eating.

'Yes, I am hungry.'

'You want *lebne*?'

Bread and *lebne* is a monotonous diet. A change would be welcome.

'Do you have potato?'

'Yes.'

As best I can I explain to him how to bake potatoes. He goes to
the kitchen and about an hour later returns with three crisply baked
potatoes.

'Do you have olive oil and salt?'

He returns with both. I break open the potatoes, pour in the oil
and lightly sprinkle salt inside. They taste delicious.

'Good?'

'Yes, very good, thank you.'

'No problem.'

Oh my dear man – no problem. No problem for your simple act of kindness. No problem for you to obey your commands. No problem to stand by as I am beaten. No problem, no problem, no problem. The words echo down the years and send a message to all who simply obey without thinking. No problem.

It's Christmas. We are going carol-singing. My mother makes sure I am properly dressed.

'Terry.'

'Yes.'

'I saw Mrs Morley today.'

'Oh.'

'She said would you call for Jane and take her carol-singing.'

Me? Take Jane carol-singing? Although she must be the same age as myself, I regard her as a magnificent woman. Like me, she is tall; she also has long, beautiful hair. I don't know what to say.

'What time?' I mutter.

'If you call at seven, Jane will be ready.'

I'm lost for words, anxious, flattered, apprehensive, shy. I go upstairs to my room, brush my hair, clean my teeth, put on my best Tootal tie – yellow with golfing symbols emblazoned on it. At three minutes to seven I leave the house. It's so cold the air hurts my lungs. I knock on Jane's door; to my horror Mrs Morley answers. She smiles. 'Jane will be ready in a moment.'

I wait – embarrassed, anxious and hopeful. Jane comes down the stairs, looking lovely, and we leave the house together. When we join the other singers, I want to stand beside her, hold her hand, tell her what I feel. But she retreats to the other side of the group. I have never seen her since.

Where is Jane now? Suddenly I also remember Ellen. She was attractive, even though she had the most appalling acne. Her adolescent self-consciousness increased her shyness, and no doubt added to her suffering. One day I heard she had been found drowned in the local canal. I had rarely spoken to her, just smiled at her from time to time. But now, as I lie here, I see her as clearly as I did forty years ago. I weep for her, for her pain, her parents' pain. For years she has been alive in my subconscious, and now I see her again and smile shyly. The years have melted away. Life, death, time have lost their linear structure. As she and I meet for a moment, we are released from our prisons. None of the constraints of this world can hold us.

My thoughts continue to move between childhood and the events leading to my capture. I remember travelling to New York and appearing at a press conference with Ben Weir. I told the reporters that the Archbishop of Canterbury, after consulting with Bishop Allin, had authorised my involvement on behalf of the Western hostages, but while I would consult with many groups, my independence as an envoy of the Church had to be maintained. I explained that it had been decided I should go public to make clear to the kidnappers that the Church appreciated the gesture they had made in releasing Ben. I made an appeal for a meeting with the kidnappers and promised that the Church would do everything in its power to resolve the hostage situation. I did not mention Kuwait, but it was my private hope that that country, having heard my comments, might grant my request to visit the prisoners held there.

Back in London, I increased my efforts to gain entry to Kuwait and visited the Kuwaiti Ambassador in London several times. Each time he told me I would not be granted a visa. These refusals caused me to question just how much backing I was getting from the British and American governments. I felt sure that if either government were to support my visit on humanitarian grounds, I would be allowed in. It puzzled me that there appeared to be so little background help, and I simply assumed it was a case of neither government wishing to provoke an oil-producing nation. Although it was reported in the press that I had been refused a visa, I myself made little public comment. I hoped that eventually I would win through. In Rome, the Vatican continued to press my case through its own diplomatic channels, and Archbishop Silvestrini continued to be a wise and good friend.

Acting on what Fred Wilson had told me, I visited the Iranian Embassy and spoke with the Chargé, asking for permission to visit Iran and speak with officials there. I was received politely but nothing appeared to happen. I remained persistent. The long-awaited breakthrough finally came in November 1985. Myron Belkind, the London head of Associated Press (AP), brought a letter addressed to the Archbishop of Canterbury at Lambeth Palace. The letter, delivered the previous day to the AP office in Beirut, appeared to have been written by Father Lawrence Jenco, and was signed by him, Terry Anderson, David Jacobsen and Tom Sutherland. It began by saying that the hostages had heard about the Archbishop's efforts on their behalf, and they were grateful. It declared that the kidnappers were willing for the Archbishop to be involved, and said that efforts should be directed towards Kuwait. The letter concluded with a note from the captors saying they were becoming impatient and threatening to kill or capture more Americans. The writer appealed to us to go to Kuwait to try and bring this matter to a conclusion.

I was quickly able to establish that the signatures on the letter were genuine. Here was a written appeal to the Archbishop from the hostages themselves, and a request from the kidnappers for Lambeth's involvement. It confirmed previous indications I had received. I discussed the letter with Dr Runcie, and he agreed that I should continue to try for a face-to-face meeting with the kidnappers; also that it was now crucial that the British and American administrations should support my application to get into Kuwait.

From time to time I had had meetings with officials from the US Embassy in London, but I gained little information about the American line on the hostages. Earlier in the year, Oliver North had suggested that it might be helpful if I met with a contact of his, who he said was in London occasionally. Such 'contacts' were always appearing in one way or another. More often than not they introduced themselves. Individuals would write to me with information which they claimed would be helpful. Almost always it was not. Others would request a meeting. As soon as they asked for money, as some did, I closed the conversation as I had no intention of paying informers. In some ways it was like assembling a jigsaw puzzle. Gradually a small part of an enormous picture appeared, but one knew the total picture would never be completed. Many informants, I am sure, used a false identity. Some gave no identity at all. There was only one who was recommended through what might be described as an 'official' American channel. One morning my phone rang and a man introduced himself as Mr Spiro.

'Mr Waite?'

'Yes.'

'I shall be in London next week. I think you have heard of me?'

'Yes, I have.'

'I would like to meet you. The early morning is best for me.'

We agreed to meet the following week over breakfast at a location near Charing Cross Station.

'How shall I recognise you?' I asked.

'Don't worry, I know you.'

On the appointed day I left home earlier than usual and waited at the main station entrance. A tall man with close-cropped hair wearing a leather jacket and an extra-large pair of sunglasses approached me. He greeted me pleasantly and we walked together to the restaurant. We chose a corner table in the empty room. I ordered a full breakfast; he settled for black coffee.

As we ate and drank I tried to sum him up. He appeared to be physically very fit and his manner was friendly. There was no trace of a foreign accent although his bronzed complexion, coupled with the name he had given, led me to assume that he came from either Cyprus or Greece. We chatted inconsequentially. He explained that he had many contacts throughout the Middle East and visited America now and again.

'If I can be of help to you I would be happy,' he said.

'How can you help?'

'I don't know yet. If we meet occasionally, perhaps there will be a way.'

We stood. He replaced his sunglasses and hurried away. Had he not been recommended to me, I doubt whether I would have seen him again.

We did meet several times in the future, usually first thing in the morning. I discovered that Spiro lived outside the UK but did not find out where until our final meeting. Regrettably, like the vast majority of such contacts, I heard little from him that I did not know already. Probably the most valuable advice he gave me was to concentrate on Iran which, he maintained, held the key to the release of the Western hostages. He urged me to visit Tehran and establish contacts at the highest level. This I failed to do. At our penultimate meeting I happened to mention that I was going to Monte Carlo to represent the Archbishop at the funeral of a mutual friend, Dick Stallard. Spiro surprised me by saying that he lived in the South of France and would meet me at Nice airport on my return home. He appeared looking relaxed and happy as I was checking in for the London flight. We sat in the lounge and discussed a scheme he was considering, designed to promote economic development in southern Lebanon. My flight was called, we said farewell, and that was the last I saw of him.

A senior official from the American Embassy visited me at Lambeth Palace shortly after we had received the letter from Beirut. I told him that I needed US backing to get into Kuwait and added that I also intended to press for a meeting with the kidnappers in Beirut; if there were any points the American government wanted to communicate to the kidnappers, I would gladly convey them. I was told that someone would be in touch with me if I was successful in arranging a visit to the Lebanon.

Laurie Lee wrote about memory in one of his essays. A wasted memory, he said, not only destroys, but can deny one's existence. Perhaps that is why I am trying so hard to piece together the past here, in this place, where I have to affirm my existence. Lee went on to suggest that the urge to write might indicate a fear of death. The need to leave messages behind for others. I have that need, but all I can do is to write in my head. If ever I leave here alive, will it be possible to remember these days – this bleak room, the eerie silence, the whispering, the unlocking of doors, the time when night and day had no meaning? Will my memory be accurate, whatever that may mean? On the subject of accuracy, Laurie Lee suggested that to record the exact dimensions of the Taj Mahal is not to possess its spirit. I swim in a pool of memory. I want to be still and float back into childhood, into security, back to the womb where I can be safe, protected, unconscious. The thought of an impending interrogation forces me to swim. The luxury of childhood must wait. Perhaps there will be a time to linger and float through the days when the sun was strong and warm, and every day held the promise and excitement of discovery. Perhaps.

In my memory I walk down the long corridor in Lambeth Palace. I smile as I see my friend and colleague Wilfrid Grenville-Grey take a cricket ball and bowl it down the gallery on the day he is leaving for another job. 'Ever since I've worked here, I've wanted to do that,' he says. 'Now I'm content.'

I walk past the Chaplain's room, the Archbishop's study, the State Room with its lovely collection of Worcester china, down some ancient stone stairs and into the chapel. Before the war, there was a magnificent painted ceiling here. In a matter of seconds a direct hit reduced the work of a lifetime to fragments.

I climb upwards on steps worn with centuries of use, lift a heavy metal latch and push open a door. The wooden boards creak as I cross a small room. I pull back a heavy curtain and look down at the silent chapel. Here in this very room Cranmer is said to have worked on the Book of Common Prayer. Stacked against the wall stands the library of the eminent theologian, Bishop John Robinson, remembered in the public mind for his popular book, *Honest to God*. I look out of the window: St Thomas's Hospital, the Thames, the Palace of Westminster. I sit in an old wooden chair and close my eyes. Tomorrow I leave for Beirut and, I hope, for a first meeting with the kidnappers. There is no turning back. I am alone and often afraid and bewildered by the complexity of events. On the table before me lies an old Prayer Book. I open it at random. The Collect for the Sunday before Lent, Quinquagesima:

> O Lord, who hast taught us that all our doings without
> charity are nothing worth; Send thy Holy Ghost, and
> pour into our hearts that most excellent gift of charity,
> the very bond of peace and of all virtues, without which
> whosoever liveth is counted dead before thee.

O Lord, keep love strong within me, poor fool that I am.

'You will write everything.'
  'What do you mean?'
  'You will write the story of your life.'
  'All my life?'
  'Yes, just as though you are writing a book.'
  I am sitting facing the wall. Behind me the man in the suit is giving me instructions.
  'We want names of people and dates.'
  'What kind of dates?'
  'Every time you have visited the United States.'
  Can he be serious? I can't possibly remember. I have spent a lifetime crossing the world. Besides I don't remember dates. I remember people, places, sights, sounds, smells – but dates! What to do? First, I will stick to the truth. I don't have to say anything that will compromise anyone. Second, I will make this whole business as difficult as I can.
  'Put out hand.' I hold out my hands and the locks are removed.

'Write.'

A blank exercise book is given to me, together with a ballpoint pen.

'Lift blindfold a little. Face the wall.'

I do as I am told. I don't have my reading glasses; I left them behind at the hotel. I can see to write, but I'll be as illegible as I can: 'I was born in Bollington, Cheshire.' I stop. If I say my father was a policeman, won't this increase their suspicion of me? I decide not to mention it. I continue to write in a cramped, small hand: 'My father, Thomas William Waite, was born in Staffordshire. My mother, Lena Beatrice Hardy, was born in Cheshire.'

The man in the suit is still standing behind me.

'Cover eyes.'

I pull the blindfold lower.

'What is this?' The book is taken from my hands.

'The story of my life.'

'What is this writing?'

'My writing.'

He snorts with disgust. 'Why do you write like this?'

The fact is that I am being bloody-minded. I reply with part of the truth:

'I don't have my reading glasses.'

'Why?'

'I didn't bring them from the hotel.'

'Write better.'

The book is handed back to me, and I continue. I have no intention of writing more clearly.

'Put name of your father's father – put date of birth.'

How can I possibly remember my grandfather's date of birth? I can roughly calculate it, but if I do that I must be able to remember what I have written. I make up a date one day and one month before my birthday and in the previous century. That should make it easier to remember.

'Writing no good.' He is looking over my shoulder again.

Even with my glasses, my writing is not good. As a left-handed child I never found a comfortable writing style. I married a left-hander, and two of our four children are left-handed. Sinister information!

'You must write better.'

Off I go again. This silly game might continue for hours.

'Stop. Give me.' He takes the book. 'You must write bigger – understand?'

'Yes.'

I start writing and fill several pages with useless detail. My interrogator is bored and has gone to the opposite side of the room to watch TV. After an hour or so he returns.

'Give me.' I hand over the book. 'Give me.' I hand back the pen. 'Sleep.'

I lie down and face the wall. He speaks to my regular guard and leaves. What will his reaction be if he is able to read my scribble? Anger, I suppose. My mind returns to his question about visits to the United States. I appreciate his suspicions. I have to be able somehow to convince him that he need not fear me. Put simply, the real situation is that I am caught between the machinations of groups in America and Hezbollah. Now I must suffer the fate of the man in the middle.

I think of my wife, Frances, gentle, determined, deeply sensitive, probably the most loyal and trustworthy person I have ever known. She has the same integrity that I first saw in my father. How hard it must have been for her to live with my restless nature. I let myself drift across the ocean of the past, into sleep, into peace, into dreams that heal and sustain.

I wake with a start. My chains are twisted and uncomfortable. My blindfold is askew. There is shouting. What in God's name? I pull myself back from sleep to the conscious world. People are yelling, running, chanting. Someone is talking to my guard. It's a demonstration in the square outside . . . If only I knew Arabic. The reaction of the guards tells me they are agitated. I lie ignorant, alone, half-awake, caught in a world of which I know so little. Motivated, I hope, by a love for my fellow human beings. We are all poor lost souls seeking our destiny, our identity, our worth, our acceptance, holding to our inadequate understanding of what we believe to be the truth. What is the truth? Where does it lie? How can we know it? It will make us free, but how can we be sure of our perception? It has so many sides, so many shades. You must tell the truth, know the truth, live the truth, be the truth. Oh God – another day.

The school in Wilmslow was not half so bad as I had been led to expect. To my surprise, I went immediately into the A-stream and was told that I would be given an opportunity to sit another examination in a year's time. That information failed to thrill me, but I determined to settle down to work as best I could.

My day started early. Soon after six I would dress and make my way to the kitchen. The previous evening my mother had prepared porridge for me to heat up. A green tin of Lyle's Golden Syrup stood on the table with the legend so well known to my generation: 'Out of the strong came forth sweetness.'

As soon as I had had a hurried breakfast, I left the house to start my newspaper round. This I did seven days a week for the magnificent sum of ten shillings. It was a small fortune to me, and initially every penny went towards paying for my bicycle. When that was achieved I could go back to buying second-hand books. Occasionally I would stop and browse in the bookshop in Wilmslow. The smell of a new book was a delight, but the price was almost always beyond my limited resources.

Family holidays were infrequent and often a source of strain rather than relaxation. At Blackpool we committed ourselves to the care of one of the infamous 'landladies'. Immediately after breakfast, regardless of the weather, we had to leave the premises and stay away until just before the evening meal. As the weather was variable, this could be an ordeal. My father took me to the top of the famous tower, and later we visited the Tower Ballroom to watch Reginald Dixon perform on the theatre organ, the organ that rose from beneath the floor with Reg improvising for all he was worth. Sights and sounds never to be forgotten.

If we did not go away for a whole week, we went for a series of day trips – to Rhyl in north Wales or New Brighton on the Mersey. In Liverpool we travelled around on the overhead railway. From this unique vantage point we could look down on ocean liners from every corner of the globe. As we crossed on the ferry to New Brighton, I imagined myself sailing the oceans and exploring the world. How I longed to do just that. Liverpool, still battered and scarred by the ravages of the Second World War, was a city of excitement. The streets were crowded with all nationalities. At lunchtime, Pier Head was full of budding orators haranguing the crowd from their soap boxes. On bomb sites, escape artists intrigued their audiences, while on street corners cardsharpers endlessly repeated the three-card trick. My mother took me to the only restaurant I ever went to as a child, in Lewis's department store.

We ate roast chicken, which we normally had only once a year on Christmas Day.

I left for Beirut in a blaze of publicity. Having made the decision to go public, there was no possibility of keeping the media at bay. I recognised that they had a job to do, and I needed their help and support.

Several months earlier Fred Wilson and I had met Louis Boccardi, the head of Associated Press in New York, and told him of our willingness to do everything possible for the hostages, mentioning the 'blood money' proposal. Lou, a highly intelligent and able man, promised his personal assistance where he could give it. A message came through that the kidnappers would communicate with me via a shortwave transceiver, and Myron Belkind, the London bureau chief, bought me a set in London and also a Polaroid camera.

The morning of 13 November was cold and foggy. I left home early to catch the 0900 MEA flight from Heathrow. The previous day I had been told that Colonel North and an official from the State Department were flying to London from the US and would meet me at the airport. They had questions they wanted me to put to the kidnappers. I checked my luggage; my flight was called. There was no sign of the Americans. I was disappointed, as I wanted to hear what the representatives of the US government had to say. An inquiry at the information desk revealed that all flights from America had been delayed by adverse weather conditions. There was nothing to do but board my flight.

Just as the cabin door was being closed, a message was handed to me. I was wanted urgently at the terminal building. A car was at the foot of the steps. I got in, and we drove through the mist to the departure gate. There I met Colonel North and a Mr Borge from the State Department. North apologised for being late. They had been delayed by fog, he said. Mr Borge shook my hand. He looked worried and said nothing apart from a brief greeting. North wanted me to put three questions to the kidnappers: Did they want money? If they didn't, what did they want? Would they be prepared to meet with someone from the US administration? There was no time for discussion as my plane was ready to depart. I climbed back into the car and within a few moments was on my way to Beirut.

I did not know what to expect on my arrival. There was always the possibility that the kidnappers, having followed developments through the media, might take the opportunity to release another hostage. I had visited Beirut only once, many years ago. I considered the questions Oliver North had asked me to raise. I thought it most unlikely that the kidnappers were after money, and was surprised that this should be suggested to them. If money were required, I would not act as an intermediary. Exchanging money for hostages went against everything I believed in. The other two questions seemed straightforward enough, although the Americans appeared to be saying publicly that they would not enter into negotiations with terrorists. Later I learnt the important distinction between 'negotiate' and 'talk with'.

There was utter confusion at the foot of the aircraft steps when we touched down. Members of different militia groups active in Beirut pushed and shouted in an attempt to surround me and lead me to a car. The ever-efficient Associated Press office had made arrangements for me to be taken briefly to a hotel, after which I was to be transferred to Terry Anderson's apartment. I left the airport surrounded by militiamen who drove at breakneck speed through the war-torn streets. When we came to a traffic jam, my escorts cleared it by the simple expedient of firing their automatics in the air. Eventually I arrived at the apartment. Terry had chosen well. The block was directly on the Corniche, overlooking the Mediterranean. In more peaceful days it would have been idyllic. Two journalists – Robert Fisk, then working for the London *Times*, and Juan Carlos Gumucio – introduced themselves. Both had considerable knowledge of the Lebanon, and Fisk was a personal friend of Terry Anderson's. An electrician from the AP office came to the flat and installed the shortwave radio. I sat down, tuned in to the agreed frequency and waited.

It must be the early hours of the morning. I have been sleeping fitfully and was awakened by what I thought was something touching my face. I can definitely feel something in my hair. I run my fingers across my scalp. It's a cockroach. I fling it across the room. It's one thing to share this space with vermin, but quite another for them to be so intimate. Now I can't sleep. I sit with my back against the wall and strain my ears for any sound. Tonight the shelling is far away. Here, in captivity, lost men dream dreams and remember days of liberty and imagined freedom. My story grows slowly in my head. Now in the deep darkness of night my past life seems as though it were lived in a matter of moments. My visits to Beirut merge into one visit. Robert Fisk bounces into Terry's flat in a humorous mood bordering on the hysterical. Then he sits quietly and reveals the depth of his intelligence and his understanding of the Lebanon.

Ghostly, disembodied souls chatter on the shortwave radio. A grenade explodes in the sea, tossed by a fisherman who will eat today and starve tomorrow; the explosion will kill all the fish. I pick out a book from Terry's full bookcase. All I can do is turn the pages. I see the words, but my thoughts swirl around in a dizzy tormented anxiety. You have been doing too much, pushing yourself too hard. Relax, man, relax. Why no message on the radio? I have the right frequency, at least the one that was given to me. The radio remains on day and night. I barely sleep. What message will they send? How will I know it's genuine? Will they trick me? God, I hate this life. Why am I doing this? Why am I here, miles from home, when I could be in my own house with my family, my own books and a comfortable, interesting job to pursue each day? There must be at least a dozen possible answers. For the moment, there is nothing to do but wait.

The message never came over the radio. Instead the telephone rang. I answered it, expecting a call from the AP office to check that everything was well. A voice I didn't recognise spoke to me.

'Mr Waite?'

'Yes, speaking.'

'We would like to talk with you.'

'Who are you?'

'I think you want to speak with us.'

'Perhaps.'

'Could you meet me at — '

He mentioned a certain petrol station in Beirut, quite unknown to me. I hesitated. After so many approaches by individuals falsely claiming to have vital information about hostages, I had learnt to be cautious. I was also concerned lest a rival gang attempt to kidnap me. It was Robert Fisk who suggested a test question which would indicate whether or not I was in touch with the kidnappers. A journalist known to Terry Anderson had a Finnish girlfriend. The kidnappers could hardly know this. I asked the caller to provide the correct name. Within a short time he phoned back: 'Christina.' The name was right. Almost certainly he had spoken to Terry Anderson. I was in direct contact with the kidnappers at last.

'Meet us tonight at the surgery of Dr Mroueh. It's near the American University in Beirut.'

The line went dead.

'M R O U E H.' I spelt out the name.

'Do you know him?'

Robert Fisk didn't know him, but we soon established that he was a Shiite gynaecologist with an apartment and consulting rooms adjacent to AUB. When I moved into Terry's flat I had asked my bodyguards to leave me alone. Although they were willing to stay in the flat with me, I preferred to be on my own. My driver, Hussain, a cheerful and seemingly fearless local employee of Associated Press, was always on hand. I asked him to be ready to drive me that evening to the doctor's surgery.

Evening came. Hussain arrived at the flat in his usual good spirits. I emptied my pockets and carried only the camera I had brought with me from London. I tried not to think of the risk I was taking. I hoped no one would be so stupid as to attempt to follow me. Earlier some members of the press corps had tried to. I had given them a general statement at the Commodore Hotel and requested them, too, to leave me alone. Admittedly it was a difficult situation for a number of people. I needed the help and support of AP and the expert advice of Robert Fisk and Juan Carlos. They faced the double dilemma of being deeply concerned about their friend and colleague Terry Anderson, and also being involved in an important news story. As far as I know, they both played that dual role honourably.

I asked my driver to go around the town first, so that we could see if we were being followed. He revved up the car and in typical macho fashion accelerated away. We drove towards the city and along several side streets.

'Are we being followed?'

'No, nothing.'

'We had better drive for a little longer.'

I was conscious of the fact that in all probability the kidnappers themselves might have watched me leave the apartment in order to protect their own security. Goodness knows who else would be observing my movements. We drove for a further fifteen minutes or so.

'OK, if you can't see anyone let's make for AUB.'

Hussain swung the car round, and we drove through the night.

'Right, stop here.'

He stopped, grinned, and shook my hand.

'Good luck, Mr Terry.'

'Thanks, Hussain. I'll see you later.'

I watched him drive away. It was dark and deathly quiet. I hitched the camera case over my shoulder, turned, and walked alone the last few hundred yards to my rendezvous.

The glass front door to the lobby had been left ajar. I pushed it open and entered. There was no sign of a porter. The elevator creaked its way upwards. I stepped out on to an empty landing and pushed the bell of the apartment opposite. There was a short delay, then the door opened revealing a slightly built, middle-aged man.

'Good evening, Mr Waite.'

His English was excellent with only the slightest trace of an accent.

'Come in, please.'

I entered.

'These are my consulting rooms. No one is here yet.'

I followed him down a corridor to his study. The room had the clinical neatness of a successful medical practitioner. Chromium-and-glass desk, black leather chairs, expensively bound volumes in a cedar bookcase. He placed himself behind the desk and invited me to sit opposite him.

'I don't know who these men are,' he began. 'They simply want me to be an intermediary. I would like to see this problem solved. Do you mind if I smoke?'

He took a pipe and filled it with tobacco. Medical certificates lined the walls. I looked at them. He smiled.

'Yes, I did some of my studies in America.'

An unopened copy of the *Wall Street Journal* lay on the desk. I put the camera beside it. On one wall was a painting of a cottage; it could have been rural Wales.

'That was my house in southern Lebanon. We had to leave it years ago.'

Along with thousands of others, I thought.

The doorbell rang. He rose.

'Excuse me, please.'

After a few minutes Dr Mroueh returned. 'Would you mind coming to the waiting room for a moment, please?'

I followed him along the corridor. He ushered me into a side room.

'I shan't be long.'

He closed the door. I assumed the kidnappers or their contacts had arrived. Within a few moments the doctor reappeared.

'I am afraid that you must be blindfolded for the meeting.'

He handed me a strip of material. I covered my eyes and tied it at the back.

'This way.'

He took me by the arm, guided me back to his study and sat me down. I was conscious of several people in the room. I thought I recognised the voice of my telephone contact. From under my blindfold I could see an expensive pair of French-style shoes. Someone spoke in Arabic. Dr Mroueh translated.

'Did you come alone?'

'Yes.'

'Are you armed?'

'No.'

'What do you have to say?'

I began by greeting my unseen audience. I told them the Archbishop of Canterbury was prepared to do all he could to bring about a resolution of the hostage problem. We were very conscious of the suffering of the people of Lebanon. Ben Weir had spoken to me of the severe hardships endured by the Shiite people of southern Lebanon. Before I could say any more, I needed further proof that I was speaking with the kidnappers. I asked if they would take me to see the people they held. There was silence for a moment, followed by discussion in Arabic. Dr Mroueh translated again.

'They say it is impossible. It is too dangerous.'

This hardly surprised me. I asked the doctor to pass me the *Wall Street Journal*, and signed it at the top. Then I mentioned the camera and asked if they would bring me pictures of the hostages, each holding a copy of the signed newspaper. There was more discussion. Finally Dr Mroueh spoke again.

'They agree to do that. You must now wait a little while.'

There was a pause. I heard footsteps as they left the room. Someone returned almost immediately.

'You can remove the blindfold now.'

Dr Mroueh sat opposite me. The camera had gone. He took out his pipe and began to fill it once more.

'They are very anxious.'

'I can understand that.'

'I am sorry that you must be blindfolded.'

'I understand their concern, but it makes it difficult to talk to them when I can't see their eyes.'

He made no reply. We waited thirty, forty-five minutes, one hour.

'They should be here soon.'

The doorbell rang once. I replaced my blindfold. Footsteps in the corridor. Something pushed into my hand. I looked under my blindfold. Four Polaroid pictures of four men, each holding a copy of the signed newspaper. Terry Anderson, Tom Sutherland, David Jacobsen and Lawrence Jenco.

At last . . .

Several men spread themselves around the room. Dr Mroueh continued to interpret. I opened the conversation.

'Thank you for getting me these pictures. Are the men well?'

'Yes, they are well.'

'What news do you have of Alec Collett? His family is worried.'

'We don't have him.'

'Do you have news of any other hostages?'

'We have no news.'

'Before I came to see you, I met with representatives of the American government. They asked me to put some questions to you. They are not my questions.'

'OK.'

'First, I was asked if you wanted money. I must tell you that if it is money you want, I will not be able to help. I do not like to exchange money for hostages.'

There was a moment's silence, then someone began to shout in Arabic. Immediately, I regretted putting the question. The atmosphere became electric. I sat quietly, cursing my stupidity.

'You know it is not money. Why you ask that question? We stop talking now.'

'It is not my question. I was asked to put it to you so that everyone can be clear about what you want.'

'America very bad. They know what we want. They know our problem.'

'You have made it clear. There is no doubt that you are not asking for money. I will tell the Americans that.'

'What other questions they ask you?'

'They ask if you would like to meet someone from the American government.'

'No, we do not want to meet. America no good. No meet.'

'Right, I will tell them that.'

'What other question?'

'They say what do you want?'

A snort of disgust from across the room.

'They know answer to that. We write letter to Archbishop and to Reagan. They know.'

'They want to be clear.'

'We want our brothers home from Kuwait. They have very bad time. If they stay in prison, they die. Their conditions very bad. Food bad. No letters or news from their family. They have very bad time. They die if we do not help.'

'The Church will try to help. We will not do anything outside the law. For a long time I have been trying to get to Kuwait to see your people. I will keep trying. If you give me letters from relatives, I will try to get them to your friends in Kuwait.'

'We will get you letters.'

'I think our best chance is to see if the payment of "blood money" to the relatives of those who were killed might help. This would not be breaking the law. I will continue to see whether we can make some progress here. I will also ask the Americans to help me get into Kuwait.'

'OK, good. If America help you – you will go to Kuwait.'

'Can you release some hostages now? That would be a good sign and might help me in my mission.'

'We have released Mr Weir. That was good for you.'

'I will speak to the Americans. I will tell them exactly what you want and will let you know what they say very soon. Please, you will take good care of the hostages?'

'Yes.'

'Thank you for this meeting and for trusting me.'

'We will leave now. You must wait for half an hour before leaving. It will be dangerous for you to leave before then. Understand?'

'Yes, I understand. Goodnight.'

I sat quietly in my chair. I heard the sound of whispering. People were leaving the room. A door closed.

'They have gone now.'

I removed my blindfold. Dr Mroueh was sitting behind his desk.

'We can wait here for a moment, then go to my flat. It's just downstairs.'

I was very tired. I had half-expected to be taken captive myself. I looked at the photographs again. Four bearded men standing against a plain white wall, looking directly ahead, a haunted, distant look in their eyes. The *Wall Street Journal* and the camera were back on the table. I picked them up and put the photographs in my pocket. Dr Mroueh stood.

'I think we can go to my flat now.'

I followed him out into the lobby. We entered the small lift and descended one floor. He took a key from his pocket and opened the door to his apartment. He called out to his wife and led me into the sitting room.

'Please sit down. Would you like some coffee?'

Coffee was produced. I have no idea what we spoke about during the half-hour or so I waited. My mind was full. I had been frightened by the meeting. Now surely I would get US backing to visit Kuwait. The kidnappers had trusted me. A first step had been taken towards the building of trust. I needed to get moving. We telephoned Hussain and asked him to meet me at the end of the street. I said goodbye, descended in the lift, walked into the empty street and met my car. It was midnight.

I have no desire to eat and no pangs of hunger. That surprises me, but I think my feelings of anger and disappointment are so strong that they take precedence over my physical needs. The thought of my first meeting with the kidnappers still chills me. In my cerebral narrative I have left out the body search, the sight of arms from beneath my blindfold. Unconsciously I protect myself. The force of their anger in response to the question about money still makes me cringe. Did the Americans really believe they could buy off the hostage-takers? They probably did: there were strong rumours that hostages had been bought by France and Libya – but the Middle East is full of the most amazing rumours. Attempting to separate fact from fantasy is a Herculean task.

When I returned to the flat, I was glad to see Bob Fisk. Naturally, he was anxious to have news about his friend Terry Anderson. I told him that four of the American hostages, including Terry, were alive and seemingly well.

The principal agenda for the Lebanese captors was undoubtedly the fate of the Kuwaiti prisoners. I wanted the Americans to know at once about their demands, in the hope that the US would back my application for a visit to Kuwait and urge the Emir not to execute the condemned prisoners. It was only much later that I learnt that Iran had a totally different agenda, which at this stage was probably unknown to their Lebanese associates.

As it was impossible to have a secure conversation from Beirut, I had to fly to London for a brief meeting with officials from the American government, among them Oliver North, and I received the assurances of support that I was hoping for. I was further told that the Emir would be requested not to proceed with the death sentences. I also had contact with others who were helping me, particularly associates from Saudi Arabia. I was informed that there was a very good chance that the captors would reciprocate the efforts the Church was making by releasing another hostage, probably Father Jenco. It was suggested that I should return to Beirut straight away to send a positive message to the kidnappers. Within twenty-four hours I was heading back to the Lebanese capital.

Now, with ample time for reflection and the benefit of hindsight, I ponder the wisdom of this second visit. I was anxious to keep the process moving forward. I wanted the kidnappers to know immediately that I had been promised powerful support in my endeavours to get into Kuwait. It was well known that the Kuwaitis were sensitive to geopolitical circumstances and could be influenced by their immediate neighbours, the Saudis, and the Americans, who acted as their protectors. There was every reason to believe that progress could be made. If I could communicate this to the kidnappers quickly, there was a chance that the situation could be defused, and perhaps conditions might improve for the four Americans.

On my return to Beirut, I had to change planes in Paris, which meant going from Charles de Gaulle Airport to Orly. As I stepped off the plane in France, I was met by a man who identified himself as a representative of the French government. He offered me a lift, and on the drive he expressed his concern for the French hostages and told me he would welcome any help I could give, especially with regard to one hostage who, he said, was suffering from a serious heart condition. I told him I had no information about French hostages, but I would certainly do what I could. The next morning the French official and a companion were sitting behind me on the flight to Beirut.

I went to Terry's flat again and made contact with Dr Mroueh. Shortly before my own capture in January 1987 I heard that a rumour was circulating that on my second visit I was wearing a tracking device supplied by the Americans. I have never, to my knowledge, seen a tracking device, let alone carried one. To meet with the kidnappers was risky enough without exposing myself to unnecessary dangers. Apart from that, although I certainly did not approve of kidnapping, I would not willingly have breached the trust the kidnappers placed in me. I also spoke to my telephone contact, who expressed satisfaction at the American response and undertook to get me letters from the relatives of the Da'wa prisoners to deliver. I asked if I might meet these relatives, but he said this was not possible. He urged me to continue my efforts on behalf of his friends and told me that no more Western hostages would be released for the moment. The kidnappers asked if they could have the shortwave radio. Not wishing to antagonise them unnecessarily, I agreed to leave it behind for them.

Back in London, I discussed progress with Samir Habiby. We decided that I ought to visit the White House to brief President Reagan on my communications with the kidnappers and the demands being made. As it happened, on the very morning suggested for the meeting I had an appointment to see Pérez de Cuéllar, the Secretary-General of the United Nations in New York. President Reagan could not see me in the afternoon as he was leaving for California at lunchtime. I had decided anyway that I wanted to meet the Secretary-General before going to the White House, as I was acting on behalf of all the hostages and not just the Americans. The Vice-President, George Bush, was asked to deputise for the President, and a meeting with him was arranged following my visit to the UN.

Pérez de Cuéllar had been known to me for some time, and I had considerable respect for him. He said he would do everything he could to assist my mission, and while I was in his office he personally contacted the Kuwaitis, asking them to receive me. He promised me his help at any time and, much encouraged, I left for Washington.

My first visit to the White House, in the early 1980s, took place during a conference of Anglican archbishops to which I accompanied Robert Runcie, and was arranged by the Presiding Bishop. At the time, President Reagan was recovering from the attempt on his life, so Vice-President George Bush greeted the party. Before leaving, the Archbishop of Canterbury said a few well-chosen words and as was his custom handed over a small gift – a framed print of Lambeth

Palace. An official quickly left the room and returned with a cardboard box which he handed to Bush, who in turn presented it to the Archbishop.

'A gift from the President,' he said. 'Something to put on your desk, Archbishop.' The Chaplain accepted the gift, and we took our leave and returned to the conference centre at Washington Cathedral where we opened the box. It contained a glass jar, inscribed with the President's initials and intended to hold jelly beans, which we were given to understand were a particular favourite of the President. The jar never made it to London as it was smashed in transit. Malicious tongues accused the Chaplain of a deliberate act of sabotage.

On my second visit to the White House, in 1985, I was accompanied by Bishop Allin, the Presiding Bishop of the Episcopal Church, and Samir Habiby. Admiral Poindexter, the National Security Council Adviser's deputy, Colonel North and several other aides were present. I took a seat by the fireplace opposite Vice-President Bush. After giving an account of my meeting with the kidnappers I outlined my reasons for wanting to visit Kuwait. I said that I believed it would ease the situation if some humanitarian consideration could be shown towards the Da'wa prisoners. The Vice-President listened carefully.

'Well,' he said. 'You know who to keep in touch with.' I understood that he was referring to Oliver North. He went on to ask me several questions about Colonel Gaddafi, whom I had met previously. I said that anyone who had remained in power for as long as he had was not to be underestimated. The Vice-President made little comment.

'The White House press corps would like to meet you before you go.' Bush walked with me into the rose garden. I answered a few general questions and returned to say goodbye. A photographer entered and performed the compulsory ritual.

Before leaving Washington, I had lunch with the British Ambassador. I told him of my meeting with Vice-President Bush and my hopes of US assistance to get into Kuwait. In New York, Samir arranged for me to meet the Syrian Ambassador, formerly the Foreign Minister, and later the Libyan Ambassador, both of whom were accredited to the United Nations. I also met the British Deputy Consul-General and the UK's First Secretary to the United Nations Mission who were deeply concerned about the fate of Alec Collett. The meeting with Collett's American wife stands out in my mind.

We met in the headquarters of the Episcopal Church, and all I could do was to assure her that I would make every effort on behalf of her husband. I often felt so helpless myself that it was not easy trying to reassure distressed relatives.

After my visit to the White House, it appeared as if we were edging forward. Samir Habiby, as energetic as ever, organised a meeting with the Kuwaiti Ambassador in Geneva. The Ambassador was extremely cautious, but he suggested that if the letters from the prisoners' relatives conformed with the requirements set forth by the International Committee of the Red Cross, it would be possible to get them through. He was hopeful of being able to arrange a 'safe conduct' family visit to the prisoners, and when Samir and I asked him to allow me to visit them as soon as possible, he agreed to pursue the request.

In Geneva we handed the letters to the Red Cross for delivery to Kuwait. They gave me a number of official mail forms to be used by the families in Lebanon on future occasions. Two or three weeks passed. No messages came from the Kuwaitis.

As Christmas 1985 approached, I decided to return to Beirut. I wanted the kidnappers to know of the favourable response we had received from the Kuwaiti Ambassador in Geneva.

Wearily I made my way to Heathrow Airport. Relatives of the hostages had given me letters and cards to take with me, and I hoped that the kidnappers would agree to let me see them at a time of year which they knew was significant for Westerners. In the back of my mind was the very faint hope that they might release another hostage to keep the whole process moving. No dramatic advance had been made since my visit to Washington, but I thought there were indications of progress, and at least none of the Da'wa prisoners had been executed.

On arrival in Beirut, I was once again taken to Terry Anderson's flat. Myron Belkind had bought me another radio, which I carried with me. When I had settled in, I made telephone contact with the kidnappers via Dr Mroueh. They were pleased at what I had to report and expressed approval of my visit to George Bush. I told them about the Red Cross letter forms which I had brought and said that it might soon be possible for relatives to visit the Da'wa prisoners. They promised to let me know about the possibility of visiting the Western hostages. A day or two went by.

One evening, just before Christmas, the telephone rang. Bob Fisk was sitting in the apartment with me and Juan Carlos Gumucio. I picked up the receiver and recognised the voice of my contact.

'Mr Waite?'

'Yes.'

'We don't like what you have done. You have forty-eight hours to leave the country. If not, we will kill you.'

'What do you mean? What has gone wrong?'

'You must leave in forty-eight hours.'

The phone was replaced. I turned to my companions and relayed the message.

'I simply don't understand it. A day or two ago things were progressing, now they seem to have turned around a hundred and eighty degrees. What should I do?'

Robert Fisk suggested I stay and see what materialised. Juan Carlos, more cautious, reminded me of the irrationalities in the situation. We decided to consult Dr Mroueh, who was in no doubt at all about what was to be done. I left Beirut on Christmas Eve, perplexed and sad. I was not to return to the Hezbollah-dominated sector of the city, West Beirut, until my final visit in January 1987.

The shelling is intense this evening. I know it's evening because a few moments ago the guard told me the time. Eight o'clock – six in London. Back home, they will be wondering what has happened to me. Well, here I am, waiting for goodness knows what. Why did the Lebanese have such a sudden change of mind during my visit at the end of 1985? One minute they were enthusiastic about developments, the next, they were threatening to kill me. The first clue came from one of my contacts: 'Mohsem Rafiqdoust, head of the Iranian Revolutionary Guards, gave the instruction that you were to leave Beirut immediately.'

'Are you sure?'

'Pretty sure.'

'Why?'

'I don't know.'

Well, now it's clear. Painfully, bitterly clear. The prisoners in Kuwait were at the top of the Lebanese agenda. First, they wanted the prisoners' lives to be saved; second, their conditions improved; and finally, their release. The Church could help them with the first two points and eventually, possibly, with the third. The Iranians, at war with Iraq, needed weapons. The hostages provided the leverage to get weapons from America. On another level, the Iranians were in the business of exporting and developing the Iranian revolution throughout the Lebanon. Beirut was full of 'advisers' from Iran working with radical Shiite groups. While the Iranians might have had some sympathy for the Da'wa prisoners, their own political agenda clearly came first. All Iran had to do was discredit me by increasing the Lebanese suspicion of my role. All America had to do was play me along.

And what of Oliver North in all of this? Churchill's words about Russia seem apt: 'a riddle wrapped in a mystery inside an enigma'. The soft-spoken military man, the family man, the man who moved in the shadows and almost became a shadow himself is now accused before the world. But shadows tonight have struck more terror to my soul than the substance of ten thousand soldiers . . .

You fool, Waite, you stupid fool. Tears come to my eyes, but I steel myself. I may be a fool, but whatever happens, my spirit will remain strong. No regrets, hear that? I thump my fist into my palm out of sheer frustration and anger. No self-pity, remember? Whatever else you feel, no self-pity.

« 4 »

'This writing not good.'

It's late at night. The man in the suit has returned with two others. I recognise the nasal tones of the old man who struck me, but I can't place the third man. To my relief the two others quit the apartment, leaving me alone with the man in the suit and my guard.

'Not good – understand?'

'I can't see without my reading glasses.'

'OK. You tell me – I write.'

With a sinking feeling I realise that I have to dictate my life story to him. While he has reasonable English, he is far from fluent. Almost certainly he will use a tape recorder. As though he can read my thoughts, I hear a click as he switches on a machine.

'Start now.'

'Where do you want me to start?'

'Start like you write a book – what you call it?'

'An autobiography?'

'Yes – right – start like that.'

I begin to speak rapidly. I am playing a game with him, and frankly I am getting tired of it.

'Stop – too quick.' I stop speaking. 'I must write – go slow.'

I begin again, trying to spin out endless useless detail. We continue for an hour or so.

'OK, enough.'

The tone of voice tells me he is tired and not a little fed up.

'Sleep.'

I lie down again facing the wall. I hear him leave. How long will this continue? How long will it be before they turn really unpleasant? The outside door opens and several people come in. My stomach tenses. It's the uncertainty that is so hard. I never know from one moment to the next what is going to happen. It sounds as if they are bringing some equipment. They talk softly to each other as they move items around the room. For some reason the guard is moving his bed. Oh God – what is happening? They must have realised that I am not co-operating and are now preparing to use tougher methods. Why am I being so bloody-minded? I have nothing to hide, nothing to be ashamed of. It's simply that I will not allow myself to be intimidated. I can and will tell the truth, of that I need have no fear. If we ever get to important questions, I can deal with them in a straightforward manner. I also recognise that I am doing my level best to continue in my role as envoy and not change to that of hostage. I don't want to accept that I am a captive.

'Sit.' I struggle to a sitting position. Someone tightens my blindfold. I feel someone else at my feet unlocking the padlocks, and the locks are removed from my hands.

'Stand.' As I get to my feet I feel weak and a little light-headed. Too much lounging about! I have to be guided across the room.

'Sit.' I sit down on a wooden chair. I feel that there are several people behind me, and someone is in front. They seem to have erected a bright light. I can't see it, but I can feel the warmth.

'Not turn head.'

I keep my head towards the front.

'Take cover from eyes.'

I remove it and am blinded for a moment by the light. As my vision returns, I see that I am facing a video camera which has been placed on a stand. A studio light is behind it. The camera operator has hidden himself by swathing his body in a long blanket. His head is carefully covered with a towel, and over the small space left for his eyes he wears sunglasses. He reminds me of the bandaged Miss Troy in *The Lady Vanishes*. From behind where I am sitting the man in the suit speaks:

'Now you say everything to video.'

This could be a lengthy session.

'Say everything. Start now.'

The operator starts the camera and moves out of my range of vision. Once again I tell my story. I get to my final visit to Beirut, and I pause for a moment. There is a noise. I think I recognise it, but it can't be. It certainly is. Behind me the man in the suit is snoring gently.

Back in my chains, I go over what I said. The problem with tapes is that they can so easily be doctored. Will my captors do that? Certainly, they are going to question me further. My intuition tells me that they are probably convinced I have been trustworthy as a negotiator, but they are uneasy about my contacts with Oliver North. This is understandable. In their position I would be uneasy. Like so many persecuted groups, Islamic Jihad borders on paranoia and actually attracts paranoid characters into its ranks. The old man who hit me is one such. The man in the suit is more calculating, but he is also subject to outbursts of irrational feeling: 'I hate the West. I hate the British, the French, the Americans. I hate them all.' The strength of his rage caught me once like a blow between the eyes. It was useless to argue with him. Useless to ask how anyone can possibly hate whole nations. But I tried.

'What else can we do?' he demanded.

'You can use your intelligence. You can put your case before the world. Every time you use violence against the innocent you turn more and more good people against you.'

'We have tried. No one listens.'

There is truth in what he says. Injustices go on and on, and few pay attention until they overflow into violence and further injustice. I made a final effort.

'But when you imprison the innocent you are not being a good Muslim. It's the same as stealing. You are stealing a life, stealing a man from his family.'

End of discussion. In his heart he must know what I have said is true. He is a man caught in a conflict. A battle for liberty. Freedom for his family, freedom for his people, freedom for his faith. A man seeking power. Power that has been denied him all his life. Can the end ever justify the means? Can injustice ever be used to herald justice?

When I was thirteen I could hardly believe that we were leaving Styal. The thought of moving away caused me almost physical pain. I wandered through the village, said goodbye to Alan and Michael, took one last look at the primary school. At the cricket field I sat alone on the steps of the wooden pavilion remembering the days when I kept the score book for the First XI and ate Saturday afternoon tea with the team: Heinz Salad Cream, lettuce and tomatoes, real cream cakes. My hope that one day I would graduate from scorer to a junior position in the team was never now to be fulfilled. I went to All Saints for the last time. Johnnie Dumbell, aptly named as he actually was a dumb bellringer, stood in the porch tolling a single peal. After the service I went back to a house full of half-packed boxes. I didn't want to leave; this was my home. I knew everyone in the village. I put my treasured books into boxes, carefully packed a stuffed snipe I had inherited and collected the scattered pieces of my Meccano set. My father had helped me make a huge working model of Blackpool Tower with these very pieces. Although we were moving no more than twenty miles away, it might well have been to the far side of the world. The removal van arrived in the morning. My parents and my brother and sister were travelling in the van. I took my bicycle and cycled away from the village for the last time; past Oak Farm, along by Ringway Airport, stopping for a moment by Castle Mill swimming pool which had been closed some years before when a polio epidemic struck the village; two of my school-friends had caught the disease. I rode on through the back lanes to Lymm and a mile or so more to our new police house in Thelwall.

I have lost track of the days. It's probably Tuesday, but I can't be sure. One day is very much the same as another. Bread and *lebne* for breakfast, one quick visit to the bathroom, and then twenty-three hours and fifty minutes lying in the corner with nothing but my thoughts. I live on sandwiches and two cups of tea a day. It's enough. The guard is watching an Arabic programme on television. Someone taps on the apartment door, and I can hear voices in the hallway. Visitors arouse my fear. Several people enter the room. I recognise the old man with the cold and the man in the suit. There is also another person whom I don't know and who says little.

'Face the wall.'

I get into a sitting position facing the wall. My heart is beating faster than normal. I breathe deeply in an attempt to keep calm. God, please help me.

'We want to know about Colonel North.'

'What do you want to know?'

'Everything.'

'I have told you everything I know.'

'You lie.'

'I do not lie. I have told you what I know. There is no need for me to hide anything.'

The old man speaks softly in Arabic. 'Sleep.'

I lie down. Someone turns up the volume on the television. Two pillows are placed over my head. The man in the suit sits on the pillows. I struggle to move my head so that I can breathe properly. Someone removes the blanket covering my feet. Oh God, give me strength. A sudden pain shoots across the soles of my feet and convulses my whole body. I want to cry out, but my face is pressed into the pillow. Another blow sears my skin, and another and another. God, how much more? The old man must be beating me with a cable. After a dozen or so strokes he stops and runs his finger down the length of my foot to see if there is still feeling. When he discovers from my reaction that there is, he resumes the beating. I clench my fists and tense my whole body. My feet hurt so much, so much. Finally he stops. The man in the suit gets up and takes the pillows from my head. I lie quivering with nervous reaction.

'Now you will tell us.'

'There is nothing more to tell.'

I force the words out with all the energy I can muster and wait anxiously for another blow. Nothing happens. The men whisper among themselves, and I hear them leave the room. The television is turned down.

'I need the bathroom.'

The sympathetic young guard unlocks my chains. I try to stand, but it's impossible. He supports me across his shoulders and half-drags me the few paces to the toilet. I stagger inside and the door is left slightly ajar. I feel sick, anxious, afraid. Perhaps they will beat me again – even kill me. Whatever they do, they will never destroy me – never, never.

Somehow my guard gets me back to my mattress and secures my chains. I lie quietly, and my swollen feet burn like fire. I close my eyes:

> *Come, sleep, and with thy sweet deceiving*
> *Lock me in delight awhile.*

'In the year 920 A.D. King Edward the Elder founded a city here and called it Thelwall.' So read the inscription on the outside of the Thelwall Arms. Thelwall hardly fitted my concept of a city. One church, one pub, one post office, one police house, three waterways: the upper reaches of the Mersey, the Manchester Ship Canal and the much smaller Bridgewater Canal. That was Thelwall. I never really settled there.

My new school was in Stockton Heath, five or six miles away. The headmaster, Kenneth Greenwood, an evangelical Baptist and a Scot, was one of the two men who had considerable influence on my understanding of Christianity. The other was Arthur Warburton, an Anglican lay reader. They were vastly different from each other.

Greenwood was a vigorous preacher who lightened the solemnity of his message with genuine good humour. Arthur Warburton was quiet, reflective and inclined towards high Anglicanism. While Greenwood was tall, lean and fit, Warburton, his opposite, died of a heart condition as a comparatively young man. True to his understanding, Greenwood preached the evangelical message that called for the hearer to respond by making a definite decision to follow Christ. Warburton, while understanding the necessity of commitment, had a deep belief in a gradual growth towards truth through the sacraments. Greenwood's sheer dynamism and excitement was appealing and touched one side of my nature, whereas Warburton was able to speak to my more reflective side. I owe them both a considerable debt.

I worked hard at my new school. I was soon made a prefect and was eventually elected head boy. But despite making good progress, I still felt a restless spirit within. Often in the evening I sat on the bank of the Ship Canal, watching the cargo boats sail through the fields. I longed to travel. I had read so much, and I wanted to see the world for myself. I joined the local Sea Cadets and once a week donned a naval uniform and attended the shore establishment on the banks of the Mersey. It was through the Sea Cadets that I had my first encounter with death. A fellow cadet was killed in an accident, and his family requested that members of the Cadet Corps be his pallbearers. Although I was only fourteen, I was tall and well built and was selected to be one of them. When we arrived at the house, we were shown into the front room where trestles supported an open coffin. We gazed down intently at the pale face of our dead friend. I felt numb. The undertaker screwed down the lid, and we struggled to carry the coffin on our shoulders through the narrow hallway and into the hearse. Being the tallest, its weight pressed hard into my shoulder. At the graveside we stood to attention while the last post was played. Together with another boy, I lowered the coffin into the grave. For a moment we remained silent, then the officer in charge called us to attention. We moved into marching position and left the churchyard, striding away to our own uncertain, unpredictable futures.

My feet are a little better today. I can now walk unaided. As I lie on my mattress, I try not to think of torture, deliberately turning my mind back to childhood. Reconstructing those years, I relive them as vividly as I can. If only I had a pencil and paper. If only I had a book

– anything. Every day I am forced to draw on my inner resources – to search for a level of reality that will sustain and support me. I remember the clear certainty with which Kenneth Greenwood enunciated his faith. He seemed to live in a world of faith without doubt. I very much wanted such a world, but in truth I had never found it.

Greenwood once took a party from my school to hear an American Evangelist preach. He spoke powerfully and at the end of his address called for those who wanted to follow Christ to stand. I felt acutely uncomfortable; guilty for reasons I could not understand. The simple act of standing would remove the guilt, and a new life would begin, the preacher said. Along with several others, I stood. I felt conspicuous and not a little foolish. Absolute certainty did not flood in, nor has it since. The Christian faith has provided me with a set of symbols through which I have been able to make interpretations, which in turn have helped me to find meaning in life. When I doubt, it's not that I doubt the healing power of light and truth. There I don't seem to falter. I don't always live the truth, far from it, but I know clearly that's where I want to be. I have some doubts about dogmas, which have perhaps become less luminous in changing circumstances. One reason I love the Orthodox Liturgy is that, within it, symbolic life is writ large. At the same time the whole action of the Liturgy centres around a profound mystery, which can never be explained. Now the mystery within me links with the mystery beyond, and for a moment I experience a deep peace and stillness.

It's night, but I can't sleep. The television was switched off hours ago, and my guard lies on his bed snoring softly. A small light burns in the room, and for a moment I lift my blindfold to look around. I see a pile of school exercise books in the corner. Could some of my captors be teachers? Outside, there is the sound of shelling that continues night after night. At first it kept me awake; now I sleep through it without any problem. Except tonight. The beating has upset me. But in a strange way it has also strengthened my determination. I tell myself over and over again that all I need to do is hold to the truth. It will set me free, heal and sustain me. For a moment I am arrogant enough to link myself with some of the people I most respect: Solzhenitsyn, Arthur Koestler, my friend Desmond Tutu. People who have suffered for what they believe. I tell myself I have now entered a new fellowship, a unique fellowship of endurance. I do this to support myself, to help me gain courage. And to inflate my importance? Perhaps. In any case I need the support of others who have suffered. I need their understanding, their courage, their dignity, their fellowship. This room is part of the university of the world. I, poor fool, have enrolled in the course and now find how tough it is. The guard stirs and mutters in his sleep, while I try to get comfortable. My chains have bound me in a foetal position. I am a baby totally dependent on others, totally at the mercy of others, totally vulnerable.

A bell rings. For a moment I stop breathing. Someone is at the door. Oh God, please not another beating, please not. I quickly pull the blindfold over my eyes, and the guard rises from his bed. He goes into the hallway and opens the door. People enter.

'Sit – face the wall.' It's the man in the suit. I face the wall. 'You have five hours to live.'

The words hit me like a blow. Five hours to live. In five hours I will move from one state to another. Five hours, five, five, five; the number reverberates through my head.

'Think hard. You have many things to tell us. If you don't tell us, in five hours you die.'

They whisper to my guard and leave the room. I lie down.

Five hours to live. My thoughts go to my family and friends. How I hate to leave them like this. They will never know how I died. They will never know my last thoughts or my deep love for them. They will always have to live with uncertainty, not knowing how I lived in these last days, not knowing how I died. I think with affection of Robert Runcie, the Archbishop of Canterbury. Damn, I am shaking. I am afraid. Stop it, man. Why be afraid? Death is an adventure. Soon you may know answers to questions you have never been able to understand, let alone answer. But I don't want to die. Please not yet. Come on, you coward. Never be intimidated by anyone – never. Oh God, I am so tired, so alone.

I must have fallen asleep. I wake and immediately remember that I may be at the end of my life. Sleep has refreshed me. I feel stronger. The outside door is opening. I hear voices in the hallway, then in the room. A radio is switched on.

'Sit.'

I do so.

'What have you to tell us?'

'Nothing.'

To my surprise my mouth has gone quite dry. I have read of this phenomenon in novels, but now I experience it for myself.

'You lie.'

'Do not call me a liar.' My voice rings out clearly. It's as though I have taken distance from myself and can stand back and hear myself responding.

'You tell us everything,' the man in the suit orders.

'I have nothing more to say.'

'You have been sentenced to death by Muslim law. You can write one letter.'

'I need to write many letters: to my wife, my children, my mother, my friends.'

'You can write only one letter.'

'Only one?'

'Yes.'

My chains are unlocked and a ballpoint pen and pad are put into my hands. I face the wall and looking under my blindfold I begin to write.

Dear Archbishop, Frances, Ruth, Clare, Gillian, Mark, Mum [I continue with the names of several relatives and close friends]

This is the last letter I shall write. I have been told that I have a short time to live and that I can send this message to you. I am sorry that my life is ending in this way. I am not afraid to die, but I don't want to die without you knowing that I am well and in good spirits. Try not to be too sad. I have done my best and can die with a clear conscience. Also try not to be bitter against my captors. They have suffered much in their lives. I love you all.

God bless and goodbye.

Terry

The letter seems sorely inadequate, but it's the best I can do. The man in the suit asks for it and takes it from me.

'Who are these names?'

'They are my family and friends.'

He reads the letter.

'You want eat?'

'No, thank you.'

'You want a last drink – whisky, brandy, beer?'

That is a taunt.

'I would like a cup of tea, please.'

The guard is sent into the kitchen to prepare tea. In a few moments he returns and hands me a plastic beaker. I sip the tea slowly.

'You want more?'

'No, thank you.'

'Stand.'

'I would like to say my prayers.'

'You can do that.'

I say the Lord's Prayer aloud and then silently pray for all those whom I love and also for my captors.

'You want to say anything?'

'No.' I am determined not to plead for my life in any way.

'Stand.'

I struggle to my feet. The radio is playing Arabic music. What a way to die. I feel cold metal against the side of my temple.

'You have anything to say?'

'Nothing.'

There is a silence. I wait. The gun is removed. The old man speaks. 'Not tonight – later.'

I sit down. My chains are replaced and locked. I lie down and within a few moments am asleep, utterly exhausted.

From my vantage point on the bank of the Ship Canal the world called to me. I had read Captain Cook, Slocum, Stevenson, and longed to explore the world beyond Cheshire. I told the Commanding Officer of the Sea Cadets that I wanted to leave school and join the Navy as a boy entrant. He urged me to continue with my studies and wait until I was eighteen or nineteen. Two years seemed an eternity. How could I wait two years in this dreadfully dull place? I plucked up courage and told my father that I wanted to leave home.

'What are you going to do?'

'Join the Navy.'

He looked at me long and hard. 'Do you realise what this means if you join up now?'

'Yes.'

'Are you sure you know? If you join up now, you will be committed until you are thirty.'

'I know.'

Our talks lasted for days and continued long into the nights. I travelled to Runcorn and wandered down to the river to look at the old Transporter Bridge. It creaked and groaned its way across the Mersey with its cargo of cars and pedestrians. Further up the street I entered an office and submitted myself to a medical and a written examination. A chief petty officer from Liverpool supervised me – the only candidate. Several days later papers arrived in the post indicating that I had been accepted. I said goodbye to my friends at school. To Jenny, the head girl, who was a special person in my life, to the headmaster and to some of the teachers. As head boy I stood at Assembly and called for three cheers for the holidays. Before I left, I went to see the CO.

'Let me tell you one thing. Be careful of your friends. They can let you down badly.'

What extraordinary advice. I couldn't understand what he meant. He limped out of the room and I never saw him again, but his last words have remained in my memory.

I returned home to face another long evening with my father. His assent was needed, and I was required to take the signed papers to the recruiting office in Liverpool. We argued for hours. Finally he put his signature to the document, and I collapsed into bed. At breakfast he said he would accompany me to the railway station in Warrington. On the bus he continued his argument. He was still talking when we arrived at the station. I bought a ticket, and we went to the platform. The train steamed in.

'Please, Terry, think.'

I put out my hand to open a carriage door and turned to my father. He was looking at me intently with his strong blue eyes shining out of his lined face. I dropped my hand and we walked together back to the exit. Doors slammed, a whistle blew, the train pulled away. We returned home in silence.

'Not tonight – later.' The last words of the old man reverberate through my head. Later – how much later? It's pointless to worry, pointless to dwell on the situation. If they kill me, they kill me.

The guard goes about his daily routine as usual. He brings me a sandwich and a cup of tea, escorts me to the bathroom, returns me to my chains

'Who were the people who were here last night?'

'I don't know.'

'Why don't you know?'

'I am a soldier.'

'Are you married?'

'My wife is dead.'

'I'm sorry.'

'She died from a car bomb.'

'In Beirut?'

'Yes. In Beirut everything expensive – except life.'

I wonder where he got that truism. Outside a battle is raging. I hear a tank rumble down the street. In the distance heavy shelling pounds repeatedly. Machine guns and automatic rifles chatter with dreadful ferocity.

As I returned from the bathroom this morning I noticed from beneath my blindfold a pile of small arms stacked in the hallway. Lebanon – an exploding arsenal.

The battle gains momentum throughout the day. I am now accustomed to the noise and no longer worry about shells hitting the building in which I am kept. To pass the time I do some mental arithmetic, calculations involving the speed of light. At first I forget numbers, but with practice I improve. I try to remember what I can about Einstein's theory of relativity, his illustration of the train. How I wish I had more knowledge of the subject; I find these theoretical speculations totally absorbing. The shelling fades away as I think about the mystery of space and time. The man in the suit and the old man do not return.

Several days pass. Much of the time I am lost in space – absorbed with numbers. It's now evening. My stomach is upset, and I need to make an extra visit to the bathroom. The guard is alone, and normally when he is by himself he will not free me to go to the toilet. On one previous occasion like this I was so desperate that I began to crawl across the floor to get to the bathroom. He heard the clank of my chains and almost shot me on the spot out of fear.

'Please. I need the toilet.'

'Later.'

'It's very urgent.'

'Later.'

'I tell you it's very urgent.'

I hear him cross the room.

'Be very quick.'

He unlocks the padlocks and guides me into the small bathroom. I remove my blindfold and stretch my aching limbs, then turn around. On the top of the cistern lies an automatic pistol complete with silencer. A thousand thoughts flash through my mind. What are my chances of escaping? Fair, I suppose. If I pick up that automatic, I must be prepared to use it. What have I said repeatedly to my captors about the use of violence? Now that I am in a tight corner, have I any right to use violence? Perhaps murder my guard? I put my blindfold back over my eyes and tap on the door. It opens.

'You have left something. You had better take it.'

I hear a sharp intake of breath. There is a clatter as he picks up the pistol and closes the door. Back in my corner I wonder what on earth really happened. Was it a test? A test to see if I was genuine? Was it a mistake on the guard's part? I conclude it was a mistake. My guard never mentions the incident; neither do I. I do not want to live by the gun.

« 5 »

MY FATHER WROTE to the Navy explaining that I had changed my mind. I felt awkward and somewhat ashamed. For months the idea of leaving home had dominated my thoughts; now I was totally unsure of what to do.

'It might be a good thing to resume your studies. It would be quite easy for you to go back to school.'

I was too proud to return.

'I don't want to do that.'

'You will need more qualifications to get on in life.'

I didn't care about 'getting on'. I wanted to live life to the full – to launch out on my own. In the quiet of my room I felt insecure and vulnerable. Although I would not admit it to his face, I knew my father was right. I needed more knowledge. I decided to do three things: first, take a brief holiday; second, get a job – any job to provide me with some degree of independence; and finally, apply for a correspondence course and study on my own. Within two years I would be required to do National Service, and this would then take me beyond my narrow confines.

I packed a rucksack, gathered what savings I had and set out by getting a lift to Dover. Once across the Channel I explored France, Belgium and Germany and finished up in Vienna, although I had been hoping to get as far as Rome. As I had very little money, I hitchhiked and stayed in youth hostels. At the railway station in Vienna I asked about the cost of a single ticket back to Calais and discovered, when I counted my money, that I had barely enough to get me across Austria! I left the station, made for the autobahn and hitchhiked home.

'Henry Milling & Company Limited, Tea and Coffee Merchants, High Class Grocery and Provision Suppliers' was written in gold lettering on the window of the head office in Warrington. Arthur Woods, the company secretary, interviewed me for a position. He had been with Millings all his working life, starting as a van boy delivering customers' orders and working his way up to the most senior position in the company. He was a kindly and sincere man who took a genuine interest in his employees. 'We can give you a good training, you can learn every part of the business,' he told me.

I accepted his offer, even though business life interested me hardly at all. I went out in the vans, served in the shops, visited customers, worked in the company office. In the evenings I studied the subjects I had cut short at school and continued to read as widely as I could. The time passed pleasantly enough, but my heart was not in my work. Millings was in any case approaching the beginning of the end. Guy Milling, 'Mr Guy' to his employees, had cause to be a worried man. Supermarkets were making their appearance, and some old-established firms were starting to recognise that they had to change their ways or go out of business. Compared with the new supermarkets, Millings was inefficient. Its management style and method of accounting had scarcely changed since the firm was founded in the early nineteenth century. If it was to stand any chance at all in the new competitive market, eventually there would have to be a total restructuring, and huge capital sums would be required. It took more than twenty-five years for the firm finally to cease trading, but signs of the end for most such family businesses were discernible in the 1950s. Years later when I was working with the Church I visited Mr Guy on his deathbed. I remember him as a good and generous man.

At the age of seventeen and a half, with my National Service just six months away, I decided that a career with Millings was not for me and I might as well leave. I applied for early enlistment and was told that if I signed on for three years instead of for the compulsory two, I would get a much better rate of pay. This time I travelled alone to the railway station, went to the army recruiting office in Liverpool and enlisted with the Grenadier Guards. My father made no comment.

Alone with my thoughts, I puzzle about the incident with the gun. Perhaps I could have got away without shooting my guards, perhaps not. Useless speculation. I have no regret about not using violence. It's now late at night, and the guard is pottering around. He seems restless. The doorbell rings, and he leaves the room. I stiffen. I hear voices that are new to me. It sounds as if several people have entered the apartment. The guard comes to my mattress, and I hear him collect my few possessions and put them in a bag: my plastic cup, toothbrush and toothpaste, a small piece of soap. At least it doesn't take long to pack. They must be moving me, perhaps even setting me free. My heart is pounding.

'You must not speak. Do exactly as you are told,' an unfamiliar voice repeats a familiar message. 'Understand?'

'Yes.'

The guard unlocks my chains.

'Stand.'

I climb to my feet. Behind me the guard collects my bedding.

'Sit down.'

I am guided to a wooden kitchen chair and hear the sound of masking tape being unwound. They are certainly moving me; masking tape is an indispensable part of every kidnapper's kit. Released hostages with whom I had spoken before my capture had described how they were almost mummified by the stuff as they were being moved. Hands hold my head, and the sticky tape is wound round and round my mouth. I feel totally helpless and fearful. My blindfold is tightened and some form of headgear is fitted on me. When they place a *burqă* over my nose and mouth I realise they are dressing me as an Islamic woman! Surely there are few females as tall as six foot seven in the Lebanon. A garment is dragged over my shoulders and fastened at the back. I am surrounded by guards; the atmosphere is tense. It seems as if a special group is employed to transfer hostages, since each time I have been moved I have heard unfamiliar voices.

'Make no noise.'

My arms are taken, and I am led across the room. I hear the front door being opened, and a hand pushes me in the middle of the back. I walk forward. We stop for a moment, and again I hear the sound of doors being opened. Once more I am pushed forward, this time into a lift. Down we go. The lift stops, and I am guided around a corner, down some steps and into the back seat of a car. Guards sit on either side of me. We drive away, and after ten minutes or so we stop. Drivers are changed, and we continue. Again we stop. The two men in the front whisper to each other. We wait for what I estimate to be about twenty minutes before we move off again. Near by, shells are exploding; small arms are hissing. We drive on silently. The car stops. A voice whispers in my ear: 'Get out.'

I am held on both sides and hurried along until we reach the door of a building, where they propel me forward.

'Go up.'

With the help of the guards I feel my way up some stairs, up and up and up. After we have climbed about thirty, my weakened muscles begin to protest. The men on either side of me half lift me by the arms. On we go. Finally we stop and walk along a corridor. Then a key is turned in a lock, and I am pushed through another doorway. To my relief, the headgear is removed, the masking tape ripped away from my mouth, the clothing taken from around my shoulders.

'Sit.'

I drop to the floor. A door closes, a key turns. I remove my blindfold. Once again I am alone.

'Report to Liverpool at 0900 hours.'

I packed my bag, said goodbye to my family and caught the train. I had little idea of what to expect, but my father had told me that the Guards' training was the hardest in the British Army. He had applied to join when he left home, but, for what reasons I never knew, he was not accepted. In the strange battle of wills that existed between us I had scored one point at least.

The recruiting sergeant sat behind a wooden desk, empty save for a blotter and pen. Two young men in civilian dress stood nervously in the corner.

'Waite.'

'Sir.'

'You're in charge of the party.'

He nodded towards the other two occupants of the room. They blinked at me. He opened a drawer and produced some documents.

'Railway warrants. Take these men to Lime Street and proceed to Caterham. Understood?'

'Yes, sir.'

He handed me the papers.

'Don't waste time, Waite. Get them there as quickly as possible.'

'Yes, sir.'

'Right, don't wait about, Waite – get moving.' He laughed at his own feeble joke and turned his head towards my new companions. 'Come on, you two, you don't have all day.'

We picked up our cases in the hallway and clattered down the wooden stairs. On the train I discovered that my comrades were National Servicemen. Like me, both were apprehensive about what lay ahead and very fed up at being forced to leave Liverpool. Neither had ever been to London before. At least I had a small advantage there. In Styal during the summer holidays, I would wander down to the railway track to watch the Manchester–London express race through the station, and I was determined to visit the capital as soon as I could. When I had saved enough from my wages at Millings, I caught the express to Euston Station. A short walk took me down Woburn Place to Russell Square where I noticed that the Hotel Russell was advertising bed-and-breakfast for twenty-seven shillings and sixpence. I booked in and spent three or four days on my own, exploring the city that years later was to become my home.

We arrived at the Guards' Depot in the late afternoon. I looked for the guardroom and presented our documents. The sergeant on duty gave us a disdainful glance, took the papers and stared at them.

'Well, what are you waiting for?'

None of us knew what to reply.

'At the double. Move.'

'Where to, sir?'

'Sergeant – not Sir – right?'

'Yes, sir – Sergeant.'

'Not "yes" – just Sergeant, right?'

'Sergeant.'

'At the double.' He bellowed the command and pointed in the direction of the main block, a quarter of a mile away. We picked up our cases and began to jog along the road. As we lumbered and sweated our way down the drive we could still hear his voice ringing out across the concrete. 'At the double – heads up!'

We were in the Army. Life would never be quite the same again.

For a moment I sit quietly. Obviously I am in another apartment building, very near the top. Across from where I sit, I can see that the room was once fitted with French windows. They have been removed and the gap covered with sheet metal. The handle on the inside of the door has been taken off. A single light bulb hangs in the centre of the room, casting a pale glow across the gloomy surroundings. There are no staples to which chains could be attached, and as yet I am not chained. I can therefore walk and thus get some strength back into my body which is very weak after so much lying around. I pace up and down the room, measuring the length and breadth, and calculate how many times I need to walk in a circle to complete a mile. I plan to walk each day and to increase the amount as I get stronger. Next, I examine the walls very carefully for some sign of a previous occupant. They are bare, but about two inches from the floor I see markings. I am tremendously excited. Here is contact, albeit remote, with another prisoner. There is a minute cross and what looks like a clover leaf. I search desperately for a name or initials but find nothing. For a long time I stare at the graffiti and draw comfort from this distant contact with an unknown prisoner.

The room is very damp and surprisingly cold, and all I have to wear are socks, trousers and a shirt. There is no bedding, but perhaps that will arrive soon. I cross to the door to look through the keyhole. It has not been blocked so I can see that there is a room opposite. The door is closed, but a light shines beneath it. Again I feel excitement. Are there other hostages in this building? Suddenly, I see a shadow and leap away as someone knocks on my door and inserts a key in the lock. The knock is a signal to pull the blindfold over my eyes. The door opens and several items are thrown into the room. As the door closes, I uncover my eyes. My foam rubber mattress and blanket lie on the floor. Beside them, to my delight, is my leather jacket.

I make up my bed and put on my jacket, then I lie down and wrap the single blanket around me. It is, alas, impossible to get warm as the damp penetrates everything. Eventually I fall asleep, only to awaken an hour or so later, shivering violently. The upper part of my body is kept reasonably warm by the jacket, but my legs are like ice. Although I am very tired, I decide that exercise will warm me, so I get up and begin to walk round and round, counting as I go. My limbs are stiff after weeks of immobility, and my skin is giving me problems. I suspect ringworm. I walk for a mile or so and lie down again. The blanket is so thin that it is of very little use.

Nevertheless I sleep again, and when I awake I can see a few beams of light coming into the room through minute gaps where the metal sheet does not quite cover the window. I get up and lift my mattress. The floor is soaking wet underneath. I roll up the mattress and use it to stand on so that I can see through one of the gaps. It is early morning. I look out at another apartment, which I assume is across a street. It has an open balcony on which an old lady is standing. I can just catch sight of her. I wonder who she is and what she would think if she knew hostages were being kept directly opposite. I gaze across the street for a long time, unbelievably happy at the sight of another human being. After a while the old lady turns and goes indoors. I step down and prop my mattress against the wall, hoping it will dry out. If only there were some ventilation, conditions in the room would improve in an hour or so. My bladder is full, but there is no bottle in the room in which to urinate. I walk round and round trying to control my need. Damn, they must come soon. Round and round I walk, feeling more and more uncomfortable. Finally I decide that I must knock on the door to attract attention. I give three taps. Nothing. I tap again and hear footsteps. I quickly secure my blindfold. A key turns in the lock, and the door opens.

'Sit.'

I sit.

'Why make noise?'

'I need toilet.'

'Not make noise – understand?'

'I need toilet.'

'Later.'

'It's urgent. I need toilet.'

'Later – not noise – quiet – understand?'

'Please, I need toilet – if not toilet, please bring bottle.'

'Later.'

'But it's urgent, please.'

The door closes, and the key turns. I feel a sudden surge of anger. How can this new guard be so bloody insensitive to human need? My insides ache. I don't want to urinate on the floor as I am loath to make the room more unpleasant than it is already. The only receptacle is my water jug, which is almost empty. I swallow the last few ounces of water and then urinate into the plastic container. I suppose I must learn to face indignity with what good grace and humour I can muster.

Two or three hours pass. Through the gap at the edge of the metal shutter, I can see that the sun is shining, but it can't penetrate the room. I know I must make the best use I can of the time I am out of chains to keep myself in shape. I have now devised a programme that will provide exercise for my whole body.

There is a knock on the door. I sit down.

'Take.'

The guard has a peculiar way of pronouncing 'take'. He says 'tek'. For some ridiculous reason I think of the Duke of Teck and decide to nickname the guard 'Duke'. I hold out my hand, and he throws something on to the floor. It's a piece of bread.

'Don't do that, please. I have to eat it.' He ignores me and pours something into my cup.

'I need a bottle, please,' I say.

'Why?'

'I need bottle for pee-pee.' I use the word he understands.

'Later.'

The door closes. I hear him move across the hallway and unlock the door of the room opposite. I strain my eyes through the keyhole to see who is there but can hardly make out anything. My blood runs cold as I see a leg and a chain. There is at least one person opposite me chained to the wall. That's a bad sign. It must surely mean that I will be chained again. When the guard leads him out of the room, I can't see the face of my fellow prisoner, only that he is dressed in white shorts and a singlet. As the guard crosses the hallway, I dart away from the keyhole. He checks my door, and then I hear him walk away. Time for breakfast.

The first days of army life are a blur in my mind. Everything was done at the double. My travelling companions disappeared at the double, and I never met them again. I found my barrack room, collected my kit and set about making it conform to the standards required by the Guards. First the boots. To get these up to scratch one needed a candle and an old dessert or soup spoon. The back of the spoon was heated over the candle, and one slowly burnt off the stipples on the leather until the surface was quite smooth. Then black polish was applied, not with a brush but with a cloth. The polish had to be rubbed into the leather, and the cloth occasionally dipped into water. It took hours for a layer to build up, but eventually a mirror-like surface was obtained. Two pairs of boots had to be treated in this way.

Every item I received was in frightful condition. The brass on my webbing was green, the battledress looked as if it had just gone through battle. Hours of work lay ahead. At first I was alone in the barrack room, but gradually others arrived: Trevelyan, a National Serviceman from Cornwall, Carstairs, a former regular soldier who had re-enlisted, Schumacher, recently out of public school, Peter and Paul, twins from east London who had joined up together.

A couple of our squad had been told that they were to be considered for the Officers' Selection Board. I certainly didn't want that as I wasn't at all ready for such responsibility. Had I known what our squad sergeant was going to be like, I might have thought differently. Lance-Sergeant Swire was very smartly turned out: his boots were immaculate; his battledress, sartorial elegance itself; his cap, doctored in true Guards fashion so that the peak came down almost vertically in front of his eyes and along his nose. It was extremely difficult for those of us who came from the north to understand his commands, even though, true to his calling, every utterance was delivered forte. He was mean, nasty and, deep down, very insecure. Keen to be promoted to full sergeant, Swire was determined that we, his first squad, were going to be perfect. We were going to pass every inspection the first time, weren't we?

'Sergeant.'

'Right, you idle bastards.' He brought his cane down hard on the table. The crash reverberated through the room like a bullet. 'You're idle – every bloody one of you – idle. What are you?'

'Idle, Sergeant.'

'You've no bloody right to be idle. What are you doing in the Guards if you're idle? No one in this squad will be idle. Right?'

'Sergeant.'

We had been up at 5.00 a.m. to prepare for our first kit inspection. Our boots were shining, the brass gleamed, our bedding was folded with the sort of precision demanded by architects and engineers. By the time we were sent off to have breakfast, it was raining, not torrentially, just enough to make life a little more miserable than it was already.

'My God,' said Carstairs, 'the Artillery was bad enough, but this is madness. Swire is off his bloody head.'

'Obsessional personality,' muttered Schumacher. 'Clearly a disturbed type.'

We trudged to the canteen, glad not to be at the double for a change. Breakfast over, we returned to our block. Our quarters were on the third floor. As we approached the room, we heard the sound of shouting. There was only one man who could bellow like that. One of us opened the door. A scene of devastation confronted us. Lance-Sergeant Swire was raging round the room like a mad elephant, overturning beds and throwing armfuls of immaculately pressed and polished kit out of the windows into the mud far below.

'You bastards! You idle bastards! Fail your bloody inspection, would you! Swines! Idle swines!'

Schumacher looked at me and winked.

'Also maniacal,' he said. 'A bad case, old boy, very sad.'

At last I am allowed to visit the bathroom. Once inside I can see that life has taken a turn for the worse. The floor is covered with about three inches of water, while only a trickle comes from the tap. The toilet does not flush and has been used by several people before me so that the odour is overpowering. To add to my troubles, I have no soap, towel or toothbrush. They seem to have been lost in transit. I wash as best I can. The skin on my arms and face is very sore indeed. It appears to be ringworm on my arms, but as there is no mirror I can't see my face. My eyelids are dreadfully irritated and feel swollen. I dry myself on my shirt, and just as I am about to replace my blindfold I notice a red plastic bucket in the corner.

If I could get that to my room, one problem would be solved. I have washed my water jug as best I can, and certainly don't want to urinate in it every day. I replace my blindfold, pick up the bucket and knock once on the bathroom door. The guard opens it, guides me to my room and locks the door. I am still in possession of the bucket. Thank God for that. I look through the keyhole. The guard opens the door opposite, and I can see him unchaining my fellow prisoner and taking him to the bathroom. He seems to be quite young with bronzed skin and wearing a gold chain around his neck, but I still can't see his face. He could be Lebanese or even French. They return, and the prisoner is locked up again.

I say my prayers and start to exercise: bend knees, touch toes, sit up, press up. Just a few of each to begin with. Tomorrow and in the following days I will increase the number slightly until my muscle tone returns. After exercise, I begin to walk. Today I decide to walk without counting so that I can think. As I move round and round, my mind wanders. The trance-like state I have known before returns. The apartment, the world, seem far away. My mind is free to roam at large. This continues for hour after hour until I stop walking, sit on the floor, and wait for lunch.

Lance-Sergeant Swire sat behind a table at the end of the barrack room. Before him, each man sat by his bed energetically cleaning his rifle.

'Today we go to the range.' The rasping south London voice cut through the air like a rusty knife. 'Where do we go, Trevelyan?'

'Sergeant.'

'What do you mean – Sergeant?'

'I didn't hear, Sergeant,' Trevelyan responded in a thick Cornish accent. He had spent the whole of his life in Cornwall and had it not been for National Service would probably never have stepped over the county border.

'What do you bloody well mean, Trevelyan? Stand up.'

Trevelyan rose. Lance-Sergeant Swire got to his feet, picked up his cane and stood directly in front of his victim.

'First, Trevelyan, learn to speak proper Queen's English. Second, wash your filthy lug 'oles out.' He stuck his cane in one of Trevelyan's ears. 'Third, smarten your bloody self up or else.'

'Sergeant.'

Lance-Sergeant Swire returned to his desk.

'Right, stand up.'

We stood.

'You need some exercise. Pick up your rifles.'

We did as commanded.

'You guard your rifle with your life, right? Don't ever mistreat it, right? Don't ever drop it, right?'

'Sergeant.'

'Right. Now throw it across the room to the man opposite who will catch it in his free hand – *move!*'

Highly polished 303 rifles, leftovers from World War II, began to fly across the room. They were heavy and not at all easy to catch in one hand. Without warning the inevitable happened. There was a clatter as some unfortunate missed a catch. Swire was waiting.

'What the bloody hell are you doing damaging army property, Trevelyan?' He cracked the unfortunate Cornishman across the knuckles with his cane. 'I'm watching you, Trevelyan – watching you very carefully. I don't like you, Trevelyan – not one little bit. You're on report, Trevelyan. You watch yourself, Trevelyan. Right?'

'Sergeant.'

'Five minutes, downstairs. *Move!*'

We scrambled to prepare ourselves to visit the range. By now most of us were able to assemble our kit quickly and smartly.

'Waite. Right-hand man.'

I took my position. Other members of the squad would take their dressing from me.

'By the right – quick march!'

We stepped out into the morning sunlight. Along the road to the back gate and into a country lane.

'Step short, Waite. Step short!'

Swire rapped me across the knuckles with his cane. I tried to reduce my long stride to regulation pace.

'Step short. How many more bloody times? Step short!'

We arrived at the range. It was a warm, sunny day. Honeybees droned their way from flower to flower. Birds sang in the hedges. In the distance cows fed contentedly. A corrugated-tin roof covered a rough wooden shed under which a large cauldron of water boiled. This was used to pour through the rifle after firing. A piece of cotton, known as a 'four by two', was then pulled through the barrel to clean it thoroughly. We took up firing positions and squeezed the trigger. The old rifles kicked and bucked like wild animals.

'Don't pull the bloody trigger, squeeze.'

Another volley sounded out. Swire strutted across the range.

'Come on, move yourselves.'

There was a whine as a bullet whistled overhead.

'The bloody madman,' said Schumacher, throwing himself to the ground. 'That's against regulations for sure.'

Swire threw his rifle to a recruit.

'Boil that through and then form up.'

We cleaned our rifles and marched back to the camp, our ears ringing, our hearts heavy at the thought of further sessions with Lance-Sergeant Swire.

'Can I have soap and a towel, please?'

'Later.'

'My skin is not good. I need to wash properly.'

'Later.'

The key turns in the lock. This morning the bathroom was a terrible mess. A steady stream of water poured through the ceiling where, for some mysterious reason, the guards had been making a three-foot hole and once again the floor was flooded. To get into the bathroom I had to pass through a cascade of water to reach a tap that didn't work and a toilet that still wouldn't flush.

This flat is at the very top of the building; I heard the guards banging a water tank above my head and also breaking through into the bathroom. I still have the plastic bucket, for which I am thankful. My companion across the hall is obviously not so fortunate. Yesterday he was knocking on the floor and making a fuss, evidently wanting to go to the bathroom. The guards came and told him to be quiet. He was clearly in distress and called out again. I looked through the keyhole as the guards returned, opened the door and proceeded to beat him.

What sort of men are they? Clearly they are under very strict orders, which implies a strong, disciplined organisation. They are, I suspect, ordinary men from the countryside or the southern suburbs. Fighters for Islam, fighters for their country. Fighters for the Iranian revolution? Very probably. At least one of the senior men has an accent which I suspect is Iranian. An ideology that sends its martyrs to instant paradise is difficult to argue with, and its practitioners know it and exploit it.

I am getting worried about my eyelids. They are so swollen I can hardly see. It must be some form of infection. The guards don't see it, of course: every time they come into the room I have to wear my blindfold. A knock on the door.

'I need some medication please.'

'Why?'

'My eyes are not good.'

'Close eyes.'

I close my eyes, and the guard lifts the blindfold slightly. I hear an intake of breath as he expresses surprise.

'Not good.'

'No, they are very painful.'

'I talk with Chef.'

He replaces the blindfold and leaves the room. I get to my feet and start to walk again. I must keep fit. I must – I must.

To my surprise I have been given an electric fire and an iron. Every morning I prop up my mattress and dry it out in front of the fire. I also dry my shirt. The electricity fails at least once a day, but it's always possible to dry my bedding. The iron does wonders for my self-respect. Although my trousers are tattered and worn, I press them daily. I am not allowed to wear shoes in the room, but I have asked for shoe polish. The guard must have thought I was mad, and I don't really expect to receive it. The lessons learnt thirty years ago in the Army have never left me and now help me to maintain my dignity. Perhaps I have something to thank Lance-Sergeant Swire for after all.

When my mattress was thrown into the room it was bound with

a piece of raffia. I plaited this into the shape of a cross and secured it to the wall. This symbol of suffering and hope gives me a focus in my drab prison. The Christian message of redemption through suffering is hard to grasp, and even harder to live! I pray for release from both the physical constraints and my inner blindness. I also pray for strength to accept this ailment, whatever it is. My face is now grossly swollen, and my eyes are so irritated that it's virtually impossible to resist rubbing them again and again. A guard, in his kindness, brought me a little bowl of olive oil, which I applied to my face. It did not help at all. I still do not have soap or a towel, and the bathroom continues to be a disaster area. But I am alive and discovering how to draw on inner strength. I laugh to myself when I remember a joke made by one of my Lambeth colleagues some years ago. He had seen a new advertisement for the British Army which read: 'It's a man's life in the Regular Army'. One day when I was complaining about something or other he turned and said, 'Well, it's a man's life in the Regular Church of England!'

'Do you remember me?'

A tall, portly figure stood behind a row of extra-large suits in the High and Mighty clothes shop in Edgware Road. His hair was grey and his moustache neatly clipped.

'Company Sergeant Major Brittan, Coldstream Guards.' He smiled.

There was a time when this gently-spoken manager was credited with possessing the loudest voice in the British Army. I first encountered him on the parade ground at the Guards' Depot, Caterham. On Saturday mornings when we practised for the Trooping of the Colour, Brittan dominated the square. He had presence and an old-fashioned courtesy combined with an iron discipline. Lance-Sergeant Swire escorted us to the parade ground, our boots so highly polished that we had to shuffle on to the square to prevent the surface from cracking before we were inspected. The band played a selection from its repertoire. Swire strutted to and fro. I stood stiffly to attention as right-hand marker. Luminaries from different regiments issued commands totally incomprehensible to such as myself. Finally we were off. The unintelligible commands of Swire rattled through our ranks. I could not make head or tail of what he shouted and relied entirely on common sense and intuition. We marched, counter-marched, slow-marched, performed every combination of the marching art known to man. It was going well, too well. Suddenly there was a crash as one of our number lost his footing and plunged to the ground. The eagle eye of Sergeant Major Brittan spotted him immediately.

'That man,' he shouted. 'Idle on parade – guardroom.'

Poor Trevelyan was hauled to his feet and escorted at the double across the square.

'I'll fix that bloody man,' muttered Swire. 'If it's the last bloody thing I do – I'll fix him.'

We believed that he would.

Waterloo Day – a time to relax for a while.

'On Waterloo Day,' said Swire, 'you will enjoy a meal. A very good meal. It will be served to you by the officers. You will get a lot of beer – free beer. You will enjoy yourselves, won't you, Schumacher?'

'Sergeant.'

'You'd bloody well better enjoy yourselves. This is a happy squad, Schumacher. I want you to enjoy yourselves.'

'Sergeant.'

We trooped into the canteen. All of us were ravenously hungry and not a little thirsty. As promised, the beer flowed freely. Finally, totally satisfied and somewhat stupefied, we returned to our barrack room and stretched out on our narrow iron bedsteads. I had been asleep for what seemed a matter of minutes when the sound of shouting penetrated my consciousness.

'Stand by your beds – stand by your bloody beds!'

Who could mistake the dulcet tones of our instructor?

'Parade in ten minutes.'

We lined up outside the block. Our feelings were beyond description. Swire put us through our routine.

'Remember,' he said. 'Always remember, you're never off duty in my squad.'

After an hour of agony, we returned to our barrack room. Trevelyan was promptly sick. Schumacher fell asleep on the floor. I got into bed and pulled the covers over my aching head. Waterloo Day had been celebrated. Tomorrow we would be back in our training routine. Three cheers for Wellington!

At daybreak, prayers are chanted from the mosque. I can't be sure as to whether they are recorded or not. The prayers help me to keep track of the time, both hours and days. Each Thursday evening a sermon is delivered, and at Friday prayers in the morning a lengthy address booms out across the area where I am imprisoned. I wish I could understand Arabic. As it is, I can distinguish only the odd word or two. I have asked for books. I ask every day, but nothing comes. I have asked for a book to help me learn Arabic – no book. I have asked for medicine – no medicine. The days stretch out interminably, and since I am still not chained, I walk. As I plod round the room I use my imagination to escape to places I have known. A long outing through New York City, starting at the Cathedral of St John the Divine and finishing at the Brooklyn Bridge. On Second Avenue I call at the Episcopal Church headquarters and talk with Jack Allin, the Presiding Bishop. Onward to Grand Central Station; a visit to the New York Public Library before walking down Broadway. I trudge round and round the bleak, damp room, remembering people, places, sights and sounds. A knock. Blindfold on. Sit down.

'Good morning, Mr Waite. How are you?'

The man in the suit.

'I am not well. This place is not good. The bathroom is not good. I have no towel or soap. I have no books. My eyes are not good.'

'Close eyes.'

He lifts my blindfold.

'What is this?'

'I don't know, but I think it's an infection. I need medicine, and I need to wash properly.'

'We have problems with bathroom.'

There is a three-foot hole in the concrete ceiling through which water cascades. No water at all comes through the taps. The toilet does not flush, and the floor is perpetually flooded. I believe him.

'What medicine do you need?'

I ask for antibiotics, some ointment for ringworm and eyedrops.

'Write please.'

He hands me a ballpoint pen and paper. I make a list of medicines which I think may help me.

'We bring for you.'

'Can you please get me some books? I have nothing to read.'

'Later.'

'I need another blanket.'

'Later.'

He takes the list and leaves the room, locking the door behind him. The days are so long. Apart from exercising my body and mind, there is nothing to do. Another knock on the door. It is lunchtime. When the guard has left, I lift my blindfold. A bowl of rice and hot water stands on the floor. As an extra bonus someone has added a chicken-bone devoid of meat. I can truly say that this is the weakest chicken soup I have ever tasted: it is nothing more than hot water and rice. As I eat, I remember those who have to live year in and year out on one bowl of rice a day. I join them for this meal, thankful to be alive, and thankful to have had a hot meal, no matter how simple.

In the late afternoon, the medicine arrives. The man in the suit can move things along when he wants to. Although I don't have my reading glasses, I can read the instructions, and I read them again and again. If only the author of these medical notes knew how avidly they would be devoured by a hostage starved of all reading material . . . I swallow one of the tablets and apply ointment to my face. My beard has grown long, and from what I can see of it, it is getting quite white. I remember a film I saw once in which a prisoner was discovered after spending years in solitary confinement. He had lost both the power of speech and his reason. I keep thinking of him as I look at my beard and feel how long my hair has grown. So many fears to be faced and lived through.

Lance-Sergeant Swire sat behind his table in the barrack room. Behind him was a blackboard covered with dates.

'When you leave this bloody squad, every man jack of you will know history.'

He swung his legs up on to the table and tapped his boots with his cane.

'Look at the board.'

We were sitting by our beds, polishing our boots. Twenty pairs of eyes focused on the blackboard.

'These, in case you didn't know, are battle honours. Grenadiers win their honours by sheer bloody guts and bravery.'

Swire pointed his cane at the board.

'Remember these dates. Fasten them in your tiny minds. Learn them so that you can repeat them in your sleep. Get that, Trevelyan?'

'Sergeant.'

'You'd better get it, Trevelyan. Get it into your thick Cornish head, Trevelyan. Right?'

'Sergeant.'

Swire stood and turned the board round.

'What's the first honour, Bellamy?'

Bellamy blinked.

'Bellamy, are you bloody well deaf as well as stupid?'

'No, Sergeant.'

Swire picked up a wooden chair-leg and hurled it down the room at him.

'First bloody honour, Bellamy. It's been staring you in the face all night. Bring that stick here at the double, you stupid sod.'

Bellamy returned the missile.

'Take a look, Bellamy. Take a bloody good look. Store that date in your mind. I'm watching you, Bellamy.'

Swire cast around for another victim.

'Trevelyan.'

'Sergeant.'

'First battle honour.'

'Waterloo, Sergeant.'

'Come here, Trevelyan. At the double, you bloody fool.'

Trevelyan stood to attention in front of Swire.

'You, lad, are a menace to the squad. You are thick, stupid and bloody useless. I'll get rid of you if it's the last bloody thing I do.'

Swire was as good as his word. The next day we heard that Trevelyan had reported sick with a mysterious injury. By lunchtime his kit had disappeared. We never saw him again.

Each morning I wake early. On waking I say my prayers. I don't make special pleas or ask favours. As simply as I can, I try to enter into the mystery that is God. Often I say the Communion service and during it bring to mind my family and friends. Then I exercise. The routine bores me, but I continue it twice daily as I know it is essential to keep as fit as I can. Breakfast arrives at different times during the morning. Occasionally it fails to appear, but that is a rarity. The diet is plain and unappetising. Bread, *lebne* and sometimes a few olives. This morning I have finished my breakfast, and the whole day lies ahead like a vast unexplored sea. I am learning to be quiet and still within, perhaps calm is a better word. I don't want too much stillness as I need a certain inner tension to keep my mind alive. I continue to produce memories of my childhood and teenage years. I discover that I can recall the names of people I have not consciously remembered for almost forty years. As an exercise I attempt to name as many members of the staff of Henry Millings as I can, and soon have a long list. Many must be dead by now, but surely some live on. I wonder where they are; how their lives have developed.

There is a knock at the door. I remain sitting in the corner with my blindfold now in place. Several people enter the room and walk around. They totally ignore me, and I stay quiet, trying to work out how many voices I can distinguish and what is going on. There is a sound that I identify as a plug being inserted into an electrical socket. Now another noise. I feel an awful sense of panic. Someone has switched on an electric drill. Oh please, not that. I couldn't bear that form of deliberate mutilation. Please, not that. The drill starts again, and to my relief I hear it being used on the marble floor. What can they be doing? Holes are drilled in two or three places, then there is the sound of hammering. Finally all is quiet, the tools are collected, and the party leaves the room.

I hastily remove my blindfold and look around. Oh no. Oh God, no. Near the wall where my mattress lies they have inserted rings in the floor. That means they are intending to chain me. And that in turn means an end to my early-morning view of the old lady standing on her balcony, an end to brief glimpses through the key-hole into the room opposite, an end to what little physical freedom and diversion I have. I get to my feet and start to walk. This may be the last walk I will have for a long time, and so I count, round and round. One mile, three, seven, round and round and round in a kind of desperation, nine, twelve. My feet are blistered. No matter, march on, thirteen . . . fourteen miles! I press on blindly, walking, walking, walking. At fourteen and a half miles, there is a knock on the door. I sink to the ground. A bowl is put on the floor, and the door closes. Rice and beans. I am ready for lunch.

There were only two or three from our squad who went on Sunday mornings to early Communion in the Guards' chapel. The pleasure of this event, for me, lay in the fact that it was possible to have a moment of peace and to know myself as an individual rather than a number. Also, I could go for a late breakfast when the canteen was quiet and help myself to platefuls of bacon and eggs. In the Army we were always hungry. The constant physical exercise developed our bodies to peak fitness. Most days we had sessions in the gym. Throughout the week we swam, boxed and played football. Every

day we marched around the square, and although Swire remained
as objectionable as ever, we had learnt to tolerate him, as one learns
to tolerate a nagging toothache. The weather grew warmer, and
Swire decided that a trip through the countryside would be of benefit
to the squad. He instructed us to assemble our kit and backpacks
and form up outside the barrack block. We were inspected and then
were off, through the camp, out of the back gate and into the country.

'At the double. Pick your bloody feet up.'

We moved into a steady jog. After fifteen minutes or so, when we
were all feeling like death and in need of a break, the instruction
came to don gas masks. We struggled to pull these relics of 1940
over our faces while maintaining a steady jogging pace. Swire trotted
alongside.

'Keep your heads up. Left, right, left, right, left, right – head up,
Carstairs, you idle bastard.'

The man next to me began to falter. Swire spotted him.

'Take his bloody arm, Waite.'

I grabbed his arm, and the man on the other side did likewise.
We half dragged our companion along the woodland path, towards
the large mental hospital that stood in its own grounds next to the
depot.

Back in the block, we stripped off our saturated clothing and
fought for a shower. As I removed my rough khaki shirt I noticed a
slight rash on my arms. I dismissed it as nothing more than heat
rash. In fact, it was the beginning of the end of my life in the brigade
of Guards.

« 6 »

THE OLD LADY dressed all in black steps on to her small balcony and turns towards the sound of morning prayers. She stands silently in the early light – the only human being I have seen for many weeks. I watch her closely through the gap in the metal screen. She, too, must live alone; I have never seen anyone else on her balcony. I think of how fortunate she is to be able to walk out into the day and warm herself in the sun. Like me, she has grown accustomed to war. When shells are exploding and small arms pierce the air, she appears on the balcony and calmly hangs out her washing. What does she make of my room? When she looks across, she must see a window covered by a metal sheet. Perhaps the locals have learnt not to ask questions and simply get on with their own lives as best they can. After she has gone indoors, I decide to walk for a while. The weather is getting warmer, but the room remains damp.

The medication is taking effect; the swelling on my face is reduced. I now also have a small towel, a piece of soap and, to my delight, a toothbrush and paste. From time to time water comes through the taps. All in all, progress has been made. I walk round and round, letting my mind wander, making the most of my limited freedom while it lasts. Suddenly a pain shoots through my body as I catch my little toe in one of the rings screwed into the floor. The pain is so fierce that I am afraid my toe is broken. Damn, there are enough problems without this. I can just about manage to walk, but it's very painful; and it will be a while before I can do fourteen miles again. How stupid I am, how careless. I sit on my blanket and wait for breakfast. The guard enters, and I anticipate getting my food. Instead I hear the unmistakable clank of a chain. He takes my foot and puts the chain around it.

'Oh no, you don't have to do that.'

He makes no reply. I get the impression that he is unhappy about what he is doing.

'Why do you chain me? I can't go anywhere.'

He continues to fasten the chain to the link in the floor.

'Chef say you must have chain.'

'Let me speak to Chef.'

'I tell him you want speak.'

The guard leaves the room. A thick steel chain, each link of which has been welded for extra strength, fastens my leg to the staple. The chain is only a few feet long so there is no possibility of walking. I can't get to the window now to see the old lady, and of course I can't reach the keyhole to see the prisoner opposite. I realise that I will miss walking so much I feel like crying at the unfairness of it. Just in time I remind myself of my vow against self-pity. I've had a blow, not a disaster. I can still exercise, and, who knows, perhaps breakfast will be tasty!

'What's this, Waite?'

Swire pointed at the spreading rash on my arms.

'I think it's heat rash, Sergeant.'

'Report sick.'

I did as I was told. By now the blisters were spreading to other parts of my body. The Medical Officer looked me over, asked me a few cursory questions, and scribbled on a form.

'This needs careful attention. Report to Shorncliffe.'

I returned to the barrack room, which was quiet. My companions were out at the range. I packed my kit, collected my railway warrant and marched through the camp gate without having an opportunity to say goodbye to anyone in the squad. I caught the train to London, and on to the seaside town of Folkestone. Shorncliffe Military Hospital was a mile or so down the coast, high on the cliff overlooking the sea.

The contrast between the Guards' Depot at Caterham and Shorncliffe Military Hospital was dramatic. While there was military discipline of a kind in the hospital, it was insignificant compared to what I had recently experienced. I was assigned to the Male Skin Ward where an elderly, fat colonel who occasionally practised dermatology inspected me. As a first shot, he prescribed the same for me as he did for ninety per cent of his new patients: a warm salt bath followed by an application of gentian violet to the affected parts. Having experienced only cold showers for months, the bath was sheer luxury. I lay back wallowing in the deep, hot, soothing water, then applied the ointment to much of my body, as the rash had spread to my neck, legs and arms. When I emerged from the bathroom and joined my fellow patients on the ward, we made a colourful group. Most of us were deep purple, and one or two were heavily bandaged.

To keep order, the majority of us were confined to bed for several hours each day. Once a week the Commandant would inspect the ward, a gentle exercise during which bed patients were simply required to lie to attention. We had little to complain about: the food was good, the Red Cross kept us supplied with books, and we all knew that, given the nature of our skin problems, we would probably not be returned to our regiments for several months. Regrettably, in my case the gentian violet had little positive effect. The rash spread, and the irritation became so intense that at night my hands were bound to the sides of the bed to prevent me from scratching in my sleep. The fat Colonel did not appear at all concerned. He prescribed more baths and a succession of different ointments. The baths provided temporary relief from the chronic irritation, and afterwards I was swathed in bandages like many of my companions. Slowly, very slowly, I noticed an improvement. Christmas was approaching, and I had made sufficient progress to be able to travel home; my arms and legs were almost clear. I donned my best uniform, put on the red tie indicating that I was a hospital patient, collected my railway warrant, and made for Cheshire.

My family had moved into a new police house at Lymm, just a few miles from Thelwall. I arrived home and immediately got out of uniform. Large areas of my body were red and inflamed: the irritation was returning with a vengeance. My parents did their best to make Christmas Day a joyful celebration, but it was impossible for me to enjoy it. The following morning I felt so uncomfortable that I packed my case and headed directly for Shorncliffe and, although I did not know it then, the end of my short military career.

'Please can I have a book?'

The days are never-ending. Now that I am chained, there is naturally very little exercise that I can do. I have, however, worked out a programme which will tone up most of my muscles. I go through the routine every morning and evening, estimating that it takes about an hour each time. I spend the remainder of the day thinking and attempt to keep my mind alive with mental arithmetic and reflections on my life.

'Please, I have nothing to read. The days are very long without a book.'

'I will ask Chef.'

The guard leaves the room, and I am alone again. The medicine has worked wonders; I seem completely cured. That at least is something to be thankful for. The wall against which I sit is an outside wall. At midday the room heats up, and by late afternoon it can be very hot. The noise of fighting continues unabated. One night I awoke to discover that the room was shaking. At first I thought the building had been hit by a shell and had visions of the ceiling collapsing while I remained helplessly chained to the floor. But since there was a lull in the shelling, I concluded that it must have been a small earth tremor.

The key turns in the lock. I hear two voices; one is the kind guard, the other I don't recognise. They are moving around the room picking up items. The new voice seems to be speaking sharply to the guard. They leave, and I remove my blindfold. The electric fire has gone, but as I don't need it now, it doesn't bother me. The iron has also disappeared, and that makes me sad. Years ago I was told never to become too attached to material possessions. Now I know what that means. I don't require much. I would like a Bible and a Prayer Book and some substantial reading matter; philosophy or history would be marvellous. This would be an ideal opportunity to read Proust, Henry James, Cervantes. In my mind I look along my bookshelves at home and pick out those waiting to be read. If only I could have them now.

A knock on the door.

'I have something for you.'

'Thank you.'

'You will be happy.'

'Good.'

The guard puts a book into my outstretched hand.

'Thank you very much.'

He leaves, and I eagerly remove my blindfold. At last a book! *Beyond Euphrates* by Freya Stark. I haven't read it before but I know other works by this remarkable traveller, and I am delighted to have it. First, I hold it to my face to capture the lingering smell of a new book. It reminds me of childhood and the sensuous smell of new volumes in the bookshop in Wilmslow. Next I see how many pages there are and count the words on each page so that I will know exactly how long it will take me to read the book. I tell myself that I must read slowly, but I know I am not capable of

My father,
Thomas William Waite,
as a young police cadet
in Chester

My mother and father
at their wedding in
St John's, Lindow, Cheshire,
22 September 1937

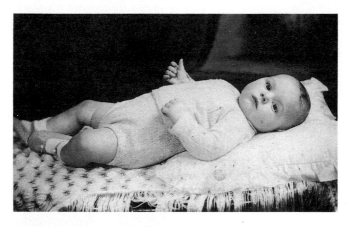

I was born on 31 May 1939;
this photograph was taken a few weeks later

A school holiday in the Lake District in 1951.
TW is third from left, back row

A very junior member
of a very senior
regiment

Student solitude, Regent's
Park, in the early sixties

Commissioned into the
Church Army by the Rev.
Donald Lynch, 1960

Marriage to Frances Watters
St Jude's, Belfast, 16 May 1964

With the twins, Ruth and Clare, in Bristol, 1965

The family in Blackheath, 1981.
CLOCKWISE: *Gillian, Ruth, Clare, Mark, Frances and Raq*

In my office at Lambeth during the Runcie years

*With Richard Chartres during the Archbishop's
official tour of the US, 1981*

Meeting Chinese leaders with Archbishop Runcie, Beijing, 1983

The meeting with Forbes Burnham in Guyana, 1984

'It's the Pope for you!'

Father Lawrence Jenco, at the Vatican,
immediately following his release from captivity, July 1986

With Archbishop Desmond Tutu,
following a meeting with Margaret Thatcher at Downing Street, 1985

such discipline. Once beyond the first page, I will want to continue until the whole joyous experience is complete. Along with the book, the guard has given me a small plastic magnifying glass as I have no reading glasses. It's hardly sufficient, but it does the job, and that's all I need.

'Let us now praise famous men, and our fathers that begat us.' So begins the first book I have read for months. I am delighted that it's an autobiography so that I can compare the book I am writing in my head with the one before me:

> Our life is in the visible track we made: but autobiography holds a memory of those ghost tracks, can tell something of the moments of choice endlessly repeated.

I follow the writer on her expedition: Baghdad, Beirut in a different age. Here in my solitary life she takes me away on a voyage and at the same time reveals something of her own inner journey. Would that I could write my story as competently as Freya Stark.

I arrived back at Shorncliffe and made my way through the half-deserted hospital to the ward. It was raining and blowing hard. I walked into the conservatory and looked down at the raging sea. The rain beat against the window-panes with indifferent elemental fury. A few tattered decorations, remnants from our pre-Christmas party, hung limply from the ceiling.

'You're back then?'

'Yes.'

Chadwick, a veteran of the Korean War, was sitting in a wicker chair, a bottle of beer at his elbow. 'It's been bloody quiet here, I can tell you.'

I sat opposite him. His feet were swathed in bandages and propped up on a stool. He was suffering from some obscure form of foot rot contracted while wading through swamps in Malaysia.

'Why come back so soon?'

I told him.

'You'll be all right, you'll get a P8.'

I didn't want a medical discharge. That would represent yet another failure in a life hardly distinguished by achievement.

'They'll give you a pension. It's clear, if you can't wear the bloody uniform, you're no use to the Army, mate.'

I wandered back into the ward and sat on my bed. Chadwick was

probably right. Civilian life could be just around the corner. Sister
Jennings, an elderly civilian nurse, bustled into the ward.

'Ah, I heard you were back,' she said cheerfully. 'Take a bath and
get into bed. Doctor will see you tomorrow.'

It took me a long time to fall asleep. I was uncomfortable, worried
and alone. Outside the gale continued, providing a natural accom-
paniment to my own turbulent state. A few lines of verse flashed
through my head:

> *All is best, though we oft doubt,*
> *What th' unsearchable dispose*
> *Of highest wisdom brings about . . .*

Would that I had the faith of Milton.

The weather is getting unbearably hot. The mornings are tolerable,
but in the afternoon the sun strikes directly against the wall by which
I sit. Since there is no ventilation in the room, the air quickly
becomes foul. When the guard opens the door to bring food, a
sudden draught of cool air floods in and gives relief for a few minutes.
It's difficult to know what to do. I feel tired and listless, and when
I lie down, I am soon soaked in perspiration. Because I am chained,
I can't move to the far wall. This slow torture has lasted for weeks;
and although I continually complain about the lack of air, nothing
happens. I exercise as best I can in the early morning when it is
comparatively cool. Although necessary, exercise is a chore. Still, I
continue it without fail and feel guilty if I miss a day. Since I was
put in chains I have stepped up the number of movements, but I
still miss my walks. Occasionally the guard will release me for an
hour, so that I can walk around the room. I drift into dreams as I
move round and round. Today I have been kept on the chain except
for my usual brief visit to the bathroom.

The door suddenly opens.

'Sleep.'

I lie down, my blindfold pulled well over my eyes. Several people
enter the room, talking in low voices. Someone drops an object on
the floor.

'Face the wall.'

I turn to face the wall. As I lie wondering what is going to happen,
I hear the sound of banging outside. One of the party is hammering
at the adjacent wall, which, I assume, faces a small balcony. The

hammering continues for an hour or so. Then something heavy is dragged into the room – more hammering. It's frustrating not to know what is happening. Finally the work is over. Someone sweeps up, and the party leaves the room. When I remove my blindfold I discover that a heavy fan has been inserted into the wall. At last some ventilation. I crawl as near to it as I can and look through the space where it has been installed. They have erected some form of screening on the balcony so that I can't see out; and, of course, no one can see in. If I strain I can manage to catch the briefest glimpse of a patch of blue sky. I gaze at it, remembering the days when I had the freedom to look at the heavens, to stand by the sea, to lie on the grass, to walk through the woodlands. Days that belong to the past, recoverable only in memory. I draw back towards my mattress.

The new equipment in my prison brings mixed emotions. On the one hand, I am relieved that some fresh air will come into the room. Although the fan is not yet connected, the hole in the wall alone makes a tremendous difference. On the other hand, I am depressed. If they have installed a fan, it must mean that they plan to keep me here for some time yet. One point I note about my behaviour in captivity is that I am constantly looking for signs and attempting to give them hopeful interpretations. If a guard is kind, I tell myself it must be because he is preparing for my release. One part of me knows that this form of reasoning is purely speculative and often ridiculous, but I continue it nevertheless. Now I see the fan as a negative sign, even though I will benefit from it in the weeks to come. The problem is that I have no information about anything, not even about the prisoner in the room opposite me. I am told nothing.

I have finished Freya Stark. Reading in captivity is sheer delight. I have time to enter into the mind of the writer, and to be caught up in the flow of her thoughts without interruption is a great pleasure. Modern life is fragmented, full of distractions. Here I can really read. Here I can discover how to convert my loneliness into creative solitude. Part of the secret, I think, is to make a companion of the experience. Although much of my life has been spent alone, the real beauty of solitude is only now becoming apparent to me. If I ever leave captivity, I will take this precious gift with me.

'Pretend to be asleep,' the soldier in the next bed whispered across to me.

I closed my eyes and pulled the sheet up over my shoulders. I waited for a few moments and then cautiously glanced down the ward. A slim figure in military uniform was making his way through the silent room. Although it was ten o'clock in the morning, every bed patient appeared to be totally unconscious and those who were dressed disappeared into the bathroom. No one stirred. As soon as the figure returned to the main lobby, slumbering soldiers sprang to life as if the resurrection trump had just sounded.

'Bloody nuisance,' muttered my companion. 'He's daft, you know, bloody daft.'

Regardless of his mental condition, the visitor was certainly not popular with the men. In the early days of my hospitalisation I had made the mistake of chatting to him. He was an army Scripture Reader, well-intentioned no doubt but totally unable to communicate except by inserting a scriptural text into every sentence he uttered.

'Good to see you, brother. I know you go to church. You are walking in the light, aren't you, brother? You have a great witness to make here. Remember John three, verse sixteen.'

How could I, or indeed anyone, reply to this jargon? I knew what he was trying to say, but why did he find it necessary to speak in such a pretentious manner? He pressed a small copy of the Gospel According to St John into my hand, together with a tract, and continued on his missionary journey down the ward. I glanced at the leaflet, which told of a conversion to Christianity that took place in the previous century. It was virtually unreadable, and I threw it away.

The winter months passed pleasantly enough. I used the opportunity to read and think about the future. Medically, I was making good progress – as long as I did not put on the khaki uniform. It looked increasingly as though I would be given a medical discharge. What was I going to do?

I made a list of the subjects that interested me: theology, philosophy, history, literature. I asked myself how I wanted to spend my life. In the past, Arthur Warburton and others had suggested that I might consider whether or not I had a vocation to the Anglican priesthood. I did consider the suggestion seriously and gave it much thought in hospital, but it did not attract me. It seemed too restricting. I also felt that I was hardly the sort of person to be looked to as an 'example' of Christian living.

Although I had little or no experience of poverty or extreme deprivation, I recognised within myself a desire to assist those who were less fortunate than I. As I had ruled out the priesthood, the Anglican Church seemed to offer few opportunities for full-time work, but one afternoon I came across an advertisement in the newspaper for the Church Army. It explained that the Church Army was a society of the Church of England, founded in 1882 by Prebendary Wilson Carlile, which was devoted to social and mission work. Young men and women who were practising Anglicans and thought that they might have a vocation to the lay ministry were encouraged to write for further information. I had never heard of the organisation, and although the name did not attract me, the type of work involved seemed appealing. That afternoon I sent a letter to the London headquarters.

Within a week I received a reply, telling me that a Church Army officer was working in the parish of St Saviour's, Folkestone, and if I made contact with him, he would gladly see me. I wrote to the officer at once and received an invitation to visit him the following Sunday afternoon. As I had no suitable civilian clothes, I put on my army uniform and set out for St Saviour's. Years later, Captain Tom Reeman told me the surprise he and his Sunday-school class received when I strode into the parish hall. My slim build made me appear even taller than I was. As Tom was below average height, the contrast was dramatic. He took me to his home to have tea with his wife Sarah and their young family. St Saviour's was a high Anglican parish, extreme even by Anglo-Catholic standards. (The then parish priest eventually renounced his orders and joined the Roman Catholic Church as a layman.) Tom had charge of a daughter church in a new housing area. Although he and his family lived in a new house, it was immediately obvious to me that they led a very simple life. Later I was to experience for myself the modest salaries paid to Church Army officers.

Tom explained the work of the society and told me something of his own life. Back in the hospital, I reflected on the meeting. Tom had impressed me by his straightforward simplicity and honest commitment to his vocation. He had little standing in the Church and was quite content to deal with the everyday problems that confronted people on the estate. He also impressed me by his non-partisan approach to the Church of England. He had worked across the spectrum of church life, from the evangelical wing to his present position. He cared about people and in his own way was able to communicate the love and compassion that lie at the heart of the Christian message. Although I had reservations about the military image of the Church Army, which have remained with me, I recognised that this was part of the organisation's Victorian legacy, and the task of attempting to make the love of Christ real in daily life appealed to my idealism.

Now that the fan is connected, the climate in the room has improved, although it's often unbearably hot. Since the mock execution, my guards have been reasonably friendly. I begin to believe that they might well release me soon. Just before I was captured, I heard that the government of the United States was proposing to conduct a public inquiry into the Iran arms-for-hostages affair. I don't believe that I will be released before the report of the Tower Commission is published, but afterwards my chances might be good.

Today another book arrived. It's a university textbook dealing with the history of slavery in the United States. I had to give back *Beyond Euphrates*, which I had read several times. I parted with it reluctantly, but perhaps it has gone to the prisoner opposite, and if so, I'm happy. Here I sit, chained by the feet, reading of men, women and children, whole generations, who spent a lifetime in chains. It's somewhat comforting to get a perspective on my own limited suffering. Alongside these poor souls, my captivity is bearable, especially now that I have a book from time to time. The guard comes in and sits on the floor with me. He is in a cheerful mood.

'Can you sing?'

'Sing?'

'Yes.'

It's a strange question. I haven't sung for months. In fact, I have always been instructed to speak in whispers.

'Sing for me.'

His request catches me by surprise. Perhaps he is fascinated by European singing. I wonder what to attempt. Then I get an idea. First I give him a verse of 'God Save the Queen', followed by a couple of verses of the hymn 'Oh God, our help in ages past'. If the other prisoner can hear me through his closed door, he may get the message that an English churchman is being held in another room. It's a long shot, as the electric fan is making a great deal of noise, and I assume there is a fan in his room as well.

'Very good.'

The guard leaves the room and locks the door. I imagine that he wanted me to sing because he was bored. I pick up the book and begin to read about places I know in Ghana and Nigeria. Then the lights fail. Electrical failure is common these days; sometimes I am in darkness for several hours. The fan stops working, of course, and the temperature soars. It's frustrating to sit on the floor knowing that it's a clear, bright day outside and that I am denied sunlight. Not enough light comes through the space where the fan is, and because the screening has now been extended on the balcony, I can't even see my small patch of blue sky any more. I miss that a lot. This apartment is old and dirty. Last night I awoke with a start when a huge cockroach walked across my face. On a previous occasion, cockroaches were actually biting my feet while I was asleep. Mosquitoes are another constant nuisance. I spend hours attempting to catch them, but they always seem to come to rest on the wall opposite, and my chain allows me virtually no freedom of movement. If there is light, I can shake my bed-covering in their general direction in the hope that they will fly within swatting distance. If it is dark, then there is no hope. My body is covered with bites and some have gone septic. The guard laughs when I mention this to him and replies in a good-natured way that mosquitoes are fond of Europeans. I tell him the reverse does not apply.

The light comes back on, and the door opens.

'Mr Waite.'

'Yes.'

'I am a student.'

'What do you study?'

'I am making a study of the Anglican Church.'

'I see.'

'I would like to ask you many questions.'

'Please do.'

My questioner's English is good. He sounds young.

'How is the Anglican Church organised?'

I begin to answer him in some detail. He listens carefully. I don't mind answering his questions, in fact, I quite enjoy talking to him. He is the first person I have spoken to in any detail for so long. I discuss the role of the Archbishop of Canterbury, the Lambeth Conference, the Anglican Consultative Council and the General Synod of the Church of England. He listens intently and takes notes. I wonder why he wants the information, and whether he really is a student, but it doesn't matter. He's quite welcome to ask me what he wishes. After three hours or so, he brings the meeting to a close and leaves with a promise to return one day.

I lie down, still thinking about the Church I know so well. Suddenly there is the most massive explosion yet, followed by another and then another. The building shakes and small pieces of concrete from the ceiling fall on me. The guard rushes into the room.

'Don't be afraid.'

He rushes out again. Another tremendous blast echoes through the streets. It sounds as if bombs are exploding in the road below. That's what it must be, it's certainly not shelling. The guard returns, checks that my chain is secure and leaves again. He doesn't reply when I ask him about the explosions. Now all is quiet. I turn on my mattress and try to sleep. Beirut, oh Beirut.

'We are going to give you a P8.' The elderly Colonel examined me carefully. 'The condition has cleared up, as you can see, but obviously you can't wear the uniform.'

I packed my few possessions, said goodbye to Sister Jennings, received the congratulations of my fellow patients, and left Shorncliffe and the Army for ever.

My final travel warrant took me first to a discharge centre near the Guards' Depot, which resembled an old-fashioned clothing store. The soldier in charge handed me a sheet of instructions stating that I was entitled to a suit or sports jacket, shoes, shirt. In short, a complete set of civilian clothing. I wandered around the store fascinated by the extraordinary array of articles waiting to be selected. The choice of hats was between a trilby or a cheesecutter. On balance I thought the cheesecutter might be more dashing and added it to my collection. The suits all looked like the one my father wore on his wedding day. I chose an undistinguished sports jacket, carefully packed it in my new cardboard suitcase and caught the train home.

Back in Cheshire my parents were sympathetic and understanding. I told them that I was thinking of working in some way or another with the Church but had not yet decided how. After a few days I travelled to Mirfield in Yorkshire to spend some time in retreat at the house of the Community of the Resurrection, an institution of the Anglican Church, founded towards the end of the previous century by Bishop Charles Gore. Its members take the threefold vow of poverty, chastity and obedience and preach and teach, mainly in the United Kingdom and South Africa. Bishop Trevor Huddleston is one of the best-known.

I had read *The Venture of Prayer* by Father Hubert Northcott, a work that helped me to understand the prayer of contemplation. Father Northcott was resident at Mirfield when I arrived and I was able to have many conversations with him. From Mirfield, I went to stay with the Cowley Fathers at Oxford, an austere group with a community house in the Cowley Road who were not, as I soon discovered, noted for the excellence of their cuisine. Members took turns cooking, and while I admired the simplicity and commitment of those who lived the religious life, I decided it was not for me. I also did not believe that I had a vocation as an ordained minister. Once again I wrote to the Church Army, expressing interest. They responded by saying that I could work for them in one of their hostels, and if the experience proved satisfactory, they would consider me at their next Selection Conference, which would take place in London later in the year. Within a few days I was on my way to Middlesbrough in Yorkshire, where the Church Army ran a hostel for ex-prisoners and the homeless.

I am very bored. In the corridor people come and go. I hear a gentle knock on the outside door, someone talking in a low voice. Now I hear a key being inserted in the lock and quickly arrange my blindfold.

'Good afternoon, Mr Waite.'

I don't recognise the voice. The English is excellent.

'We have something here that is very interesting, to you and to us.'

He flips through the pages of a book. The pungent smell of new paper reminds me of bookshops and freedom.

'What is it?'

'A report, Mr Waite. Your name is mentioned in it.'

'Can I see, please?'

He doesn't reply but continues to leaf through the pages.

'It's an American report, Mr Waite. It tells of what the Americans were doing.'

I think he is attempting to frighten me.

'I should be interested to read it.'

Again he doesn't reply immediately.

'What have you to say, Mr Waite?'

'There is nothing to say except I would like to read what has been written.'

'Are you sure you have nothing to say?'

He closes the book with a snap and leaves the room with it still in his possession. I return to my boredom.

There is a lot of activity today. Several people have arrived and are moving things in the hallway. The guard hasn't yet brought my breakfast and it's quite late in the morning, judging by the regular prayers offered from the mosque. I wonder if the activity is associated with the explosions last evening. There was a great deal of noise throughout the night, but nothing to compare with what happened earlier.

The door opens. Several people enter. Even though I am blindfolded, their tension communicates itself to me. My chain is unlocked.

'Stand.' My arms are seized. 'Walk.'

We move across the room, turn left into the corridor, left again into what I assume is the kitchen.

'Sleep.'

My arms are gripped tightly, and I am guided to lie down in some sort of box. I imagine it is what my mother used to call an ottoman, a form of settee with a hinged lid over a space for storing blankets. I lie in this box as best I can. I am too large to lie on my side, and when I lie on my back, my knees stick up. Someone tries to close the lid, but it's impossible. There is much excited conversation. Further attempts are made to close the lid, this time by sitting on it. Then it is flung open.

'Stand.'

I climb out of the box and am guided back to my room and the chain.

'Are you going to move me?'

'No speak.'

The door closes. My thoughts race, and the familiar anxiety returns. It grips me in the stomach, and I can feel my heartbeat accelerating. The door opens again. Once more I am led out of the room into the kitchen.

'Get inside.'

I am pushed towards what I sense must be a refrigerator. All the shelves have been removed. They push me inside and force the door shut. A few moments ago this machine was working, the sides are still cool. The door opens, and I am pulled out. I hear the dreaded sound shut. A few moments ago this machine was working, the sides are still cool. The door opens, and I am pulled out. I hear the dreaded sound of masking tape being unwound. That noise will surely remain with me for the rest of my life. My hands are taped together.

'Are you going to move me in the fridge?'

'No speak.'

'There is no air in the fridge. It's very dangerous. I might not be able to breathe.'

'No problem. Not long.'

'It doesn't take long for the air to finish.'

'No speak.'

Tape is wound around my blindfold and over my mouth. My feet are bound together at the ankles. I am pushed into the refrigerator and the door closes. There is a small ledge and I rest on it. If I didn't have this support, the pressure on my legs would be unbearable. Already the machine is defrosting and water is sloshing around my feet. Suddenly I am tipped backwards as they prepare to move me out of the room. Water splashes everywhere, and I am drenched. I slip off the ledge and immediately feel an awful strain on my legs. I must get my hands free, if only to support myself. If I can get them free, I might be able to open the door. It's a hope, if nothing more. I am thrown around as they manoeuvre the fridge out of the flat. Now it is vertical, and once again I slip. I struggle and struggle with my hands. Suddenly they are free. Thank God. Gradually I lever myself back on to the ledge and support myself with my hands. It's possible for me to push the blindfold and tape towards my forehead so that I can see. It's pitch black. So the light does go out after all!

I hear the elevator gates opening. We are on the landing, waiting to go down. Other people are standing by the lift. I can hear two women speaking, also a child. They may belong to our group, or they may be complete strangers. It's too dangerous to knock on the wall of the fridge: my captors would shoot first and think afterwards. The fridge tilts again, this time forward. I am caught by surprise and hit my head on the side. Now we are in the lift. Now we stop. I tilt backwards. Now I am being carried down some steps. It's getting terribly hot in here. I am soaked with water from the fridge and my own perspiration. Down we go. A short rest. Down again. Now I am being lifted up. Now silence. I am fighting for breath. This is madness, sheer madness. Stories flash through my mind of children being trapped in old refrigerators and suffocating to death.

An engine starts. So, I must be on the back of a truck. I balance my body as best I can and with two thumbs press hard against the rubber seal around the door. A sudden rush of cool air enters, giving me immediate relief.

The man at the wheel is driving like Jehu. From the sound of the engine, we must be racing through the streets. I try with all my might to open the door, but it's useless. All I can do is keep up the pressure on the seal to make sure I stay alive. The air is barely sufficient, but I won't suffocate while I keep the seal parted. Now we stop, and I hear voices – a roadblock? On we go, then stop again. Now we are reversing. The engine is switched off. I pull my blindfold down and slip my hands back into the tape. The door is opened, and the air hits me like a shower of cold fresh water. I take deep draughts of this life-giving elixir.

Several hands pull me out.

'Be quiet.'

I have no energy to be anything but. I can hardly stand. From under my blindfold I can see the ottoman next to the fridge. Have they brought my unknown companion along? I crouch, panting for breath.

'Come.'

I am guided off the lorry on to what feels like a small platform and across an open space. This is probably an underground car park. I can smell the petrol. Onward through some gates.

'Sit.'

Looking down, I see a foam mattress lying on an earthen floor. I sit down and am properly secured.

'No speak.'

The guard leaves, and I hear him lock a door. I lift my blindfold all the way and look around. I am in an underground room, probably the storeroom in a car park. There are metal partitions on each side of me, and a small light outside casts a faint glow in my space. Perhaps the unknown prisoner is in the cubicle next to me. I can't reach the partition to knock softly, and to shout would be madness, so I don't know how I can find out. My clothes are wet through, and I am shivering. I wonder how long I will stay in this miserable place and what tomorrow will bring.

≪ 7 ≫

THE TRAIN TO MIDDLESBROUGH meandered through the Yorkshire countryside. At one moment I was entranced by the bleak beauty of the moors; at another, a sudden chill passed over me as if a cloud had crossed the sun. I was both excited and apprehensive. I wanted to give my life to the service of God and my fellow men. My experience of life was negligible, but I had seen enough to be aware of suffering in the world. The Church would surely give me an opportunity to assist others. But was my faith strong enough? I had read the Bible, but it had never captivated me in the way it seemed to grip some Christians. I had always attended church and had enjoyed singing in the choir, but I had never considered church services as such the most thrilling experiences in life. If I was now on my way to test a vocation that would perhaps lead to a lifetime within the Church, ought I not to feel more certain, more secure in the faith? The nagging doubts about religion that dogged me spoiled what inner peace I might have had. It was as though I was being pulled from within. On the one hand, I wanted absolute security of the kind I imagined a religious order might offer; on the other, I wanted freedom, freedom to explore worlds within and without.

I felt in the inside pocket of my demob jacket and pulled out my army pension book. Seventeen shillings a week disability pension should provide me with some security for a little while.

My first impressions of Middlesbrough were unfavourable. The streets were dirty, and there seemed to be a general air of depression. I crossed the road and found Wellington Street close by. Number ten was the Church Army hostel. A massive door, rather like the main entrance to a prison, was securely fastened shut. To the side of it a small door led to the front office. I entered and put down my cardboard suitcase. An elderly man looked me over and asked me my business, then picked up the phone and spoke to a Captain Kinsey. In a few moments a middle-aged man in a grey uniform bustled into the office. I was immediately struck by the fact that half his face was covered by a purple birthmark. This must have caused him considerable embarrassment throughout his life, but I never heard him refer to it. He was brisk, and I suspected at once that he did not suffer fools gladly.

'Come and have a cup of tea, lad.'

His house was next to the hostel, and his wife, a cheerful Yorkshire woman, soon had me sitting at the table in front of a homemade cake and a steaming cup of tea. She asked if this was the first time I had visited Middlesbrough and I replied that it was.

'It's a mucky town, but the people are grand.'

When she smiled, her whole face shone, and her eyes sparkled with good-natured amusement. In her quieter moments she betrayed a reflective sorrow which must have come from living close to suffering for many years.

When tea was over, her husband rose. 'I'll take you to your room,' he said to me. 'It's not grand, but it's private.'

We went down the concrete pathway past the workshop, where one or two men suddenly leapt into action when they saw us, and into the hostel. My room was on the first floor.

'On Sundays you're welcome to have your meals with us. For the rest of the time you can get what you like from the canteen. If you would like to come to church with us tomorrow, you're welcome.'

When he had left, I sat on the iron bedstead. A table, a chair and a wooden cupboard completed the furnishings. I unpacked my few belongings, stacked my books on the table and looked out of the window. Outside a parade of smoking chimneypots stretched to the horizon. I searched in vain for a sight of some greenery and finally decided to go for a walk. Crossing the railway, I passed a succession of cheap furniture shops and came eventually to the town hall, a massive structure which stood like a Greek temple surrounded by semi-derelict ruins, a symbol of the prosperity that had condemned hundreds of workers to live under a pall of smoke and eke out a living in the steel mills and shipyards. There was nothing else to see, so I returned to the hostel. Captain Kinsey was behind the desk.

'Well, lad, had a good walk? There's not much fresh air around here, I'm afraid. The great thing about Middlesbrough is the countryside and the sea. They're close by, and you should get out there on your day off.'

He opened a huge ledger. 'Full again,' he sighed. 'It's not often we have spare places these days.'

I asked him about the residents.

'A mixed bunch. A good number of recently discharged prisoners, quite a lot on probation. Many men from broken homes. Men look-ing for work. A very few long-term residents.'

I asked him about an unusual-looking man I had seen in the court-yard wearing a tweed jacket, plus fours and rough woollen stockings with sizeable holes in the heels. Captain Kinsey smiled sadly.

'A Cambridge graduate, grandson of a bishop, been here for years. Was a heavy drinker, but that's over now. He's quite content to stay on. Never sees his family.'

The man's grandfather was known to me by name. I had sung hymns written by him countless times. When an opportunity pre-sented itself, I attempted to speak to his grandson. Under his tweed jacket he wore an old green pullover with holes in several places. When I asked how he was, he stared at me from beneath a shock of pure white hair with the wary eyes of a trapped animal. He opened his mouth to reply, but no words emerged. He tried again, his eyes darting to left and right. 'Er, er, er.'

That was all he could manage. He made a half-bow, turned and escaped to the privacy of his cubicle. I never had an opportunity to speak to him again.

My first night Captain Kinsey showed me the canteen. It was full of men seated around tables covered with sheets of coloured plastic. Kinsey spoke to several of them, and they replied deferentially, like soldiers to an officer, prisoners to a warden, tenants to a landowner. He took me to meet the cook, standing behind the serving counter dressed in the regalia of his trade. Conscious of his power, he grinned and joked, passing a plate of stewed meat and potato to a resident without once looking at him.

We left the canteen and walked upstairs to the dormitories. They were very clean, with about twenty beds to each, but there was the unmistakable institutional odour that later in life I recognised when I visited prisons around the country. Several mattresses were placed against the wall.

'Bed-wetting,' Captain Kinsey explained. 'We don't allow drink in the hostel, but there's no way to stop them bed-wetting.'

'Do you get much trouble?'

'The occasional fight, illness of various kinds, epilepsy, that sort of thing. We rarely have to call the police.'

'Can you help many of them?'

He looked at me and smiled.

'This is not spectacular church work. It's a long, hard slog. Year in, year out, we are here to give a home to those who have little or nothing. We help them by just being here. Mostly we can't help more than that.'

I looked around at the drab dormitory and then at Captain Kinsey. I tried to imagine what it must be like to spend a life drifting between prison and hostels, to be caught in a routine that offered little joy. How could Kinsey maintain his optimism year after year, seeing little result for his efforts, facing constant disappointment and let-down? I respected him for his commitment and determination. Working against all the odds, he was showing a compassion for his fellow men more powerful than a thousand sermons. I doubted that I had the qualities to serve humanity as he had served it for the past thirty years or so, and it made me pause.

The next morning I went with him and his wife to St Columba's Church. The building was like a huge ark in the midst of an industrial sea. The service was high Anglican, as though emphasis on colour, incense and drama could provide an antidote to the dreariness of the surroundings. Captain Kinsey acted as master of ceremonies, which meant that he had a responsibility in the Liturgy to see that the ritual forms were correctly observed. While I was no stranger to Anglo-Catholicism, I felt uncomfortable in the church. The congregation was small, elderly and apparently exhausted. Father Hooper, the parish priest, overawed me with his austere solemnity. I decided that I would look for another church to attend on Sundays, even though the church members I met did their best to welcome me.

My work in the hostel was simple enough. There was plenty of time to listen to the residents' stories of unhappy childhoods, broken marriages and prison life. I puzzled in my mind over the problems they raised. Did the fault lie with the individual, the family, society, or was it a bit of each? The hostel was so crowded that all we could offer was first aid. I wondered if the Church should put its efforts into developing smaller units where intensive individual help could be given. This I concluded might suit some, but there were others, like the Bishop's grandson, who could live only in a large, anonymous hostel.

As I grew to know the town, I understood Mrs Kinsey's early remark that the people were 'grand'. I met Jean, a nurse at the local hospital, who lived in one of the terraced houses near the hostel, and we occasionally went out together. Ultimately we became good friends, although we hardly communicated once I left the town. Middlesbrough opened my eyes to the complexity of human nature, and I learnt something about the cost of human compassion. I wasn't at all sure that I could pay such a price, but I knew I wanted to continue.

The metal door opens, and I hear footsteps crossing the earthen floor.

'Tek.'

It's the Duke. I hold my hand out and receive a sandwich and a can of something or other. When I remove my blindfold, I discover it's a soft drink and a sandwich bought from a roadside stall. The guard has also brought me a piece of material I can use for a sheet. Now that my clothes have dried out I am much warmer, but the real problem is mosquitoes. The sheet will provide some protection, but not much. The guard returns.

'No speak – very quiet – understand?'

'Yes.'

He removes my bonds and guides me through the metal door.

'Be quick.'

Another hand takes my arm, and we set off at a brisk pace. From beneath my blindfold I see that we are crossing a paved area. Suddenly we stop.

'Be quick.'

I am pushed forward and hear a door close behind me. An overpowering odour tells me that I am in a lavatory. When I lift my blindfold I see it is very dirty, probably a public lavatory in a car park. I use the facilities. When the knock on the door comes, I fasten my blindfold and am hurried back to my cubicle and secured.

'Sleep – no speak.'

As soon as I lie down I am attacked by mosquitoes. I do my best to wrap the material around the exposed parts of my body, but it's virtually impossible to prevent myself from being seriously bitten. I fall into a light sleep until a sudden noise draws me back to consciousness. I have lifted my blindfold, but it's so dark I feel as though I can touch the blackness. Someone is moving – perhaps my unknown companion is being taken away. There are footsteps in the darkness; a whisper; a softly closing door; silence. I drift back into sleep, my feet and legs stinging from repeated insect attacks.

When I awake, it is morning. A little light filters dispiritedly into the room. There is another roadside sandwich, another trek to the lavatory, another long, uncomfortable day shared with mosquitoes, spiders, flies and cockroaches. Then it is evening.

'No speak.'

I am released from my chain.

'Stand.'

I get to my feet. My legs and ankles are swollen from innumerable mosquito bites. My unseen captors wrap a cloth around my shoulders. They are dressing me up for another move. Thank God I don't have to spend a second night in this pit. A headpiece is fitted. Once again I am being dressed as an Islamic woman. Out we go, across the paved area.

'Get in.'

I step into the back of a van.

'Sit.'

I sit on some sacks, and a blanket is thrown over me. The door is closed, and we set off. One of the guards is speaking into a walkie-talkie. We are following the usual procedures: stop – wait – drive – stop – wait – change driver – start – stop.

'No speak – sleep.'

I do my best to lie on the sacks, but it's most uncomfortable. The night air is cold, and I'm shivering. A guard throws another blanket over me. We wait for a long time – two hours? Three? The guards whisper softly. Occasionally I hear a car pass, but most of the time it's silent. The radio crackles into life; my captors stir and take away the blankets.

'Stand.'

They smooth out my clothing.

'Close eyes.'

They remove my blindfold.

'Move slow.'

I step down from the van and walk forward. Through half-closed eyes I see a small party approaching. A man, a woman and to my surprise a small child holding the man's hand. I must be the long-lost aunt from the country, and they must be my family. The man greets me and picks up the child to give me another pretend greeting for the benefit of anyone who may be watching. The child knows full well that she does not have an aunt who is six feet seven inches tall, and she pierces the night with a scream of terror. Immediately the situation is galvanised. The welcoming party turns and enters an apartment block. Hands push me from behind, and I follow. Inside the lobby I am propelled into a small elevator along with two companions. Several people set off up the stairs. We ascend in silence.

A letter from the Bryanston Street headquarters of the Church Army informed me that I had been accepted for the annual Selection Conference. I was asked to go to London and be prepared to stay for several days. Mrs Kinsey cooked a farewell Sunday lunch of roast beef and Yorkshire pudding, and I went out with Jean in the evening. We were sad to part, and although we agreed to write, we somehow knew that we would never see each other again.

I returned to my room in the hostel with mixed feelings. During my brief stay in Middlesbrough I had been able to get beneath the surface bleakness of the city and experience the genuine warmth of the people. I had grown both to respect and to like the Kinseys. Captain Kinsey told me that if I wasn't accepted for training, he would welcome me back at Middlesbrough, but he thought my chances were good.

In London I met some of the other candidates: David from Yorkshire; Idwal from south Wales; Ian and Marion from Ireland; Judith from Lancashire; Len from Middlesex; Harold from the West Indies. We ranged in age from nineteen to mid-thirties and came from a wide variety of backgrounds. None of us quite knew what to expect from the Selection Conference as we made our way along Edgware Road to the college in Marylebone where we were to be accommodated.

The first morning we began a long series of personal interviews with different Church Army officers. These concluded some days later in a meeting with the college principal, the Rev. Donald Lynch. Before we came to London, we had all submitted various pieces of written work, and there were further examinations during the week. As the end of the conference drew near, a number of us were sitting in the common room after lunch.

'They say the test tonight is the critical one.'

Several pairs of eyes focused on the speaker.

'What's so special about tonight?'

'Hyde Park. Everyone has to speak for at least five minutes.'

The thought of standing on a box at Speakers' Corner terrified me.

'What if I dry up?'

'Dennis Oxley will make sure you don't.'

Captain Oxley, an intense man and a dynamic orator, was a legendary figure in the Church Army. A regular speaker at Hyde Park, he was responsible for taking candidates through their ordeal. When we arrived that evening, the action was in full swing. A speaker from the Coloured Workers Association was haranguing a large crowd of listeners. Near by, a bald man, his head and face completely covered with tattoos, presented his philosophy of life. The Catholic Truth speaker was engaged in a complex explanation of the doctrine of transubstantiation. But the largest crowd by far was gathered around the Rev. Donald Soper, the doyen of the park. He was expounding the Christian faith with force and humour, convincingly applying each to issues of the day. We put up our stand and stood awkwardly around while Dennis Oxley prepared to sing a hymn. A small crowd gathered. Dennis launched forth. Somewhat falteringly, we followed, one by one. Before I knew it, I was on the stand facing a sea of interested and amused faces. Just as I was about to open my mouth in public for the first time, a heckler beat me to it.

'You buggers have got gold in your teeth. I can't get meat in mine.'

The crowd laughed good-naturedly. Another voice shot out from the back:

'Repent and pay the rent.'

My wit was too dull to give an appropriate reply. I stood there desperately attempting to pluck up enough courage to begin. Dennis was at my elbow.

'Take no notice. Get going.'

I took a breath and started. I have no recollection of what I said. When I climbed down, I was trembling but inwardly rather pleased that I had taken the first tentative step towards public speaking.

It is all very puzzling. Last night we stepped out of the elevator and I was guided into another apartment. They led me into a room and told me to lie on a sofa and sleep. I was ordered not to remove my blindfold, but I could see from under it that the room was fully furnished. My foot was chained to a radiator.

This morning I heard a man and a woman talking in the hallway. Someone whose voice I had never heard before brought me breakfast on a small plastic tray. He spoke kindly and apologised for the fact that I was chained. After I had finished breakfast, he returned, and

I was moved into another room which had been completely cleared of furniture. So here I sit on the floor in what I know is a lived-in apartment. For the first time in months the room is lit by natural light; there are no screens over the window. It's wonderful to have sunlight in the room and to feel the breeze blowing through a half-open window. My feet are still painful. I started to count the number of mosquito bites on my left foot and gave up at one hundred and forty-six.

At lunchtime the man returned, closed the window and switched on air conditioning. Sheer luxury. I asked for some lotion for my feet, and he promised to get it. I also asked for books, and he said he would try to find some. Furthermore he told me that he thought I would be released soon.

'How soon?'

'I don't know, not long.'

'One week, a month?'

'Perhaps just a few weeks.'

Can that possibly be true? I don't know what is happening as I have no news of the outside world at all. Someone is tapping on the door. I secure my blindfold. Several people come in and talk quietly between themselves. I recognise only the voice of the man whom I identify as living here. Tools are brought into the room, and work begins. My heart sinks as I hear an electric drill used on the window-frame. After one brief day of natural light, I am returning to darkness. The work is finished, the room empties. I am alone again. A metal sheet has been fastened over the window so that no daylight enters. The electric light is on, but that will be intermittent as always. The American writer Emerson once said that the sky was the daily bread of the eyes. I seem to have been hungry for a long time.

'Do you need to keep me chained?'

The owner has returned. He takes a key and unfastens the lock.

'Thank you.'

'I have brought you some food.'

He places a tray on the floor and leaves. The food is the best I have had in captivity. A few fresh vegetables, fruit, meat, potatoes. I eat as slowly as I can. The owner returns.

'Would you like to see TV?'

I tell him that I would. He wheels a trolley into the room and sits on a chair behind me with the automatic TV control in his hand.

'OK, lift blindfold, but do not turn head.'

To my surprise it's *The Benny Hill Show* with Arabic subtitles. I can't imagine how any non-English-speaking viewer could possibly understand Hill's verbal humour. The owner laughs at the slapstick comedy, but as soon as scantily dressed women appear on the screen, he changes to another channel. As women occupy much of the programme, we spend most of the time darting back and forth between a political discussion in Arabic and Benny Hill's *double entendres*. Finally the extraordinary show finishes, and the news is announced. The television is switched off immediately.

'Can I watch the news?'

'No, Chef says no news.'

'Why not?'

'I don't know.' The trolley is wheeled out of the room.

The doorbell rings, and I hear several people enter the apartment. For a while they talk in the corridor and then come into my room. As they enter, one of the party gives an exclamation of surprise at seeing the chain hanging loose. While they are talking among themselves, it is replaced around my foot.

'That is not necessary.'

'Chef says you must have chain.'

'What news do you have?'

'Good.'

'What do you mean, "good"?'

'Good news for you. Soon you go home.'

'Is that true?'

'*Inshallah* – much good news about you in newspaper.'

'What does it say?'

'It says you may get Nobel Prize.'

'Me? I can't believe that.'

'Look.'

He puts a newspaper in front of me. I look under my blindfold and see a picture of myself and several others. As the script is in Arabic, I can't read it.

'What does it say?'

'Your name goes for Nobel Prize. Very good.'

They leave the room. Are they being truthful? Why would they lie about such a thing? I don't think for a moment that I will be awarded the prize even if my name has come up. My achievements are modest to say the least, and with all the uncertainty as to how I have behaved in this whole affair, it would be more than surprising.

This news could, however, explain the reason for the better conditions I now enjoy, even though life is still somewhat restricted. I hear the party leave, and my guard enters.

'You want anything?'

How can I answer that?

'No, thank you.'

'Goodnight.'

I lie on my mattress, close my eyes, and look back on a day that has taken me from light to darkness, from Benny Hill to the doors of the Nobel Prize committee. One more surrealistic day in captivity.

8

Back at home in Lymm, I waited for the results of the Selection Conference. Since I would not hear for two weeks, I decided to see something of Scotland. With my rucksack on my back I hitchhiked to Inverness where, alone in the rugged beauty of the Highlands, I considered the conference. My fellow candidates represented all the different strands within the Church of England. The majority, however, could be described as 'middle of the road' Anglicans, which was how I regarded myself. The down-to-earth friendliness of the officers I met in London impressed me, and I was in sympathy with the practical approach the Church Army took towards individuals. Its Victorian military image still bothered me, but my doubts were not strong enough to dampen my enthusiasm. Recognising that I was at a major crossroads in my life, I tried to define what it was that drew me to a vocation within the Church.

My experience in Middlesbrough had reinforced my feeling that I was not right for the ordained ministry. I believed then, and still believe, that a clergyman must maintain tradition within the body of the Church. I recognised that it was vital to have an appreciation of the history and tradition of the Church, and indeed I greatly valued both, but I did not see myself spending my life defending them. Also, I didn't want to be locked into a stereotyped role.

Another part of me, however, considered ordination for all the wrong reasons. I imagined that if I was ordained I might find the security for which I was searching. I have always been grateful that I rejected that erroneous notion. I tried to dig deeper. What was it about the Church that attracted me? Eventually my thoughts settled on the ministry of Jesus: his wisdom, compassion and life of service. That was the heart of the matter. His example captured my youthful idealism, and I felt called to follow him. Having acknowledged that, my insecurities came to the surface again. If I joined the Church Army, I would have to live simply – very simply. What if I married? Could I ask my wife to live in the way I had seen Church Army families live? Going on from day to day with hardly a penny to their names. As a layman I would never 'advance' in the Church.

Promotion 'through the ranks' would be denied me. That might be all very well in my twenties, but what about in my forties?

Something within me told me to put these considerations aside and follow my instincts. The Church Army and the wider Church would provide me with a base for service. I decided that if I was accepted, I would give it a try.

When I returned home, I found a letter of acceptance waiting for me. Along with the letter were instructions on what I would need for college. I set about collecting some of the books: C. B. Moss, Bicknell, a hefty commentary on the Bible, a Concordance, and struggled along the Marylebone Road weighed down by all of these volumes.

The college stood on the corner of Cosway Street, almost directly opposite the Marylebone Magistrates Court. I was assigned a third-floor room, which was dominated by an extra-long bed kindly obtained for me by the college principal.

Downstairs in the common room, I met David and Idwal, my friends from the Selection Conference. Meals were formal and segregated by sex. The Training College Captain, Dennis Oxley, and the Matron presided jointly. As we ate, I surveyed the gathering. I recognised many of the faces but several were new to me, and it looked as if a number of people I had got to know at the conference had been turned down. I was quickly brought out of my daydream by Dennis Oxley rapping on the table with the back of a soup spoon. He got to his feet and began to address us with the same intensity that he had demonstrated in Hyde Park:

'The rising bell will sound at six-thirty a.m. Chapel is at seven. From seven-thirty until eight you will be in your rooms for your private prayers. Breakfast is served promptly at eight. We listen to the eight o'clock news during breakfast, after which you may talk. Until then you are expected to keep total silence. From eight-thirty until nine you will clean your rooms and parts of the college. Lectures will occupy you during most mornings and some afternoons. You should use as much free time as you can for private study. There will be a rota for washing-up after meals. Every week you will be given a personal allowance of twelve shillings. You will also be given a uniform, and your clothes will be laundered each week. Are there any questions?'

There was an uncomfortable silence as we each considered what we might ask.

'What about speaking to the ladies, Captain?'

Bob Kennedy's cultured tones rang out across the dining room. He was a witty and cheerful Anglo-Catholic. As a youngster, he had featured in several BBC plays and had an exceptional speaking voice.

'It is not encouraged. There will be times of course when it is necessary, but normally there will be no fraternisation.'

Although men and women studied together in the same building, they were strictly segregated except for lectures and chapel services, and even then they were not allowed to sit together. The men were at the front of the lecture room; the women, at the back. In chapel women sat on the left, men on the right.

Kennedy grinned.

'What if there's a fire, Captain?'

'That would be an occasion when you would be expected to use your common sense, Kennedy.'

We stood. Grace was said, Matron left the table, we filed upstairs, subdued by the prospect of a life that promised only silence, segregation and hard work. I was reminded of Kipling's poem:

> *These are* our *regulations –*
> *There's just one law for the Scout*
> *And the first and the last, and the present and the past,*
> *And the future and the perfect is 'Look out!'*
> *I, thou and he, look out!*
> *We, ye and they, look out!*
> *Though you didn't or you wouldn't*
> *Or you hadn't or you couldn't;*
> *You jolly well* must *look out!*

The owner of the apartment unlocks my chain.

'You can walk a little. No problems, please.'

He locks the door, and I begin to exercise. Better food and cleaner living conditions have improved my health considerably. My hair and beard are now very long indeed. As I am not allowed a mirror I have to imagine what I look like, and I must be a fearsome sight. A built-in wardrobe stands at one end of the room, one side firmly locked, the other open. Inside I discover my clothes hanging neatly on a coat hanger. I am dressed in shorts and a vest, and it is far too hot to wear anything else, but it is comforting to see my own clothes waiting for me. Could this be another sign pointing towards an imminent release?

The door opens.

'Sit down, please.'

I sit on the floor.

'I have some books for you. You must read them slowly.'

'Thank you very much.'

The owner places two or three paperbacks in my hand.

'If you are going to keep me for a long time, I would like a Bible, please.'

'If we keep you long, you will get a Bible.'

'Will you keep me long?'

'I don't know.'

Although I want a Bible, I hope they won't bring one. On the other hand, nothing is certain. They might bring me a Bible and release me the next day. It's so frustrating never to get information, never to know if anyone is telling the truth. The door closes. At least I have three books. I remove my blindfold and open the first. What a bitter disappointment. It's a children's story written for students of English with a vocabulary of about a thousand words. The second and third books are in the same series. The householder has obviously made an effort to find a shop selling English books, but he apparently didn't know what to buy, or perhaps he wanted to improve his own command of English. It will take me no more than fifteen minutes to read all three books, after which I will be left to my own thoughts again.

The first book is very curious. It tells the story of a young British soldier in Northern Ireland and seems to be straight propaganda. It's illustrated in full colour, and it takes me only a few minutes to read it from cover to cover. The other two books are fables from Aesop's collection, the kind I read to my children when they were about three.

Ruth, Clare, Gillian, Mark, where are you now? I hope to God I haven't caused you too much suffering. Frances, how are you coping? I can't allow myself to keep thinking about you all – it hurts too much, and there is the danger of falling into over-sentimentality. You are all strong. You will survive, whatever happens. I pray you survive well. I think of the difficulties many families have to face: chronic illness, divorce, death. Will I see my wife and children again? Will no one tell me? Will no one put an end to this horrible experience of not knowing? How long must I stay here like an animal, locked away from all human companionship? How long, God? How long will you allow me to exist in this situation? A year? Two years – three? Well, I have almost managed a year, but two years would be very hard. Please not two years.

The door opens. I hear the owner speaking to another man.

'Sit near wall.'

A new voice. The chain is fastened around my leg.

'Why do you do that?'

'Chef say you must have chain.'

The owner speaks to his companion in Arabic and then to me.

'I am sorry.'

'It's not good to be chained all day. I am not an animal.'

'I am sorry.'

'The books you have brought me are for children. Can you please try and get me some different ones?'

'I will try.'

The door closes.

How I wish I could reread Byron's poem, 'The Prisoner of Chillon'. How does it begin?

> *My hair is grey, but not with years . . .*
> *My limbs are bow'd, though not with toil . . .*
> *I suffer'd chains and courted death . . .*

At least I can remember a few lines, but most of the poem has gone. I could try to compose in my head. Poetry, music perhaps. Why can't they give me a pen and paper? That's harmless enough surely. It's one thing to keep me like this, but to deny me books and writing materials as well as companionship seems heartless. Perhaps I don't crave company so much. There are times when I would be happy to talk to someone else, but being alone is not too bad. But how much longer can I survive without being able to read and write? Will I go mad? Why should I? Why should solitary confinement make me lose my reason? My body may get weaker: I can't do much about that, but I can keep myself sane.

'. . . be transformed by the renewing of your mind . . .'

St Paul writing to the Romans. If I keep my mind alive and my soul free from bitterness, I'll survive. Perhaps even discover what it means to be transformed. God, please help me.

*

The college gave us a thorough grounding in theology and provided me with a body of knowledge which was to prove invaluable throughout life. I particularly enjoyed studying church history and Christian ethics, which the Rev. Ralph Baldry brought alive in his stimulating seminars. I wasn't an outstanding student, I had too many interests that diverted me from concentrating on achieving the highest grades. I continued to read widely and to follow my musical interests. There was not enough time to pursue everything, but I tried to expand each day and often read late into the night. Apart from academic work, we were expected to go to Hyde Park on Saturday evenings and speak at the Corner. As time passed, this became easier, and I grew to enjoy meeting the various characters who spoke and heckled each weekend. On Sunday evenings, several of us would stand in the Edgware Road and invite people to attend the service in the Church Army Chapel in Bryanston Street. This was so acutely embarrassing to me that I avoided it whenever I could, slipping away to spend time chatting with the old lady who sold newspapers next to the Odeon Cinema. She regaled me with tales of London life, and I kept in touch with her for years afterwards.

In the summer, instead of taking a long vacation, we took part in the Church Army summer trek. We would assemble at a cathedral city and after a service conducted by the Bishop, make our way in teams of six or so to a coastal resort. Some teams walked the whole way, pulling their belongings behind them on a cart. I was fortunate and made my journeys in a Bedford Dormobile which stopped each day in a different parish where we would hold a service in the church and move off the next morning. The whole tour took two or three weeks. Whatever value it had for the parishioners upon whom we descended, it enabled me to develop a sound working knowledge of the Church of England and its people. I experienced every kind of churchmanship imaginable. In some parishes, Holy Communion would be celebrated by the clergyman standing at the north end of the Communion table, a position which made it quite clear that the service was a memorial and not a sacrifice. In another parish, the Communion service would be conducted with such elaborate ritual that a casual visitor would be unable to distinguish it from a Roman Catholic Mass.

During these tours I met people from widely different backgrounds and got to know large areas of the British Isles. One summer we camped in the church hall of a seaside town and spent several weeks conducting services on the beach. Initially, I had some reservations about this type of activity, as I was loath to disturb the privacy of the holidaymakers who may not have wished to be presented with a church service on the sands. But my fears were proved groundless when a large number of people turned up each day especially to take part.

Our days were full. We emerged from our camp-beds in the church hall at about 6.00 a.m. and went for an early-morning swim. Not surprisingly at this time of day, the beach was deserted. It was a wonderful time to bathe. On returning we either attended a service in the church or conducted our own morning prayers before preparing breakfast. The remainder of the day was spent on the beach, with a service at eleven, a children's hour at three, and an evening meeting at seven o'clock. The attitudes of the local Anglican clergy to these events varied. Some would join us for one evening of the week and even pluck up enough courage to speak. Others would sit on the seawall and join in the hymn-singing. The majority would offer their support from a distance.

As I lie in chains, my mind goes back to the freedom of those days by the sea. I stand on a soap box and speak about the love of God for mankind. The wind blows in my hair, and I fill my lungs with the fresh, salt air. Even then I would tell myself to be careful about speaking of states of being which I had not experienced myself. I warned myself not to talk glibly about love or suffering, reminded myself that I knew very little about life. In some ways it seemed almost an arrogance to speak about such profound mysteries, but I did it with the hope that I might one day grow in the faith.

In our final year each of us went through a series of interviews to help determine in which part of the society we would be best suited to work after completing our studies. In the sixties, the Church Army was engaged in extensive social work. It had hostels for men and women in many towns; officers worked in prisons; there was a housing scheme for low-income families; and Church Army Sisters staffed a number of homes for young, unmarried mothers. Substantial work was done to provide shelters for the elderly; a large number of officers worked in parishes all over the country; and there was the itinerant work of preaching and teaching. All these areas required further specialised training, which took place in Church or secular establishments. As an inveterate traveller, I found the itinerant work most appealing, and to my delight this was the sphere to which I was assigned.

As the final months in London sped by, I began to see the value of the highly structured college life I had initially rebelled against. It provided a platform from which the individual could begin to create a framework for his or her own life. Once away from the college, officers would be required to work in situations which demanded that they develop a high standard of personal discipline. I never conformed to the pattern of life or prayer that I learnt at Cosway Street, but it helped me find my own pattern in later years.

Captain Alan Chambers, head of the Mission Department at the Church Army, was my new superior. He smiled broadly as he ushered me into his office in Bryanston Street.

'Well, welcome to the department.'

I sat down by his desk.

'I don't know if there will be enough room for you; we can but try. You might enjoy some months on the York van.'

The Church Army had a number of caravans assigned to various dioceses. Each van was staffed by two officers who spent their time moving from parish to parish, conducting preaching and teaching missions.

'At the moment it's in the Vale of Cleveland. John Cooper is in charge – you'll enjoy his company.'

I took the train to York, and as I stepped off I found a wiry, tousle-haired man in his mid-twenties waiting for me.

'The journey will be a bit draughty, I'm afraid, but it won't take too long.'

We walked across to an old motorcycle and sidecar. He arranged the luggage as best he could and I climbed into the sidecar. Soon we were out of town and deep in the marvellous Yorkshire countryside. John shouted across to me.

'Let me know if it feels insecure. The car came adrift recently, but I think I've fixed it properly.'

'Was anybody hurt?'

'No – it had a soft landing in a hedge.'

As we chugged gently through the hills, I held on to the bike just in case. When we arrived at a hamlet, John steered around the back of a magnificent Norman church, down a small track and stopped in front of an antiquated caravan.

'Home again. Come on, let's get something to eat; I'm starving.'

He opened up, and we carried the luggage inside. I could hardly stand upright, but thankfully the bunk beds seemed long enough. John opened a stove and threw on some fuel.

'It gets pretty cold at night so I keep this fire going. Shall we have eggs and beans?'

He started to cook while I unpacked my belongings. He had cleared a space on the shelves for the few books I had brought with me, and there was an empty cupboard for my clothes. My thoughts went back to my childhood and to Romany of the BBC. Romany, otherwise G. Bramwell Evens, was a naturalist and a Methodist lay preacher. From time to time he would set out in his caravan, or 'Vardo' as he called it, and write and broadcast about his experiences. Usually he visited the English Lake District. I collected all his books, and later I discovered that one of my mother's bridesmaids had been his secretary for many years.

Over supper John explained his way of life. He usually got out of bed at six-thirty and went to early Communion in the parish church. If there was no service, he used the time for his private prayers. Two or three hours each day were reserved for study. If he was conducting a teaching mission, he would stay in the parish for ten to fourteen days, run classes for children during the late afternoon, and speak at services for adults in the evening. As if that weren't sufficient, the early afternoon was normally taken up with home discussion groups. He depended on the church members to supply him with most of his meals, which they did cheerfully enough, and to tow his van to the next village.

'Do you work at this pace all the year round?'

'It's not so bad. We take some days off between engagements and get a break in the summer. We're completely booked up for several months ahead.'

He poured the last of the cocoa.

'A lot of the clergy live quite isolated lives. Some get pretty depressed at continually ministering to small congregations. Our work can give them a bit of a boost, as we can always draw fairly large congregations. But I'm not convinced that we should be so concerned about large numbers. If we can get people to think about their faith and perhaps help them learn how to apply it, we shall have done well.'

We washed the dishes in a small sink.

'How do you like working in Yorkshire?'

'Terrific. The people are great. Very straightforward and hospitable. Let's call on the Rector.'

We stepped out of the van and walked along the pathway towards the church. John pushed open the heavy oak door.

'Take a look at this.'

He pointed to some new woodwork, finely carved and obviously created by a master craftsman.

'Look round the back.'

Almost out of sight was a small mouse carved unobtrusively into the design.

'Mousey Thompson. He's famous round these parts. He leaves his trademark on all his carvings; you'll find it all over Yorkshire.'

Father Barker sat in his study smoking an old cherrywood pipe. He urged us to draw our chairs closer to the fire.

'It gets quite cold here in the winter, but it's bracing.'

He was well advanced in years. The latter part of his ministry had been spent in Middlesbrough; now, as incumbent of a small country parish, he was as hard-working as ever. His wife, a small plump Yorkshire woman, bustled in with a pot of tea.

'If you need anything, let me know,' she said. 'When you want a bath, just ask. We've always plenty of hot water.'

She placed a tray on a side table and left. Plain, direct, unobtrusive.

Father Barker brushed ash off his cassock and looked across at me.

'Will you serve at Mass tomorrow?'

'I'm sorry, Father, I don't know how.'

He looked surprised.

'I'll teach you – it's very easy.'

That was that. Father Barker taught me to serve, and from that day to this I have hardly ever served at Mass again. Assisting at church services has never held much appeal for me.

Back in the caravan, John and I discussed the forthcoming teaching week. We planned to hold a special service each evening when one of us would deliver an address on different aspects of the faith. In order to bring some life and interest to the proceedings we decided that while I was in the pulpit holding forth, John would bang on the church door, walk up the aisle and question me. At the appropriate time I climbed into the pulpit and John slipped outside. After I had been speaking for five minutes or so, there was a tremendous crash, and the church door flew open. The noise was so loud that even the solid natives of Yorkshire stirred in their pews. John stormed into the church and marched down the aisle. He had taken no more than a few paces when the churchwarden seized him and rapidly propelled him towards the exit. After some explanations we were able to continue, much to the amusement of the congregation.

As the week went on, the evening congregation increased in number. Virtually all the children in the village attended the daily meetings planned for them, and the afternoon discussion groups were equally popular. The Yorkshire people were generous with their hospitality, and we were served dozens of Yorkshire puddings and countless high teas. At the end of the week a farmer hitched the van to his tractor and towed us to the next parish, where we started all over again.

When winter came we were tucked away in a village in the Dales. During such breaks John would leave a space of several days in the calendar so that he could visit other parts of the diocese. While he was away, I remained in the van, reading and preparing for yet another week of speaking. Often I spent the time alone, surrounded by the most magnificent countryside and quite content with my books and solitude.

In the morning the householder leaves, presumably to attend to his business. His wife usually remains at home, and now a young man sits outside my door throughout the day. He is probably a student, as he chants from the Koran for hour after hour. When he is not chanting he conducts a conversation with the owner's wife. She remains in the front of the apartment, and they shout to each other down the hallway. Perhaps they are related. This morning he takes me to the bathroom as usual. There is a very small window above the bath – far too small to escape through. In any event, we are three or four floors up, so escape would be very difficult, especially as my guard waits outside nursing an automatic pistol. Today he has overlooked the fact that the window is slightly ajar. I can just see out. Opposite is a very modern-looking office building, and beyond that the blue, blue sky. A gentle breeze is sweet and wholesome. I remember more of Byron:

> *And mine has been the fate of those*
> *To whom the goodly earth and air*
> *Are bann'd, and barr'd – forbidden fare . . .*

How I long for freedom. How I long to feel the wind and gaze into the sky.

'Be quick!'

A staccato command quickly brings me out of my dreams. I put on my pyjamas, adjust my blindfold and tap on the door. The guard guides me back to my room and fastens the chain around my feet. As he is new, I try to engage him in conversation.

'Is it true that a follower of Islam should not steal?'

He is quick to reply.

'No steal – to steal very bad. Muslims not steal.'

'Why then do you keep innocent hostages? You are stealing us from our families. You are stealing our lives.'

He is silent for a moment.

'Chef say no speak.'

He leaves the room, locks the door and resumes his chanting. I start my own morning prayers, remembering from a lifetime lived with the Book of Common Prayer:

'If we say that we have no sin, we deceive ourselves, and the truth is not in us: but, if we confess our sins, he is faithful and just to forgive us our sins, and to cleanse us from all unrighteousness.'

So help me God.

The starkness of winter gently gave way to the advances of spring. We continued our travels through Yorkshire, meeting hundreds of people. In the late summer each year John spent several weeks in the south-east working among the hop-pickers. As soon as the season arrived, we closed the van and set out for Paddock Wood in Kent. Thirty years ago hop-picking provided an annual holiday for the East Enders of London. They packed a few possessions and spent several weeks in the Kentish hopfields, making money and enjoying a simple holiday. In fact they earned little, but the fresh air and companionship compensated them somewhat.

Arriving at Paddock Wood, we made our way to the field. The hop-pickers were allocated rough wooden cabins with corrugated-iron roofs. We found our cabin and moved our few possessions inside. Apart from a raised wooden platform to accommodate a mattress, the room was quite bare. We had brought sleeping bags with us, but for some reason had forgotten mattresses. Our next-door neighbours, a family from the East End, took pity on me and invited me to spend the first night in their cabin. They had filled a huge sack with straw and reserved me the end position in the bed. I spent a crowded and somewhat restless night. Cooking facilities were non-existent, and all hot food had to be prepared over a fire outside the cabin. One tap provided water for thirty or forty people. For the whole of the hop-picking season, John and I lived in the camp and gave advice on a multitude of problems, and on Sundays conducted church services around the camp-fire. I made friends with many of the hop-pickers and long afterwards visited them in their homes back in London.

At the end of the season I didn't return to Yorkshire with John. Alan Chambers asked me to call and see him and told me that I was to be transferred to London to join the Flying Column, a team of four Church Army officers, usually three men and a woman, who were based in the capital and travelled throughout the country, conducting programmes such as we had done in Yorkshire. Another young officer and I found a top-floor flat in a Victorian house in Queen's Park, several stops beyond Paddington.

One day after spending a week in a parish in the south of England, I decided to hitchhike to Cheshire. My father had been ill, and it was some months since I had seen my family. My salary was so small that hitchhiking was the only possible way for me to make private journeys. I took the tube to the end of the line and stationed myself by the side of the road. It wasn't difficult to get a lift, and within a short time I was in the Midlands, waiting for what I hoped would be a final lift to Cheshire. A small estate car passed me and pulled up when the driver saw my signal. I clambered in, and we set off.

The back of the vehicle was filled with cardboard boxes and cases. As we talked, I discovered that the driver was the Rev. Harold Wilson, Secretary of the Adult Committee of the Church of England Board of Education, on his way to conduct a conference in the north. He was particularly interested in new methods of adult education and was currently involved in studying the ways in which small groups functioned. Before he dropped me off near my home, I had secured an invitation to a conference on a subject which interested me greatly.

I quickly realised that my father was far from well. He was smoking Woodbines as heavily as ever and had developed a cough that alarmed me. To add to his troubles, he was engaged in a dispute with his chief constable which was to result in his early retirement from the police force on medical grounds. While my father was probably the most straight and truthful man I have ever known, he could be difficult to live and work with precisely because of these qualities. There were many times when he expressed his disgust at what he perceived to be corruption in the police force, and whenever he came across it, he tackled it head on. Although I have long since forgotten the details, I don't believe he was speaking of major corruption. It was the day-to-day bending of the law by some of his colleagues that he regarded with acute distaste. His strong stance cost him any possible promotion in the force and brought him much unhappiness. Now that I had been away from home for a few years and had begun to establish myself, I found I could talk to him on more equal terms, and I began a long campaign to get him to consult a doctor.

'You're not well, Dad. That cough is getting worse. If you deal with it now, you might put it right. Leave it, and anything could happen.'

He made no promises, and I returned to London worried and unhappy for him and my mother.

The conference I attended at Elphinsward, a conference centre in Haywards Heath, West Sussex, marked a major turning point in my life. Harold Wilson had invited a number of educationalists from the United States and assembled clergy and lay workers from every part of the Church in the British Isles. There cannot have been a single participant who was not initially puzzled or confused by the conference, and in some cases downright hostile to it. Most, if not all, had been brought up with inflexible, traditional attitudes towards leadership and education. The conference was to stand many of these ideas on their heads!

Delegates were assigned to what were known as T- (for training) groups. Each group had no obvious agenda other than to study the dynamics of group development, that is to say, interpersonal relations and personal behaviour in groups. I found the work fascinating because it taught me a great deal not only about my own leadership style but also about organisation, dealing with conflict, and learning. At the end of the main conference I was invited to stay on for further study with a smaller number of participants, and I left Elphinsward determined to develop my understanding of group dynamics. The Church of England Board of Education provided such opportunities, and in a year or so I had gained considerable experience. Although I continued to work with the Church Army, more and more of my time was spent with the Board of Education. I joined a training team as a junior member and travelled around the country conducting courses for clergy, teachers and social workers.

I have finished my prayers, and the day stretches ahead. At first sight it appears empty, but in this solitary space the past, present and future merge and my concept of linear time changes. At one moment I am a child wondering at the mystery of the universe, at another, a young man uncertain and compulsive. Who am I? What am I? It's painful to be introspective, to see myself in the light of truth. In this solitary dark space, the light of truth shines brightly; so brightly that it hurts. My mind goes back to my early years, to the first painful separation from my parents. That must be one reason, if not *the* reason, why it has been so difficult for me to accept rejection; why I am such a complex mixture of defensive introspection and an outgoing desire to please, to be accepted. But why look for explanations? Why not be straightforward and accept the fact that pride, envy, lust, hate are as much a part of me as their opposites? It is so easy to slip into despair, to dwell on failure – failure to love, failure to be generous. I must hold on to what I really believe. God, I need you – your healing, your grace, your love, your forgiveness. Thank God, my faith relieves me of morbid soul-searching and offers hope. Belief that God is truth, and that truth will heal. Oh God, show me your compassion.

9

BRONDESBURY ROAD, Queen's Park, was a dull but convenient part of London in which to live. The tube was three minutes from the house, and I could be in central London in less than half an hour. Just as the conference at Elphinsward proved to be an important landmark in my career with the Church, so Brondesbury Road was the place where my personal life took a new direction. The house was owned by an Irish couple, Eamonn and Margaret. Eamonn worked in a pub in Covent Garden and left the house in the middle of the night to serve drinks to the market porters at four in the morning. He and Margaret lived in a couple of rooms at the back of the property and let all the others. I and my Church Army colleague lived at the top of the house; beneath us was a young Irish couple, Edna and Tony, both of whom were teachers. I made friends with them and often called in for a drink and a chat. One evening as I climbed the stairs, I passed Edna, who greeted me in her usual cheery way.

'Back again, I see. Drop in later, we've an old friend staying with us. You might like to meet her.'

After supper I went downstairs. Edna showed me into the sitting room.

'Frances, this is Terry Waite who lives upstairs. Terry, this is the sister of an old schoolfriend of mine, Frances Watters.'

Frances shyly shook hands with me. She looked serious, even worried. I was immediately struck by the beautiful shape of her face; she could easily have stepped directly out of a portrait by Modigliani. We chatted together, and I learnt that Frances was staying with Edna while she looked for a job in London. Born in Belfast, she had lived most of her life in Northern Ireland. She told me that she was about to write a letter of application for a job at London University.

'Let me help you,' I offered, anxious to make an impression. She seemed reluctant, but I persisted.

'It's no trouble at all. I've got a portable typewriter upstairs. You tell me what you want to say, and I'll type it immediately.'

Before she could reply I had darted upstairs and collected my

Olivetti portable. It was rather battered but worked well enough. I swept back into the room, where Frances sat quietly by the table.

'Now you dictate, and I'll type.'

I didn't do too well. I could type notes, but neat, precise job applications were outside my range. Frances was patient and finally accepted one of my drafts. After I had left, I believe she discarded it and sent in her own handwritten application. Anyway, she got the job.

As I lie on the floor it's hard to imagine what Frances is now experiencing. I smile to myself when I remember that evening. I was so outwardly confident, she so apparently diffident. We first went out together to a 'Ban the Bomb' meeting in Trafalgar Square. It was packed with demonstrators, so we left and walked through the streets of Whitehall, glad to be away from the noise and turmoil of protest.

Later Margaret offered Frances a room on the ground floor. She took it, and when I returned at weekends, she would cook me a meal. We hardly ever ate out; neither of us had the money to spare. Sometimes we would go to the Everyman Cinema in Hampstead, where we saw *The Childhood of Maxim Gorky* and *Nanook of the North*. In the summer, I went with Frances to Belfast to meet her family. The thought of the visit caused me much apprehension. I was shy too, although I appeared to be full of confidence. Perhaps that is why I was so attracted to Frances. We went down to the Ards Peninsula, a wild and lovely location, where her family rented a cottage each summer. Denis, Frances's father, was a solicitor, the son of a solicitor, and a highly intelligent man. His wife, Joan, was English, and Frances bore an amazing resemblance to her. Packed into the cottage were the three other daughters, Ann, Ruth and Sheelagh, along with Aunt Mary from England and Ruff, the family dog.

I was totally unaccustomed to large, intimate family gatherings and felt somewhat self-conscious despite everyone's friendliness. The days were long and leisurely. I was introduced to soda bread and potato bread. We went fishing and caught dozens of mackerel, which we took home and cooked in oatmeal. Now, in this dark room, I remember those days so vividly: the smell of the sea, the little fishing boats bobbing in the harbour at Portavogie; Tommy, the one-legged fisherman at Strangford Lough; the holiday that was both an end and a beginning. It was the last summer the Watters family spent in the Ards Peninsula. The following year they took a cottage in the

Mourne Mountains to which they returned every summer until Denis became too ill to travel. Frances recognised this holiday as closing a chapter in her life. A new chapter was beginning. I realised that I loved her and wondered where I might find the courage to ask her to marry me.

The owner of this flat is a kindly man. He does his best to make sure that I am served good food, which he often brings to me himself. Although he has made it obvious that he doesn't like to see me chained day and night, he has clearly been overruled by the mysterious Chef. He conducts some of his business from home but spends a number of hours away each day. I have no idea what his business is, although from the few crumbs he offers, he may be in the import–export trade. As virtually every Beirut businessman claims to be in that field, such information tells me nothing. Last night he had a visitor. I heard them chatting in the room next to mine. After a while there was a knock on the door, and I secured my blindfold.

'How are you, Mr Waite?'

'OK.'

'This is my friend. He is a businessman.'

A hand was offered me, and I shook it.

'Tomorrow he goes to London.'

Thoughts raced through my head. Why was he going to London? Was his journey connected with the hostages? Would he bring back news?

'How long will you be in London?'

'Two weeks.'

'Will you bring me news of my family, please?'

'Your family good. No problem.'

'I would like some news from them – a letter, anything.'

'No problem – your family OK.'

He handed me a piece of paper.

'What is this?'

I looked beneath my blindfold at what he had given me. It was a Scottish banknote. I told him so.

'Is it good in England?'

'Yes, perfectly good.'

He took it back and returned it to a bulging wallet. He pulled my blindfold down over my nose.

'Can you please buy me some books?'

'It's very difficult – I will try.'

They left the room. No one else came to see me that evening. I did my usual exercises and got into bed. The boredom was killing, deadening. All I could do was close my eyes and travel back over the years. Like a child playing imaginary games, I pretended I had a pen and paper and once again I began to 'write' . . .

Frances's elder sister, Ann, lived in Paris. Although our funds were limited, we decided to accept her invitation to go and stay with her for a week. My thoughts went back to my schooldays in Wilmslow. Our French teacher told us that the best way to learn French was to visit France. He organised a school party at £15 per head. I was so eager to see a foreign country I couldn't wait to get home and tell my parents about the trip. In those days £15 was a small fortune to my father. He told me it was impossible to find the money. One warm sunny afternoon I sat in the classroom with one or two others. Outside in the playground the party prepared to leave. Wistfully I watched them walk through the school gates to board the coach that would take them to the coast. There goes my chance, I thought. Now I would never see France.

Frances and I left from Lydd airport on the south coast where a plane took us to Beauvais, some thirty miles outside Paris, and a coach carried us into the city centre. This was by far the cheapest way to travel to Paris in the early 1960s. Ann had a large, elegant apartment near the Étoile. In one week we visited all the main sights. We spent the night walking through Les Halles, had onion soup at three in the morning, and walked to Sacré Coeur to watch the sunrise. Shortly before we left Paris, we prepared a picnic lunch and went to sit by the Seine. It was a perfect day, warm with a gentle breeze. As we sat together watching the river flow by, I asked Frances to marry me, and she accepted.

For a moment I can 'write' no more. I am too full of emotion. I can't help but look back on our life together and consider how difficult it must have been for her to live with my unsettled, searching nature. Frances, quiet, shy, and now possibly thrown into the public eye because of me. She was able to accept me with all my restless vulnerability and show me the real meaning of love. It has taken me over twenty-five years to learn how to relax in her love. I am still learning.

We returned to London, and before we bought an engagement

ring we went to Belfast where I followed the old-fashioned custom and asked Frances's father for permission to marry her. I felt awkward and acutely embarrassed, but Denis was charming and did his best to put me at ease. He told me he was delighted, as did Joan. They were both rather surprised that Frances was the first daughter to marry; she was the most reserved of all the girls. We returned to London, our savings depleted by travel. In Kensington Church Street we discovered a small jeweller's shop which stocked a number of second-hand rings. Frances chose one, and we became officially engaged.

I must have dozed off. Normally I don't sleep too badly, although the chain around my feet is uncomfortable. When I turn, it pulls and wakes me. My dreams are surprisingly comforting. Their richness seems to compensate for the drabness of my waking life. Tonight I have been travelling in regions unknown. For a long time I sailed the oceans, my small boat well stocked with food, books and music. I looked along the shelf at the different authors: Hemingway, C. P. Snow, Thomas Mann. Just as I was about to take a book from the shelf, the boat tipped to one side, and I felt something tug at my ankle. That was when I awoke. I close my eyes and try to re-create the scene, but it's useless. I am awake now, and my boat, together with my treasured possessions, has gone. My disappointment is acute. Why should I wake up at the very moment when I was going to read – why should I be denied such a simple pleasure? The boat and the books were so real I have difficulty believing they are gone.

I lie still, listening to the sounds of the night. The apartment is quiet. I can just hear the guard breathing gently on his mattress outside my room. Somewhere in the distance a dog begins to bark. Soon it is joined by another, and another. Their barking cuts across the unusual silence and somehow emphasises the loneliness of the night. In these nocturnal hours I inhabit a world which is hardly charted. Where is my guard tonight? Is he sailing the oceans, fighting battles, reading books? Where is my family? They appear and disappear in my dreams. My friends pass by at times, so real that it seems as if I could touch them. Now they leave me alone in my half-conscious state. Somewhere deep within lies the secret of my survival. It lies beyond family, beyond friends, beyond simple desires and hopes. Somewhere, somehow, I must touch the mystery that is God.

*

My work with the Board of Education continued to absorb me. John Adair began to apply the insights gained from group studies to leadership training at the Royal Military Academy, Sandhurst, where he was a lecturer; Mary Drinkwater, a former college principal, worked with teachers and educators; Harold Wilson and Laurence Reading concentrated on bishops and clergy; I worked with all of them and gained considerable experience. I visited the new prison at Grendon Underwood and talked with the staff who were hoping to use group work in their rehabilitation programmes. Conflict-resolution and the dynamics of interpersonal and intergroup conflict interested me, and occasionally I was asked to assist groups that had problems. One such event stands out clearly in my mind as my report on it read rather like a detective novel.

A new incumbent in a rural parish had fallen out with his council, and the parishioners had become totally divided. Eventually the parties involved decided to ask for outside help, and I was approached. I suggested that we all go away for a residential weekend at the Diocesan Conference House, and the fact that this suggestion was accepted led me to believe that progress was possible. Progress was made, but not in the manner I had expected.

One dark autumnal evening I arrived in the cathedral city where we were to meet. The cathedral stood high on a hill, dominating the landscape, with the conference house quiet and secluded in its shadow. The participants arrived, found their rooms and assembled in the dining room for dinner. My suggestion that we have a very brief meeting after dinner was greeted with relief. At the meeting I told the company that I would do my best to help them make an objective analysis of the situation and, I hoped, decide what, if anything, they wished to do about it. The meeting finished at about ten o'clock, and everyone made for bed. I stayed behind in the panelled sitting room, writing my notes and preparing for the next day. The house was quiet and in semi-darkness. As I was putting my papers together to go upstairs, the door opened and one of the house staff entered.

'Excuse me, sir, have you seen the caretaker?'

I told her I had seen no one for at least forty-five minutes.

'He went out a while ago and hasn't returned.'

I told her not to worry, I would go outside and check. I opened the huge front door and stepped into the courtyard. It was deathly still and pitch black. The woman handed me a small flashlight, and I set out. I walked around the house without seeing anyone. Down below in the town a few lights flickered; up on the hill the darkness covered the buildings like a shroud. As I passed one of the participants' cars, I noticed what I thought was an old coat on the ground. I walked nearer and shone my torch in its direction. It was an elderly man lying quite still. Quickly and anxiously I knelt by his side. He was dead. I hurried back to the house to telephone the police, and in no time they appeared.

'How many people at the conference, Mr Waite?'

'Twenty.'

'Where are they?'

'I expect they are all in bed.'

'Why aren't you in bed?'

'I was just about to go. I had been preparing for tomorrow.'

'Tell me exactly what happened this evening. Explain your movements step by step.'

I repeated the events of the evening as best I could.

'When you went outside, did you see anyone?'

'Not a soul.'

'Did you hear anything?'

'No.'

'A car or anything like that?'

'No, it was totally quiet.'

'I would like you to wake the members of the conference and ask them to assemble in the meeting room.'

'Shall I give them a reason?'

'No, just ask them to come downstairs immediately.'

I climbed the broad wooden stairs and knocked on each door. To my surprise, not one person asked why they were being summoned to the conference room at midnight. One by one they descended. One by one they were called into the study and interviewed by a police officer. Finally, in the early hours, the interviews were concluded. The Bishop arrived to comfort the grieving widow. The body was photographed and removed. We got to bed as the first grey fingers of dawn were stretching out to warm the ancient stones of the cathedral.

When we met for a late breakfast we were told that we were free to leave should we so desire. For the moment, we had been cleared. The house staff was obviously unable to continue with the conference, so we decided to bring it to an end. We packed our cases, said our farewells and left for home.

Was the caretaker murdered? It was thought not. The police concluded that while he was making his rounds he disturbed an intruder, either a peeping Tom or a person attempting to break into a car; there was a brief scuffle, and the caretaker, who was known to have a weak heart, dropped dead. No one was ever apprehended. As for the Parish Council, the shock of sharing such an experience together was enough to set them on the road towards a resolution of their differences. As I remember, the Vicar and his council found a new harmony, and all was well.

I returned to Lymm for the Christmas holidays. My father was thin and gaunt, and his cough racked his wasting body.

'Dad, please, you must stop smoking.'

'It's my only pleasure.'

'It's killing you. Every time you smoke, you cough and cough.'

'I've always had a bad cough.'

'If you can't stop smoking, at least go and see Dr Hughes.'

'I'll be all right.'

Along with a cough, my father had always had what he called a 'weak stomach'. Now he was scarcely able to eat. My mother attempted to cook dishes that would be easy on his digestion, but it was of no use. To add to his troubles, he was still embroiled in the dispute with his chief constable. Every night he sat in front of his typewriter, pounding out page after page, working like a man obsessed. At times he would stop and attempt to explain his argument to me. I did my best to understand but failed. It was too complex. He had been granted legal aid to fight his premature retirement on medical grounds and was in communication with a leading counsel in London.

I returned to London deeply worried, about both his health and the fact that I had never been able to establish what I considered a satisfactory relationship with my family. That Frances seemed to have a different, richer form of family life added to my discomfort. Before I went to Ireland to ask her father's permission to marry her, I told my parents of my intention. They appeared pleased, and eventually Frances came with me to Cheshire. She was exceptionally patient and caring with my father and made a good impression on everyone. We decided to get married in May of the following year.

As I developed expertise in group work and leadership training, I received more and more requests to conduct conferences and seminars throughout the British Isles. In the diocese of Bristol in the west of England, Canon Basil Moss, then Director of Post-Ordination Training, had recognised that the Church needed an articulate and informed laity if it was to fulfil its task in the world and had written an outline programme designed to be discussed by groups of clergy and laity across the diocese. This he named SALT, an acronym for Stewardship and Laity Training and also an indirect reference to Matthew 5:13: 'Ye are the salt of the earth.'

A weekend conference was organised under the chairmanship of the Right Rev. Clifford ('Jim') Bishop, then Bishop of Malmesbury and Suffragan Bishop of the diocese, and I was invited to attend. Arriving at the Bishops' house on a warm summer afternoon, I could hear shouting and laughter in the back garden as I walked up the path. The Bishop's large and cheerful family was splashing about in an old rubber paddling pool. It was only a matter of minutes before I joined them, and thus began a lasting friendship with Jim and Ivy and their marvellous children. I have long since forgotten how I dealt with the conference, but my suggestions must have appealed to the participants since later in the year I received an invitation from the Bishop of the diocese, the Right Rev. Oliver Tomkins, to take up a new appointment as Lay Training Officer.

This narrative has been running on and on. I don't know how long I have been writing in my mind – one hour, two, three? As I tell myself the story, sitting cross-legged on the floor, I attempt to conjure up a picture of those days almost thirty years ago. I can see Oliver Tomkins before me: tall, with piercing but compassionate eyes, always careful in his choice of words. When he invited me to visit him at Bishop's House in Clifton, I was extremely nervous. I arrived in Bristol early and walked through the town, up the main street, stopping to look in George's Bookshop, past the university and then around the corner towards the Downs. Outside Bishop's House stood a Rover limousine, standard issue in those days to diocesan bishops. A chauffeur in a peaked cap emerged from the car and went in through the main gate. I looked at my watch: two minutes to the hour. I opened the gate and walked up the short drive. The doorbell was answered by the Bishop's secretary, who ushered me into the house and offered me coffee.

'Bishop will be with you in one moment. He is just finishing a telephone call.'

Exactly on the hour the door opened, and Bishop Oliver emerged. He greeted me warmly.

'Come in, sit down. Alice will bring us some coffee.'

I sat in an armchair by the fireplace. The Bishop collected a file from his desk and sat opposite me. For a moment he read from it and then looked up.

'Tell me something about the work you have been doing.'

I told him.

'Both Basil Moss and Jim Bishop would like you to work in the diocese.'

I said that I would be happy to.

'How would you organise your work here?'

I explained that I would first arrange a series of residential courses for the diocesan clergy, during which we would investigate new educational methods. I would also want to conduct conferences for lay people which would deal with the fundamentals of Church life, and I would like to encourage the formation of specialist groups: lawyers, teachers and so on, to discuss the relationship between their work and their faith, and the impact of one upon the other. The Bishop took careful notes. Later I realised why it was that he always seemed to have time for people. He was an excellent manager of his own time. Whenever I went to see him, he could look up his notes and immediately recall our last discussion. The hour together passed quickly.

'As all my diocesan team are clergymen, it would be good to have a layman such as yourself working here. There are problems, of course. A clergyman can always be given a small country living and be free for half of his time to work in a diocese. In your case we would have to find a house and a salary from our central funds. However, that is not your problem.'

He smiled and rose, indicating that the interview was over.

'I shall be in touch with you shortly.'

As I walked out into the warm sunshine, I decided that I really did want to work in the Bristol diocese.

Change was in the air. Eamonn and Margaret wanted to redecorate my flat and let it out at an increased rent. I needed to save every penny if I was to marry the following year. The Church Army came to my aid. In Seymour Place, round the corner from the Magistrates

Court, the Church Army owned a pub. The Walmer Castle, built at the turn of the century, had been given to the society by the owner, who decided it should be used for a more sober purpose – and it continues to be a base for social work. The room designed as the public bar was used as a storeroom. Upstairs, in a series of small rooms, lived various single Church Army officers. I was offered a room at the very top of the house and eagerly accepted it. There was one minor difficulty. In order to prepare a meal I had to climb up a small fire escape, cross a flat roof and then descend several stairs into the kitchen. One night I came home very late after taking part in a conference somewhere outside London. I unpacked and made for the kitchen to get something to eat. As I went back across the roof I was suddenly blinded by a piercingly bright light. At the same moment a voice boomed out into the night.

'Stay where you are – don't move.'

I stopped and looked over the parapet. In the street below stood several police cars. I shouted down to them,

'I live here. I've just been to cook my supper.'

'Stay where you are.'

Eventually I was joined on the roof by a policeman to whom I explained the unusual geography of the building. The very same episode was repeated several weeks later when finally the message got through to the local police station that a figure would frequently be seen crossing the rooftop at midnight, and that his business was lawful.

I remember Seymour Place for another incident. One afternoon I had clambered across the rooftop with a plate of cheese on toast. As I ate and listened to the radio, an announcement came over the air which hit me with a force I can still remember vividly.

'News is coming through that President Kennedy has been shot while visiting Dallas.'

I leapt to my feet. I was stunned. For some reason I felt I had to tell another person. The house was empty. I went out into the street and made for the off-licence on the corner. Although I rarely bought anything from the shop, I frequently called in to have a chat with the manager. He was incredulous. Neither of us could believe that the President of the United States had been assassinated. I returned to my room and listened to the details as they unfolded.

10

THE DAYS PASS so slowly. The householder continues to be
polite, the young guard continues to pray. At times he disturbs me
by sobbing hour after hour. As he chants, he cries as though his
heart will break. I cannot escape his religious emotions. They invade
my room and penetrate my soul, making me puzzled, sympathetic
and angry all at once. If he has such feelings, why can't they be
expressed in human terms by showing compassion for innocent hostages? Finally he stops, and there is quiet. A ray of light enters the
room through a minute space between the metal window cover and
the wall. Gently it pierces the darkness. It shines with a steadfast
intensity and gives me hope. Light is stronger than darkness. Hold
on to light. Let it strengthen you.

A few days ago the guard came into the room with another man
whose voice I did not recognise.

'Mr Waite?'

'Yes.'

'Nobel Prize given to American.'

'Oh.'

'We are sorry not you.'

'I never expected it would be.'

'Nobel Prize political.'

I make no reply.

'America control Nobel Prize.'

'When will you release me?'

'I don't know.'

'Why do you keep me?'

'I don't know.'

'Do you think I am a bad man?'

'No, Mr Waite. You good man. We know.'

'How long then?'

'Perhaps not long.' The usual reply.

'Can you please bring me some books? Long books, please. I sit
here all day with nothing to read. Please, I need books.'

'We try for some books.'

'Please try. The days are very long.'

Several days have passed, and no books have arrived. The small light continues to shine, and I continue to hope for freedom, and if not freedom, then some relief from crushing boredom. I hear the front door of the flat open and recognise the familiar voice of the owner. He speaks to the guard, and I hear the key being inserted in the lock of my door. Automatically I adjust my blindfold. The man enters.

'Mr Waite, you good?'

'OK.'

'I have book for you. Good book. Bible.'

My heart sinks as I remember the conversation of several weeks ago when the guard said that if they were going to keep me for a long time, I would certainly get a Bible.

'Thank you.'

I take the book in my hand, and the householder leaves. I look at it and experience a second disappointment. It's a modern translation. It seems churlish to have such feelings after having been deprived of books for so long, but I am starved for beauty. The King James' Version would have provided me with the beauty of language. I could have learnt whole chapters by heart and taken delight in their rhythm and flow. A modern translation is useful for study purposes, but I crave the music of language which would breathe harmony into my soul. I light a small stub of candle, pick up my plastic magnifying glass and begin to read from the book of Genesis, a book of beginnings:

'"Let there be light" and there was light. God saw that the light was good.'

The beam of light fades as evening approaches. The candle flickers in the gloom. I close the Bible, lie down and shut my eyes. Hold on to light. Hold on and never let go – never.

Frances and I were married on 16 May 1964 in Belfast. The sun was shining, but a cool wind reminded me that the city was on virtually the same latitude as Moscow. Harold Wilson flew over from London to assist Canon McKelvie, the local incumbent, in the wedding service. John Cooper, awkward like me in his hired morning suit, was my best man. We had both stayed the night in a local hotel and in the morning made our way to St Jude's Church, Ormeau Road. In the traditional fashion, my family and friends sat on one side of the church, Frances's on the other. There were long rows of empty pews behind my family group. Northern Ireland was the other side of the world to my relatives. My mother, brother and sister were present, but not my father, which was a great disappointment.

'These occasions are not for me,' he said, when I asked him to attend. I half knew he wouldn't come before I suggested it to him. He was far too shy and uncomfortable in unfamiliar surroundings.

Canon McKelvie took the wedding service, Harold, the Communion. The reception was held in the hotel at which I had been staying, and then at last Frances and I were free. We took the train to Londonderry where we boarded a local bus which carried us into the Republic and deep into Donegal. From Burtonport we caught the little ferry to Aranmore and stayed in the only pub, which closed whenever the landlord felt so inclined. The last part of our honeymoon we spent in the Watters' cottage in the Mourne Mountains.

Before our wedding, the Bishop of Bristol had formally offered me the job in his diocese. The Church bought a small new house in Woodcroft Close, Bristol, for two thousand pounds, and Frances and I moved into our first home, virtually penniless but filled with excitement and hope.

One week before Frances gave birth for the first time, we were told to expect twins. Strangely enough, I had frequently said that our firstborn would be twins, but when we received no medical confirmation of this prediction, I forgot about it. On the evening of 11 July 1965, I drove Frances in our Ford Anglia across Bristol to Southmead Hospital. About three miles from home, the heavens opened, and it rained so hard that water in the engine brought the car to a halt. Mercifully, the rain stopped and the car dried out sufficiently to get us to the hospital, where Ruth and Clare were born the following day. As the birth was difficult (they were both face presentations) I was not with Frances during the delivery. Just over a year later, Gillian was born at home in Woodcroft Close.

The Bristol years were full and demanding. With three girls under the age of two, our meagre finances were stretched to the limit. My work continued to take me away from home for days at a time, and a great deal of the responsibility for the children fell on Frances.

We always made a point of getting away in the summer for a family holiday. A friend gave us a caravan so that we could have inexpensive holidays. We kept it in a large vicarage garden in Devon, and, supplemented by a tent, it accommodated all of us in reasonable comfort. One summer, Jim Bishop and his wife Ivy lent us their cottage in Norfolk. Another year friends offered us a cottage in Devon. Although we had little money, we had good and generous friends.

In the early years of the children, I did much of my reading at night while bottle feeding one of the girls. We upgraded our car to a Ford Cortina Estate and fitted three safety seats in the back. To give Frances an occasional break, I would sometimes strap the children in and drive the two hundred or so miles to see my parents in Cheshire. My father was now seriously ill and unable to work. Although he was always pleased to see his grandchildren, he was quickly exhausted and often had to retire to bed. One weekend he seemed particularly depressed.

'What information does the consultant give you?' I asked.

'Not much. He just tells me to continue the treatment. I start a course of radiotherapy next week.'

My heart sank.

'Has the doctor told you what the problem is?'

'No.'

'Would you like me to speak to him?'

'Yes, I would.'

I went to a local telephone box in order to have some privacy and called the hospital. The doctor was in his office, and I was able to speak directly to him.

'I am calling on behalf of my father, Thomas Waite, one of your patients. I would like to come and see you if that's possible.'

'I don't think there is much I can tell you.'

'Could you tell me what he is suffering from, and what the prognosis is?'

'He has a severe pulmonary condition. The prognosis is not good.'

'Is it cancer?'

'Yes.'

'Have you told my father?'

'No.'

'Do you intend to?'

'No. It would upset him too much.'

'I think I must tell him.'

'You know best, Mr Waite. It might come easier from you.'

'How long has he to live?'

'It's impossible to say. Six months, perhaps a year.'

I replaced the phone and left the phone box. I was afraid and deeply upset, but I knew that my father had to be told the truth. When I reached the house, he was sitting by the fire, coughing over a Woodbine.

'Did you get through?'

I nodded.

'Well?'

'It's not good news, Dad.'

He looked at me, waiting for confirmation of what he surely knew. 'Go on.'

'He says you have cancer of the lung.'

'And?'

'It's very serious. You may have only a year to live, but he can't be sure about that – nobody can.'

He remained silent for a moment. I wanted to cry but held back my tears.

'Well,' he said finally, 'that's that.'

I stretched out my hand and found his. He looked up.

'Thank you,' he murmured.

I remember a year of intense activity. Growing, demanding children; hectic visits to Sainsbury's supermarket; conferences throughout the diocese; hurried trips to Cheshire. I helped my father put his affairs in order, and as the months went by a totally new relationship developed between us. For the first time in my life I was able to relate to him as a friend and not as an authority figure. He wanted his body donated to medical research. I obtained the necessary papers, and he signed them. My mother nursed him at home as best she could, even when he was completely confined to bed. The local GP visited daily and administered heavy doses of morphine to ease his constant pain. I tried to get to see him every ten days or so, often travelling from Bristol to Cheshire and back in the same day. As the motorway was still unfinished, the journey was arduous.

One Friday evening I returned home exhausted after a training conference in Swindon and told Frances I would not go to Cheshire the following day as I had planned. Late the following night the phone rang. It was my parents' next-door neighbour. My father had died a few minutes earlier. Frances came downstairs, and we sat together in the sitting room. For a moment I couldn't speak, and then the emotions came rushing to the surface. When I was calmer,

I packed a small suitcase and made my way to the car. As I drove through the night, I castigated myself for choosing to stay at home on the very weekend he died.

The house was silent when I arrived. Upstairs, my father lay in bed covered by a sheet. I gently pulled it from over his head and looked at his tired, worn face. His life had been hard – very hard, and only in the past year had I been able to discover a real relationship with him. The truth both hurt and healed. I said a silent prayer and, in my new role as head of the family, went downstairs to comfort my mother and make the final arrangements for the funeral.

Writing a book without pencil and paper, without being able to make notes or consult records, is peculiar. I sit chained to an iron radiator with nothing but my thoughts. Some memories stream back like great pools of light. I see people I have known and feel the warmth of their company. Other days are lost to recall, waiting for the magic touch which will bring them to life again. I remember Proust saying that it's a vain labour to attempt to capture the past, that intellectual effort is futile; the past is hidden beyond the reach of intellect in the sensation obtained from some material object. Chance alone determines whether we come upon this object before we die.

This seems partly true for me. I allow myself to float across memory into that wonderland between the world of what we call conscious life and the world of dream. If I can't bear the construct I put on reality, I shall go mad, doomed to ramble for ever in a netherland filled with people and objects obeying laws that disturb and fascinate me. There are no material objects around me to bring back the soul of a past known to me. My clothes have disappeared, my wedding ring has been taken, also my watch. I remember telling myself before the last journey to Beirut: Take an automatic watch. If you are captured and have a battery watch, it could run out on you. Now they won't let me have my watch. Why? Why not let me have this simple, harmless toy?

Stop this endless protesting and questioning, I now tell myself. What does it matter? I am haunted by thoughts of death. My father is dead, gone after days spent in a semiconscious haze of half-existence. The University of Liverpool did not want his body. So Bill Burroughs, the local undertaker, took over. On the evening before the funeral, I went alone to the undertaker's chapel. Bill

ushered me in and left me alone. I wept in solitary silence. The
funeral service was at the local crematorium. I read the Lesson and
went home with my mother, sister and brother. Life went on.

'Would you like to see a video?'
   I would. I am bored beyond imagination. I have had quite enough
of remembering.
   'Yes, please. I would like that.'
   'OK, tonight we bring.'
   The anticipation I feel reminds me of Christmas as a child. My
mother was in her element at Christmastime. A box of decorations
was produced from the attic; we had had the same ornaments for
years. She festooned the living room with them until it resembled an
oriental grotto. The kitchen grew full of pungent smells: mincemeat,
Christmas pudding, sage and onion stuffing. She loved cooking, and
Christmas provided her with the one occasion on which she could
be justifiably extravagant. The Christmas cake was virtually solid
with fruit and covered with a good half-inch of marzipan. My father
always brought home a goose; a local farmer delivered a chicken,
which my mother plucked and cleaned expertly. I don't remember
the Christmas presents, but I do remember the excitement and the
wonderfully coloured wrapping paper. How could we possibly wait
until Christmas morning for permission to open these treasures?
   Would I like a video? I can't wait.
   At last, evening comes. A tap on the door. Blindfold on.
   'You have the video?' My excitement has reached fever-pitch.
   'Soon.'
   I am given food. Another tap on the door. Blindfold on.
   'You have the video?'
   'Yes.'
   A trolley is wheeled in, and I hear the connection being made. A
switch is turned on, and my captor leaves the room. The door is left
slightly ajar. I lift my blindfold. The video begins. A helicopter
sweeps across a desolate landscape, men in camouflaged uniforms
swear at each other in undertones as they lie concealed in a dugout.
Then the shooting starts. It's Vietnam. The violence is indescribable.
I can't bear it; it assaults my sensibilities. Finally it comes to a miser-
able, bloody end.
   The door opens. Blindfold on.
   'Good?'

'No, I don't like that video.'

'Why? Video very good.'

I don't want to argue. I simply ask him not to bring me any more. He wheels the trolley away and locks my door. I am left alone again with my memories.

The mentality which makes sex a forbidden subject and yet tolerates graphic expressions of violence is hard for me to understand. Yet these cheaply made films are churned out in America and distributed along with the other accoutrements of Western life. I find them obscene. It is the glorification of violence which disturbs me so much. Violence, death, mutilation produced and marketed for entertainment sickens me.

At least I now have a Bible to read, but it brings me little or no comfort. I am so desperate for signs of hope that I play the silly game of opening it at random and with my eyes closed letting my finger come to rest on a text. I have vague memories that this form of divination was practised by one of the English monarchs before he engaged in battle. Charles I at Edgehill? Perhaps. I don't remember. My intellect tells me that this way of treating the Bible is ridiculous, but deep within there is a desperate need for something to pin my hopes on.

My first attempt lands me in the middle of a genealogy, my second in the midst of Solomon's building exploits. Enough. I am always looking for signs of hope. I listen to every inflection of the guard's voice. I ask questions. I heed every sound. I strain my ears to listen to the radio and TV which occasionally play outside my room. Sometimes I still hear my own name mentioned, but the context always eludes me.

The Bible not only does not give me a sign, it makes me angry. I start by reading the Old Testament; in many respects it's as bloody and violent as the video. Not only that, outside the room in which I sit, people are being slaughtered daily. I read of the same happenings in the very same location three or four thousand years ago. I know that the Bible is an accurate portrayal of human nature, but at present I can't bear too much reality. I am battling with my own anger, a deep primitive fury which I must have carried for years. I am angry, childishly angry. Angry for a multitude of rational and irrational reasons.

There is a tap on the door. Blindfold on. The guard comes in and begins to gather up my few belongings.

'What are you doing?'

He doesn't reply.

'Am I going?'

'I don't know.'

'Are you going to let me go?'

'You must ask Chef.'

He shuffles around and leaves the room. I remove my blindfold. My Bible has gone along with my soap and toothbrush. My heart begins to beat faster. I am going. Perhaps I shall be freed at last. It must be December by now – home for Christmas, thank God.

Tap on the door, blindfold on.

'Hello, Mr Waite.'

I recognise the voice of the householder. Other people are with him.

'Now you go. Be very quiet.'

My body is shaking as my chain is unlocked.

'Stand up.'

With difficulty I get to my feet.

'Put this on.'

From beneath my blindfold I can see a tracksuit which I struggle into. I hear the removal gang whispering together.

'Be very quiet, please, very quiet. Goodbye, Mr Waite.' The house-holder shakes my hand.

'Goodbye. Thank you for your kindness.'

'It is my duty.'

My arms are grasped. We move down the hallway and into the small elevator. We descend. I can hear the heavy breathing of my escorts. Out of the lift. Turn right. Down some steps. Stop. A door opens. Move forward. I feel the night air. I am shoved quickly into the back of a car. Someone on my left and on my right. Doors slam. We move off rapidly.

'Put head down.'

I lower my head. The car stops. The driver changes. We move off again into the night, into the unknown future.

« II »

AFTER THE LONG STRAIN of caring for my father, my mother adjusted to life without him surprisingly quickly. I made sure that she was properly settled, then resumed my work in Bristol and with the Board of Education. One day in the late sixties I received an exciting invitation. Would I like to go to Uganda for two or three weeks as the British member of an international team which was to conduct a series of training conferences for the bishops, clergy and senior laity of the Church of Uganda? The team was to be made up of staff members from the Episcopal Church in America, the Church of southern Africa and the United Kingdom. I accepted eagerly.

Canon Eric Hutchison, a Canadian national who was working in the Department of Philosophy and Religious Studies at Makerere University and also acted as an adviser to the Archbishop of Uganda, had a key part in organising the conference. He had realised that Uganda was facing major changes in virtually every area of life — social, economic, political, and religious. The first task, as he saw it, was to develop the indigenous leadership of the Church so that it could move from overdependence on external aid towards self-reliance and a position of interdependence within the worldwide Anglican Communion. The Church of Uganda was a lively body. In the early days, when the first missionaries visited East Africa, Ugandan Christians had suffered death and mutilation for their new-found faith, and their blood had indeed proved to be the seed of the contemporary Church.

The BOAC jet swept low over Lake Victoria. From the cabin window I could see the last vestiges of night disappear as the sun gently stretched across Africa. I followed instructions and fastened my seat belt. Five-thirty a.m. I had slept fitfully, but now I was wide awake. The plane bumped along the tarmac and came to a halt opposite a ramshackle collection of airport buildings. Our location, ENTEBBE, was painted in large letters across the top of one of them. The pilot switched off the engines, and we waited. In the distance two or three Africans listlessly manoeuvred a flight of steps in our direction. Another party seemed to be considering whether or not they ought to apply themselves to hauling a luggage cart. The cabin door was opened. No one seemed in a great hurry to leave.

I descended and stood for a moment on the tarmac. The early-morning air was cool and fresh, and everything was wonderfully quiet. The vast dome of the heavens was breaking into a multitude of colours: orange, red, yellow and green. I could feel the temperature rising as the sun ascended higher over the horizon. The luggage party passed me with their trolley. One of them clambered into the hold and began to throw suitcases towards his companions. I strolled towards the terminal building while two soldiers wearing thick army greatcoats and carrying ancient 303 rifles gazed vacantly at me.

The handful of passengers who had disembarked were met by relatives and friends and quickly disappeared. I looked around for a sign that someone might be meeting me. There was no one in sight. I inquired of an official how far it was to Makerere University.

'About twenty miles,' he replied. 'You can take a taxi.'

A battered Peugeot 404 stood outside.

'I'm looking for Canon Eric Hutchison,' I said hopefully. 'He works at Makerere, but I'm not sure where he lives.'

All I had was a post-office box number.

'Probably at Katalemwa. We shall find him.'

As we left the airport, Uganda captivated me. A light mist covered the lush green landscape. Spirals of woodsmoke curled upwards as villagers prepared an early-morning meal. Bougainvillaea made a riot of colour against the brown mud of small thatched huts. Sights, sounds, smells filled me with a multitude of new sensations. Eventually, we came to Katalemwa.

'He will be here,' said the driver confidently.

He stopped and pointed to a small white board planted near a hedgerow. The name HUTCHISON was painted on it in bold black letters. The driver beamed, and I congratulated him. A sturdy Ugandan wearing khaki shorts and a brightly coloured shirt appeared at the door and confirmed that this was indeed the residence of Canon Eric Hutchison. I said goodbye to my guide and went through to the dining room. Eric, his wife Elspeth and their young children were sitting at the breakfast table. As I entered, the Canon leapt to his feet.

'Good heavens,' he exclaimed. 'I didn't realise you were coming today. How did you find us?'

As I sat down to breakfast, he put brown bread into the toaster;

his wife poured coffee; and the children tucked into fresh pawpaws.

After breakfast Eric suggested that I go with him into Kampala, first to take the children to school, then to the university where we could have a brief discussion. We got into an ancient Volkswagen Beetle and bumped our way into town.

We dropped the children and drove on to the university campus. I continued to find Uganda an amazingly beautiful country. While there was evidence of considerable poverty and underdevelopment, one immediately sensed the friendliness of the people. We drove through the main gate of the university to Eric's office where we discussed the outline details of the forthcoming conferences. One week would be spent in Kampala, the capital; another in Mbale in the east of the country, some two hundred miles away.

'You must meet Philip Turner,' Eric said, when he had gone over the itinerary. He bounded to his feet with, I was soon to learn, his customary amazing energy.

We found Philip at the main hospital in Kampala where he had been visiting patients. A clergyman of the American Episcopal Church, Philip was also on the staff of the university. As we stood on a balcony overlooking the city, he told me he was married with a young family and had recently returned to Uganda after spending a sabbatical year studying social anthropology at Oxford University. Within a few moments he was briefing me on the complexities of Ugandan life: the tribal tensions, the ongoing feud between the Kabaka, the tribal ruler of the Muganda, and the President, Milton Obote; the differences between the northern tribes and their southern compatriots.

It was all fascinating, but much of it went unregistered. The heat of the day and the night journey were catching up with me. We said good-bye, and I went to rest. Within a few hours of landing, I had met two men who were to become both close colleagues and lifelong friends.

Uganda surprised me. I had never expected to be so enthralled and fascinated by Africa. Later I was to learn many hard lessons in that beautiful and tragic country.

I can hardly think at the moment; words fail to capture the depth of my despair. I have been moved to another building somewhere in Beirut. I am in a room which has been used to accommodate prisoners before, I know, because metal staples have been driven into the wall; three sets in all. It's possible that previously people were kept together here. The usual large metal sheet covers what were once French windows, leading, I assume, to a small balcony. I was pushed into this room a short while ago and chained by the foot to one of the staples. A bulb hangs from the ceiling casting a dim light across the room, but it does not cheer me. I am next door to the bathroom, which I asked to use when I arrived. The bathroom has a small window about one foot square. This too has been covered by a metal plate, which is locked in position.

I doubt that they are going to release me now. My hopes were high when I was with the householder, but now I am back in an apartment which I assume is used exclusively by the kidnappers. There may be other hostages here. I have heard nothing yet but will, no doubt, tomorrow if they take people to the bathroom.

Outside it is quiet. Tomorrow I should be able to get some sense of where I am from the street noises. I am not too far from my previous location, but just how far is hard to tell, as the car stopped and started several times during the journey.

A tap on the door, a key turns. My bedding has arrived.

'You have my Bible?'

'Later.'

'My toothbrush?'

'Later.'

'How long will I stay here?'

'I don't know.'

The door closes and is locked again. I listen carefully and hear another door being unlocked down the corridor. I strain my ears but can make out no conversation. The door is locked. Silence again. I make my bed, which involves nothing more than spreading out the foam rubber and covering it with a blanket. I wish I had a pillow – just a small pillow. It's quite cold. I wrap myself in the blanket and close my eyes. Tonight my soul is heavy, very heavy.

'It's difficult to get a Ugandan to admit that there are tribal problems in the country – tribalism is a taboo word – but there are, believe you me.'

We were sitting in the Speke Hotel in Kampala. My companions had arrived from overseas, and we had gone out for a meal together to discuss the work we were to do. Our informant was a longtime resident of Uganda who had lived in most of the principal towns.

'The Muganda hate Obote – hate him. You know that, don't you?'

We listened.

'First, you must get the language straight. You are in Uganda. This part is called Buganda. It's peopled by Muganda. They speak Luganda. That's easy enough. It gets more complicated later!'

We listened with growing fascination as he recited his party piece.

'When the British came, they formed an immediate alliance with the Muganda. Why? Simple. There was a traditional monarchy; the British know all about that. The Muganda could be very diplomatic and charming; that appealed also. An alliance was quickly formed, and the British used the Muganda to control the whole of the country. The northerners, with a totally different language and tribal structure, suffered not a few humiliations. Can you imagine the rumpus when Obote usurped the Kabaka, the King of Buganda?'

We could. That morning both Eric and Philip had given us a detailed briefing on some of the issues facing the Church of Uganda. When the ecclesiastical province of Uganda, Rwanda and Burundi was created, the Church was able to elect its own African archbishop. A house was built on Namirembe Hill to accommodate the new incumbent. Offices were opened, staffed by officials who were to serve the whole province. Namirembe was in the very heart of Buganda. The newly elected Archbishop, Erica Sabiti, came from Toro and from a totally different tribe. Since the house at the top of the hill was occupied by the Muganda Bishop, the Archbishop had to take a lower position further down the slope. The tensions were palpable. It would be a long time before the Church could begin to work effectively as a national body rather than a collection of independent diocesan tribal units. And the Church's problems were merely a shadow of those that dominated national and political life. Our job was to take one small step towards helping the Church leadership to understand some of the dynamics of conflict and intergroup relationships. If the conferences were successful, it was hoped that a long-term educational programme could be developed.

Beforehand, I wanted to understand how the Africans felt about the situation. This was a difficult task, as they were understandably cautious about expressing their views to strangers. To a large extent I had to depend on intuition. It seemed to me that many African leaders had an ambivalent relationship with the European missionaries. On the one hand, they valued their expertise and ability to attract funds and resources from overseas. On the other, there was a certain resentment. Europeans were better paid and enjoyed better conditions. The tensions were not expressed overtly, but they were certainly close to the surface.

Missionaries, especially those who had lived in Uganda for some time, faced unique difficulties. Some had attained a job level in Africa that they would never have achieved at home. Over the years, their contacts in, and knowledge of, the UK dwindled. In their hearts they knew they ought to be 'working themselves out of a job' to enable local men and women to take over, but if they did, what about their own futures? Where would they go? Even though they might have a better salary than many Ugandans, they were far from being affluent. The anxiety-level was very high indeed for those who had given their most creative years to Africa. As we planned the conferences, we decided that we should try to provide a 'safe' environment in which these and other potentially explosive subjects could be discussed and analysed.

We were driven out to the site of the theological college at Mukono, several miles from Kampala. It was a beautiful setting. The American Church had invested heavily in making sure that the Ugandans had good facilities. The whole site, several acres in all, was well equipped and maintained. The staff, housed in pleasant bungalows dotted across the campus, was mostly drawn from Europe and North America. It was easy to understand why some expatriates were reluctant to transfer their responsibilities to the locals. But the clock could not be turned back. Several Ugandans were studying abroad, preparing to return and take senior positions in the college. Questions were now being asked about the wisdom of sending men and women overseas for training. Why could they not do their training in Africa? In essence the answer boiled down to money and facilities, but there was a strong desire among the clergy for a genuine African Church to emerge, not a European one.

The conferences conducted by the international staff were considered successful. Although we had not previously worked together, we all had had sufficient experience to enable us to adapt our ways of working and co-operate as a team. The participants, drawn from all parts of the country and representing every aspect of Church life, entered into the experience with enthusiasm. As I think back now, several people stand out in my memory: Janani Luwum, the young Provincial Secretary who was later to become Bishop of Gulu, then Archbishop of Uganda, and is today remembered throughout the world as a great African martyr; John Wasikye, a clergyman from

Mbale, who was murdered during the final days of the Amin regime; George Lubega, a Muganda, who was to become my close working colleague, and who suffered terribly during the dark days of persecution and warfare against the Church . . . the list goes on. As we worked with these men, we had, of course, no idea of the terrible price they were going to pay in the future. For my part, I gained more than I contributed. The brief visit to Uganda gave me only a glimpse of the immense problems facing the Church and the country, but these were the sort of issues I wanted to know more about and help resolve. My chance to do that came sooner than I expected.

There is another prisoner in the apartment with me. This morning I heard a door being unlocked and then footsteps passing my room. The bathroom door was opened, locked, and I heard the sound of running water. After five minutes or so, someone tapped on the bathroom door, a sign that the guard considered enough time had been spent washing. Once more footsteps passed my door, again I heard a key being turned. Someone else is also being kept in solitary confinement.

I have a new guard. I think I have met him on a previous occasion, but I can't be certain. He speaks quite good English, and from the sound of his voice he is in his early twenties. As he crouches down to unlock the padlock securing the chain around my foot, I can see that he has powerful arms. He escorts me to the bathroom. His companion stands guard at a distance. He carries a pistol in case I try to make a break for freedom. The bathroom is a grade down from the one in the private apartment, but it's adequate. As usual, the mirror has been removed so I have no idea how my appearance has changed over the months. I have lost weight, but I am not in bad condition. My teeth have given me problems ever since I cracked that one on an olive stone. When I was captured, I was halfway through a course of dental treatment and had a temporary filling. It is still in place, but as I brush my teeth I wonder how long it will stay there.

Who can the other prisoner be? Is there any hope of communicating with him? I can't think of any way I could leave a message in the bathroom, but perhaps an opportunity will occur later. A tap on the door. I adjust my blindfold and am guided round the corner and into my room.

'Can I have some exercise, please?'

'Later.'

'Can you please bring me some books?'

'I ask Chef.'

'Can you bring me my Bible?'

'Later.'

He fastens the chain around my ankle.

'That is too tight.'

'Good.'

'No, it's not good. Not good at all. Look.'

It is far too tight. The metal links bite into my skin. He unlocks the padlock and fastens it again, this time giving me a little more space.

'It's not good to be chained. Why do you do it? The door is locked, the room is guarded.'

'Chef say you must have chain. I am sorry. You want anything?'

'Yes, please, I want books. Plenty of books. Please, I need to read. I sit all day – nothing to read. Please, I need books.'

'I ask Chef for you.'

'Thank you.'

He leaves the room and locks the door. I remove my blindfold and am grateful for the ray of sunlight that comes through where the metal shutter does not fit exactly. When I am off the chain, perhaps I will be able to see through the crack. I can hear traffic noises and people in the street below. This seems to be a busy area and very near to a mosque. I was awakened at daybreak by prayers. The voice over the loudspeaker was exactly like the voice of the young man who guarded me and prayed with such fervour in my previous location. Could it be one and the same person?

If they are going to keep me on the chain for twenty-four hours a day, I must continue to follow a regular programme of exercise. To introduce variety, I try to remember some exercises which I read in a Canadian Air Force manual years ago. First, I lie flat on my back and raise both legs in the air. I do this several times. A key turns in the lock. Blindfold on.

'What you do? Sit.'

I get into a sitting position. Someone is standing behind me while someone else is inspecting the chain.

'What you do?'

'I am doing some exercises. I must stay healthy.'

He continues to check the chain.

'Not make noise, understand?'

'I didn't make a noise.'

'We hear noise. Not make noise. Understand?'

'Yes.'

The guards leave the room. I suppose the chain did clank as I lifted my feet, but who is going to hear that up here? I stand and try other exercises that do not involve moving my feet. I am determined to keep fit, no matter what. After about an hour, I stop and sit down. What to do now? I have said my prayers. They were simple. I remembered my family, my friends, my fellow hostages, my captors. I wish I could be more profound in my spiritual life. I am still very much a child in my understanding of my faith. I have no deep thoughts, no great insights, no outstanding qualities. I am a very ordinary man chained to a wall and attempting to struggle through another day of boredom and uncertainty.

'Among the stones I stood a stone,' Byron wrote. I understand that.

> ... *All was blank, and bleak, and grey;*
> *It was not night, it was not day* ...
> *A sea of stagnant idleness* ...

God, give me a break, please.

ON MY RETURN from Africa I found it difficult to settle back into my work in Bristol, so strongly had Uganda caught my imagination. Its problems offered a challenge that appealed to me. Our conferences had been well received, and the majority of participants had indicated that they wanted more along these lines. Archbishop Sabiti and his advisers had since decided that they would like to organise an ongoing programme to further Church leadership and development in the province. They hoped to find a director who would start the programme, train his successor, and then leave. As the Episcopal Church in America had agreed to fund the programme for a period of time, it was to America that they looked for such a person. Philip Turner, however, opposed the idea. Given the historical relationship between Uganda and the United Kingdom, he felt that a British director would be preferable. Unknown to me, he submitted my name and pressed my case. Initially, the Americans were understandably cautious. As they were paying for the programme, they not unreasonably felt that they would like their own man to head it. Philip continued to press, and eventually I received an invitation to apply for the new post of Provincial Training Officer in Uganda.

Looking back on those days, I am surprised that Frances and I agreed so quickly that we ought to go. We reasoned that if we were to go overseas temporarily, it should be while the children were still young. We had been in Bristol almost five years and had settled down. But I was no longer in a mood to settle. I discussed the offer with my bishop, Oliver Tomkins. He said he would be sorry if I left the diocese, but he thought it would be valuable for me to get overseas experience. He himself had been born in China of missionary parents and had travelled extensively as a young man. The work I had been asked to do in Bristol was now well established. A small Advisory Committee under the chairmanship of Elizabeth Ralph, the City Archivist, had been functioning for some years. New forms of lay and clerical education were flourishing. I could either leave now and allow my successor to develop the next stage of the programme, or I could stay for another three years or so. The decision

was easy. We packed up most of our furniture and stored it in a
Bristol vicarage, said goodbye to our families and friends and together with our three small daughters made our way to Heathrow
to catch the BOAC night flight to Entebbe.

Later, all I remembered was a packed aircraft. Frances remembered being served kidneys in Madeira sauce in the early hours
of the morning. The children, always good travellers, excelled themselves on this occasion. We arrived at Entebbe as dawn was breaking.
This time Eric was waiting to meet us. We climbed into his Peugeot
404 and set off along the dusty road towards Kampala.

'Why have you brought me here?'
'I don't know.'
The guard has come with my breakfast: a piece of unleavened
bread, some cubes of cheese, a few olives. He pours tea into a
coloured plastic picnic cup.
'How long will I stay here?'
'You must ask Chef.'
'I never see Chef.'
'He will come and see you soon.'
'Will you please bring me some books? It's over a year now, and
I have had so little to read.'
'I will try to get you book.'
'Please try. I need books very much.'
He leaves the room. The bread is fresh, and the cheese is good.
I have to eat very carefully because my teeth hurt. I think an abscess
is developing under the tooth that was cracked by the olive stone. I
eat slowly and drink the tea. The food is adequate but monotonous.
I miss not being able to choose my own food; I miss fresh fruit and
vegetables. I never used to eat much fruit, now I long for it. Fruit
is indeed the only food I crave. I would so enjoy an apple, an orange
or a banana – an orange best of all.

I try to restrict my requests to the guard to books, so that if he
thinks of me after he has left my room, he will think of books. I
need books more than I need food. If I were given a choice between
more food or a plentiful supply of books, my decision would be
immediate. My mind wanders to the Uganda Bookshop in Kampala.
It was owned by the Church of Uganda and was surprisingly well
stocked with a great variety of volumes. Upstairs was a small coffee
shop where one could sit on the verandah and watch the world go

by. Most mornings Denis Hills would spend half an hour or so there with his newspaper and a cup of coffee. Hills, a British author and lecturer, was later sentenced to death for criticising Idi Amin and eventually liberated by the Foreign Secretary, James Callaghan, who paid a flying visit to Kampala for that precise purpose.

I have not had coffee since my capture; plain tea and water only. Water is kept in a red plastic jug by my bed. I have a bottle in which to pee, a plastic brush for my hair, a toothbrush, soap and a towel. That, my restored Bible and my bedding complete my kit. I have developed a daily routine. When I wake, I can get some idea of the time from two sources: the mosque and the sun. The mosque tells me when it's daybreak; the small beam of light gives me a further guide, should I sleep through the morning prayers. I usually start the day with a short prayer, after which I pack up my bedding. As the room is damp, I lean the mattress against the wall and fold my blanket as precisely as I did years ago in the Army. I consider it vital to maintain as high a standard of personal cleanliness and order as possible. Then I begin my exercises. Each day I increase them slightly, ten, fifteen, twenty press-ups, touch toes one hundred times, swing arms. I have worked out a programme which makes me sweat and sometimes takes more than an hour to get through. I like to complete it before breakfast if I can, so that I can wash properly on my daily visit to the bathroom.

I have one tracksuit, which I wear day and night, and two sets of underclothes. These I wash in the handbasin, but as the guards are always impatient, there is never time to get them properly clean. It takes days for anything to dry in my room, and the guards won't dry anything outside for me. When I return from the bathroom, I sit cross-legged on the floor and say the service of Holy Communion. At first my limbs were stiff, but now I can sit quite comfortably in the lotus position. I continue to follow the practice I started right at the beginning, of locating myself in my imagination in a church or some special place I have known in the past. It's a great comfort to follow a regular pattern of words in my prayers; it saves me from falling into a state of self-pity.

After the service, the day is before me. Usually no one comes into the room until lunchtime, which is about two or three in the afternoon. I fill the time by writing my book in my head, but I can't do that all day. At times I take flights of fancy. I travel by train to Hong Kong, by boat around the world. I make a list of all the supplies I will need for these journeys and carefully pack them. I design a house; I play *Desert Island Discs*, and select my favourite recordings for an enforced sojourn on a tropical island. I attempt to compose music. I discovered early on that mental arithmetic was a way of keeping myself totally absorbed, and by now I am doing calculations which sometimes continue for three or four hours. When I arrive at an answer I attempt to prove it via another route. My memory must have been improved by this exercise because, to my surprise, I find I can remember a long string of numbers without too much difficulty.

Lunch arrives. Today, it is a plate of rice, canned mixed vegetables and one or two pieces of fatty meat. A hot drink is never served at midday. After eating, I lay out my mattress and lie down for a while. I was correct in assuming there is a balcony outside my room. Earlier, two or three guards were sitting in the morning sun talking together. I could hear them dragging chairs across the balcony. Now they sit in the hallway, chatting and laughing. I drift into a light sleep. I don't want to sleep too much, otherwise I will be awake all night. After half an hour or so I sit up. The electricity has failed, so I sit in semi-darkness. Supper is still several hours away and will probably be another cheese sandwich, after which I will do my evening exercises. The day drags on. My life goes by, and all I seem to do is relive the past in my memory.

It was late in the afternoon when I climbed into my car to leave Gulu for Kampala. The journey of some two hundred miles was largely on unmade roads, murram roads, as they were known locally. From time to time a grader smoothed over the surface, but when the rains came, deep ruts developed, which could make driving hazardous. The sun was already low in the sky as I left the outskirts of the town and headed for the open countryside. The first few miles would be lonely, and I didn't expect to see any other traffic until I came to Soroti, seventy miles away. The previous day I had left Kampala to attend the consecration of Janani Luwum as Bishop of Gulu. Frances stayed behind with the children, and as we had been in the country such a short time, I wanted to get home as soon as possible so as not to be away from my family any longer than was necessary.

The consecration took place in the Gulu football stadium, which was packed to bursting point. The whole scene was a riot of colour.

Tribal costumes, Ugandan flags, political party colours merged together in a kaleidoscopic pattern of celebration. Milton Obote, the President, was in attendance. He had been brought up in the same district as Janani, and for a time they had been at school together. Both had been taught by Phoebe Cave-Browne-Cave, a missionary who had spent most of her life in Uganda and was a living legend throughout the country.

The creation of the new diocese of Gulu and the election of Janani Luwum as the first bishop was of great significance for the people of the north. It represented their coming of age. I left immediately after the service, but the celebrations would continue until well into the night. The vast majority of the crowd lived in considerable poverty, but they knew how to celebrate and unconsciously recognised the importance of doing so. I could not help but be caught up in the atmosphere of jubilant pleasure. My visit gave me further insight into some of the complexities of Uganda. In colonial days, the national boundaries were drawn with little or no respect for tribal territory. I heard of a tribe in the north which was split up into three: one-third in Uganda, another in Zaïre, and the remainder in the Sudan. Each group was expected to have different national loyalties, while their primary loyalty lay with the tribal unit. This single piece of information threw a great deal of light on the difficulties the country was experiencing in creating a national identity.

I drove along the flat dusty road to Soroti with my mind full of the sights and sounds of celebration. Before leaving Kampala, I had been given some elementary instructions about driving at night. Car theft was a continuing problem, and thieves used ingenious methods. A highly dangerous but apparently successful one was for a man to lie across a narrow roadway. When the car stopped, thieves would emerge from the bush, attack the driver and make off with the vehicle. Some taxi-drivers adopted the simple expedient of driving over the body. Other, less daring bandits placed rocks in the road or fastened a rope between two trees, but these methods were not so popular because they could damage the car.

I had been warned to keep a sharp lookout and not stop. Twenty miles or so from Gulu, on a narrow stretch of road, the Peugeot's headlights picked out something in front of me. I slowed the car. To my horror, it was a body stretched full-length across the narrow track. It was impossible to drive around it. I stopped the car some distance away and opened the window to listen for any noise. Total silence. What should I do? I could not follow the taxi-driver's example, but I had to get through: this was the only road home. Gradually I edged the car forward until I was within a few feet of the body. An African wearing khaki shorts and a torn shirt lay quite still, his head facing away from me. Leaving the car engine running I gingerly opened the door and stepped out. Not a sound. Cautiously I moved towards him, hardly daring to look into the bush. I touched him with my foot. He didn't move. I bent down. He stirred and mumbled something. The stench of stale alcohol hit me immediately. Never was I more delighted to meet a drunk. Carefully I dragged him to the side of the road where his ancient bicycle lay in the ditch. I made him as comfortable as possible and continued my journey.

Our house in Kampala was on Namirembe Hill, adjacent to the Provincial Office. When we first arrived, we stayed with Eric and Elspeth Hutchison for a few days before moving into a house on the university campus whose occupants were on home leave. When they returned, we went out to the theological college at Mukono and finally moved to Namirembe when a house there became vacant. It was a simple and unpretentious single-storey building with a lovely garden and magnificent views over Buganda. Although Frances preferred not to have help in the house, we soon learnt that we ought to employ someone in order to provide them with a living. We took on Wilson, a young man from western Uganda who helped in the kitchen, and Dick, a local schoolboy, who tended the garden in return for money to pay his school fees. We also inherited Peter, a large black Labrador, as some protection against burglary which was rife in the capital.

One of my first tasks was to try to find my successor. I wanted someone who would work with me from the start, and if at all possible I wanted the programme to be under local leadership and self-supporting within three years. The Rev. George Lubega was suggested. He was a Muganda, brought up in a village several miles from Kampala, the son of an impoverished coffee farmer. As a boy he had suffered major hardships and was the only survivor in a family of twelve children. The other eleven had died in youth from various diseases. George had had no opportunity to go to school until he was fifteen, but he proved to be an exceptional student and qualified to enter the theological college. He was ordained and, among other appointments, worked as a hospital chaplain in Kampala. I liked him as soon as we met and was struck by his critical and probing mind. He said he was definitely interested in working with me, but there were difficulties. His bishop was reluctant to let him do work for the province. Also, given the history of domination by the Muganda, some people were unhappy about a Muganda occupying a senior national position. These obstacles were overcome largely by George's personality, and within a short time he joined me on a full-time basis.

To celebrate his appointment, George invited my whole family to visit his home in Luwero. We drove out one Saturday morning. After a mile or so, the tarmac ran out, and we bumped along on a murram highway. In Luwero, we turned off the main road and drove down a narrow track to his father's house. George's wife and children greeted us. She had prepared a chicken steamed in banana leaves, which she served with *mutoke*, boiled mashed green plantain, a staple food of the Muganda. The meal was delicious; the hospitality and friendship overwhelming. I was, however, appalled at the conditions in which George's family had to live. The mud house, although clean, was in a most fragile condition. Most clergy of the Church of Uganda were paid pitiable salaries, and many had to depend on farming to feed their families and pay their way. When I compared the difference between the house we were occupying in Kampala and this small shack in the bush, it was hard to accept such discrepancies. I was determined that I would somehow find the resources to enable George to accommodate his wife and children properly while he was working with me throughout the country.

Memories of Uganda have taken me completely away from my chains. For the past hour I have been a young man again, standing on the grass in front of our house in Kampala, watching my daughters laugh and play; such happy children. Now they run indoors squealing as the rain begins to fall. Heavy rain. It beats on the iron roof of the house, drowning our conversation and filling the air with a musty smell of damp earth. In Africa one lives close to the earth.

'Why?' someone once said to me. 'Why do you think Europeans are so distant from Africans?'

'Fear. They are afraid of Africa, afraid it will swallow them. It's too vast, too mysterious, too earthy. Many Africans prefer to walk barefooted – to be in direct touch with the earth. Europeans wear shoes and cover the ground with concrete. One day Africa will be covered with concrete, and the spirits which fail to escape will be entombed for ever.'

I remember standing on the bank of a lake in Buganda feeling vulnerable, frightened, alone. There is a great silence – a huge silence. The lake stretches out as far as my eyes can see. Why do I feel so vulnerable, so threatened by the magnificence of my surroundings? I sense the spirit of this place, a restless consuming spirit seeking to draw the unwary back to the earth from which they came. A small breath of wind stirs the gnarled branches of a dying tree. A wisp of woodsmoke spirals high into the sky. I smell the damp dark atmosphere of this place, and it disturbs me.

Today I was allowed to take a shower. The water was warm and relaxing. Standing in the bath, it was just possible to see through a small gap in the shuttered window. The flat I'm in is probably on the sixth or seventh floor. I assume this because I can see another block opposite mine, and I simply count the floors until they reach this level. Down below is a busy road severed by a roadblock manned by bearded young men carrying machine guns. It's a bright sunny morning, and there are people walking in the street. I yearn for the freedom to walk, to see the sun and the sky, to feel the wind and the rain. I am certain that I am in the southern suburbs of Beirut.

Back in my room, the lights have failed yet again. The guard has brought me a candle, but as I have nothing to read, it remains unlit. Someone is tapping on my door. Blindfold on.

'Hello, Mr Terry.'

'Hello, who is that?'

I hold out my hand and someone takes it.

'How are you, Mr Terry?'

'OK.'

'You want anything?'

'I want books, please. Also I need exercise.'

'OK, soon we bring you books. Plenty books. Tomorrow you have exercise. One hour. Good?'

'Yes, thank you.'

'You good, Mr Terry?'

'OK.'

'We want you to be good, Mr Terry. We not treat you like others. You good man. We know.'

'Please, can I have my watch?'

'OK, no problem. Today you get watch.'

'I would like some fruit, please.'

'No problem. We give you fruit. You want anything else?'

I decide I have asked for enough, but I try one final question.

'When will you let me go home?'

'I don't know. We hope soon you go.'

'Who does know?'

'I don't know.'

'OK, thank you.'

The door is locked, and I remove my blindfold. My visitor must have been a 'Chef' of sorts. I don't recognise his voice, but he is definitely Lebanese. So, I am to get my watch. That will be helpful; I will be able to keep track of the date. It is quite difficult to work out the exact date without a watch. I am told it by one of the guards, but as I have no way of recording it, I quickly get confused. If I make marks on the wall, the guard spots them and for some odd reason gets agitated. Another tap on the door. It's the regular guard. Blindfold back on.

'Take.'

I hold out my hand. It's my watch.

'Thank you.'

'No problem.'

'Who was the man who came to see me?'

'Little Chef.'

I smile. At last I have been visited by the popular restaurateur in person.

'Take.'

I hold out my hand again. It's a banana.

'Thank you very much.'

'No problem.'

The door is locked again. My watch lies in my hand. It's a heavy waterproof model I bought years ago to keep out the dust and humidity of Africa. I turn it over and see that there are scratches on the screwdown back cover. Someone has obviously been giving it a thorough inspection. Then I notice that the seconds hand has stopped. I manage to take off the back cover and find a small piece of wood, probably part of a matchstick, jammed in the works. Why on earth do that? I remove it and replace the cover. Let's hope it works. The seconds hand moves round the dial, and now at least I have some control over my solitary days.

*

George Lubega was a quick learner and a most congenial companion. We travelled all over Uganda together and gradually developed a training programme. The Rev. Peter Chapman, warden of a community centre in Mbale, joined us on many occasions, and we were able to conduct residential conferences at his base. I was pleased with developments.

At home, the girls started infant school in Kampala and quickly settled down. All was not well in the country, however. Kampala was suffering a crime wave of exceptional proportions. It was so severe that a number of my colleagues questioned whether there was a deliberate attempt to break the infrastructure of the country. One evening Frances and I had gone to bed when we heard the sound of an alarm. Some weeks earlier a group of us had bought a number of alarm canisters, the kind used to sound distress signals at sea. As thieves frequently came during a rainstorm, any alarm had to be exceptionally powerful to be heard above the sound of the deluge. Several of us had agreed that we would go out to investigate immediately if we heard an alarm sound. There was a door in our bedroom leading directly to the garage. Quickly I started the car and drove down the driveway in the direction of the noise. I arrived at the house of one of our African neighbours to discover an amazing scene. The householder was a widow who lived with two or three of her children. Thieves had broken into her home by placing a large stone in a sack and swinging it against the front door. The eldest son had waited for them behind the door with a long broad-bladed knife known as a *panga*. When the first man entered, the boy swung the *panga*, splitting the man's head open. Now he lay in a pool of blood on the floor, unconscious and on the point of death.

His companions must have fled when they heard my car approaching. The police were called. A uniformed officer arrived with a man in plain clothes who was clearly drunk. There was nothing we could do for the injured thief, and by the time the police had arrived he had died without regaining consciousness. The plainclothes man staggered around the room and kicked the body two or three times.

'Cover him over, madam,' he said to the widow. 'We'll take him away tomorrow.'

The widow was clearly not happy with this proposal.

'What about my door? Anyone will be able to enter.'

The constable volunteered to board up the door. A blanket was produced, the body covered, the door boarded, and we left.

Back at home it took me a while to get to sleep. Just as I was drifting off, an alarm sounded again. By now it was dawn. I leapt into the car and drove off. To my surprise, the alarm was again coming from the widow's house.

'What's happened now?' I asked the eldest son.

'The thieves came back to find their friend.'

Before he could say more, a small group of Africans appeared, surrounding a terrified-looking man who was secured by a piece of rope. They were shouting and every few moments struck the captive a smart blow on the head. I went to meet them.

'Who's this?' I asked.

A large man carrying an ancient blunderbuss answered me.

'It's one of them. We caught him in the road. He doesn't live here. None of us know him.'

'But you can't be sure he's a thief, can you?'

'We know. He is a bad man. We know.'

'Ask him, please, who he is.'

The suspect could not, or chose not to speak English. Someone put a question to him.

'He says he is a stranger here. He was going to look for work.'

The crowd roared their disbelief.

'He lies. Kill him.'

The large man punched his victim in the mouth. Blood began to trickle from his lips.

'Stop!' I shouted. I pushed my way through the group and stood between the roped man and his accusers. 'You can't be sure he is a thief. Call the police. That's the best thing to do.'

The large man raised his shotgun.

'Move or I will shoot him and you also. You are European. We know this man. We will kill him.'

I was thrust to one side. They took their victim and bound him to a tree. I heard his bones break as they hit him with heavy sticks. When I returned in the morning his broken, bruised body lay on the grass. The other body was still inside.

I stood silently, feelings of anger, sorrow and revulsion threatening to engulf me. I turned and walked quickly back to my car and drove home. The girls were playing happily in the early-morning sun. Frances was preparing breakfast. My feelings were so deep and powerful that I had to suppress them. If I didn't, I knew I would drown.

As Frances frequently had to stay alone in the house with the children while I was in different parts of the country, we decided to hire a nightwatchman. One evening, a thin, elderly man reported for duty. He wore an ex-army khaki greatcoat, a knitted woollen cap and a pair of worn leather boots. In one hand he carried a *panga* and in the other a bow and arrow. He grinned cheerfully.

'*Jambo, Bwana.*'

We greeted him, and as our Swahili was limited, we asked our gardening boy, Dick, to translate. The man told us he was quite fearless and that we need never worry again about our security. He never slept at night. He was always awake, and no one would ever get past him. Although he spoke confidently, we had our reservations. However, we made him some tea, and he positioned himself by the side of the house. Anxious to impress us, every ten minutes or so he would march past the living-room window sporting his bow and arrow, looking determined and ferocious. As we were expecting friends for dinner, we asked Dick to warn the guard, which he duly did. At about eight o'clock we suddenly heard the sound of shouting. I ran out and found the man in a highly excited state, standing at the top of the hill lobbing stones into the darkness. Dick, hearing the commotion, also came out of his quarters.

'What on earth is he doing, Dick?'

'He says some people tried to come here, and he has chased them away.'

I asked Dick to try to calm the watchman and hurried down to the road below. Our guests, mercifully uninjured, were cowering in the shadows.

The nightwatchman didn't last long. His claim to be eternally vigilant proved empty. He left, and we never saw him again.

Violent robbery became so bad in Kampala that several of us who lived on Namirembe decided to take turns standing guard at night. A demoralised and inadequate police force provided no protection whatsoever. It was easy to see why so many people decided to take the law into their own hands, often with tragic consequences.

Michael Sams, a member of the Church Missionary Society, lived near by, and he and I often remained awake at night to patrol the houses on the hill. We became convinced that much of the trouble was being caused by soldiers from the barracks on the Entebbe road. It was common knowledge that machine guns could be obtained from the barracks for the payment of a small sum. Often thieves would travel together in a car to a district they had targeted. The driver would cruise around and drop off his party one by one, arranging to collect them later at a pick-up point. A VW Beetle had frequently been seen in our district on the nights when burglaries were committed.

One night, when I was at home talking to a Ugandan colleague, we heard the familiar sound of an alarm in the distance. We jumped into my Peugeot and almost immediately saw a Volkswagen speeding down the hill. Desperate to put an end to our misery, we gave chase. The VW left the paved road and slipped away down a rough murram track. I was soon able to draw alongside the smaller car and gradually edge it into the ditch. We jumped out and pulled open the door of the Beetle. The driver, who was alone, seemed half dazed. We assumed he had taken drugs of some sort. He made no attempt to resist us, and we drove him directly to the police station. The officer in charge checked our captive's identity documents and stared at us.

'This man is a soldier. We can't do anything.'

Although we had no proof to link the man with robbery, we did expect that he might at least be questioned.

'We can't do anything. Sorry.'

The frightened policeman turned away. I conferred with my colleague, and we decided to take the man to the barracks. After a good deal of delay we finally met the Commanding Officer. He was a huge northerner wearing a multicoloured shirt and an expensive wristwatch on each arm. He laughed and invited us to have a drink with him. We refused. He said there was nothing more to be done. We left and made our way home. At least we never saw the VW again, and for a week or so there was a respite from robbery on our hill.

George Lubega, Peter Chapman and I spent a lot of time visiting the rural areas of the country to assist in the setting up of local development programmes. From time to time I invited colleagues from Europe or America to assist us with major residential conferences, and later George travelled to England to work with the Board of Education for a while. The first such visitor to Uganda was an American from the Episcopal Church. On his first night in Kampala, Frances and I decided to take him out for a meal, together with George and another member of our team, Clement Janda, a refugee from southern Sudan. We all climbed into my car to drive into town. Opposite the restaurant was a car park. I pulled in, and Frances and the others got out. Just as I was about to open my door, I noticed an African jumping around and waving a machine gun. I lowered the window.

'Get out! Get out!' he shouted.

Stupidly I thought that I had parked in a prohibited area, and that the man was some sort of guard. I started the car.

'No, you fool,' someone shouted. 'He wants you to get out of the car!'

I got out. The man took my place and drove away. Shaken, we made our way to the restaurant where the proprietor, who had witnessed the whole scene, offered us drinks on the house.

The American, who had never been in Uganda before, was shocked. We explained to him that the country was on the verge of a major crisis and that we anticipated trouble for some time to come. The Peugeot was never recovered.

Sitting here in the half-light of my room, my mind remains in Uganda. The dramatic events of those years are still sharp in my memory. I can feel the tensions of the country as it stood on the brink of social revolution. Everyone who lived in the capital felt the strain of sleepless nights and stark, bitter brutality.

From time to time, we would escape for a day or so across the border into Kenya. We stayed at Kitale on the edge of the White Highlands or, when we had more time, in Mombasa on the coast. Once we were returning to Kampala after several days spent in Kenya. The children were asleep in the back of the car, and Frances and I were chatting quietly in the front. We approached the border checkpoint near Tororo. The Kenyan authorities waved us through, and we drove the several hundred yards across no-man's-land to the Ugandan post. To our surprise the barrier was open, and the office was completely unmanned. Not being an enthusiast for border posts, I drove straight through and made for home.

That night we were disturbed by the sound of shouting and what appeared to be distant artillery fire. No local alarms were sounded, so I turned over and went back to sleep. The next morning when we tuned in to the World Service of the BBC, we heard reports of a coup in Uganda. I dressed quickly and went to the Archbishop's house. Erica Sabiti had received only sketchy information via the radio. Yona Okoth, then Provincial Secretary of the Church of Uganda and a supporter of Milton Obote, had heard nothing of significance. The hill was unusually quiet, and the Archbishop sensibly suggested that everyone stay indoors until there was more information available. A couple of days earlier, Philip Turner had left Uganda to attend a conference in Nairobi, leaving his wife and children in their home at Makerere. I decided that I ought to go and check up on them (they had no phone), and then attempt to telephone Philip with first-hand news.

Kampala was like a ghost town. Travelling towards the city, I passed a body in a hedge and another by the side of the road. The Turner family was in good spirits. We chatted for a while and then I set out for home. As I drove down the road leading from the university to the city, a huge tank rumbled towards me. I slowed the car. The turret of the tank revolved slowly until the barrel of the gun was pointed directly at me. The heads of several soldiers appeared at different portholes. I lowered the window and did the first thing that came to mind: I smiled, waved and greeted them. Immediately they beamed and waved back. Later I heard a tank story with a very different ending: when the Army stormed the airport at Entebbe, a tank fired a shell at the portrait of Milton Obote which hung above the reception counter. The explosion killed several people in the room, including a friend of mine, a Roman Catholic priest, who was attempting to get a colleague away on the last plane.

We didn't have a phone at home either, so I went into the Provincial Office to try to get through to Philip in Nairobi. The building was deserted. I went to the switchboard and dialled his number. As I was dialling, shooting broke out around the building. I sat on the floor and after about two hours of repeated dialling, finally made contact with him. Philip told me that he had heard of the coup and was deeply concerned about his family. I assured him that all was well and suggested that he shouldn't try to return until things were calmer. Then I went back home, wondering just what trouble lay ahead.

« 13 »

I AM AGAIN ALLOWED one hour of freedom from the chain every day, when I return from the bathroom. For some reason I am still interested in how far I walk, so I count the number of paces. As I count, the familiar trance-like state comes over me. At the front of my mind I am counting, elsewhere I am dreaming of all manner of things. At times the dream takes over, and I lose track of the distance I have walked. Why do I have this desire to measure? Now that I have my watch, I also measure the passing of the days. Perhaps it gives me a little security, but it does not bring comfort, except the comfort that comes from having a familiar possession. The watch has been with me on my travels throughout the world, and it is the only personal item I have now. It helps me organise my day. It's become desperately important to arrange the day according to a pattern. If this is disturbed by the guards, it upsets me out of all proportion to the disturbance. I need a structure: wake, pray, eat, wash, exercise, pray, think, eat, and so the day passes. By creating a pattern in the vacuum in which I live, I exercise my choice, affirm my identity. Even when the guard tells me that I am to be chained again, I have a schedule for the remaining hours of the day.

Although books have been promised, I still have only my Bible. I am disappointed that it doesn't bring me greater comfort, but perhaps I am beginning to acquire a more profound insight. Comfort won't come from without. I must find my own inner harmony, my own internal balance. I long for a deeper peace and liberation. Perhaps the desire for tangible reality leads me to take the Bible too literally. I know it can be read on several levels, as history or literature, but now more than ever I need to be able to read it with the eyes of faith. My faith has been exposed for what it is – uncertain, questioning, vulnerable. It was a friend, Christine, who once intuitively told me on a country walk that in seeking the liberation of the hostages I was in reality seeking my own liberation. Frances also knew this, and realised that I had to work out my own salvation in my own way. What does inner liberation mean? Freedom from fear, darkness, anxiety? How remarkable that a casual comment can rest in the mind and be resurrected years later in this dark outpost.

During these last days while I have been reliving our years in Uganda, the strong emotions associated with that country have returned with the memories: the joy, the fear, the restless searching and striving for harmony. I saw the soul of Africa, the great mother soul, which nurtures and destroys with a dreadful consuming passion. In the emptiness of the desert I saw my own emptiness. In the darkness of the forest I recoiled from the dark recesses within me. I know now why we seal ourselves from our vast and mysterious unconscious. Deep within we are nurtured or consumed, enhanced or destroyed. My inner self knew the soul of Africa as though it understood it was returning home, back to an origin long lost to conscious recollection and recognised in a world known only by dream or intuition. Who or what had called me to a continent to meet the very same demons that haunt my subconscious? No magic will tame them, no pact pacify. I step across ancestral soil, through caverns of recollection, by shores of instinctive longing. My mind knows transformation through the power of symbol, but within I am too young even to have touched this reality. Journey on, sleep, eat, exercise, tell stories. One day perhaps I may understand. One day . . .

A pick-up truck moved slowly along the road by our house. Streamers flew from the windows, tin cans attached to the vehicle by lengths of string bounced along the tarmac. Ten or more Asians stood in the back shouting and laughing. Frances and I watched as they disappeared across the hill.

'Madness,' I said. 'Sheer madness.'

I walked up the hill to Archbishop Sabiti's house. He was sitting in his drawing room overlooking the garden, clearly worried.

'I hope all your family are well. We think everyone on the hill is accounted for, but are not quite certain. We should know very soon.'

I accepted his invitation to sit opposite him.

'I am not at all happy about the events of yesterday. We have known Amin for a long time. I doubt very much that he is the man for this country.'

I listened carefully. The Archbishop, an African chief, revealed only a fraction of what he knew.

'We must pray hard, these are dangerous times.'

I accepted a cup of coffee and continued to listen.

'You know the British High Commissioner, I think.'

I nodded.

'I would like you to go and see him for me. Simply tell him of my concern. I think he should be very cautious. Tell him that.'

I knew Erica Sabiti would not be more specific. I also knew that while he had his own tribal loyalties, his actions would not be governed by tribalism, nor by the fact that Idi Amin was not a Christian. I made an appointment and drove to the High Commission building in town. The High Commissioner met me and escorted me along a corridor to a meeting room. We entered, and he locked the door. I conveyed the Archbishop's message. He listened carefully, looking worried. He was clearly under strain. I explained that the Archbishop was expressing the views of many Ugandans and not only his own opinions. As our conversation drew to a close, the High Commissioner looked at me intently.

'Amin, as you know, is a former British soldier. We think he can be controlled.' He smiled wanly and shook my hand.

The government of the United Kingdom was the first to recognise the administration of the former army boxing champion, General Idi Amin.

Yona Okoth, the Provincial Secretary, was among those missing, and rumours were rife. Some said that because he was a prominent Obote supporter, he had gone into hiding; others, that he had been arrested by the Army. A few claimed that he had been shot. Yona's wife, a large, matronly woman, believed he had been taken by the Army for questioning. She was right. Yona was being held with several dozen other men in a camp close to the city.

We pressed for his release and were finally given permission to visit him and the other internees. Early one morning I accompanied Archbishop Sabiti to the prison. Soldiers pulled open heavy gates, and we entered a guarded compound full of prisoners who crowded around us, anxious for news of their families and friends. Several men lay motionless on the floor. Guards prevented us from going near them. We learnt that it was not uncommon for drunken soldiers to pick on a prisoner and beat him unconscious.

Yona was cheerful, although clearly concerned about his fate and the fate of his companions. Someone produced a small wooden box. We placed a silver cross on it, and surrounded by the ragged group of prisoners, the Archbishop began the Communion service. At the distribution of the elements the Archbishop administered the chalice and I the host. Many members of the group openly shed tears as they received Communion. Afterwards we took the names of as many as we could and promised to give their families news. We were to return to the prison several times before Yona was finally released.

The Bishops of the Church of Uganda, disturbed by the increasing violence in the country, asked General Amin to come to the Archbishop's house and listen to their concerns. As an adviser to the Archbishop, I also attended the meeting. The General arrived in full military uniform. To my surprise, he appeared apprehensive. He was welcomed with typical African courtesy and sat while the Archbishop read from a prepared text. The Archbishop expressed the concern of the Church at the breakdown of law and order in the country and appealed for a return to constitutional government. The General listened, his eyes darting from one member of the group to another. When it was his turn to speak, he produced a script and began to read in halting English. He made promises to put the country on its feet after what he said had been years of corrupt government. Sitting in that room listening to the General was the Bishop of Gulu, Janani Luwum. Years later I visited the chapel of the twentieth-century martyrs in Canterbury Cathedral and saw the memorial to Janani. I remembered this brave successor to Erica, cruelly murdered because he would not give up his opposition to brutality and injustice.

The Bishops asked a few questions. The General gave perfunctory answers. The meeting broke up. Many had their suspicions that Uganda was approaching a period of extreme difficulty. Few realised the extent of the decline that the country was to face.

As time passes, I have the impression that I am entering a new phase of my captivity. The initial suspicion and hostility has gone, and the guards now treat me as half-guest, half-prisoner. I cannot understand why they have failed to release me. The householder seemed convinced that I was going home. All I can imagine is that some event, about which I am totally ignorant, has happened in the world outside, and my release has been blocked. The guards have a television set in the corridor, and from time to time I can hear the sound of English programmes. They still practise the maddening habit of turning the sound down when an English commentary comes on the evening news. They are so well drilled they never make a mistake, and they seem determined to keep all information from me.

I am preparing myself for a long-drawn-out wait here. It appears that provided I do not cause difficulty, they are going to continue to treat me with some humanity. As well as letting me take exercise, they have said they will bring me more books. All I can do is to live one day at a time. I am becoming accustomed to a solitary life. Most of the day I continue my inner dialogue with myself, telling myself the story of my life. I debate with myself, and converse with people I have known in the past.

I keep wondering what has happened to my family and friends. I hope my children have continued with their education. Whenever my mind goes to those close to me, I get upset. Now I understand why so many long-term prisoners cut themselves off completely from their families. The pain can be too hard to bear.

I must concentrate on discovering the positive aspects of solitude. My unknown, unseen companion who lives down the corridor probably experiences feelings similar to mine. I hear him pass my door each day, to and from the bathroom, then the key turning in the lock. Who can he be? After a while I don't torture myself with that question. I have absolutely no way of finding out, so I let it rest. There are only the two of us here at the moment, of that I am sure. The number of guards varies between two and four, but only one comes into my room. He is quiet, and I wonder to myself how he ever came to be involved with this business. Occasionally he will talk a little, but I can never be sure of the truth. He told me his father was a wealthy businessman. Who knows? He is better-mannered than some of my previous guards. I assume that he comes from Beirut and not from the rural south, but again, I don't know. I know so little. While I am exercising I often try to look through the small space in the shutter, but I can see nothing. Since the handle of the door has been removed and a plate fixed over the space, it's also impossible to see through the keyhole. The days are very long.

The question of memory continues to fascinate me. Are all the experiences of my past life retained in my unconscious, awaiting recall? How do I select what I remember? There is no one for me to impress with inflated accounts of my life. But I may be trying to impress myself, bolster my courage. I am acutely aware of the human being's capacity for self-deception. Still, why should I deceive myself in this place? I want to be true, but the meaning of truth eludes me. Classical, philosophical definitions of truth do not satisfy me. I want to know what it means to live the truth. I want my flawed nature to be whole. Why should I long for these goals? Perhaps I need this period of solitude to allow myself to settle after years of activity. If I can embrace solitude as a friend, I might find healing.

I remember thinking that very same thing months ago, and still I struggle. Now it is becoming even more difficult for me to articulate the experience through which I am passing. Words seem inadequate; they fail to capture the mysterious nature of my solitary life. I recollect seeking solitude before my captivity and never finding it. Gibbon spoke of it as 'the school of genius'. But these are disjointed thoughts, mere ramblings on the surface of a mystery. Now, for better or worse, I have been given the gift of solitude. I must live it as fully as possible.

Frances and I had one more brush with death. We had been in Kampala and were returning home. As we drove through the darkness, Frances remarked that she was sure we were being followed. Our garage, which adjoined the house, was at the top of a steep slope. I had left the garage door open when we went out, and I told her I would drive quickly up the hill and directly into the garage. The car Frances had noticed was still behind us. As we drove up the slope, we saw to our horror that the wind had blown the garage door closed. I got out of the car to open it, and as I did, another vehicle came up the drive behind us and several armed men leapt out.

'Put up your hands!'

A pistol was pointed at my head.

'Give me the keys.'

I handed over the keys, and one of the party jumped behind the wheel. Suddenly the man with the pistol saw Frances in the shadows behind the car. For one dreadful moment I thought he was going to shoot her. She stepped forward, and he noticed that she was pregnant. He lowered the gun, climbed into our car, and they sped away. All I could do was to emulate our former nightwatchman and throw a rock after the disappearing vehicle. I missed. Once again we were without a car.

We went indoors where my mother, who was spending a month with us, was looking after the children. We decided not to alarm her, and she did not find out about the car theft until years later. Perhaps we were being over-protective as she had a most amazing series of adventures when she herself travelled in remote areas of

Uganda with a Church medical worker. On her return to England she was in great demand as a speaker at a variety of local groups.

As time went by, General Amin seemed to consolidate his position in the country, apparently by force of arms. Milton Obote was given refuge in neighbouring Tanzania. Many people questioned why Obote had chosen to leave Uganda to attend the Commonwealth Prime Ministers' Conference in Singapore when he knew that there was considerable unrest at home. One theory, which was widely believed, was linked to the decision of the newly elected Conservative government in the United Kingdom to resume the sale of arms to South Africa, a policy which caused dismay throughout the continent. Julius Nyerere, then President of Tanzania, wanted African Commonwealth heads of state to join together to oppose the planned sale. It was said that he had persuaded Obote to go to the conference in Singapore, even though Obote was reluctant to do so. While he was away, the coup was engineered in Uganda.

This was only one of the many stories which surrounded the events of the coup. Both Israel and the United Kingdom were accused of aiding Amin. International and inter-tribal conspiracy theories were rife. Whatever the truth, Uganda staggered from crisis to crisis, and the lot of the vast majority of people in the country was not improved by the political changes.

As I travelled to towns and villages all over Uganda, my convictions about our training programme deepened. It became even more vital to equip local people for survival. The situation was as stark as that. Often the clergyman was the only individual in a village who had received any advanced education. Our programme was specially designed to enable him to utilise his local resources to the maximum. Wherever possible, we encouraged the initiation of co-ordinated preventive medical, educational and rural development programmes. It was uphill work, but slowly we trained a nationwide network of men and women who understood the fundamental principles of self-help and were able to apply them.

On my travels throughout Uganda I met many Roman Catholic groups, including the Society of Catholic Medical Missionaries. The Medical Mission Sisters, as they were known, told me that the leaders of their community from around the world were to meet in Uganda for a conference, and knowing of my work, they asked if I would organise it for them. I knew little about the Order, but the Sisters assured me that they wanted someone who would help them examine and rethink their working assumptions. I agreed to assist them, little realising that once again my life was on the point of change.

At last another book, and what a book! I hold it in my hands and feel genuine happiness for the first time in weeks. *The First Circle* by Alexander Solzhenitsyn. After weeks of pleading, hoping, waiting, I have a book, and one I have always wanted to read. I examine it in detail: the date of publication, the publisher's blurb, the back cover. I count the number of words so that I know how long it will last me. I want to savour the book, to enter into the mind of the writer. Solzhenitsyn came to Lambeth Palace once: bearded, angular, marvellously individualistic. A sentence jumps out from the page: 'If one is forever cautious, can one remain a human being?' The words of Volodin, whose humanity sent him to the camps.

I can give you an answer to that, Innokénty Volodin. A clear, unequivocal, resounding 'no'. I have so wanted to be cautious, to play for safety, not to take risks, but something within has always nagged me to push forward. I can't possibly compare myself to the stalwart victims of the gulag, but I know what you say when you speak. I feel the iron in my soul. I am pierced by self-doubt, I am a fool, but I desire life, freedom, justice, truth. I want them passionately, but they terrify me with their absolute demands. I can't imagine a better book for the moment. The light bulb flickers and goes out. I have a box with three matches inside. I light my stub of candle, pick up my magnifying glass, and begin to read.

'I have sought for rest everywhere, but I have found it nowhere except in a corner with a book.' So, rather surprisingly, wrote Thomas à Kempis in an autobiographical note. Today that experience has been mine. I have been able to leave my own life, travel with others, listen to their conversations, share their sorrows. Today I have experienced the beauty and peace of solitude. No extra visits from the guards, no shelling outside, just a candle, a book, and my imagination.

Despite the privations and misery of the characters who haunt the pages of *The First Circle*, I can't help but envy the measure of freedom they have. They can move around the camp, exercise, keep intellectually alive. Even with those freedoms it's dreadful for them, but the book gives me courage and hope. There are days when I feel myself sinking into depression, when an event from my past triggers memories of my frailty as a human being. But the human spirit and the desire to survive are strong, and I feel that inner strength today. I suppose I am learning to accept myself, even to love myself. I think I know what else I may be doing. In repeating my story, I am affirming my existence; convincing myself that I am a person with a past, with relationships. I have thought these thoughts many times before, but they return more strongly now. I remember again how Africa touched me.

It wasn't the politics of Africa, although they were complex and interesting. Africa spoke to my unconscious in a profoundly disturbing way. I saw that my own 'civilised' behaviour was little more than a veneer covering a world I had hardly seen, let alone explored. I could drown in hidden oceans, be carved in pieces by aggression, be totally overwhelmed by passion. Uganda showed me life in all its fullness. Love, hate, laughter, tears were close to one another, just as they are in a child. But Africa is no child. The many faces of Africa smiled at me, stared at me and threatened me. They told me I had many faces, too. They urged me to take courage and examine my own tragic, comic nature. Africa confirmed within me the desire to take an inner journey.

Now in this Lebanese prison, where the electricity has failed and my candle has burnt out, I tread carefully. All my human guides and supporters are far, far away. The outer and inner journeys have at last met, and both must be made alone for a while, perhaps until the end of my life, for I may never leave this place alive.

The Turners and the Hutchisons both left Uganda. Philip went to the United States, and Eric to Cambridge University. Wilson, our cook, experienced severe difficulties. He believed that he had been bewitched, took to his bed and prepared to die. I tried to talk with him, but it was useless. He refused all food and began to decline quickly. I consulted a clergyman, one of his fellow tribesmen, who said that the only remedy was to send him home so that he might consult the local medicine man. A depressed and ailing Wilson finally summoned enough courage to put a few belongings together and make for his home district. A week later he returned, quite his old self. The spell had been broken, and he was completely well. Not long afterwards he left our employ to return home permanently, and we took on William, an excellent cook, who had worked for the Hutchisons for ten years or so. William remained with us until we finally left the country in 1971.

The Amin regime did nothing to halt the reign of terror practised by bandits in Uganda. Night after night I left the house because an alarm had sounded. The scenes of brutality I witnessed then have been imprinted on my mind for ever. Even householders who barred their windows were not immune from the ingenuity of thieves who engaged in what was known as pole-fishing. They would take a long bamboo stick and fix a hook on one end. In the dead of night they would poke the stick through the bars and collect what they could. One night a neighbour of ours lost his trousers together with his wallet, which was in the back pocket! Really unpleasant pole-fishers would insert razor blades in the pole so that if the victim awoke and grabbed hold of it he would be injured, and thus delayed in giving chase.

The conference with the Medical Mission Sisters (MMS) took place at Fort Portal at the foot of the Ruwenzori Mountains. Before attending I had done some homework and learnt that the community was founded in the last century by Dr Anna Dengel, an Austrian woman of considerable spirit and determination. She started work in India, and the MMS developed at such a pace that by the 1970s its network was worldwide. An American, Dr Jane Gates, had recently been elected Superior of the community, following the retirement of Anna Dengel. She had initiated a complete review of the life and work of the Society, in response to the major changes which the Roman Catholic Church was experiencing in the wake of the Second Vatican Council of 1962–5.

At the same time, many pioneers in the health field were suggesting that there ought to be greater emphasis throughout the world on preventive health programmes, rather than the traditional concentration on large curative establishments. At Fort Portal, these issues were discussed, but they proved to be so complex that many of those present felt that further analysis should be made by the community, together with competent practitioners drawn from the health, educational, medical and religious fields. A conference in Rome was arranged, and I was one of several 'outsiders' invited to attend.

14

'IF YOU SAID THIS to the Romans they would be highly insulted, but let me tell you, Africa and Europe meet in Rome.'

We were approaching Fiumicino Airport. My neighbour, who had slept for most of the journey, was telling me about his adopted city.

'You have only to travel a mile or so from the airport and you will see people living in conditions worse than Uganda.'

The plane levelled out and flew along the coastline. A cold, grey sea lapped listlessly against black volcanic sand.

'It's a city of contrasts. You'll love it and hate it. Its inhabitants are the rudest people in Italy. They've very little time for the Church, even though they give it grudging support. They have to, it brings in the visitors.'

The plane touched down in what appeared to be the depths of the countryside. We rumbled along to the terminal building. My informant bade me goodbye.

'Hope you have a good visit. If you have time, get out to the hills. Drink the local wine, eat roast lamb and forget Rome the city.'

He pushed his way to the front of the plane while I collected my belongings from the overhead rack. During the flight I had attempted to read my papers for the conference, but they were so numerous that I gave up halfway through. I didn't know any of my fellow participants: a specialist in community health care from Holland, a behavioural scientist from India, an educationalist from the Philippines. I was looking forward to the experience, and especially to visiting Rome which I had been wanting to do ever since the hitchhiking tour when I had got only as far as Vienna.

A car was waiting for me, and we drove out of the airport and on to the Anulare, Rome's circular road. The conference was to be held in the Generalate of the Order, which was situated just off the Via Aurelia. The outskirts to the south-east of the city seemed to be a sad clutter of ugly, half-finished apartment blocks, mere concrete shells topped by a roof. I learnt later that most of them had been erected without permission, but providing the builder could get the roof in place he was safe, at least for a while. We raced around the track, but even though the driver was no laggard, we were constantly passed by other vehicles, great and small. Finally, our lap completed, we turned off on to the Via Aurelia and then into a country lane marred by a pile of old mattresses and household refuse casually dumped in the hedgerow.

The Generalate, a brick building of recent vintage, would not have qualified for an architectural award. Rome, I discovered, was littered with new religious houses built before the Second Vatican Council when men and women were expected to come to the city in their thousands to train for the priesthood and the religious life. But increasingly Churches around the world had preferred to have their candidates spend more time at home. This, coupled with the decline in vocations, had resulted in many huge buildings standing three-quarters empty for much of the time. The Medical Mission Sisters had not fallen into that particular trap. They rented half a house and maintained only a small administrative staff on the premises.

During my days in Rome I had little time to get to know the city, and none at all to escape to the hills. The Sisters were a hard-working group, determined to get as much as they could from the conference. They outlined their work throughout the world. When the Order was started in India, all the major positions in a hospital were taken by the religious Sisters. Their dedication, professional skill and willingness to work all hours of the day and night meant that they quickly established a reputation for excellence. More patients were attracted to the hospitals, which thereby flourished. However, difficulties were accumulating for the next generation. As hospitals grew in size it became impossible for religious Sisters to occupy all the key positions; lay staff had to be employed. This immediately increased expenses since lay staff, unlike the Sisters, had to be paid competitive salaries. Most lay staff also had families and outside responsibilities, which made it impossible for them to be committed in the way the Sisters were. Further staff was required simply to keep the units functioning. The Sisters soon found themselves managing multi-million-pound institutions.

Along with these complexities, other questions arose. The Medical Mission Sisters had started out with a clear commitment to the poor, but certain hospitals now seemed to be catering largely for those who could afford to pay for medical treatment. Many members of the community seriously questioned whether working in a hospital was the most appropriate way for them to deal with the root problems of poverty and poor health. They argued that in many situations hospitals failed to resolve fundamental health problems. A patient would be admitted to a hospital in Africa suffering from a disease caused by malnutrition, inadequate water supply or something similar. The patient would be cured, return home, and within a month or so be queuing for readmission. Many Sisters felt they must be freed from their institutional responsibilities in order to follow their first vocation, which was to serve the poor, in particular those who did not have access to adequate health care.

Running alongside the institutional questions were others concerning the religious life of the Order. The Second Vatican Council had sent tremors through the Church, and they were felt keenly within many religious communities, which were forced to reconsider the nature and style of their commitment. Soon after the Council, the Medical Mission Sisters gave its members a free choice about wearing the religious habit. The vast majority chose to adopt lay dress. At this tumultuous time, the community was faced with the enormous task of enabling its members around the world to redefine their priorities and match these with new directions in their work, or the apostolate, as it was commonly known.

As we discussed these issues together, we could see that the community as an institution had come full circle in its development. The pioneers had started very simply with a direct commitment to the poor. The work had become institutionalised, and now, following the retirement of Anna Dengel, the founder, the original inspiration needed to be rediscovered and reapplied to meet the needs of the latter half of the twentieth century. It was felt that, to fulfil this task, the community needed to engage in a worldwide educational programme supported by external consultants drawn from relevant fields. I was asked if I would consider co-ordinating such a programme for a period of two or three years.

Back in Kampala, I discussed the proposal with Frances. The idea of a new challenge excited me. George Lubega had returned from England and was ready to take over my position. Teams had been trained and pioneer projects established. On the other hand, I was apprehensive about leaving the Anglican Church, even temporarily, as I knew I would miss the supports that were offered. If I took the job, I would visit virtually every part of the world and would certainly get to know the Roman Catholic Church well, but Rome might prove to be a much lonelier position than Uganda had ever been.

Frances and I realised that the longer we stayed there, the more difficult it would be for us to leave. Our children would begin to get established in school, and I could find myself unable to do what I had intended to do from the start – namely, work myself out of a job. Finally, with mixed feelings on both sides, we agreed that I should accept the new position.

It was late in the afternoon of 16 October 1971 when we walked together across Namirembe Hill, turned on to a small track alongside the cathedral and within a few minutes found ourselves at the hospital. Earlier in the day Frances had experienced labour pains and decided that the time had come to book into the ward. That evening we had planned to entertain a representative of Oxfam of Canada at dinner. Frances insisted that I go ahead with the meal and visit her later. Immediately after dinner I went back to the hospital. It seemed to be deserted. Frances was in a small side ward, already in labour. I rushed into the corridor to find a nurse, but there was no sign of anyone. By the time an aide finally arrived, our son was half delivered. We named him Mark. I looked at the handsome baby peacefully sleeping in his cot and felt proud that we had a son. After a day or so, we carried him home. We wanted him to be baptised in Uganda before we left. As George was away at the time, Clement Janda, my colleague from the Sudan, baptised him in the University Church at Makerere.

By now the days were rushing by. A flat had been found for us in Rome and would be ready for occupation after Christmas. We decided to sail from Mombasa to Trieste. The Suez Canal was closed at the time, and we would have to journey around Africa and up the Atlantic, four weeks in all. We hoped it would give us a break before stepping into our new life in Italy.

Last night it was very cold and wet. Rain blew into the room through the industrial extractor fan which was installed in an outside wall some time ago. As in a previous location, two or three men entered the room, bashed a hole in the wall, fitted the fan and left. It was helpful during the last days of the summer, but it is never used now. Even then it was of limited use because the electricity supply failed constantly. There was so much water on the floor this morning that my mattress was soaked. I have been chained to another wall, away from the damp, which enables me to peer under the door into the corridor outside. Now I can see the feet of my unknown companion as he passes my room. I can also see the feet of the guard when he stands outside my door, listening for noises in my room. I can't sing or speak aloud to myself. If I do, he knocks on the door or comes in to tell me to be quiet.

My whole existence has to come from within. I find myself wondering, if I have to live like this for a long period of time, whether I will ever be able to form human relationships again. How long can I bear being alone? This question constantly passes through my mind, but I try not to dwell on it. I wonder if the other hostages are being kept together. Some were, I know. Perhaps I and my unseen companion are the only ones in solitary.

I have enjoyed revisiting Uganda. Although we lived in the country for only three years, life there was so full, it now seems like a lifetime. The Archbishop arranged a garden party for us just before we left, so that everyone could say goodbye. Neither of us was looking forward to the occasion; we would have preferred to leave without too much fuss. As it turned out, we were able to miss the farewell party. The Lloyd Triestino ship on which we were to sail usually went to Karachi and then returned to collect passengers at Mombasa on the way back to Italy. Because of the war in Pakistan, the boat terminated in Mombasa, and we received a cable saying we must be ready one week before the normal departure date. We decided that we could just make it. Dick, who had become almost one of the family by now, went out and bought a Moses basket from the local market. We put Mark – then six weeks old – into it and loaded him, together with our three girls and our few possessions, into a Volkswagen van and set out to drive the eight hundred or so miles to the Kenyan coast for the last time.

It was an early December morning when we left our house in Kampala. William and Dick waved us a sad goodbye. Peter, our gentle black Labrador, had gone to another family the previous day. We passed the bungalow which had belonged to an Obote supporter and had been looted following the coup. I remembered watching from our garden as a gang smashed the front door and totally stripped the building. They carried their pathetic spoils of victory down the lane, singing and laughing as they went. We had said our farewells to our friends the day before; now we passed their silent houses waiting for the first warming beams of the morning sun to bring them to life.

An old lady stood by the side of the road, a large water-pot perfectly balanced on her head. Her face was lined with the marks of a long life of suffering and sorrow. In the taxi-park, drivers were vying for trade. They would wait until they had crammed eight or ten passengers into a dilapidated Peugeot and then fly like the wind to every corner of the country. Accidents were frequent. Once a taxi overturned on a main road and came to rest upside down. The passengers were so tightly packed in that despite this unusual manoeuvre, they remained firmly jammed together – shaken but unhurt.

We passed Mukono, our second temporary home when we first arrived in the country. We laughed as we remembered how alarmed we had been when we heard a piercing scream during our first night there. It was nothing more than a hyrax, reputed by locals to be the nearest living relative to an elephant, and noted for its blood-curdling cry. We soon reached the Nile and crossed it at Owen Falls dam. Just a few hundred yards upstream was a stone marking the source of this mighty river and its discovery by Speke in 1858. Many an argument took place about that tablet. Africans would deny Speke's claim, saying they knew about the river all the time. Others would respond that they may have known of the source of the river, but they didn't know it was the mighty Nile, the source of life for the Sudan and Egypt. Some years after the day we last crossed the dam, my friend and former colleague John Wasikye was shot by soldiers as he travelled to Kampala. His body was thrown into the river at this point to join the thousands of others who were interred in the seething waters of Owen Falls.

We approached the border post, stopped, and produced endless documents indicating that we had paid our taxes and were entitled to leave the country. Once through the formalities, we breathed a sigh of relief. We entered Kenya and remembered our holidays there. On one memorable occasion, we had travelled with the Turners to the small settler town of Kitale. Our hostess, Mrs la Riche, a daughter of one of the first European settlers, allowed our children into her kitchen to witness the birth of a small deer known as a dik-dik. Near Kitale we had seen our first herd of elephants and twenty or thirty giraffes walking in lofty pride across the bush.

Arriving at the Equator, we stopped to take photographs, standing in the white circle which marks this boundary. On our way to the highlands, at nine thousand feet, our car engine spluttered as it strained to cope with the change of compression. Young men stood by the side of the road selling sheepskin coats and hats. The air was clear and cold and the sky a brilliant blue. Pine trees towered above us in stately splendour. At Naivasha, pink flamingoes covered the lake, providing us with a sight which never failed to impress and defies description.

We remembered travelling along this road with Frances's sister, Ann, who came to stay with us for a holiday. Since the car was full, we put her suitcase on the roof rack. To our dismay, when we stopped for a break, the case had disappeared. Although it was a very long shot, we turned around and retraced our route. After about twenty miles or so, we came to a village consisting of about six mud huts. To our amazement, a young girl emerged from one of them most elegantly dressed.

'Hey,' shouted Ann, 'she's wearing my pants suit.'

Indeed she was. The girl had been travelling behind our car in a bus and had seen the suitcase fly off the rack. Naturally, she considered this to be good fortune and took it home. I was all for letting her keep the suit, but Ann, who was travelling light, needed it. The girl returned it, I gave her something for her kindness, and we continued on our journey. Unfortunately we were not able to trace any of the other passengers who had benefited from the unexpected windfall.

As night fell, we arrived in Nairobi. We decided to be extravagant and made for the Hotel Intercontinental, where we could all get a bath and a good night's rest. Mark had that day completed five hundred miles of his first African safari. He had crossed the Nile, traversed the Equator, climbed into the highlands and entered Nairobi. Throughout, he had slept soundly.

The next morning we took the long straight road to Mombasa. When I first travelled this route, it was still a murram track; now it was paved. On one occasion, a huge deer had leapt in front of my car and was killed instantly. A passing bus stopped, and a dozen or so passengers hauled the animal on to the roof and made off. Presumably it would provide most of them with plenty of meat for some time to come.

Almost all the way from Kampala, the road and the rail track ran together. A wonderful book, *The Maneaters of Tsavo*, tells of the building of the railroad and how the labourers were terrorised by lions as they crossed what is now Tsavo National Park. We always kept a sharp lookout here, but never once saw a lion. Several miles from Mombasa, the air changed, and one could smell the sea. At this point we always played a game: 'The first one to see the ocean'. The girls would strain their eyes until one would shout: 'There it is, I can see it!' Sure enough, a glint of blue-green water, a clump of palm trees and the promise of a holiday. We drove into Mombasa, passing under the huge imitation elephant tusks which acted as a gateway to the city, along the main street bustling with life and down to the ocean.

I am now allowed to take a shower every day providing I am quick. This is sheer luxury. The temperature of the water varies; one day it is scalding hot, another quite cold. No matter. To be able to enjoy a daily shower is marvellous. If I ever leave this place, I hope I will never forget how much pleasure very simple things gave me. Today, as I stood under the shower, I glanced through the gap in the metal shutter at the street below. A car was parked off the road in an empty space intended as a shop unit; children walked together in the sunlight; a lady carried some flowers. Although the street was drab and ordinary, it was also full of life and colour. Even at this distance, seven floors up, squinting through a minute crack, I could see the colour of the flowers. I hardly took notice of flowers before, but now they appear exquisitely beautiful. I have been starved of colour for so long, just as I was during the years following the war. I wish I could see some pictures. Now there would be time to look at and absorb them. If I ever get out of here, will I make time to stand and stare? Will I still find pleasure in what is simple? I hope so, I truly hope so.

Back in the room, the guard fastens the heavy chain around my ankle.

'I have finished my book.'

'You read very quick. You must read slow.'

I wasn't conscious of reading quickly. I had simply lost myself in the writing.

'Give me.'

I hand him *The First Circle*.

'Can you bring me another book, please?'

'I look.'

He leaves the room. It's terrible to part with a good book as I have no idea what, if anything, will take its place.

He returns.

'Tek.'

A slim volume is put into my hand.

'Thank you.'

The door is locked. Blindfold off. It's a paperback published by
Mills & Boon. Well, as I have never read a romantic novel from this
publisher, I might as well give it a try. It is soon read. A young
teacher, a handsome doctor, a Swiss count parade through the pages.
True love wins after many trials. I hope I don't get too many more
in this genre, but it won't be replaced today. Nothing else to do but
return to my own book and continue writing in my head.

On our first visit to Mombasa, we stayed in a curious house which
we named 'the Signal Box'. It was perched on a slope overlooking
the channel and had been especially constructed with large windows
to give good views of the shipping – hence the name. After that we
went farther up the coast and rented a small house directly on the
beach. They were wonderful holidays. Now, on our final visit, we
stayed for a night or two in a small hotel near the town. George
Lubega and Folmer, a Danish volunteer who had joined our team
some months earlier, had been away at a conference and were due
in Mombasa a few days after we sailed; they would collect the van
and take it back to Kampala.

We boarded our ship several days before Christmas. As the voyage
took about four weeks in all, both Christmas and New Year would
be spent at sea. Very few passengers had been able to make the
advanced departure time, and for the whole journey there were not
more than two or three people in first class and about a dozen of us
in second. The crew suggested that, as this was an exceptional voyage,
all passengers might move to first class. This prospect delighted us,
not least the children, as there was a very large swimming pool in
first, compared to a much smaller one in second. Alas, none of us
was promoted. An elderly first-class passenger stated that she had
paid for her privacy, and that was what she wanted. We stayed on
the lower deck.

We sailed away from Africa, along the channel, past the Signal
Box, and out to the open sea. Standing on the rear deck, we watched
until the palm trees gradually disappeared over the horizon. Africa
had marked me in ways I could never have anticipated. It would take
me a lifetime to digest the lessons I had learnt.

We steamed into Durban early one morning. Two gangplanks

connected the ship to the dock: one for whites and the other for non-whites. We felt a sense of shame as the single non-white passenger in our small party was obliged to descend alone. She was an Asian lady who was returning to her home in the Republic. She smiled graciously when we expressed our feelings.

'I am used to it,' she said quietly. 'There are things one must accept.' She disappeared into a dockside building, leaving us to ponder on a system which condemned millions to servitude.

We walked by the beach. 'Whites only' was blazoned on seats, public toilets, taxis. This was my first visit to South Africa, and I felt a mixture of shame and anger coupled with pity for those who had to protect themselves and profit from Africa by adopting such methods.

We sailed on to Cape Town, leaving yet another of our small party behind. He had decided to hire a car, drive across the country and rejoin the ship there. Cape Town was decidedly more liberal than Durban, but the dreadful shadow of racism continued to haunt what was an extraordinarily beautiful country. I took the girls to the top of Table Mountain from where we looked down on the splendour of the ocean. I wondered if, like me, years later, they would look back on Africa and remember. What would they remember? Violence and terror, or joy and generosity? Thunderstorms or bright clear days crammed with colour and life?

We returned to the ship and set sail. Our adventurous companion had literally missed the boat! We were quite a distance from the shore when we spotted a motor vessel speeding towards us. It pulled alongside, and with much laughter and good humour our missing comrade was hauled aboard. Although we were so few in number, the purser attempted to run the ship as though everything were normal. Each night a small band assembled and dutifully executed its repertoire. Initially, most of us felt obliged to spend some time dancing, but as the days passed, it became more and more of a chore until we realised that we were attending solely to encourage these stalwart troupers. We suggested that they might like a rest from playing, but they responded by saying that they were under orders to play nightly whether passengers attended or not. Thereafter, relieved of our responsibility, we would often hear strains of distant melodies echoing through the ship as we sat out in the cool night air.

The crew did their best to be cheerful, but it was hard going. A dozen passengers of limited means would certainly not be able to tip the scores of attendants adequately. They knew that, and we knew that.

We crossed the Equator, and the traditional ceremony was duly performed in the swimming pool. Christmas and New Year were quiet and cheerful, but hardly exuberant. A Christmas party and dance in the main dining room for half-a-dozen adults and a large number of disconsolate officers was a test of the Captain's benevolence. Wisely he pleaded that urgent matters required his personal attention and disappeared to the bridge.

We approached Gibraltar in the early morning. On the bridge Frances and I caught our first sight of the Rock from the ship's radar. The weather was growing noticeably colder and we looked forward to a day in Barcelona where we could buy warm clothes. Our stop in Spain provided us with just enough time to replace the children's flip-flops with adequate shoes and get the clothes we needed. Then we were back on board for the final leg of the journey.

There was thick fog as we steamed up the Grand Canal in Venice. Virtually every passenger had now left or was about to leave the vessel. Instead of travelling on to Trieste, we too decided to disembark and fly from Venice to Rome. When we arrived at our apartment early one winter's afternoon, it was just about ready for occupation. We stood on the balcony and looked down at the street. We had no Italian, knew hardly anyone in the city, and once again were setting out into the unknown.

There are no more books for the moment. I imagine that the guards only have a very few and want to spin them out as long as possible. Today I feel anxious for no obvious reason, apart from the absurd situation I find myself in. Despite a tense sickness in my stomach, I can still manage to smile from time to time; but my inner journey is proving to be very difficult because I have no means of recording my thoughts and dreams except by committing them to memory. I forget dreams very quickly unless they are exceptional. My dreams seem to nourish me, even make me laugh; I awoke last night in such good humour. Perhaps my unconscious is buoying me up, keeping me afloat as I sail across uncharted seas. It might be more accurate if I said 'without charts'; many have travelled this route before me and survived. My unknown companion is making the same journey. How does he manage?

I do not feel the presence of God. I wish I didn't have to say that, but it is true. All I do is cling to a simple hope and belief, very simple, very basic. I will be sustained and supported from within, and I will not be destroyed. If this is the dark night of the soul, so be it. One day I will find light.

15

'TURN RIGHT, and it's on the right.'

I acknowledged the policeman's directions, and continued down the gloomy streets of south London. Within twenty-four hours I would be back in Italy. A garage with row upon row of black cabs stood on the corner. A man in overalls greeted me cheerfully, and we walked together along the rank of twenty or so vehicles.

'I need one in good condition. It's got to get me to Rome,' I explained.

'They're all pretty good,' he replied. 'They have to be to pass the regular checkups.' He stopped. 'This should do.' He slapped its front mudguard. 'Two hundred and fifty quid.'

I climbed into the driver's seat. To my left was an open space for luggage, behind me a glass screen with a sliding window. I turned the ignition key, and the diesel engine sprang to life.

'No problem with this one.' He lifted the bonnet. 'We've serviced it regularly. Plenty of go left in it, but they all must come out of regular service after ten years.'

I agreed to buy it.

'Any problems – just bring it back. Bit far though!' He laughed, and promised to have it ready the next day.

The following morning I was back at the garage.

'It's against the law to have locks on the rear doors of taxis in service.' He handed me the vehicle documents. 'But now it's in private use, you might like to get them fitted some time.'

Gingerly, I edged the vehicle into the busy London street. The meter and registration plate had been removed; otherwise it was identical to the hundreds of other cabs in London. Near Waterloo Station I stopped at traffic lights. Suddenly an elderly man opened the rear door and settled into the passenger seat, shouting an address at me.

'This is a private car,' I said. 'I can drop you at Lambeth Bridge.'

He accepted the offer. I dropped him, refused payment, and went immediately to get locks fitted. The journey to Rome was slow and sure. Although it was February, I crossed the Alps without difficulty and within a couple of days was driving into Rome.

The taxi proved to be an inspired buy. We filled it with the children's schoolfriends and deposited them at birthday parties around the city; in the summer we loaded it with tents and camp-beds and made for the south coast of Sicily. After a few years, afraid it might soon require parts unobtainable in Italy, I sold it and bought a ubiquitous Fiat, but the taxi always remained the family's first love.

There were two Anglican churches in Rome. All Saints catered for the Church of England, St Paul's for the American Episcopalians. The Anglican Communion also maintained the Anglican Centre, which housed the most comprehensive collection of Anglican books in Europe. We tended to go to St Paul's, where there was a young congregation, and from time to time I would take the girls with me to the Russian Orthodox Church.

Gradually we explored the city. In the late summer we paid at least one visit to the open-air opera held in the Terme di Caracalla. *Aïda* was a favourite as the spirited performances always included live animals – horses or even giraffes. We would sit in the cheap seats, take a picnic and enjoy a spectacular evening. As I remember the fun and enjoyment of *Aïda*, I suddenly recall the famous double scene where Radames awaits his fate in the dungeon. The stage is on two levels: the upper floor of the temple bathed in light, the dungeon beneath lost in darkness. The miraculous happens, and Aïda, Radames' lover, who had hidden herself in the prison, makes her appearance. A nice thought, but not very helpful in this place, I'm afraid. My mind drifts to the small prison near the Forum in Rome where it is said St Paul was kept. Prisons, dungeons . . . I seek escape in my narrative and am constantly brought back to the reality of chains and darkness.

Rome, as I had been warned, had considerable poverty. Like Africa, the family provided a basic unit of support, but many of the elderly and infirm who happened to be without immediate relatives lived in terrible situations. It came as a surprise to us to see a small booth in our local post office manned by an elderly scribe who completed official documents for the considerable number of illiterate customers.

The drug problem, along with prostitution, was widespread. Prostitutes camped by open fires on the Anulare, and Frances, walking alone with Mark in her arms, was occasionally propositioned by motorists. The Italian education system was a disaster. Pupils attended on a shift system, and those who were unable to get extra coaching were in difficulty. The University of Rome was grossly overcrowded and often in turmoil. The health system was little better. Even Pope John Paul II received contaminated blood following the attempt on his life in 1981. The stories of inefficiency in the Italian bureaucracy were legendary and, regrettably, true.

We were advised to do our best to keep away from any official form, document or device, as the government was in complete disarray. We did our utmost to follow this advice and so managed to avoid a great deal of trouble. One of the country's most obvious aberrations – ugly speculative development which ruined much of the coastline – was due to the lack or avoidance of planning control. In many places environmental pollution was a nightmare. Frances and I had constantly to remind ourselves that, like Uganda, Italy was a comparatively young nation. Actually it was still an amalgamation of competing city-states and regions. The Vatican State, in the heart of Rome itself, stood as an example of political compromise and accommodation.

Despite all the problems, Italy was a pleasant country in which to live. We enjoyed the friendliness of the people, the climate and the food, and quickly settled down.

Most weekends when I was at home we would eat out, frequently at our local pizzeria and occasionally in the Alban Hills outside Rome. We soon discovered that the simple establishments were the best places to eat. The local wine rarely left the village and was cool, crisp and delicious. Fish would be caught that morning from the lake and served at lunchtime. For once, the stereotype of rustic bliss and reality coincided.

Together with Dr Jane Gates, the Superior of the Medical Mission Sisters, and her assistant, Annamaria de Vreede, I began to plan my journeys. Before leaving Africa I had made a brief visit to the Philippines to attend a planning meeting, but apart from that, I had little first-hand knowledge of the work of the Society.

I needed to visit the Medical Mission Sisters throughout the world to introduce the educational programme to the members. It was believed that an outsider, such as myself, would be able to help them step back from the immediate demands of day-to-day responsibilities

and rediscover the essence of their religious commitment and involvement with those whom they wished to serve.

One of my first visits was to Pakistan where the MMS was responsible for three of the largest, most respected hospitals in the country:
Holy Family Hospital in Karachi, Holy Family Hospital in Rawalpindi and a large hospital in Dacca, East Pakistan. All three units
were suffering from the difficulties we had pinpointed at the conference in Rome: work had started modestly and then developed on
such a scale that these hospitals had become national institutions
in an Islamic state. A handful of Medical Mission Sisters bore the
responsibility for the administration of units increasingly staffed by
laymen and women, almost all of whom were Muslims. To their
great credit the Sisters managed the hospitals with considerable skill
and good humour. However, times were changing.

Political forces were challenging foreign control of the hospitals.
Some of this nationalistic fervour was stirred up by local doctors,
who saw in the hospitals an increasingly lucrative source of income.
The Catholic Church, on the other hand, wanted the hospitals to
remain as clear, living symbols of the Church's presence. Catholics
were a very small minority in Pakistan. Initially, many members from
the lower castes had come to the Church, so it was not overendowed
with highly-trained personnel. The chances of the local community
replacing the foreign staff were remote indeed. The Sisters themselves were in a dilemma. Many had worked in Pakistan for years,
were proficient in the language, and genuinely cared for the people
of the country. They were no longer being supplied with staff from
overseas, and the pressure of work they had to face was considerable.
They were in fact being forced into a situation which would be
difficult whatever future policy the MMS adopted.

I flew to Dacca on a civilian flight from Karachi. Because of the
war between East and West Pakistan, planes were forbidden to fly
over India, so I had to make the long detour around the southern
tip of the subcontinent. There were six or seven passenger seats at
the front of the plane. It was rumoured that the back was full of
arms, but since it was completely sealed off, there was no way of
verifying this. Returning to Karachi, the back of the plane was full
of wounded soldiers on their way home for treatment.

East Pakistan was deeply depressing. Poverty, humidity and the
scars of war combined to make a grim canvas. The outside of the
hospital, a large undistinguished concrete building, was disfigured

by what appeared to be green mould. As in West Pakistan, one could not fail to be impressed by the dedication of the small community which was keeping this place going. The Sisters genuinely cared for the patients who streamed through the hospital doors every day.

In Dacca, a decision had already been taken to hand the hospital over to the local authorities, and several of the community had moved to a rural location to develop a public-health programme. I was taken around the city to see the conditions in which thousands found themselves. Families lived in structures made of cardboard and plastic; children were born on the streets. We passed an ancient Hindu site where the historic temples had been razed to the ground during the fighting; there were no reliable records of the numbers killed in the conflict. On the flight back to Karachi, the scenes of warfare and poverty were vivid in my mind. I was no stranger to poverty; I had worked to relieve it in Uganda. The problem in Asia, however, was on an altogether different scale. It was one thing to see a picture of poverty on the television screen, quite another to walk through streets and smell the stench of deprivation; to stand in a hospital and watch a young mother with her dying child in her arms; to see an old man crying by the ruins of the rubble he had once called home.

In Karachi, I again met the staff of Holy Family Hospital and we examined the management structure with the board. It was clear that the community was already attempting to translate idealistic goals into practical objectives. As we tried to work and study together, the hospital continued to make its all-consuming demands; the machinery never stopped. The wheels turned relentlessly, fuelled by a need so great that it seemed overwhelming.

When I had finished the seminars in Karachi, I left for the hospital in Rawalpindi. As I approached it, I saw a young European sitting by the main gate. He was barefoot, his jeans were torn and dirty, and his shirt hung on his bony frame like a cloth on a broomstick. His head was between his knees. A member of the community went over to speak to him. He lifted his head to reveal skin as yellow as old parchment. She helped him to his feet and assisted him indoors. Afterwards we sat talking.

'Rawalpindi is the end of the line for so many,' the Sister said sadly. 'They come from Europe seeking a mystical East and affordable drugs. They get this far, and sickness catches up with them. I can't tell you how many have died here during my time. He's an American – hepatitis, of course.'

I went to the bus station and squeezed myself into a seat intended for a person half my size. The whole busload of passengers burst into good-natured laughter tinged with embarrassment. The bus shook like an old dog as the driver started up and moved the long gear lever into first, and we rattled along the potholed road. Every few minutes, the driver reached out of the window and gave several sharp blasts on a brass horn. We shambled through the outskirts of the city and onward to Peshawar. In the market-place we stopped for hot sweet tea while crowds of metalworkers attempted to sell brass and copper articles of every description. An elderly passenger scrambled aboard with a magnificent copper samovar, which the irate driver insisted should be placed on the roof. Then we were off again, climbing through a bare rugged terrain towards the Khyber Pass. The air was cooler now. On the crown of the peak I could see a solid square fortress, reminder of an Imperial past.

'There is rock to the left, and rock to the right, and low lean thorn between . . .'

Kipling's words describe this place exactly. We approached a border post. Bewhiskered patriarchs swathed in sheepskin and holding vintage muskets guarded a pile of rocks. They examined my camera and made a note in an exercise book, the driver sounded his horn and we pulled away. More rocks, more thorns, then the silver sparkle of a river. We charged along a narrow highway. The waters crashed and cascaded alongside. Snow-capped peaks towered in lonely splendour on either side of us. A reclusive shepherd waved from his solitary vantage point. It was late afternoon when we passed the University of Jalalabad – nothing more than several slabs of concrete emblazoned with broken windows – and pulled up at the bus park. The journey had convinced me that Afghanistan was best approached by bus, even though I descended the steps feeling as though I had travelled by mule.

The contrast between the MMS's work in Pakistan and in Jalalabad was considerable. I was taken to meet the small community, whose members were living in a simple local house. One room had been set aside as a chapel and contained the reserved Sacrament, which, as there was no church in the town and no local priest, the Sisters used for their Communion service every Sunday.

The community's principal work was health education, training the local nursing staff and developing public-health programmes. Its members, isolated in the midst of an Islamic culture, firmly believed that their vocation was to be of service to those in need, regardless of faith or nationality, and one could not fail to respect their commitment. A day or so later we set out for Kabul. The journey was even more spectacular than the drive from Pakistan. Again, the road followed the course of the river, which wound its way through awe-inspiring mountain ranges. Years later, this territory was to become a bloody battleground where Soviet troops experienced the difficulty of combat in such a terrain and against such a courageous people.

I am lying on my mattress with my eyes closed, walking in my imagination through the Kabul I remember: the wall by the river spread with carpets in rich dark colours; water splashing over the stony river-bed; donkeys laden with wicker baskets; the magnificent backdrop of the Hindu Kush.

A knock on the door. I sit up and fasten my blindfold. Two people enter the room. Every time there is a change of routine I feel anxious. Why should two men visit me at this hour of day?

'Cover eyes.'

I adjust the blindfold so that it comes farther down over my nose. There is a clatter as someone opens a folding chair. A guard bends down and unlocks my chain.

'Stand.'

I get to my feet. Hands grasp me from behind and I am guided across the room.

'Sit.'

I sit down in a wooden chair. Then I hear it. The dreadful sound of masking tape being torn from a roll.

'Close eyes.'

The man behind me fastens my feet to the chair with a chain. Someone holds me by the shoulders and another person unties my blindfold.

'Close eyes. No look.'

Cotton-wool pads are placed over my eyes and secured in place by masking tape. I can see nothing at all. A plug is inserted into a socket and I hear an electric motor start.

'We give you haircut. Hair very long.'

Although I would like a haircut, I deeply resent this violation. I dig in my heels.

'I don't want a haircut.'

'Chef say you have haircut.'

The electric clippers are applied to my beard and, eventually, to my head.

'Please don't make it so short.'

'Good. Haircut good.'

They finish, clean up and leave the room. My face and head feel cold now that the growth of many months has disappeared. I imagine that I now look like everyone's stereotype of a prisoner: shaven head, rough beard, ragged clothes and a chain.

'How long do you wish to stay here, Mr Waite?'

The questioner looked as though he had stepped from the cast of a black-and-white film *circa* 1940. His short hair seemed glued to his scalp, his upper lip sported a neatly clipped moustache. Immaculate white shorts, long woollen stockings and sturdy brogues completed the picture. Several pens were neatly positioned in the breast pocket of his crisply laundered shirt.

'Ten days, please.'

He thumbed through my passport, found my photograph and looked up. His eyes betrayed nothing apart from detachment.

'You have been to South Africa before.'

That could have been either a question or a statement. I took it as the former.

'Briefly.'

My passport was stamped and handed back. The official gave me one final impersonal glance and held out his hand for the documents of the next person in line. I took the airport bus into Johannesburg.

A bell rang from a nearby church, reminding me that it was Sunday morning. The city was almost deserted. An elderly African wearing a woollen cap and wrapped in a multicoloured blanket sat in a shop doorway. A sudden gust of wind blew down the empty street, catching an old newspaper and sending it momentarily soaring before it came to rest in a pool of water. Solly's Liquor Store was barred like a fortress. A tall thin white, wearing a trilby and carrying a plastic bag, looked longingly in the window, then walked away, his ill-fitting shoes revealing that he had no socks.

In the railway station, several more poor whites sat on a bench. I checked the timetable. The train to the Orange Free State didn't depart until evening. I wandered out into the street again. If this had been a Latin city, it would have been bustling with life; instead, the dead hand of dogmatic Calvinism held it in a grip of iron. A police van with a square cage-like structure on the back rumbled past. It was manned by two black policemen. I tried to imagine what it would be like to be poor and homeless in this city. Worst of all what it would be like to be poor, black and homeless.

I found my way to Rosetta, the headquarters of the Community of the Resurrection in Johannesburg. It was a simple house, with a school for Africans attached. I was given a cheerful welcome.

'Are you able to have a mixed community life?' I asked.

The priest looked at me and smiled.

'Our black priests can stay here if they are registered as servants. We are all servants, so what does it matter?'

We drove out of the city towards Soweto.

'You really ought to have a permit to enter this township, but I don't think we will be stopped.'

We entered Soweto without question. The burnt-out shells of several cars stood rusting on a strip of open land.

'Visitors to South Africa hardly ever get to the townships. They step off the boat, visit the parks and vineyards and never see the conditions the majority of the population live in. You might say that this housing is not too bad. Much of it isn't. That's not the point. It's the loss of liberty. The attempt to rob men and women of their dignity and freedom. This country can't continue like this. It must change one way or another. I wish I could see some way of avoiding violence.'

The priest sighed and put the car in gear. We drove back into town. Each morning thousands of black South Africans trekked along this route to their places of employment. Each night they returned to their separate existence.

I bought a ticket for Welkom and booked a sleeping compartment. The milk train, like its counterparts the world over, was slow and noisy. Dawn was breaking as we pulled into the station in the Orange Free State. I had hardly slept.

The mining hospital for black workers was a showpiece. A small group from the Medical Mission Sisters worked here. One was the Matron, another the Senior Tutor.

'We frequently get criticised for continuing to stay in South Africa.'

The Matron, a kindly native of the Netherlands, poured me a cup of tea.

'It's difficult to know what to do at times. We believe that we do more good by staying than by returning home. The nurses are all male. They are very good nurses indeed. We attempt to give them the best possible education.'

After breakfast I went on a tour of the hospital with the medical director, a good-natured former rugby player.

'We get a lot of mining injuries. We are very keen on accident prevention. At one time many miners suffered from heatstroke until we improved underground ventilation. The company does listen when I make suggestions.'

We donned overalls, helmets and boots and made our way over to the mine-shaft.

'This is one of the deepest gold mines in South Africa. Let's go down.'

We entered a segregated cage with an upper and lower compartment. The Medical Officer laughed.

'An unpopular white foreman was descending in the lower section one day. The blacks standing above him peed on him all the way down!'

I assume that this apocryphal story is told to visitors in mines all over South Africa.

We rode on a small train and then walked for a distance. It was very hot. Large canvas pipes carrying air lined the tunnel.

'If a man collapses with heat exhaustion, as sometimes happens, his colleagues cool him down with these pipes before bringing him to the surface.'

He handed me a sample of ore.

'Not very impressive, is it? But it pays a lot of wages. The blacks are well paid. Not as much as the whites, of course, but they are well paid.'

The African workers sweated in their subterranean oven. When work was over, most of them would return to their single existence in the mining hostels. Family life was a luxury few enjoyed. We returned to the surface, and I went back to the house. The Sister Tutor was waiting.

'You might like to have an informal session with the nurses. I'll arrange it for tomorrow.'

The male nurses who assembled in the hospital for the meeting were a highly intelligent group. I had been told that they would be cautious in what they said: first, because they didn't know me; second, because they had become accustomed to informers. The old trick of compromising a black worker and then getting him to report on his companions was believed to be widespread. I decided to begin by speaking about Africa, the Africa they had never seen. I spoke of Uganda and the Sudan. I detailed the various problems that faced Africans in black Africa. They were passionately interested, and we met for a further session the following day. Back in the community I discussed the experience.

'Many of that group could easily qualify as doctors,' said the Matron. 'The sadness is, there are no opportunities, but we can help them to be the best possible nurses.'

I had little doubt that that was being done.

Driving from Welkom to Bloemfontein and onwards to Lesotho, I began to get the feel of southern Africa. I crossed mile after mile of open farmland broken by small villages, the townships cleverly placed so as not to offend the sensibilities of passers-by. Although the Free State is not considered one of the most scenic parts of the Republic, it has a beauty all its own. A visitor coming from London or New York could not fail to be impressed by the fact that it is possible to see from horizon to horizon without interruption. I crossed the river and the railway and entered Maseru, the capital.

Apart from a desire to visit the country, I wanted to meet the Anglican Bishop of Lesotho, Desmond Tutu. I found him and his wife, Leah, at their home in the small city. My recollection of our first discussion has long since gone from memory, but I vividly remember Desmond's vital personality and remarkable mixture of humour, compassion and intelligence. Underpinning all his actions is a natural spirituality. Even on a first meeting it was not difficult to see how this impish man could sting politicians with the incisiveness of his ministry. Later, as I got to know him better, I realised just how much the battle for justice had cost him, and how his faith had sustained him when he was under attack from all sides. Once when I stayed with him in South Africa, I could not comprehend how he withstood the pressures on him and his family. He was kept under constant surveillance; his character was attacked; in 1982, he and the South African Council of Churches were subjected to an official government inquiry conducted by Justice C. F. Eloff. Throughout he maintained a simple faith coupled with a certain knowledge that he was fighting for truth and justice.

As I sit against the wall of my prison wrapped in a blanket, my mind is full of my friend Desmond. His actions and faith, which I have seen at first hand, help me now. I take comfort in the fact that he has had to withstand so much more than I have, and has shown me how it is possible to live through suffering. I need to be able to look back on people I have known, people who, unknown to themselves, have given me so much. I say a small prayer of gratitude.

Before leaving South Africa, I visited Swaziland and Botswana. David and Jinny Burney, friends from the theological college in Uganda, had moved to Botswana, and they were able to brief me on the country. In Swaziland, I had meetings with the Medical Mission Sisters, and it was there that I first experienced the loneliness of my work with the Roman Catholic Church. The Sister Doctor in the community was an outstanding woman. Although advanced in years, she worked at a pace that astonished everyone. Apart from performing routine surgery in the small hospital (she was acknowledged as being able to perform a hysterectomy in record time), she acted as police surgeon and was regularly called upon to perform post mortems. Like so many of her Dutch compatriots, she concealed a great warmth and concern under a somewhat tough exterior. When visiting the MMS I attended their chapel services but normally did not communicate. On this occasion, since there was no Anglican church near by, the Sister suggested I should take Communion along with the others. When I went up to the altar to receive, the priest (an Englishman) passed me by. At first I felt foolish and regretted going forward, but later I realised that I was merely facing reality. Our Churches were divided. Naturally, the Sister was furious and made her views known, but the priest responded that he was following the rules. So he was. I resolved not to put myself, or any other person, in such a position again.

Before leaving Swaziland I was taken to visit the recruiting camps where mineworkers were interviewed and assigned to various locations in the Republic. Care was taken to give each mine a thorough 'mix' of workers, to make it difficult for them to take concerted action against the system. Apartheid was thorough and ruthless at every level.

*

Dr Harry Smythe, an Australian priest, was director of the Anglican Centre in Rome, and I kept in occasional touch with him. The aims of the Centre included providing facilities for students who were studying Anglicanism and promoting inter-Church dialogue. Harry invited me to lecture at the Centre from time to time, and it was while I was speaking to a study group there that I first met a quiet clergyman from the diocese of Durham, Dr George Carey. Students at the Centre were accommodated in various religious houses in Rome including the Casa di Clero, which had been converted to provide permanent accommodation for foreign priests working in the Vatican and temporary housing for visitors. Several of my Anglican friends from Uganda stayed at the Casa. I was there visiting Misaeri Kauma, then an assistant bishop, later Bishop of Namirembe, when we received shocking news.

Misaeri, a few other Ugandans and I were discussing the situation in the country: Erica Sabiti had retired, and Janani Luwum had been elected to succeed him as Archbishop; most institutions were in turmoil; the Asian community was being victimised; murder and brutality were on the increase. The Churches were doing their best in difficult circumstances, and their leaders had suffered greatly. Misaeri mentioned friends who had been killed or were missing, but despite the sad picture he painted, he displayed amazing courage and optimism. As we were talking, the telephone rang. He picked it up and began to speak in Luganda. When he put the phone down, his face was stark.

'Janani is missing. No one is sure what has happened, but they think Amin has had him arrested.'

Naturally, and quite spontaneously, the Ugandans bowed their heads and prayed for their friend and archbishop. Janani, a schoolfriend of Milton Obote, had been under constant suspicion, but he refused to be intimidated and had continued to speak out against the terrible happenings in the country.

A little later, there was another phone message. Janani was believed to be dead. Killed, they said, in a car accident. No one in the room accepted that explanation. They knew that he had joined the long list of Ugandan martyrs.

The noise of fighting has been particularly bad during these past few weeks. Hour after hour the air is filled with the sound of exploding shells and machine-gun fire. Normally I can sleep through it, but lately I have been lying awake in the night. To be deprived of sleep upsets me. Sleep is a refuge. In sleep I am no longer chained. I am free to walk and fly, to laugh, to sing. Now these freedoms have gone. I doze for a moment, then consciousness rushes back as an explosion shakes the building. My guards are also awake; they chatter outside the door, make tea, cook themselves a snack. If I fall asleep during the day, I am disturbed by further explosions and anxious guards who rush into the room and order me to sit up.

I have a most painful earache. A few days ago I made myself a pair of earplugs from tissue paper. At night I pushed the tissue into my ears and lay down. The plugs were uncomfortable and ineffective, but I kept them in. In the morning, after yet another disturbed night, I removed them and decided not to use them again. Now I am deaf in one ear and experience a deep throbbing pain which makes me feel sick and dizzy. I asked the guard for a little olive oil, which I poured into my ear, but that seems to have made it worse. I am afraid of sickness. I am managing to tolerate the isolation and boredom of captivity, but to have to bear physical illness without medicine scares me. I have tried so hard to keep well. Each day I exercise. My teeth hurt but the pain is bearable. Now my head throbs and throbs. There is nothing I can do. I imagine that a small piece of the tissue has become detached and is lodged deep inside my ear. I take a matchstick and try to shift it but succeed in removing only a fragment. The pain continues. What if I lose my hearing? This is how the elderly must feel as they gradually lose their faculties, but at least they have access to medical help. Then I remember the millions who don't.

Suddenly the pain in my ear transports me back to Africa. I am walking through the steep streets of Addis Ababa. The air is thin and cool. Tiny Fiat taxis hurtle along, hardly causing a stir among the fiercely independent Ethiopians. I enter the huge covered market, unlike any other market I have seen. A stall displays Ethiopian crosses made of wood, brass or silver. A small cross, intended to be worn around the neck, is shaped like a spoon at the base. When I ask what it means, the stallkeeper demonstrates how it can be used to remove wax from the ear! If only I had it now.

Another stall is full of paintings and icons painted on wooden panels. The canvases portray an Ethiopian feast where diners are gorging themselves on raw meat. I am reminded of James Bruce, the Scottish explorer, who saw several Ethiopians steal up to a grazing cow, secure it, and then and there remove a steak from its hind-quarter. After this gruesome operation, the hide was put back in place, and the cow, albeit painfully, continued to graze. Bruce recorded this bizarre event in his published journals and was laughed at by his readers.

I leave the market and walk around the outside of the Royal Palace. Lions are reputed to roam unchained within the grounds. Outside a church an aged priest lectures a group of boys. This country is strangely different from the other parts of Africa I have visited. The language, appearance and behaviour of the people speak of another continent, of a history where Solomon and Sheba continue to be remembered and portrayed in folk art.

I am met by members of the Medical Mission Sisters and driven along a rough track to a small brick building some sixty miles from the capital. It was formerly a college attached to a church; now it has been taken over by the Sisters and provides the only medical services in the region. The Sisters tell me of a recent cholera epidemic when they were justifiably proud of not losing a single patient. Night and day they administered intravenous fluids until the battle was won, and the disease abated.

'One day a mother brought her baby to the clinic.' A Sister demonstrates with her hands the fragile size of the infant. 'It was anaemic and emaciated. We couldn't understand what was wrong until we looked into its mouth. There at the back of the throat was a leech. The mother had obviously been giving the child river-water to drink.'

Such stories were legion. I had never seen so many flies before. They swarmed across the faces of the local people, who appeared quite unconcerned. Wisely, the Sisters were developing a public-health programme while providing simple emergency care at the base. They were attempting to keep hospital services to a minimum, but were under considerable pressure to expand. Expansion would necessitate more money being spent on hospital staff and curtail the development of preventive work. They were obliged to steel themselves to make difficult decisions.

My guard has entered the room with the evening meal: a piece of bread, a spoonful of jam, and a small slab of cheese. He pours tea into my plastic beaker.

'You want anything?'

'I have a bad ear.'

'I tell Chef.'

'When will you see Chef?'

'I don't know.'

He leaves the room. The key turns in the lock. I eat my solitary supper. Outside the noise continues. I lie down, close my eyes and do my best to endure the pain.

Today I feel terrible. My head continues to throb, and I am feverish. This morning I suddenly lost my balance and fell over in the bathroom. The door opened a crack, and I heard the familiar threatening whisper of the guard.

'No noise. Quick, quick.'

Back in my room I curse my stupidity. I am responsible for this latest problem. I pushed the wretched paper into my ear; I have only myself to blame.

'You silly fool, Waite.'

Another side of me speaks within: 'Stop. Be gentle. Don't be so angry. Don't make life harder for yourself.'

That's exactly what I have done. If I had had a little more patience, a little more tolerance, I would be well now.

Self-pity edges nearer, carrying the empty promise of comfort. I am so terribly lonely. It seems as though I haven't seen anyone for years. I don't know where I am. I feel ill, lost and desolate. I challenge myself:

'Are these new feelings?'

'No.'

'You've experienced them before?'

'Many times.'

'When?'

'In Africa, in Rome, on my travels.'

'What worries you?'

'My insecurity, vulnerability, childish desire for acceptance.'

'What else?'

'Everything, every bloody thing. The inner turmoil, the lack of real peace, the constant struggle to find meaning; the knowledge that inwardly I am a child still craving approval and acceptance. I have no centre, I am hurting myself. If I don't leave here soon, I will go mad, dissolve in pieces. They will attack me from without, and I will destroy myself within. Isn't that enough to cause me to worry?'

'Can't you pray?'

'What the hell is prayer? Nothing more than a way of attempting to soothe myself by believing everything is fine. "God is in control. Don't worry, old boy, He is at hand. Pray and trust, trust and pray." You tell me to pray while I am drowning? You tell me to pray while my head feels as though it will explode? How dare you tell me to pray?'

'You are a child. Your prayers are the prayers of a child. Your faith is nothing more than superstition. Your love is self-love. You had better grow up.'

I lie shivering in my corner. I touch my ear and press from the outside, hoping to dislodge the blockage. My forehead runs with sweat, my scalp is damp.

Outside I hear the mechanical tones of prayer from the mosque: 'God is great. God is great.' A darkness descends over me. I want to die.

It was late evening. The sea lapped gently against the deserted quay. Earlier in the afternoon there had been a gun battle not two hundred yards from the hospital I was visiting. The Filipino Army had opened fire on a small boat, which they believed was carrying arms for the Muslim rebels or freedom fighters. I was spending time in the extreme south of the Philippines where a group of Catholic priests and Medical Mission Sisters provided the only social and medical facilities for the scattered population. Guerrilla warfare had been the norm in this region for years. Most of the population had moved farther north to escape the constant skirmishes. Now, when all was quiet, mosquitoes appeared in their hundreds: 'Nature's guerrillas', as one priest described them.

The small island hospital was empty; the last patient had been evacuated that afternoon, and only a handful of medical staff and a few clergy remained behind. Suddenly, my companion looked up.

'Do you hear anything?'

I listened. Apart from the stirring of the palm leaves and the gentle rhythm of the ocean, I heard nothing.

'There it is again.'

This time I heard it, the squeak of an oar moving in a rowlock. We strained our eyes. A small light flashed on the wooden jetty. There was whispering, the sound of footsteps. A group of men approached. They carried a home-made stretcher on which lay an elderly man. They stopped, and one of them stepped forward. He addressed the Sister who knelt by the side of the patient. She lifted a blanket and revealed an arm, black and swollen like a misshapen tuber. She turned to me.

'It's not good. He has been badly infected by some form of sea urchin. They have been travelling for twenty-four hours to get here.'

The fishermen carried their friend indoors. In a few moments the Sister returned.

'It's gangrenous. I shall have to amputate. I shall need your help.'

I scrubbed my hands and donned a gown and rubber gloves. The patient lay motionless on the table.

'It's really very easy. The trick is to leave enough flesh so that it can be sewn over the bone. I'll do the difficult bits. If you would do the sawing, I would be grateful.'

The tiny Filipino doctor began to work. I picked up a saw and did my part. She neatly stitched the wound. A couple of days later we went to see the old man, the sole patient in the small hospital ward. He smiled, and mumbled something in his own language. The Sister turned to me and laughed.

'What does he say?' I asked.

'He says, thank God the white doctor was here from England!'

My unseen companion has gone. No longer do I hear footsteps each morning. No longer the muted knock on the door when he has finished in the bathroom. He has gone, and I am totally alone. Late in the night I heard whispering outside my door. A candle flickered; several pairs of feet shuffled down the hallway. A door opened and I heard the noise of a chair being moved, the unmistakable sound of masking tape being torn, a whisper, another door opening, then silence. I lay still, my eyes staring into the darkness. Perhaps they have released him. Perhaps he is now on the way to his family. Who could he have been? I tried so hard to communicate with him. When I used the bathroom first, I would mark my initials on the cake of soap. On days when I followed him, I checked to see if he had left any sign for me, but I never found anything. After a while I abandoned these attempts and accepted the fact that we would not be able to reach each other. Now he has gone, and I miss him. I shudder when I consider that they may move me next. The thought of a move to another place fills me with anxiety. The only move I want is to be set free. Today I was given some drops for my ear, but it is still terribly painful. Along with the medicine were plastic sticks tipped with cotton wool. The inside of my ear is too inflamed to use them, but they might be useful later. I have been promised more antibiotics.

The shelling is lighter for the moment. Pain rather than gunfire keeps me awake during the nights now. The guard outside the door snores contentedly, rises at daybreak to chant his prayers, and returns to his slumbers.

I continue to repeat my request for books. As the Mills & Boon volume was not quite to my taste, I asked the guard to look out for Penguin Books.

'Penguin, what is Penguin?'

'You have a pencil?'

He put a ballpoint pen in my hand. I looked under my blindfold and drew a penguin as I remembered it being reproduced on the front cover of those familiar volumes. I wrote PENGUIN in capital letters. I thought of suggesting Pelican Books also, but I didn't want to complicate matters. Besides, I couldn't draw a pelican.

'Penguin Books are very famous,' I said. 'Very good books. Please try.'

'OK, my friend will look.'

Today he entered the room.

'Tek.'

I held out my hand and received a book. Glancing down, I could see it was a Penguin Book, a novel by P. G. Wodehouse. A wave of pleasure swept over me.

'Thank you, thank you very very much.' I was overeffusive in my gratitude. 'This is a Penguin Book, a very good book, thank you.'

I could sense that he too was pleased.

'Read slowly, we not have many books.'

'I will try.'

It was a slim volume that could be read in a matter of hours. This made me reluctant to begin. I read the book cover, counted the number of words, read details of other books advertised at the back, and finally started the first chapter. Today, I was certainly one of Allen Lane's most grateful beneficiaries.

My guard won't disclose how many books they have. All he will say is: 'Read slow.' I read the Wodehouse very slowly, but still the book was finished in no time at all. I enjoyed it, and for a while it enabled

me to escape from introspection and the bleakness of my surroundings. If I could choose, I would ask for more substantial books, but,
of course, I have no freedom in the matter. Today I handed the
book back and was pleased to receive another Penguin. This time
it's a collection of short stories by Somerset Maugham. I am reading
his perceptive accounts of colonial life in Malaysia. His writings
bring back a flood of memories. We lived in Africa at the very end
of the colonial era and so were able to appreciate what it must have
been like. Maugham portrays so clearly an age which has gone for
ever, but he reminds me that my life is slipping by. One day passes,
and another; I follow the same routine, broken only by upsurges in
the fighting and the constant nagging pain in my ear. I have been
given what I assume is an antibiotic, but it has yet to take effect.

In an attempt to extend the life of my book I put it down for a
while and sit quietly. In recent days I have been full of anger, pain and
frustration. Wodehouse and Maugham have succeeded in tempering
these feelings. It must be an inevitable part of the inner journey,
which I have spoken about so glibly. If I succeed in finding my own
centre, will I find stillness? And if I find stillness, will any creativity
I have be extinguished? That would be disastrous; I have so little
creativity to start with.

What did I mean when I said I wanted to die? I think it was a
very simple desire to escape from misery and discomfort. Could it
be something deeper? Could it be that deep inside me there is a
death wish? One of the alarming features of these days is that while
I have known in theory that I, in common with all human beings,
am a mixture of opposites, I realise I must now confront them in all
their power: love matched against hate, calm against turmoil, faith
against disbelief. I feel the power of these forces and recognise my
ignorance. It's as though I am blindfolded within as well as without.
I stumble along a pathway with little or nothing to guide me. An
individual with greater faith than I have would remind me that a
Bible is at my elbow and contains all the help I need. It's too easy
for me to tell myself that. I am somehow obliged to struggle through
the darkness and not allow myself comfort unless it is rooted in inner
experience. I cannot take faith, contentment, peace or love cheaply.
I desire them so much, have so often in the past sought them outside
myself. Now I have no option. It's as if I am passing through a very
narrow gateway, completely naked, totally alone.

16

THE ANTIBIOTICS HAVE succeeded in fighting the infection in my ear, and it has stopped discharging. This morning I was able to remove a piece of tissue paper with one of the plastic probes. Now I can hear properly again. The inner turmoil of the last few days has also subsided. Altogether, I feel much better and ready to face the future a little more cheerfully. In many respects it's a good thing that I am alone here; I would hate to inflict my depression on others. I remember reading somewhere that the first three years of solitary confinement are the 'make or break' years. There is still a long way to go, but this morning I feel as though I will be able to get through it if I am kept that long. I continue to hope for release and still look for signs. I imagined that the removal of my unknown companion might be a sign that I was also due to be set free, but obviously it was not. It's probably better not to worry too much about release. What I need to do is accept the moment for what it is.

I have been searching my memory for the books that have left their mark on me over the years. I remember Augustine in *The Confessions* struggling with the concept of time, and I try to recollect his whole argument. How marvellous it would be to have works of philosophy and theology with me now. At home my shelves are filled with books read, reread, half-read and not yet read. My present thoughts are disjointed, and I flit from subject to subject like a butterfly. The best I can do for the moment is to continue my autobiographical journey and return once again to Africa.

My first visit to West Africa was to Ghana. The Medical Mission Sisters had started work in a remote region of the country, virtually without services of any kind. The pattern seen the world over was repeated here. From a very small beginning the hospital had developed into one of the finest in the country. Nurses and pharmacists were in training. A Sister surgeon was able to cope with virtually any procedure. In many respects, the hospital was an effective subculture within the country. But the same questions applied here as elsewhere. Was it possible to maintain it at its present level when overseas staff would not be forthcoming in the future? If it was handed over to the Ghanaians, who would take responsibility for it? Lay doctors could not possibly have the same commitment as Sister doctors, nor would they have access to the overseas resources which helped support the hospital. To maintain the hospital at the level of excellence at which it was currently operating would require either a long-term commitment of personnel by the community, which it was hardly in a position to give, or a massive change in the country as a whole. One of the very few certainties in the situation was that there were no quick and easy answers.

Over the years, I visited Ghana many times to help with these questions. Co-ordination between the various health units in the region was developed. Rural pharmacies were established where, under strict control, simple drugs and medicines could be produced. The management structure of the hospital was changed to make it possible for local people to have an increased responsibility for their own hospitals and medical centres. Progress was not spectacular, but progress was made.

In Ghana, I developed a tremendous admiration for the lay volunteers who worked there, under very difficult circumstances. Some would stay for a year or so and then return to their country of origin. Occasionally, an individual would become so close to the Ghanaians that he or she would make the same commitment as the Medical Mission Sisters and stay permanently. Dr Ineka Bosman was one such person. After practising in Holland she came to Ghana and decided to give the rest of her life to medical work in the country. I remember seeing her sitting at a table in the shade dealing with two or three hundred outpatients, after which she would do hospital rounds, followed by routine or emergency surgery. A young doctor in Ghana had to learn the whole range of medical practice very quickly indeed.

On another visit to West Africa, I took local transport and went to the edge of the Sahara desert. Had I had the time I would have loved to travel across this wild open space. As I stood by the side of a rough track, gazing over the sand, I thought I saw a figure approaching on a bicycle. I had seen mirages in Africa before, but not quite like this. I waited, and, sure enough, it was a bicycle ridden by a European.

'Hello,' he said cheerfully. 'Can you direct me to the coast?'

He was unmistakably English.

'Well,' I said, 'you're on the beach, but you've a long way to go!'

In fact there was only one way forward, and that was along the track he was already following. It turned out that he had crossed the desert, at times with his bicycle on a lorry, at times riding. He was sending articles to a journal in England to help pay for his trip. We said farewell, and he pedalled off in what we believed was the direction of the coast. He made me glad to be English.

My ear has cleared at last. The doubt and despair I have recently been battling with has exhausted me, but I am through that for the moment. I remember now what Augustine said: 'I am divided between time gone by and time to come, and its course is a mystery to me.' He recognised that his thoughts and the life of his soul were disrupted by the havoc of change. He held on to the love of God. That is all I can do. I must hold fast to love. Looking back on my life once more, I evoke people who have inspired and helped me, often unknown to themselves. In Rome I got to know the then Superior of the Christian Brothers, Brother Charles Henry. Known as the La Salle Brothers, the Order ran schools throughout the world. It was a marvel to me that this very busy man could always make time for people. He understood the isolation of my position in Rome, and he went out of his way to support and assist me. Brother Vincent was another such person. The world is full of saints, individuals whose names are rarely, if ever, mentioned in the media, but who are truly the salt of the earth. Now, as I remember them, they bring me comfort. I recognise that I am in danger of swinging too violently in my emotions and must try to maintain a balance. Today my guard came in and sat with me for a little while.

'You good?'

'I am better, thank you.'

He took my hand and shook it. He is not without compassion.

'You want anything?'

This must be the most frequently-asked question of all. It means very little; perhaps it is a way of trying to be kind.

'I would like another book, please.'

'Tomorrow. Would you like TV? Chef says you can have TV.'

'Thank you.'

'No problem. Chef says no news, understand?'

'No.'

'You not see news on TV.'

'Why can't I watch the news?'

'I don't know. Tonight I bring TV.'

He asks me once again if I want anything and then leaves. Strangely enough, I am not overly excited by the prospect of television, especially television without news. Half the time it will be unworkable because of constant electrical failure, also many programmes will probably be in Arabic, but at least it will be a diversion. I would have preferred a plentiful supply of books, but now I am being churlish. Television is better than nothing.

This evening he comes into the room carrying a small white portable TV. He plugs it in and switches it on.

'No touch.'

'OK.'

He leaves the room. The screen flickers in the gloom. I gaze intently at some of the first human beings I have seen for two years. A man in a suit is talking with another man in a suit. Their conversation is in Arabic. I watch every gesture, observe every movement in a vain attempt to follow what they are saying. It is hopeless. Apart from an occasional word, the conversation is meaningless. After half an hour or so, the programme fades, and an announcer says that in a few moments the news in English will be broadcast. At this very moment the door opens. I hastily arrange my blindfold and hear the set being carried out.

This is terrible. To be so near to hearing something of the outside world and to be denied it is one more form of torture. A part of me wanted to tell the guard not to bring the TV back until I could watch the news. Another part urged patience. I chose the latter course, and when he returned with the set later, I said nothing.

The television set is brought to my room every evening now. At the exact moment the news is about to be broadcast, the door bursts open, a guard enters, and the set is removed. As the days go by, I feel increasingly angry and frustrated. I appreciate the fact that the guards are obeying orders. The reason they are able to keep hostages for so long is that they belong to a structure with an iron discipline, but why won't they let me hear anything about the world outside? I am desperate for news of my family and friends, and what is happening in Beirut. Day and night I hear the sound of shelling, but I have no knowledge at all of what is taking place. Slowly, I think of a way to get access to news. The first step is to reach the controls of the television set. It is near enough for me to touch, but I am under strict orders not to do so.

After a week or so, just before the news comes on and the guard enters, I lean across and switch the set off. The guard comes into the room, removes the set and makes no comment. Every night, I repeat this until he is accustomed to my behaviour. One night he enters, sees that I have switched the set off and closes the door, leaving the TV in the room. I sit quietly, my back against the wall. After a few moments the door is flung open. The set is off; he closes the door. This ludicrous performance is repeated for two or three weeks. Gradually his behaviour changes. Now he only makes sure that I have switched the set off. The spot checks become more and more infrequent.

I let another week pass, then decide to put my plan into action. If I turn the brightness down, it looks as if the set is switched off. If I turn the volume right down and put my ear to the loudspeaker on the side of the set, I can just manage to hear the broadcast. The trick is to have one hand on the ON/OFF switch, my ear to the loudspeaker, and my eyes fixed firmly on the crack beneath the door. Gingerly, I perform this contortion. For the first time I hear news; the local news in English. The woman announcer tells of meetings conducted by officials of the Lebanese government. She simply says that 'A' met 'B', and they exchanged views, but gives no details whatever. I see a shadow beneath the door. With a speed that surprises me I turn the set off and snap into a sitting position just as the door crashes open. Silence. It closes again. There is no sense tempting fate, so the set now remains off.

I continue this pattern for weeks. The tension is awful, and I wonder if the scraps of information I get are worth the emotional energy expended. There is another consideration, which I try to dismiss from my mind but it won't go away. I hate the deception involved in these manoeuvres. If I want to listen, I have to lie to my guards, and I honestly don't want to do that. My personal integrity is all I have, and in this place it means everything to me. I can't claim, nor do I, to be an example to anyone. My past is full of failings, but here I must live as near as I can to the truth. I am almost obsessed by this desire and increasingly worried about my behaviour. Of course, I twist things.

'You not watch news?'

'No.'

True, I didn't watch the news, but I feel that these small deceptions will eat away at my inner being in ways that will damage me. And although I don't want to lie to these men, my desire to listen to the news remains as strong as ever, even though I get nothing but scraps. I have now found that by moving the tuner to the end of the band, I can receive a pop radio station with English announcements. To my disgust they never give an item of news, not a squeak. There ought to be a law stipulating that all stations give at least the headlines!

Despite my misgivings, I continue to listen surreptitiously. Often, just as the English news is starting, the electricity fails. Why, oh why, when the light has been burning all afternoon must it go out at one minute to six o'clock? Once I heard a headline about hostages. Just before the item was broadcast, there was a power cut. One night a new guard came on duty. Immediately before six he came into the room and removed the plug from the socket. When he left, I replaced it and prepared to listen as usual. I had heard hardly a sentence when I saw feet outside the door. I yanked the cable out of the wall and was sitting bolt upright when the guard entered the room.

'What you do?'

'Nothing.'

'What you do?' he repeated menacingly.

'Nothing.'

He took the set and placed it on the far side of the room. The door closed.

For the next week or two I resisted the temptation to listen. The set was returned to me, and I kept it off during the news period. Finally I could hold out no longer. One evening, when all seemed quiet, I tried the old trick. A moment passed, and I saw the ominous feet outside. I snapped to attention. The door burst open.

'What you do?'

'Nothing.' I hated the petty lie.

'We know you lie. Look.'

He held something so I could see it under my blindfold. It was a transmitter microphone.

'We put in room. We hear everything.'

Although the room is virtually bare, it would be possible to hide such a small device.

'What you say?'

I remained silent.

'We tell Chef. Big trouble for you.'

The set was taken away. The door closed. Damn! The news I had caught was barely worth hearing. That wasn't my problem; I was angry at my own deception and sorry at the same time that I would no longer be able to watch the Saturday evening programme of Arabic music and dancing. As for trouble, I was in enough trouble as it was; I didn't see how it could be increased. I made up my mind to have nothing more to do with TV until they allowed me to watch everything, including the news. Even if they begged me to take it back, I wouldn't.

In a short, perceptive article written years ago, Graham Greene wrote that any journey is like a form of dreaming. The past is felt like a pain, and travel is an attempt to express the pain in harmless images. Greene quotes a novelist who, speaking about Africa, said that the interior signified not only the heart of the continent, but the heart of the mystery leading to comprehension of self in space and time. That could be why I constantly return there and remember my travels.

They have not been the travels of a spectator. I have been drawn in to witness and experience the life of the people. Images there have been: the Pyramids, the Nile, the rock churches, but I have pressed beyond these to experience the soul of the country. I have not found travel a palliative. It has deepened my feeling for the human condition and increased my pain.

I can be angry now with my captors, but I can also weep for them. Like me, they struggle and stumble through life holding on desperately to religious symbols to give them meaning and direction. I do the same, but I have been forced to test the symbols; to experience their ambiguity, to struggle like a drowning man to give coherent meaning to life.

In Benares, I stood by the Ganges early one morning. The streets were crammed with the sick and dying, those who had come to spend their last days on the banks of the holy river before being burned and scattered to return to their elemental origins. Four men carrying a litter pass by. The corpse, covered by a linen sheet, rocks to and fro as they half-run, half-walk along the dusty track. A wild pig rummages in a pile of refuse. To my utter horror I see that it is eating the body of a dead child. I turn as a nauseous spasm grips my stomach. Children and holy men are not cremated; their bodies are thrown into the holy river. Questions I can't answer rush at me. All

I can do is stand and watch, and experience a profound agony of spirit.

Although the wrath of the Chef was threatened, nothing happened. After two or three weeks the guard sat with me for a conversation.

'You good?'

'Yes.'

'You like TV?'

'Can I watch the news?'

'Chef say no news.'

'I take TV when I can watch the news.'

'No news.'

'Why?'

'I don't know.'

'Then I prefer not to have TV.'

'TV good.'

'It's not good if I can't watch what I want to watch.'

'You not want TV?'

'No.'

'TV good – very good films.'

'No, thank you.'

'OK, no problem.'

He leaves the room. I sit quietly. I will not accept television on such ridiculous terms. It was enjoyable, in parts, in the past, but I can do without it. The door opens again. I hear something being dragged across the floor.

'No touch. Understand?'

I don't understand what I am not supposed to touch. As I am chained, and whatever it is is on the far side of the room, I don't stand much of a chance of touching it. However, I still get up to an hour of freedom from the chain each morning, and that would, I suppose, be my opportunity to discover what it is.

'Tek.' A book is put into my hand. 'You want anything?'

'No, thank you.'

The door closes. In the corner is a large cardboard box covered with a cloth. I stare at it like a dummy. Originally, the box housed a colour television manufactured in Taiwan. The guards are well looked after; they have TVs, video players, radios. I look at my book: *Busman's Honeymoon* by Dorothy L. Sayers. I am pleased. I love the writing of this witty, erudite woman. A novelist once said that a good writer of fiction needs to have respect for his or her characters. Dorothy Sayers went further; I suspect she was in love with her creation, Lord Peter Wimsey.

The difference between the warm, funny, descriptive writing of Dorothy Sayers and the cerebral style of Agatha Christie is marked. I have always found it difficult to appreciate the writing of the so-called queen of the detective novel. The fact that I made the mistake of choosing an Agatha Christie novel as an introduction to this genre put me off crime novels for years. Christie characters seem to have been cut from the back of a breakfast cereal packet. Sayers draws wonderful human caricatures. Now I can settle down and lose myself in a world created through words for the remainder of the day.

My morning routine rarely, if ever, changes. This morning, the covered cardboard box commands my attention. After taking me to the bathroom, the guard returns me to my room and locks the door, leaving me free to exercise. I start to walk round the room, my blindfold tied around my forehead like a sweatband. If the door is suddenly opened, as it often is, I can quickly pull the material down over my eyes. Each time I complete twelve paces I pass the box. After ten minutes or so the guard flings open the door. I adjust the blindfold and sit on the floor as I have been instructed. Most guards check at least once during the exercise period. The more intrusive and unpleasant check several times. This one stands in the doorway without speaking and, temporarily satisfied, closes the door. I resume walking.

The box continues to fascinate me. What can it contain? I stop in front of it and stare. I go on walking, then stop again. Gently, I lift a corner of the cloth covering the box. There might be another microphone in here so I must be extremely careful. A sound in the corridor outside my door makes me drop the material as though it were red hot. After making a few more circuits I stop and, holding my breath, lift the cloth. The box is full of books! I can see several of the old Penguin Crime series, distinctive in their green-and-white covers. There is a volume from the Penguin Classics series, Herodotus' *The Histories*. Wonderful, a dream come true! Then, to my utter amazement, I am sure I can see a book I first held in my hands several years ago in New York. It lies at the top of the box in a corner, a small white presentation Prayer Book. I quickly drop the cloth and resume walking. What good news! At last I will have books to read. There must be at least a hundred in the box, enough to last

for a few weeks. The Prayer Book intrigues me. Eventually, it might
be given to me, and then I will see if it is the one I know. When
the guard next opens the door, I am walking, full of happiness at the
thought of so many good things to come. He fastens the chain around
my ankle and snaps the padlock shut.

'You want anything?'

'I have finished *Busman's Honeymoon*.'

'No problem.'

I hear him cross the room, and rummage in the box. He puts a
book in my hands and utters the usual warning: 'Read slow.'

When I remove my blindfold, I almost leap with delight. It is
Dostoevsky, the first volume of *The Brothers Karamazov*. I hold it
before me rather as a child might gaze at a precious object. *The
Brothers Karamazov* translated by David Magarshack, published in
Penguin Classics – price seven shillings.

I am not at all conscious of the passing of time. The morning has
gone by, and I am lost in my book. Normally I read quickly, but
now I try my best to go at a slower pace. Lunch is brought into
the room, the usual rice and canned mixed vegetables. I eat and
immediately return to the book. In the middle of the afternoon I
hear someone enter the apartment. Then there is talking outside my
room. The key is turned. I arrange my blindfold.

'Hello, Mr Terry.'

I recognise the voice of the Little Chef.

'Hello.'

'You good, Mr Terry?'

'I am very happy to have a book.'

'We try to get books for you. You read too much.'

What can I reply to that? He seems in a good mood, so I decide
to see if I can get something else from him.

'There is something I want, please.'

'What you want?'

'I have a Bible. I read it each day.'

'Good. Bible very good.'

'I would be happy to have a Prayer Book.'

'What is Prayer Book?'

'It is like a Bible. It is a special book to say prayers to God.' Here
I slip in something which I hope will work: 'Often a Prayer Book
has a white cover.'

The guard says something in Arabic to the Little Chef. I hear him cross the room and rummage in the box. He returns and puts something in my hand.

'This good?'

I look at it under my blindfold. It is the Prayer Book.

'Yes, very good indeed. Thank you.'

'No problem. You want anything?'

'No, thank you. I am happy with books.'

'You want TV?'

'No, thank you.'

'OK. Goodbye, Mr Terry.'

Carefully, I opened the small presentation Prayer Book. I was right; I held this very book at 815 Second Avenue, New York, where I had gone to visit the new Presiding Bishop, Edmond Browning, before returning to Beirut to continue my efforts for the hostages. Samir Habiby suggested that Bishop Browning might care to sign the book for all the American hostages. He did so, and I carried it to Beirut where again I met my contact in Dr Mroueh's surgery. I remember our conversation.

'I would like you to give this Prayer Book to the hostages.'

He looked at me suspiciously and took the volume in his hand.

'What is it?'

I explained.

'What is this?' He pointed to the signature and message of greeting. I explained again. 'What are these? Is this a code?' He indicated the coloured markers attached to the binding.

'Of course not,' I said. 'They are bookmarks. I hope you will give this book to the hostages.'

He said nothing but took it away with him.

Now, years later, the book has come back to me. The spine is broken. The coloured markers have been ripped out. The page containing the signature is missing. There is a small scrap of paper in the Prayer section. It is blank. I look at the page and see the heading 'Prayers to be said during a time of sickness'. Silently, I close the book and put it beside my Bible.

As a child, the 'Golden Numbers' fascinated me. During the sermon, as I sat restlessly in the choirstalls, I would take hold of a Prayer Book and look at the numbers printed near the beginning: 'A Table to find Easter Day'. I could not imagine anyone ever using such a table when the date of Easter was so easily discovered in diaries or calendars. The battered Prayer Book I now have by my side contains the Golden Numbers, and forty years on from my days as a chorister, I use them. The Prayer Book is invaluable, a wonderful bonus. It helps to give a greater structure to my life. Now I can live the liturgical year. It can also be used as a calendar since it contains readings for each day. All I need do is get the correct date from the guard and make a small mark in the book.

I take it carefully in my hand, examine every page to see if the previous user has left any mark in it. Apart from the one blank bookmark placed so poignantly, I can find nothing. The fact that I now have the book could mean that Terry Anderson, Tom Sutherland or others have been released. I do hope so. I return to the Golden Numbers which enable me to find the date of Easter until the year 2099. That should see me out all right!

Now that I have books, I can find a little more balance to the day. I plan it. After exercise I will say my prayers, then I will meditate for a while. Afterwards I will allow myself time to read until lunchtime – that should give me four or five uninterrupted hours, providing I have light, of course. After lunch I will think about what I have read and then spend an hour or so on my own mental writing. Then I will say my evening prayers and perhaps do some further reading until it is time to sleep. It sounds good. If the books in the box are all of the quality of the Penguin Classics, life should be cheerful. Relatively speaking, of course!

I am approaching the end of *Karamazov*, volume one. During the last hour I have been lost in the Legend of the Grand Inquisitor and swept along by the passion and force of the writing. Freedom, authority, miracles, the very matters with which I struggle, are expressed so eloquently. I have read Dostoevsky in the past, but in captivity books appear to have a new power and force. The intensity with which they are read reveals depths which were previously hidden. I am gaining a deeper insight into my own being.

The questions of authority and freedom raised by Dostoevsky send me back in memory to Rome. During my years there, many of the religious communities were struggling to give expression to the heart of the message delivered by the Second Vatican Council. This brought several of them into direct conflict with the authorities in the Vatican and caused much distress. On one side was a desire to discover effective structures for religious life which would encourage the personal development of members and enable them to work constructively with the poor and the deprived of this world. On the other side, many in the Vatican feared that too much freedom would lead to the disintegration of religious life and thus, eventually, to an ineffective ministry for everyone. The Vatican kept a watchful eye on the communities, and many communities kept a watchful eye on the Vatican!

Although I worked so closely with the Roman Catholic Church and developed an affection and respect for many of its members, I was not tempted to change my allegiance to Rome. Seeing the Church at work in all parts of the world, as I did, enabled me to recognise the tremendous diversity of belief and practice within it. The framework, so long as members stayed within it, seemed to provide a haven I longed for, but in my heart I could not accept that form of security. I was, however, and continue to be, deeply impressed by the compassion and understanding of human nature which I discovered in the Roman Catholic Church. I could not agree with much of the social teaching, but I learnt at first hand that I was in company there with thousands of Roman Catholics.

For the final few years in Rome I had my office in the SEDOS building. SEDOS, a centre for study, documentation and research for religious communities, was presided over by my friend Brother Charles Henry. He, together with Brother Vincent, suggested that when the work with the Medical Mission Sisters was properly established I might consider working with other communities which were facing similar issues. I was interested and followed up the proposal. My focus changed somewhat, from health to education, but I kept in regular contact with Ghana and continued to visit it and assist in the development of a co-ordinated voluntary health sector. Meanwhile, time was passing. We had been in Italy more than six years. The children were growing rapidly, and their only knowledge of their home country was drawn from occasional visits to England during the holidays. I was tired; constant travel throughout the world was wearing and far from glamorous. I also knew that I didn't wish to remain an 'outsider' in the Roman Catholic Church for much longer. I valued my independence, but I was finding the loneliness of the position an increasing strain.

We were prompted to make a change by the chance remark of a friend. All my family were regular visitors to the Lion English Bookshop in Rome. During weekends we would browse through the stock, and Mark would be allowed to play with the cuckoo clock behind the proprietor's desk. The owner and his wife were an English couple who had lived in Italy for many years. They had two children, a year or so older than our daughters. One day, in casual conversation, the owner told me he had just received a nasty shock. His children, both of whom had gained a university place in England, would be subject to huge fees as they were designated non-residents. He didn't see how it would be possible for him to find the considerable sums required. Ruth and Clare were now approaching thirteen years of age. I had no intention of continuing in Rome indefinitely, and given the fact that we wanted the children to be settled and with an adequate opportunity to pursue further education if they wished to, we decided it was time to return to the United Kingdom.

Once we had reached a decision, we lost no time in making the necessary arrangements. I was committed to overseas projects for nine to twelve months ahead, but there was no reason why these could not be managed from London. As we had lived away from England for so long, we had no idea at all about the housing market. Frances and I went to London and trekked around, eventually finding a house we liked in Blackheath. We put in an offer, which was accepted, and I had to leave for a conference in the United States. While I was there, I received an urgent telephone call from Frances. We had been outbid. My conference extended over two or three weeks with a long weekend break, but it was vital that we find a place to live as quickly as possible. We had given notice on our flat in Rome, and time was rapidly running out. I contacted a friend who was a surveyor with the Church Army. He worked frantically on our behalf and produced a list of eighteen possible properties in south London. I flew home on a Friday evening, and on Saturday morning we went to see all that seemed to be suitable. Late on Saturday evening we made an offer for a Victorian house in Blackheath which was accepted, and I flew back to America totally exhausted.

The journey from Rome to London reminded me of our trek to Mombasa years before. We loaded the boot and roof rack of the Fiat until the car sank on its springs, and hitched our camping trailer, also loaded to overflowing, behind.

Once in London, Frances took the children to stay with my mother in Cheshire and I hired a large van which I immediately drove the thousand miles back to Rome. Friends helped me load it with our furniture and I set out for London again, the third such journey in ten days. In London there was just enough time to unpack everything before I rushed to Heathrow to catch the plane to India where I had another conference to conduct.

As I half expected, volume two of *The Brothers Karamazov* is missing. The guard sorted through the box and failed to find it. I haven't given up entirely; he knows so little English that he could easily have passed it by.

He shouted at me across the room, 'We not have.'

'No problem,' I replied, unconsciously adopting his own catch phrase. 'See if you can find me another big book.'

There was a further sound of searching, and a book of some considerable proportions was put into my hand.

'This good for you?'

The book was the same size and weight as our family Bible.

I said it was very good.

'You want anything?'

'No, thank you.'

'OK.'

He left the room and I removed my blindfold. Excitedly I looked at the title – *The Encyclopedia Americana*: *M to Mexico City*. When playing *Desert Island Discs* I had spent much time in considering the book I might take with me to an island and had often thought of requesting an encyclopedia. Now, having only the one volume, it was a puzzle to decide how to read it. Should I start from the first entry and work my way through? Should I trace themes? I studied the book carefully with my chipped magnifying glass and leafed through the pages. Ah! maps. A map of Maine; how wonderful. I identify places that I have visited. A memory of walking the Freedom Trail in Boston returns, then fades. I wander along the highways: Manchester, Portland, Bath, Belfast. If only the people who lived in these cities knew how intently they were being considered from a Beirut prison. I follow the coastline and swing inland. An hour must have passed, and I am still absorbed with a world beyond my place of confinement. I turn to the entry on Mathematics. Perhaps now I will be able to master this subject, which has fascinated me for years. Then I discover the limitations of having access to only a single volume. First, the entry assumes a greater knowledge of the subject than I possess. Second, it refers the reader to other volumes for definitions essential to comprehend the entry. What I need is the book that was in my briefcase when I was captured: *The Mathematical*

Experience by Davis and Hersh. That book was a pleasure to read, in sharp contrast to the entry before me. I decide to read the volume systematically, turn to the first page and concentrate on the history and development of the letter M.

Moving to London when we did meant that the children were able to start the new school year without interrupting their studies. In our spare time we set about decorating and doing the thousand-and-one things that are required in a house built in the 1880s. My father was an expert at do-it-yourself work. I am exactly the opposite. Laying floors, painting and doing minor items of woodwork was an agony to me. Laboriously, slowly, the house became more of a home, and we liked it. One of the first things we did was to make a family outing to a pet shop in south London and buy a springer spaniel. We named him Raq after Romany's dog – the naturalist whose books I used to read as a child.

The first year in London was full. I completed my engagements overseas and worked betweentimes on the house. We retrieved our furniture from the vicarage in Bristol and gradually settled in. I appreciated having my books together in one place for the first time in years. I did not want to take another job immediately. I felt that I needed time to adjust to life in England after so many years and to digest the experiences of those years, and also time for further study. Finance was a problem, but I hoped to be able to get some form of scholarship. I wasn't sure whether I wanted to continue in the full-time employ of the Church, but I had gained a considerable first-hand knowledge of the world and of development issues, and while I needed a sabbatical period, I was still as concerned as ever about such matters. When, to my surprise, I was approached by the British Council of Churches to ask if I could spare a few days each week to assist them on the Africa desk, I agreed without hesitation. I knew something about that continent, and I wanted to learn more about the state of the Church in the British Isles.

The Rev. Brian Duckworth, a Methodist minister responsible for the work of the department, was always so busy that I saw little of him, but when we did meet on my occasional visits to the office, I found him to be a warm and stimulating colleague. My task was to assemble material detailing the current situation in southern Africa. It was a routine desk job, and I did not consider my contribution to the survey to be of great significance. Others, like the Rev. Brian

Brown, who had lived in South Africa for years, had a far greater knowledge of the workings of apartheid than I. As I had hoped, however, I did begin to get to know the English Church once more during this period.

I met again the Secretary-General of the Anglican Consultative Council, Bishop John Howe, who had occupied that position when we went to Africa and been a friend and supporter across the years. Bishop Oliver Tomkins, now in the last years of his episcopate in Bristol, also discussed possibilities for the future with me. The question of offering myself for the ordained ministry of the Church fleetingly crossed my mind and departed as quickly as it had entered. I still did not believe that I had a vocation to the priesthood.

Several organisations within the Church made informal approaches to ask if I was interested in a senior position with them. I wasn't. In fact, I didn't know what I wanted to do other than to put to good use the experience I had gained during the past decade. It was at this time that I first heard of Robert Runcie.

As summer turns to winter again and I feel the chill of the cold in my bones, I read the encyclopedia from cover to cover and try not to think too much about my family and friends. As another Christmas approaches, Frances is very much in my mind. She is such a quiet, private person, totally committed to the family. Once I start to think about her I castigate myself for not having had more understanding. At times, living with me must have been like living with a madman. Always on the move, curious to see new countries, anxious to meet new people. Behind me stood Frances with an unshakeable loyalty and love. Despite my resolve, I begin to cry tears of self-pity and remorse. Crying at what I have made my family endure. I have to stop myself. If I continue to follow this line of thought, I will be dragged down into total despair.

How is it that we fail to appreciate love and loyalty when we have them? This experience as a hostage is rather like suffering a bereavement. I look back and berate myself for not having shown more love and care when there was an opportunity. What agony prisoners suffer. Torture is bad and can be destructive. Inner self-torture can be equally so. If I know Frances at all, she will bear this experience with the same stalwart determination that has enabled her to face the hectic life we lived. She will put her own feelings to one side and devote all her time and energy to caring for the children.

'Run rabbit, run rabbit, run, run, run.' Why have you been running so fast, Waite? Where to? From what? One thing seems clear. You're certainly not going to be able to run for a long time to come. Not, I suspect, for a long, long time.

17

ON ONE OCCASION, while visiting the Philippines, I was taken to an organ concert in a small parish church. The organ was unique. Constructed entirely from bamboo, it had been restored in Germany. Peter Hurford, formerly the organist at St Albans Abbey, had flown out from England to play at the concert to celebrate its safe return. I was reminded of this musical evening on the other side of the world as I stepped off the train in St Albans and walked out of the station. A small shop selling antique clocks caught my attention, and I lingered to admire the restored timepieces on display in the window. I wandered down the road and asked directions. I was on my way to meet the Bishop of St Albans, the Right Rev. Robert Runcie. His appointment as Archbishop of Canterbury had been announced a week or so earlier. His name was vaguely familiar to me, but we had never met, and I knew very little about him.

A tall cleric opened the door of Abbey Gate House and introduced himself as the Chaplain, Richard Chartres. We went upstairs to his study. I instinctively liked and trusted Richard, and this first impression was to be confirmed time and again when we worked together at Lambeth Palace. He explained that the Archbishop-designate was considering what staff he might require when he moved to Lambeth. The Archbishop has several main responsibilities: one with the diocese of Canterbury, another with the Church of England, and also the role of *primus inter pares* – first among equals – in the worldwide Anglican Communion. Given the growth of Anglicanism throughout the world, the third role was assuming a greater prominence, and the new Archbishop had been recommended to consider appointing a staff member to advise him in this area, someone with international experience of the Church. Shrewd and incisive, Richard quizzed me about my background. After forty minutes or so, he indicated that it was time for us to go downstairs.

There was activity in the hallway. Workmen were being directed by a female voice which emanated from what I assumed was the kitchen at the far end of the corridor. Richard picked his way through the household items awaiting despatch, explaining the geography of the house as we proceeded. A door opened, and a tall slim clergyman emerged. He took a pained look at the chaos around him and was about to retreat when Richard caught his attention and introduced me.

'I'm terribly sorry to keep you waiting.' He shook my hand and led me through into the study. 'There is so much to attend to at the moment. I'm sorry I can't give you lunch, but Richard will look after you. Do sit down.'

The workmen had not yet begun to dismantle the study. I sat by the fireplace. The Archbishop-designate sat opposite. As with Richard, I liked Robert Runcie immediately. Our conversation covered much the same ground that I had previously traversed with the Chaplain.

'I can't be sure if we really need a new appointment at this stage.' He was drawing the interview to a close. 'I need to take advice from others, but I will be in touch as soon as possible.'

He ushered me back into the mêlée. Richard rescued me, and we went together to the kitchen. A lady appeared and was introduced as Mrs Runcie. She apologised for the confusion and invited us to sit down at a table in front of the Aga. The three of us had lunch together. Just as I was leaving, Richard told me that he was moving from his position as Chaplain in St Albans to be the Archbishop's Chaplain at Lambeth. I congratulated him. He gave me a quizzical look but made no reply.

As I walked back to the railway station, deep in thought, I again stopped to look at the antique clocks in the shop window. It was four o'clock in the afternoon. Once again, I was standing on the threshold of a major change in my life.

'Can you tell me the date, please?'

The familiar guard has been away for several days. His replacement is detached and appears somewhat surly.

He replies curtly, 'Twenty-four December.'

He snaps the padlock on my ankle and leaves the room. Tomorrow will be Christmas Day. One year ago I sat in this same room on my second Christmas in captivity. It is very cold. Normally, I sit all day with my legs crossed like an Indian tailor. I wrap a blanket around my shoulders and read. The electricity is very inadequate now, and much of the time I read by the light of a candle. Next month I will have been a hostage for three years – the crucial 'make or break' period. It seems impossible. Three years since I had a normal conversation with anyone; three years since I saw the sun or felt the wind and the rain; three years in chains. How much longer can this go on?

I plan my Christmas celebrations. Tonight, when I think it is near to midnight, I will celebrate the Holy Communion. I am lucky to have a Prayer Book and a Bible. I take one of the paper tissues I have been given and fold it into the shape of a cross. I put this safely in my Bible. The day passes slowly. I don't allow myself to think of those whom I love. I read and read and read. At supper-time the guard gives me a sandwich. I save a small piece of bread and put it in my Bible. I eat my meagre supper and read some more. I dare not leave the service too late or the guard will come in and tell me to extinguish the candle. After an hour or so, I begin. I place the cross on the floor, pour a little water into my plastic cup, and lay the bread on a clean tissue. It is very quiet. A few miles from where I now sit, Jesus was born on this holy night. 'A man full of sorrow and acquainted with grief.' The candle flickers in the cold night air. I have no strong feelings of joy or sorrow tonight. I start to read the service quietly. The Gospel of St John rings out: 'And the light shines in the darkness . . . and we beheld His glory . . . full of grace and truth.' I say the prayer of consecration, then sip the water and eat the bread. The candle has burnt out. I close the book, wrap myself in my bedding, lie down and sleep.

In my office at the British Council of Churches, I continued assembling information about South Africa. A week or so went by, and I heard nothing from either Robert Runcie or Richard Chartres. I knew that my name had been put forward as a possible candidate for the post of Assistant for Anglican Communion Affairs but I imagined that there were many other people who were also being considered. Then everything happened very quickly. I was told I had been appointed and was asked to visit Lambeth to discuss the details of my employment. John Miles from the Church of England Information Office arranged for my photograph to be taken for the Church press. Although I was known in Church circles because of my work in Bristol some ten years earlier, I was totally unknown to the general public, and my appointment passed with little comment in the media.

*

Today is Christmas Day, and there is no electric light. The guard brought me a new candle, which he lit and placed on the floor by my mattress. Breakfast was a piece of unleavened bread and some cheese. The guard on duty bothers very little about food, so I don't anticipate much of a midday meal. It is very cold. Sometimes, when the electricity is working, he brings me a small electric fire, but as the power failures last for days at a time, it is now useless. All I can do is wrap the blanket round me and try to distance myself from my circumstances.

Lunch arrives in mid-afternoon: a cold boiled potato, a tomato and a piece of bread. Before my capture I used to say that if I didn't have food or drink, it wouldn't worry me. I find that it doesn't, providing I can keep well. I eat and continue reading. It is so long since I led a 'normal' life that I must now be living from deep within. I have a better hold over my feelings, and there are not such violent mood swings. At times, I wonder if I will ever be able to bear the demands of human company again and will forever crave solitude. I can't say. All I know is that I am alive, quite cold, and in basically good heart. That's enough for today.

The first weeks of 1980 were weeks of great activity at Lambeth. The enthronement of the Archbishop in Canterbury Cathedral did not take place until 25 March, but before that there was much to do. At first, the new Archbishop did not have his own press officer in Lambeth Palace. John Miles had to exercise this difficult role from Church House in Westminster. As a temporary measure I was asked to liaise with John until media arrangements were worked out more satisfactorily. Most of the archbishops of the Anglican Communion came to England for the enthronement, and each wanted a private discussion with Robert Runcie. I was kept busy preparing briefings and looking after the visitors. One was Bishop Bezaleri Ndahura from Zaïre.

Archbishop Runcie had ordained Bezaleri five years before in St Albans. The fact that he was now to be elevated to Archbishop of a new province incorporating a part of Zaïre, Rwanda and Burundi indicated the rapid pace of development of the Church in Africa. Largely because of his personal association with Bezaleri, Robert Runcie accepted the invitation to attend Bezaleri's enthronement in Bukavu, and he asked me to plan the journey and to accompany him. I had recently been in Rome for a few days and heard from friends that Pope John Paul II was to be in Africa at the same time as the Archbishop's proposed visit. I mentioned this to Robert Runcie and suggested that Africa would be an ideal location for a first meeting with the Holy Father. The proposal was discussed with Canon Michael Moore and the Rev. Christopher Hill, both highly experienced in ecumenical matters and responsible for inter-Church relations. They were enthusiastic. The Archbishop decided to pursue the possibility.

The logistics of getting from London to Ghana and then across to Eastern Zaïre, all within the space of a few days, were a nightmare. The Lambeth staff worked late many nights and finally came up with a timetable which involved using a combination of commercial and charter flights. Christopher Hill had discussions with the Vatican, and sooner than we could have hoped everything was ready for the historic meeting. The plan was for the Archbishop to fly to Ghana accompanied by Richard Chartres, Christopher Hill, John Miles and myself. Following the Papal meeting, John Miles and I would fly with the Archbishop to Zaïre. We arrived in Accra and went directly to the residence of the British High Commissioner where we were to stay.

The meeting with the Pope took place early one morning in May at the small residence of the Papal Nuncio. We assembled in the drawing room, and the Pope entered. He looked robust and cheerful and greeted the Archbishop warmly. The Archbishop introduced his staff.

'This is Terry Waite. He has worked in Rome and also has much African experience.'

We exchanged a few pleasantries, then the two men went upstairs for a private conversation. After forty-five minutes or so they returned, and the Pope came into the room to say farewell. He shook us all by the hand once more and gave us each a medallion as a memento of the occasion. When he came to me, he looked up and smiled. 'Goodbye, African experience. Goodbye.' His eyes twinkled.

The next time I met him, he was a shadow of his former self, having survived the ravages of an assassin's bullet.

Returning to the High Commissioner's residence in the car, the Archbishop discussed the meeting. As expected, it had been little more than an opportunity for the two leaders to get to know each other and discuss general issues facing the Churches. The principal purpose had been achieved and the ground laid for a future meeting with, it was hoped, greater depth of content.

Back in London, the Archbishop of Canterbury was in the unique position of being able to brief Cardinal Basil Hume on the Holy Father, as the Cardinal had yet to meet the Pontiff for a personal discussion. Cardinal Hume had telephoned Lambeth while the event in Ghana was being arranged: 'What I can't understand,' he said to the Archbishop, 'is why the meeting is taking place in a car. Most extraordinary.'

'Accra,' replied Runcie, pronouncing it carefully, 'Accra.'

The night is very still. The holy month of Ramadan has begun. The guard brings me food as usual and tells me that he is fasting during the hours of daylight. Now, as I lie on the floor, I wonder what it was that disturbed me. It wasn't gunfire – there has been a lull in the fighting for the past few days. Then I hear it. Outside in the street someone is beating a drum while a male voice chants a haunting melody. The voice echoes through the darkness, recedes into the distance and returns for the last time. It is an hour or so before daybreak, so the chanting must be designed to wake those who wish to eat.

It lingers in my mind. After listening to countless hours of preaching and recorded prayers from the mosque, it is wonderful to hear such a simple, beautiful melody. An alarm rings outside my door, and I hear the guard stir. He will prepare his breakfast and go back to sleep until much later in the morning. I try to make myself comfortable. My foam rubber mattress has worn thin, and I am virtually sleeping on the floor. I still don't have a pillow. I try to arrange part of my blanket so that it gives my head some support, but it's difficult since I have to keep well wrapped up to avoid the cold. I do the best I can and try to sleep again. The tune continues to haunt me, and I thank the anonymous singer for his unexpected gift. When I awake, I am cheered by the shaft of light which penetrates through a crack in the metal shutter. I must have slept through the dawn prayers. Usually I am woken by the strident call, but today I was spared. The guard enters, and I arrange my blindfold. He hands me a sandwich and pours hot tea into my plastic beaker.

'You good?'

'Yes, thank you.'

'Tek.'

He hands me something. It feels like a piece of card.

'What is it?' My blindfold is pulled down over my nose so I can't see under it.

'A letter.'

My heart leaps. After all these years, a letter. Could it be news from my family at last? He leaves the room, and I quickly lift the blindfold. It's a coloured postcard. I think it's a representation of a stained-glass window. John Bunyan sits at a table looking through the bars of his cell in Bedford jail. My hand shakes as I turn it over. It is addressed to me by name, but the address has been scratched out and the postmark is too blurred for me to read. However, the message is clear:

Dear Terry,

You are not forgotten. People everywhere are praying for your release, and that of the other hostages.

With best wishes,
Joy Brodier

Joy Brodier. I stare at the signature; it is not quite clear. Is it Brodier or Bradier? It hardly matters, as I don't know anyone of either name. I reverse the card and look once more at Bunyan. He is wearing his own clothes, has pen and paper, sits on a chair at a table and looks out over Bedford from behind a barred window. You're a lucky fellow, Bunyan, although I suspect the stained-glass window is a romanticised impression of your true condition.

Why, after years without mail or news from the outside world, should this single postcard find its way to me? Once again I turn it over and stare at my name. I still have no idea as to where it was sent. Well, Joy Brodier, or Bradier, thank you very much. I place the card carefully in my Bible. I'll remember your name. Maybe we will meet one day. Maybe.

The onward journey to Bukavu was exhausting. Even on a commercial flight, travel across Africa can be difficult. Timetables dictated that we took a night flight from Ghana to Kenya, then a charter flight from Nairobi to Eastern Zaïre. Those who begrudge an archbishop first-class travel do not know how gruelling a foreign tour can be. After a full day in Accra, complete with an evening function, cases were packed, and we departed for the airport. At some unearthly hour we stopped in Kinshasa where stalwart members of the British

Embassy and the local church had assembled to greet the Archbishop. After photographs and a brief word with the press, we departed for the next leg. The only sleep the Archbishop would get in the following forty-eight hours would be what he could snatch on the plane. On arrival in Nairobi, we found that a local clergyman had arranged an unscheduled breakfast meeting attended by at least a hundred people. The Archbishop, needing nothing more than a bath and a light meal, was obliged to face the gathering and once more say something to the press. We then crammed ourselves into the small charter plane run by a group known as the Missionary Aviation Fellowship. Before the pilot started the engine, he turned round and addressed us:

'I always pray before a flight.'

The Archbishop looked mildly surprised but made no objection. The pilot bowed his head; we followed his example.

'Oh Lord, if it be thy will, help us to successfully rise above the low clouds, and grant us a safe journey.'

We looked nervously at the threatening cumulus. Dr Runcie turned to me. 'I think,' he said, 'I prefer less qualified prayer.' He smiled.

The pilot revved the engine, and we prepared ourselves for several hours of discomfort. As we took off, we could see the breakfast party leaving for home. In no time at all I had fallen into a fitful doze.

The Church of Uganda had been responsible for preparing the new province for its independence, and while they had done their best, Bishop Ndahura was inheriting a very fragile structure. The Church was virtually penniless and involved in a complex disagreement with the National Protestant Church of the country. The enthronement took place in the open air, in a local sports stadium, and could hardly have afforded a greater contrast to the enthronement I had attended several weeks earlier at Canterbury. A small canopy had been erected to provide a few of the participants with some shelter from the sun, but the Archbishop, in full cope and mitre, had to endure hour after hour of sweltering heat while having snatched only a few hours' sleep during the journey. At the end of the service we staggered back to our guesthouse for the briefest of breaks before attending a great feast.

The journey home was not without interest. Our expert charter pilot had to spend so much time circling to avoid bad weather that he was forced to land in Mwanza to refuel. He filled the small plane from a hand pump and tested the mixture carefully.

'I must do this,' he said. 'Last month there was water in the fuel, and a plane came down in the bush.' As we approached Nairobi airport, he turned to John Miles. 'Look out for big jets,' he shouted. 'If they get too near, they can flip us over.'

'Good heavens,' yelled John. 'There is one!'

John was right. The pilot took the appropriate avoiding action, and twenty minutes later we were safely on the ground. This first, hastily arranged visit of the Archbishop of Canterbury taught us all a great deal. Not least, the necessity of adequate planning and proper control over a programme. Such matters were to occupy much of my time in the future.

The postcard continues to puzzle me. The guard seems genuinely surprised when I tell him I don't know the person who sent it.

'You not know?'

'No, I've no idea.'

'Why then they write?'

'Perhaps this is a kind person who remembers hostages.'

'Why?'

'Many people remember prisoners.'

He leaves the room, and I replace the card in my Bible. I don't want it to be seen in case it is taken from me.

I am now reading a novel by the American writer William Styron, *Set this House on Fire*. A curious title, but a powerful work which confirms my view that America has produced some of the finest novelists of the twentieth century. How does a writer sustain such creativity for page after page? Beside such a book, my own work seems puny. How I long for pen and paper, but if I had them I wouldn't be able to express myself freely in this place. I would always be conscious that someone was looking over my shoulder, that one day my scribbling would be taken for analysis by some unseen 'Chef'. Better to write in memory, to make a conscious attempt to remember the sounds and smells of these days: the rattle of machine-gun fire in the street; the earthy smell of tea as it is poured into my cup; the stale dank odour of my blanket; the sickly aroma of perfume as the guard splashes cheap aftershave over my head.

'Good, very nice.'

It isn't very nice. It's an indignity to sit while someone douses me in such a manner. I mutter, 'Thank you.' My real feelings remain hidden.

Styron deals with forceful themes and at times is almost unbearable to read: murder, suicide, the age-old battle between good and evil. Am I too sensitive? I think not. I can be blindly insensitive. My finer feelings must spring from living with constant insecurity. Never knowing what to expect – having such limited choices. But this is the lot of many people in the world. Now I know what it is like to face poverty and deprivation, although my circumstances are not so bad as many suffer. I get food at regular intervals, have books, can think about anything I wish. Again I ask myself, Will I go mad, lose my reason? I take out the Bunyan card and look at it again.

What a marvellous irony that this man accused of holding services not in conformity with the Church of England should now bring me comfort. Bunyan managed to turn his captivity to good effect. But he had a strong, certain faith; a rock-like belief. I think of other prisoners. Koestler comes to mind; I struggle to remember what he wrote about solitary confinement. Something about having to enter into a dialogue with existence, with life and with death. 'The spirit is not indestructible,' he wrote, 'but in hell one can get a sight of heaven.' All that has happened to me is that a lifelong struggle has now been concentrated and must be faced within. Styron disturbs because he points to powerful creative and destructive forces which I recognise. I know them, feel their power. They shake me with their intensity and threaten me with madness. Madness would be a retreat; a luxury in some ways. No longer having to battle, no longer having to reason. But I won't go mad, at least no more so than I have been throughout my life. I will press on.

I emerge from the Italy of Styron's book. He captures the country well, and I imagine he must have lived in the south for some time to write as colourfully as he does about Naples and Salerno.

What would I want to say to such a writer if I could meet him today? I would say, keep a space in your mind for the man or woman in prison; the individual who will read your book with the same sort of relish with which a starving peasant seizes a loaf of bread. This is the individual who will penetrate to the heart of your writing. He is your critic, your disciple. He will sit with you for hour after hour, and will hear your own soul speaking through your words. Be aware of this lonely man or woman as you write.

*

It took none of the Lambeth staff long to realise what considerable demands were made upon the Archbishop's time. The only way his life could be made manageable was to keep a strict control over engagements and make sure that foreign tours were carefully planned well in advance. The journey to Zaïre had convinced us that, in most cases, it would be necessary for a member of staff to visit the country where a tour was due to take place at least twelve months in advance. It was hoped that such a visit would enable priorities to be drawn up, and a realistic programme to be arranged.

Another part of my work was to keep the Archbishop briefed on developments throughout the Anglican Communion. I had hardly settled into my office when disturbing reports began to come in about the situation facing the Anglican Church in Iran. This comparatively small community was led by Bishop Hassan Dehqani-Tafti, an Iranian national and a most courageous man.

Long before the Iranian revolution, a group of extreme fanatics, based in Isfahan, had been causing problems. They made no secret of the fact that their aim was to break the Church and destroy the diocese. The revolution which brought Ayatollah Khomeini to power enabled them to step up their activities, and following the Shah's overthrow, on 18 February 1979, the senior priest of the Anglican Church, the Rev. Aristoo Sayyah, was murdered. Threats against other churchmen increased as the fanatics used every opportunity to cause trouble. They managed to intimidate a member of the Church and forced him to spy on the clergy, threatening execution if he failed to obey. He moved to Tehran, hoping to escape from their clutches, but was soon picked up by the network in the capital. As the year wore on, the persecutions increased. Several Church institutions were illegally commandeered, and the Church's bank accounts were appropriated by the fanatics. Bishop Dehqani-Tafti had to suffer the frightening experience of appearing before a Revolutionary Court where summary execution, after the briefest of trials, was the order of the day. He was reprieved, but an attempt was made on his life at a later stage.

In the midst of such dramatic events the Bishop and his wife, together with Jean Waddell, the Bishop's secretary, travelled to Cyprus to attend the Synod of the Church. Afterwards Jean returned to Tehran and the Bishop and his wife went to London to attend a meeting of Anglican Primates. Here they received news that the American Embassy in Tehran had been occupied and hostages were being held. The Primates and the Church leaders in Iran strongly urged the Bishop not to return immediately. Reluctantly he took their advice. His wife arrived back in Tehran to find that the Isfahan fanatics had strengthened their position by joining with the hard-liners and were continuing their campaign to seize all the Church's assets.

Badly forged documents which suggested that the Church was a nest of spies began to appear. By this time, information from Iran had started to arrive on my desk daily. It was, of course, difficult to know what to do or how to aid the brave group. I learnt that the campaign was being stepped up. Jean Waddell, who was single and worked in Iran with the support of the Church Missionary Society, opened the door of her flat in Tehran one evening, and several men rushed in. She was shot, half strangled, and left for dead. Only the prompt action of a doctor saved her life. While she was recovering, she was arrested and put in the notorious Evin prison where an Iranian colleague, the Rev. Iraj Mottahedeh, was also being held.

The two remaining Iranian clergymen, the Diocesan Administrator and two other members of the Church Missionary Society, Dr and Mrs John Coleman, were arrested at the same time as Jean and Iraj. But the cruellest blow of all was to strike the Bishop and his wife when their only son, Bahram, a talented journalist, was murdered in May 1980. Later the Bishop was to write about this experience, and his words stand as a living testimony to the depth of his compassion and Christian belief.

While the detention of the American hostages continued to dominate the headlines, I struggled to discover ways to assist the Church hostages. As I knew little about Iran, I began to read up on the area in what spare time I could find. I met many people who knew the country at first hand and got them to brief me, and since part of my responsibility in planning the Archbishop's tours was to keep in touch with the Foreign Office, I asked my contacts there for information. It was useful to develop an historical background, but no one was able to tell me more about the current situation than I had already gleaned through my own channels at Lambeth. Nor, it seemed, could anyone advise me as to the best way to proceed.

The months passed, and the situation in Iran continued to be difficult. I kept the Archbishop up to date on the information I received, and we both hoped that the problem would be resolved by the intervention of the Foreign Office. Bishop Dehqani-Tafti was forced to remain in exile in England where his wife joined him. The Colemans' large and caring family in London kept in regular touch with me, and although I was almost fully occupied with other work, Iran and the situation of the hostages was always in my mind. I struggled to think of a way to solve the problem. Finally, when it seemed that no progress was being made, I discussed with the Archbishop the possibility of making a personal visit to Iran in the hope that I would be able to move things along. He was concerned about the dangers inherent in the situation but felt it might be worth an attempt. He sent a personal letter to Ayatollah Khomeini, and I applied for a visa.

As Christmas approached and nothing happened, I became more and more doubtful about the visa. We made another special plea to the Iranian authorities to let me visit the hostages at Christmas. There was no reply. Finally, during the afternoon of Christmas Eve, I went out to do some last-minute shopping. When I returned to Lambeth Palace, it was full of activity. A phone call had confirmed that I had been granted a visa, and I was already booked on a flight to Tehran the following morning, Christmas Day. The Archbishop was about to leave Lambeth for Canterbury where he normally spent Christmas. I went to see him, and we had a short discussion. He urged me to be careful.

The books I have received during the past weeks have been curious. I handed back Styron and received a Western in return. It was the first novel of that genre I had ever read and I didn't enjoy it, even though I tried to approach it with an open mind. Unfortunately, several more followed. Once the guard has given me a book, I am stuck with it for a couple of days. I never know what he has given me until he has left the room and I can remove my blindfold. This morning it is yet another tale of cowboys and Indians. I read bits and then retreat into my own thoughts. Back home on my bookshelves, I have the collected works of Carl Jung. Twenty volumes in all, together with the Freud and Jung correspondence and numerous related books. I have read the letters and large parts of the works, but I can't pretend to have studied them in great detail. It would be marvellous to have them with me now.

I first began to read Jung in the Bristol years, and more intensely in Africa when I was made aware of my inner turmoil. His *Memories, Dreams, Reflections* was powerful and led me on to more of his writings. On one occasion, I visited Jung's house in Zurich, which was then being used as a training centre for psychotherapists. Eric Hutchison, who, when he left Africa, trained and eventually practised in this field, met and talked with Jung in Switzerland. What I remember of Jung's work helps me now. I look to my unconscious to help me through these days. I abandon myself to it and let it guide me gradually towards my own centre. I know, now, that solitude need not destroy me. What I am afraid of is physical deterioration. Most of my life I have been exceptionally healthy, but I wonder how long I can maintain good health under present conditions. My skin is deathly white, having not seen the sun for years; my teeth are broken and hurt constantly; my eyes are getting weaker. From time to time I suffer agonising stomach pains when it feels as if my insides are being pulled apart. Some guards are sympathetic and let me use the toilet immediately. Others keep me waiting while I experience an agony that brings on a long cold sweat. I suspect I may have developed intestinal parasites; that would explain some of my problems. But Jung helps me keep well in my mind, and I am grateful to him for that.

When I left Heathrow Airport on Christmas morning, I had no idea what to expect. In Paris I changed planes and boarded an Iranian airliner, wearing my cassock. It was the only way I could think of to mark me out clearly as an emissary of the Archbishop. The plane was full, and my sober ecclesiastical dress blended with the traditional Islamic robes worn by the majority of the passengers. I believed my chances of achieving a breakthrough were good. The fact that I had been given a visa to enter the country suggested that perhaps someone in a high position wanted to see the problem resolved. When we landed in Tehran, a tall, bearded man met me at the foot of the aircraft steps.

'Mr Waite, you are welcome.'

Thus began an elaborate game, which was to last for several weeks.

My hotel room had a magnificent view of a mountain range beyond which lay the Caspian Sea. I sat down and wondered how matters would unfold. Before leaving London I had obtained the telephone numbers of several members of the Anglican community in Tehran. As all their leaders were either in exile or in prison, they had not met together for a church service for some time. I decided to take the initiative. I found my list, picked up the telephone, and called several members of the congregation. I told them that I had been sent by the Archbishop of Canterbury and would like them to meet me in the church so that we could share a Christmas service. I was aware that in all probability my telephone conversations would be monitored, but I saw no reason to be secretive about my mission or my intentions. In the evening, I made my way to the church. It was a small modern building surrounded by a few flats for churchworkers, and some small offices. An elderly man welcomed me, and we walked together into the building.

'I don't know how many will come,' he said. 'These are difficult days for us.'

He switched on the lights and revealed a modest church interior. Gradually people began to appear, and the church was soon pleasantly full. As I am not a clergyman, I could not celebrate the Holy Communion, so I had planned a service of carols and prayers which included a space for me to address the congregation. Before leaving Lambeth Palace, I had knelt while the Archbishop gave me his blessing. It occurred to me that this group of Iranian Christians needed to be assured that they belonged to a worldwide family which cared about their difficulties. I told them of the Archbishop's concern and asked them to come forward to receive a blessing. As they knelt at the altar rail, I placed my hands on their heads and asked that God might bless and protect them. There were tears in the eyes of many as they returned to their seats. We sang another carol, then I climbed the steps into the pulpit. The old man who had first met me acted as interpreter. I explained the purpose of my visit – to bring encouragement to the Church and to seek the release of its leaders. I had been speaking for no more than five minutes when there was a clatter outside the main door. Several heads turned anxiously in the direction of the noise. Suddenly, the door burst open and a group of bearded young men entered. They wore army boots and military-style uniforms and carried automatic weapons. The front pew of the church was empty. They sat down, dropped their rifles on the floor and stared up at me.

There is considerable activity outside my room. I heard the front door of the apartment open and could see several pairs of feet under my door. I can't quite work out what is happening, but it may be they are preparing to move me, or that someone is being moved in. A moment ago, I thought I heard the dull metallic clank of a chain in the room next to me. If a hostage has been moved into the next room, there might be a chance to communicate with him by tapping on the wall. I remember Koestler explaining a code in *Darkness at Noon*. He divided the alphabet into four groups of five letters and a final group of six. One tap indicated group one, which was then followed by up to five taps to indicate the letter. Two initial taps indicated the second group, and so on. That seems to me useful only if one has pen and paper. Without them, a straightforward one for A, two for B, might be more manageable. But my mind is leaping too far ahead. I don't know if anyone is next door yet, and I won't be sure for a couple of days. There is the sound of a chain – no doubt about it. Now a door closes. Silence. I press my ear against the wall and strain to hear more. Nothing. I lie back wondering what is happening and how long I must stay here.

A generator has been placed on the balcony, and it is kept running for long periods since the local electricity supply is now virtually non-existent. At first it was pleasant to have continuous light, but the drawback is that exhaust fumes come into my room, and I am sure they are affecting my lungs. I have a cough that will not go away. I wake in the night coughing and have been alarmed to see blood in my sputum. I don't think it's TB, but naturally the thought crosses my mind. Almost certainly I am developing a lung infection. I have asked for medicine, but nothing arrives. If only they would move the generator so that I am not constantly poisoned by the fumes. I press my ear to the wall again. All is silent. Tomorrow I may know.

I looked down at the bearded men sitting with folded arms in the front pew. They stared back at me. The old man who had been interpreting gave me a nervous half-smile and moved to sit down. I stopped him.

'Please stay a moment. Our visitors have missed the first part of my address. I would like them to hear what I have to say.'

He was understandably anxious, but he bravely stood his ground. I began again from the beginning. The old man translated. The congregation sat transfixed. I introduced the final carol, brought the service to an end, and went across to the latecomers. A stocky young man, with a full black beard, introduced himself.

'Mr Waite, we like what you say. We take you to see your people.'

I could hardly believe what I was hearing. A dozen thoughts flashed through my head. Were they genuine Revolutionary Guards? Were they about to kidnap me? I had letters and cards for the hostages back at my hotel, and I mentioned this.

'We not have time to go to hotel. You must come now.'

Most of the congregation had slipped quietly away. The old man remained. It would not have been fair to ask him for advice. I had to make my own decision.

'Right, I am ready.'

'We take this man with us.' They took hold of an Iranian with an unruly mop of hair. 'We must blindfold him. You OK, you not know Tehran. He know, so we blindfold him.'

They produced a strip of material and covered his eyes.

'Come.'

We went outside. In the road by the church stood a Mercedes. They pushed the man into the back seat, with guards on either side of him. I was ushered into the front. The driver started the engine, and we sped away into the night.

18

T HERE ARE PEOPLE in the room next to me, although I can't make out how many. It's either two or three, certainly no more than three. I can tell by watching under my door when they are taken to the bathroom. I thought I counted three trips today, but I may have mistaken one of the guards for a hostage. I have tried tapping gently on the wall, but I get no reply. I assume they are chained away from the dividing wall and therefore unable to hear or respond. My opportunity will come if they get an exercise period, as I do, when they are free to walk about. I am curious to find out who they are and what they know, and desperate for some human contact.

I am trying hard to remember the names of those who were hostages when I was taken. I continue to experience the strange phenomenon of being able to recall childhood companions with startling clarity and yet forget names I thought were imprinted forever on my mind just three or four years ago. Am I ageing prematurely? I don't know. My breathing is now giving me a problem. I have had to abandon my daily exercises because my lungs are not working properly. I can walk around the room if I take it gently, but all vigorous exercise is out.

This upsets me a great deal; I have worked so hard to keep physically fit, and exercise gave me a sense of well-being. Now two or three times a day I have to fight for breath. The guards will not remove the generator. They tell me they have put it in a new place, but the fumes still penetrate my room, causing me spasms of prolonged coughing. From now on I am going to need extra willpower. I can manage my toothache and my stomach ache, but this is different, and it frightens me. I don't know what medicine to ask for, and I don't suppose they would bring it to me for a long time. With the captives next door, two or three new guards have appeared. One I don't like at all. He speaks French with just a few words of English. Even though I can't see him, his manner is offensive. One day he is ingratiating, the next totally callous.

'You cough. No problem.'

He slaps my hand and laughs as I struggle to get my breath. I am

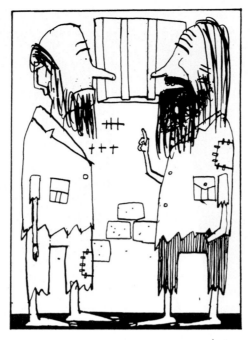

THINGS MUST BE BAD. I'VE
JUST SEEN TERRY WAITE

A cartoon by Barry Fantoni in The Times, *1985,
one of the many to have appeared over the years*

*With the Rev. Iraj Mottahedeh (now Bishop in Iran), Jean Waddell,
Dr John Coleman, Audrey Coleman and others immediately
prior to their release from captivity in Tehran, February 1981*

*Stooping to greet Colonel Gaddafi in his tent,
during the hostage negotiations, Tripoli, 1984*

At Gatwick with the Libyan hostages, February 1985

8 Nov 85

To The Archbishop of Canterbury

Your Excellency:

We have read and heard about your offer to help negotiate our release, and we praise and thank you. Our captors have indicated they are willing for you to be involved, but say that your efforts should be directed to Kuwait. Our government apparently has tried to exert pressure through Syria and other countries without success. Our kidnappers are adamant – we will be released only in exchange for the 17 prisoners in Kuwait.

But they say they are amenable to any reasonable arrangement once such an exchange is agreed to. For instance, they suggest Kuwait could unilaterally release some of the 17, and some of us would immediately be freed here. Or the 17 could be turned over to the International Red Cross, and they would do the same with us four. The details, they say,

Terry Anderson

Father Lawrence Jenco

Beirut, the first visit, 1985: Polaroids of the hostages holding a copy of the Wall Street Journal *signed by TW, together with the letter they sent to the Archbishop of Canterbury, 8 November 1985*

Tom Sutherland

David Jacobsen

are unimportant. But they are becoming impatient, and have threatened to kidnap, or even kill, more Americans We appeal to you to go to Kuwait and do your best to persue the Emir to have mercy on us and our families.

The Lord be with you.

Fr. Lawrence Martin Jenco, OSM

Terry Anderson

David Jacobsen

Thomas Sutherland

Discussing the hostage situation with Vice-President George Bush at the White House, 1985

At Lambeth Palace after the release of Jacobsen, Weir and Jenco, November 1986

In Beirut surrounded by protective Druze
after a visit to the Grand Mufti, January 1987

Meeting the press outside the Commodore Hotel, Beirut, January 1987

With Samir Habiby on the eve of departure for Beirut,
Christmas, 1985

The last picture before captivity, January 1987

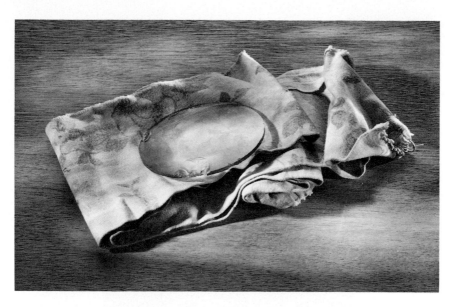

The blindfold and magnifying glass, which were with me during captivity

The Bunyan card which was sent to me by
Mrs Joy Brodier, the only communication from the
outside world in four years of solitary

The first photograph following my release, taken in Syria with Tom Sutherland, 18 November 1991

In better shape in Blackheath, 1992

sure he believes I am only pretending to be ill. Now he turns unpleasant and orders me to be quiet. He tells me I cough too much and too loudly. How can I help it? He pushes me.

'Silence.'

I sit, legs crossed, blindfolded, attempting to control my spasmodic breathing.

'You no good. Silence.'

I despise this pathetic man. He is arrogant and stupid. I must calm myself. If I get angry or upset, my breathing problems get worse. Could they be psychosomatic? Quite possibly. It may be a combination of things – fumes, infection, stress. I suppose it could even be a heart condition. I try deep breathing, but once I have got the oxygen into my lungs I have to use a great deal of energy to expel it. I involuntarily make the most awful noises, which must be heard through the wall. It's so difficult to control. God, please don't let me sink now. How awful to have survived for so long, only to succumb to illness. If only they would move the bloody generator. Please move it, please, *please*.

It sounds like exercise-time next door. I must try again to make contact with someone. It's going to be difficult, and there are risks. First, I won't know if they are alone in the room, or if there is a guard with them. I must make sure that I hear their door close before I tap. Second, I must keep an eye under my door when I tap in case a guard is listening. Third, I must choose a code. Everyone must know the straightforward 'one for A' code, so that will be the one I'll keep trying. I lie down, fasten my eyes on the crack beneath the door and begin to tap with my fingernail. One – two – three – four ... TERRY WAITE. Why, oh why, should so many letters in my name be at the end of the alphabet? I stop. Nothing. I try once more. Silence. Enough for today. I'll try again tomorrow.

A light drizzle was falling as we drove through the deserted streets of Tehran. Electric lights cast a watery yellow glow across the pot-holed road. Occasionally we passed small groups of Revolutionary Guards huddled around open fires. We stopped briefly at a checkpoint where a word from the driver was enough to get us through. I felt apprehensive but not unduly worried. We turned into a small road and came to a gateway. Guards emerged from the shadows, and once again we were waved on. I peered through the gloom. It seemed as if we were in the grounds of what had been a large estate.

We passed a number of small buildings and came to a stop in front of one of them.

'Wait here.'

The driver slipped out of his seat and went inside. I could hear the heavy breathing of the man in the back seat. It worried me that they had brought him along. If they kept him, I would feel responsible. The driver returned.

'Come.'

'What about my friend?'

'He stay in car.'

'You are not going to keep him?'

'Come. Now.'

I climbed out and we entered what seemed to be a single-storey block. I glanced to my right. A number of men in dark tracksuits sat on the floor guarded by young men with automatic weapons. We moved on.

'In here.'

I was ushered into a bare room. A European couple and several Iranians stood looking at me.

'Hello,' I said. 'The Archbishop of Canterbury has sent me to see if I can help. A happy Christmas.'

They smiled broadly. A European wearing an old pair of trousers and a tattered shirt stepped forward.

'I'm John Coleman. This is my wife, Audrey, and these are our Iranian colleagues.' He introduced each by name, and we shook hands. I looked around and to my horror saw the arrival of the young man who had been brought with me from the church.

'They are not going to keep him, are they?' I asked.

John Coleman explained.

'He is one of us. They let him out to attend the service. He was the only one they would take.'

I was relieved at the information. We sat down on the floor, and the guard brought us hamburgers and Coca-Cola.

'This is a real treat,' John said, as the food was handed out.

'I have letters and Christmas presents for you back at the hotel. I had to come here in rather a hurry, but I'll try to bring them soon.'

'We knew somebody was coming out to see us, but we didn't know who it would be. We were allowed to telephone our son on Christmas Day, and he told us.' John smiled. 'It's very good to see you.'

The guard sat in the corner as we ate. There was much I wanted to ask, and much, I assumed, they wanted to tell me. Naturally, we were cautious. I did learn, however, that until Christmas Day the group of five had been kept apart from one another. John had lived for weeks without knowing where, or how, his wife was.

'There is something important I have to say,' John announced when we had finished eating. 'We are five here: Audrey, and myself, and our three Iranian colleagues. We don't want to be released until we are *all* released.'

John's point was very much in my mind. Although I did not mention it at the time, I was aware that there were still Jean Waddell and Iraj Mottahedeh to track down. I could not leave the country without doing my utmost for all seven prisoners, and I gave the group that assurance. We continued to talk together. Finally the guard indicated that it was time for me to leave. We all said a prayer, and I promised to return with the Christmas gifts as soon as I could. We embraced, and I went into the corridor and out towards the car.

'Come,' said my Revolutionary companion. We climbed into the Mercedes and drove back to the city.

Here, hidden away in Beirut, memories of Iran come flooding back. Arriving passengers were greeted at the airport with a huge notice on the side of a hangar proclaiming 'Down with America'. Israel and France were denigrated in the reception area. I remember looking anxiously for a denunciation of Britain, but we apparently didn't qualify for one. Demonstrations were frequent. I was driven around Tehran by the Revolutionary Guard, and we frequently stopped on the edge of mass meetings attended by hundreds of young men chanting their revolutionary slogans.

'You don't understand us,' said my guide. 'America only interested in oil. America very bad.'

He took me to meet his family. We drove down an unlit street and stopped outside a shabby house. Inside it was spotless. There was little furniture, but the floor was covered by a magnificent carpet. A television set flickered in the corner of the upstairs room.

'When you meet my wife, please do not shake hand.'

A woman swathed from head to foot in traditional Islamic dress stepped forward. She said a few words and left as quickly as she had appeared.

'Please sit.' I sat on the carpet. An old man came into the room. 'My father.'

We greeted each other.

'He does not speak English. I am sorry.'

A huge dish of rice, meat and vegetables was brought in.

'Eat. You must eat plenty. We happy you eat with us.'

We ate from the dish with our fingers. I could hear the voices of women and children in the corridor outside. The dishes were removed. A large photograph album was put into my hands.

'Look. My brother. Dead. Killed by Shah. Look. Another brother. Killed. See, young brother. Prison by Shah.'

I turned the pages. Young men posed proudly for the camera. Most of them now were smiling, or weeping, from beyond the grave.

'Shah good for rich. For poor people, no good. Very bad. That is why we have revolution. America not understand: America very bad.'

'Why do you imprison our Church people? They have done nothing wrong.'

'They are spies. We know. We have many papers from church. We see people from British Embassy go into church. We watch for a long time. Bishop make much money. He has money from England.'

'He was given money for the blind school and for medical work.'

'We think he is not good.'

Before going to Iran I had heard that some people in the country chose to believe that Bishop Dehqani-Tafti was a convert to Christianity from Islam and thus working against the interests of the country. This was untrue, but the story circulated.

'It is not good to keep innocent people,' I said. 'You know that.'

'We know. We shall look at problem again.'

I expressed my sorrow at the troubles his family had faced.

'They now martyrs. Good for them.'

We drove to the Martyrs' Memorial on the outskirts of the city. Hundreds of graves marked the resting place of fighters for the revolution. Family groups wandered among the tombstones.

'We very strong.'

I had to admit that a group of people ready to die for their beliefs possess a unique strength. We returned to my hotel.

'Tonight, you see your friends again.'

I collected together the cards and gifts for the hostages. That evening we drove out of the city and into the compound.

'Come.'

We had stopped outside a palatial building and entered an enormous hall. Crystal chandeliers hung from the ceiling. Ornate gilded furniture lay broken and scattered around the room. Iron cooking pots full of rice stood on what had once been a highly polished table. Young Revolutionary Guards milled around.

'Wait here.'

I sat on a bench and thought of the French Revolution. My arrival had caused some excitement among the bored Revolutionaries. They crowded around me and commented on my size.

'You very strong?'

'Perhaps.'

'How big?'

'Two metres.'

They gave low whistles.

I placed my elbow on the dining table and challenged one of them to a bout of arm-wrestling. His friends laughed and urged him on. He rested his machine gun on the floor and propped his elbow opposite mine. I managed to win the first round and was relieved when my guide appeared from a side room before there could be a second.

'Come. We go.'

The Revolutionaries bade me a cheery farewell.

'Whom did you visit?' I asked.

'A bad man. A spy. We shoot him tomorrow.'

We got into the car and drove to the building where the hostages were being held.

'I hope you will let them go soon,' I said as we drew up outside. I was acutely conscious of how volatile the situation was, how the mood could change in a moment.

'I don't know. Perhaps.'

The hostages were well, and this time we were able to have a private conversation. They said their conditions had improved since Christmas Day, and John told me that he had managed to obtain a small radio from one of the guards, and now he listened to the World Service of the BBC during the night. All the members of the group had only the clothes in which they were detained. John and Audrey

Coleman, despite the indignities they had suffered, were serene and quietly confident in their faith. I respected them for their dignity and honest goodness.

Back with the guide I asked him why the hostages were not being released immediately.

'We must look into their case. It is not easy. I must visit important people.'

It was difficult to know what game the Iranians were playing. The intervention of the Archbishop of Canterbury had almost certainly led to an easing of the situation. My guess was that they were looking for a face-saving formula which would enable them to free the hostages. No demands had been made to me for their release, nor were any ever made. I had to be patient and keep pressing forward, one small step at a time.

I continued to seek permission to visit Jean Waddell and Rev. Iraj Mottahedeh in the Evin prison. It was not easy. Revolutionary Guards told me that Jean and Iraj were being held by another authority, and it would be hard for me to get access to the prison. I said that it would be impossible for me to leave Tehran without having seen them. I had to be satisfied that they were alive and well. The guard who had taken me to his home continued to be helpful, and on 29 December he drove me to Evin. I had heard many terrible stories about this grim fortress, and I wondered how Jean was surviving after her horrific experiences in the recent past when she had been shot and half strangled. We parked next to the prison, and the Revolutionary Guard handed me over to a prison official who guided me to a waiting area. Eventually I was escorted along a maze of passages and into an upstairs room. Two men in civilian clothes sat at desks. A door opened, and a frail-looking woman entered. She looked bewildered for a moment, but her face lit up when she saw me.

'Hello, Jean. I'm sorry I couldn't get to see you earlier.' I embraced her.

'How are my family? I am so worried about them.'

It wasn't until she was released that I realised the full significance of her question. In captivity she was told that members of her family had come to Tehran to visit her and been thrown into prison. Jean became convinced that she could hear the voices of her family in the cell next to hers, and this psychological pressure worried her more than anything else. I was able to reassure her that her family was at home in the United Kingdom, and all were quite well. We chatted for a while, then the door opened again.

'Iraj!' Jean exclaimed. 'How good to see you.'

This was the first meeting between them since they were arrested, even though they had been kept in the same prison. Up to that point, Jean had feared that Iraj had been executed. Under the circumstances she had to restrain her feelings at seeing him alive.

I had been given vague promises that the case of the Church hostages would be considered again, but warned that it would take some time. I returned to London to discuss matters with the Archbishop. The release of the American hostages in early 1981, after more than a year in captivity, gave us fresh hope that the Church hostages, too, would soon be freed. Nothing was certain, however, and, given the instability within Iran, their continued detention was worrying.

I went back to Tehran in February and once again made contact with the Revolutionary Guards. The young man who had first taken me to see the hostages was hopeful that all of them would be released 'very soon'. I needed to have the information communicated to others, so I asked him if he would be prepared to give this assurance to the Archbishop of Canterbury over the telephone. The Guard's English was limited but adequate, and he agreed to do so. He would not commit himself to a date for their release, but he did assure the Archbishop that the hostages were not in any danger.

Later the Archbishop told me how strange he found it to be sitting in his study in the Old Palace at Canterbury, speaking to a Revolutionary Guard in Tehran.

I wanted the Guard to give the same information to the British authorities in Tehran with whom I was in touch: the last-remaining British diplomat and the Swedish Ambassador, who was responsible for British interests in Iran. At first the Guard was reluctant, but eventually he agreed. The Swedish Ambassador suggested that I bring the Guard to the residence for lunch. On the appointed day, the Guard collected me at my hotel in his Mercedes. We drove out to the Swedish residence, and I explained again the object of our visit. As we drew up outside the house, the Guard leant across and opened the glove compartment. Inside was an automatic pistol. I stiffened.

'What are you doing?'

'I must take this.'

'You can't possibly go armed into the Swedish Ambassador's house.'

'I must.'

'I'm sorry, but I can't allow that.'

'Then I not go.'

'Look. I have an idea. Put the pistol in my briefcase. I will carry the case and keep it with me.'

He thought for a moment and agreed. I placed the weapon in my briefcase and snapped the lock shut. We walked together to the front door. As I rang the bell, we heard a dog bark somewhere in the house. The Guard drew back.

'What is that?'

'It's a dog.'

'A dog?' He looked incredulous.

The door opened, and a dog the size of a rabbit rushed out and began to snap at the Guard's heels. The Guard did a small dance, then sent the animal skidding across the polished floor of the hallway with a well-aimed kick. The Ambassador looked as if he was about to explode.

'My dog, my little dog. What have you done to my little dog?'

I held tightly on to the briefcase.

'A moment please.' The Ambassador retrieved his pet and shut him in a back room. When he returned, he had recovered his composure. 'I am so sorry. Please come in.'

We entered.

'I think we might have lunch right away and talk afterwards.'

In the dining room, the table was elegantly laid. A servant in a white mess-jacket stood in attendance. The Ambassador sat at the head of the table with me on his right, facing the Guard. I wedged my briefcase firmly beneath my chair. The incident with the dog had got us off to a bad start, and the Guard was now determined to make a small demonstration.

'What is this?' He pointed to the place-setting before him.

The Ambassador looked surprised.

'It's a knife and fork and spoon,' he replied politely.

The Guard gave a disgusted glance at his host and collected up the silverware.

'Here.' He beckoned the attendant. 'Take these.'

The surprised waiter put the cutlery on a side table, reappearing quickly with a large dish of rice. The Guard helped himself, shovelling rice on to his plate with a large serving spoon.

'Leave it on the table,' he said. 'We might want more.'

The Ambassador nodded, and the dish was placed on the table. Other dishes appeared, and the waiter received identical instructions. The Guard picked up the serving spoon again and began to shovel food into his mouth. He wiped his lips on the back of his hand and helped himself to more. I remembered his gracious behaviour when I had eaten with his family some weeks before. It was clear that he was now deliberately putting on an act. The Ambassador's diplomatic small talk was being strained to the limit, but he conducted himself with the utmost courtesy throughout the meal.

'Let us go and sit somewhere comfortable,' he finally suggested.

We moved to another room. I kept an eye on the briefcase. The Ambassador sat opposite me, the Guard to my right.

'Well,' I said, anxious to get out of the house. 'If you could tell the Ambassador what you have told me, we can leave.'

The Guard, having made his protest at the table, began to speak. He said that the case concerning the hostages was almost resolved, and he expected them to be released soon. Sensing that that was as far as he was prepared to go, I put my hand down by the side of my armchair and gripped the briefcase.

'Come,' I said. 'That's enough, we had better go now.'

Once we were clear of the residence, I returned the pistol to the glove compartment, thanked the Guard for his assurances and arranged to meet him again the following day. Then I retired to my hotel room, somewhat shattered.

'The case is almost closed. We have caught the man who has caused much trouble for your people.'

The Guard spoke confidently.

'Who is he?' I asked.

'A member of your Church.'

'I would like to meet him.'

'You shall.'

We went to the offices next to the church where I had first met the Revolutionary Guards at Christmas. The door opened, and a man was pushed into the room sobbing loudly. He was an Iranian. He fell at my feet and began to plead incoherently for his life. After a few minutes he was taken away, still crying and pleading.

I sat with the Guard.

'He is not well. I doubt if he is responsible for his actions,' I said.

'He has been giving false information against your people. He has caused much trouble.'

The Guard appeared stern and angry, but I knew that underneath he was sympathetic.

'We will keep him for a little while, then he will go home.'

I nodded. They had found a face-saving formula.

A few days passed, during which I was unable to visit the hostages. I took a day off and travelled to the ski slopes on the outskirts of Tehran which, despite the revolution, were full of activity. The Papal Nuncio invited me to dine with him, and I kept in close touch with the Swedish Ambassador. Despite the comedy of errors at the residence, he was exceptionally helpful to me in every respect and always at hand to do anything he could to assist in the release of the hostages.

John Coleman told me later what had happened to them during these days. The poor man who had been brought to me and accused of spreading false information about the Church was also led, blind-folded, to the hostages.

'This is the man who has caused your imprisonment.' The Guard pushed him forward.

John Coleman spoke for the group, 'We forgive him.'

The Guard was totally unprepared for such a response.

'How can you? You can't forgive him for what he has done. He is not even human.'

'That is our faith,' replied John. 'We forgive him.'

Later I questioned the man in greater detail about his activities, with John acting as interpreter. There was little doubt in my mind that he was mentally frail and had been made use of, and I said so to the Guards. He was desperately afraid that he would be executed, but he was eventually set free.

Late one night, John told me, Guards came into the room where the hostages were and ordered them to prepare to leave. They were taken, first in a car, then in a van without side windows, to a place where they were reunited with Iraj and Jean. It was here that I next met all of them. Although I had been told that their release was imminent, we had to wait several days. I visited them daily, and on one visit made a surprising discovery. I was sitting in an armchair talking to them when, for no reason, I put my hand down between the upholstered cushions. I pulled out a scrap of paper bearing the name of an American hostage who had been released some weeks earlier. I assumed from this that the Americans had at some time been kept in the same building.

The Guard insisted that Amit Roy, a journalist who was then working for the *Daily Telegraph*, be allowed to take an exclusive picture of the hostages prior to their release. He arrived and did so. The Guards then instructed the hostages to prepare to leave for the airport. Both John Coleman and I said that we would not leave until we knew that the Iranian captives were also on their way home. We were given this assurance, and the promise was honoured, although the clergymen were forbidden to leave the country. The remaining British diplomat hastily arranged passports, and with him we set out for the airport. I was very anxious, acutely aware that anything could go wrong at the last minute. The first shock came when we had a minor traffic accident while passing through the centre of Tehran. I thought we were being hijacked, but it was indeed an accident. The major blow struck after we had completed the airport formalities and stood waiting to board the flight. An official approached us and broke the news.

'I'm sorry, you can't leave.'

There are two people in the next room. I have counted the journeys to the bathroom for the past three or four days, and I am certain. I am also convinced that they are not chained to the wall against which I sit. Therefore my only chance to communicate with them will be during their exercise period. Today I follow the usual routine, and when all seems quiet, I lie down so that I can keep an eye on the crack beneath my door. I begin to tap gently. One – two – three – four – five . . . If I see anyone outside, I will have to leap to my feet immediately, for they will expect to find me exercising, and any deviation from my routine will excite their suspicion. It takes an interminably long time to tap out my name. I add the information that I have been alone for over three years. The tension is high. I am excited at the prospect of getting a reply and terrified of being discovered. Then, for the first time, another human being, another hostage, responds. One – two – three – four – five . . . My eyes remain riveted on the door. I count carefully. Whoever it is seems to be tapping so loudly that I am certain he will be heard. A B C D E F G H I J – a space. A B C D E F G H I J K L M N O – another space. A B C D E F G H – John. M C C. Of course, you fool – John McCarthy! I am so excited that I lose track of the counting and fail to catch the name of the other hostage. The tapping stops, and I get to my feet. John McCarthy, another Englishman. Human contact at last.

After days of waiting, the news that we were being prevented from leaving was too much. I let it be known in no uncertain terms that I was very angry.

'Now,' I said, with some force, 'now, we are all hostages. If anything happens to any one of us you will be held directly responsible.'

The Iranian official appeared frightened.

'There is nothing I can do,' he muttered.

We saw our flight leave.

'There is plenty you can do. You can make sure we are all on the next flight out. And you can take us all to my hotel and provide us with an armed guard.'

He did as I requested. The hostages enjoyed a couple of days of luxury after their 200-day ordeal. Then we were taken back to the airport and flown to Athens on 27 February. We spent one night in the British residence there and the next morning flew to London.

John Coleman, always cheerful, continued to make me smile right to the end of this difficult experience. I suggested that he might want to visit the duty-free shop before returning home so as to stock up on supplies. He disappeared into the shop and came out with a little carrier bag. I looked inside and burst out laughing.

'John,' I said, 'you are the only person I know who has ever gone round a duty-free shop and come out with just a bag of peanuts!'

A few years later I returned to Iran in an attempt to help the Church retrieve its confiscated assets. I did not succeed. None of the former hostages was rearrested, however, and eventually Iraj Mottahedeh was made a bishop. One bright, clear morning I set out with him and the two other Iranian clergymen to visit the grave of Bahram, the murdered son of Bishop Dehqani-Tafti. The burial ground was a simple plot outside the city. We found the grave, even though vandals had knocked over the headstone. We put it in order, and one of the clergymen conducted a short service. We stood quietly for a moment before walking away along the dusty track, each of us reliving in our mind days long past.

19

IMAGES AND IMPRESSIONS flash across my mind. Africa, China, America, Burma. Sitting here in my room, it's in some ways as though I have died. All I have is myself and what I have been. As I look back across the Lambeth years, the many journeys I made with the Archbishop fuse together into one continual voyage. Christopher Hill prepared for tours to other Christian Churches, I arranged visits throughout the Anglican Communion. The Archbishop, his Chaplain and I travelled together. Very occasionally, the Archbishop's wife would accompany her husband, but as she had no great love for official visits and was a busy and dedicated music teacher, more often than not it was only the three of us. Constant travelling under situations of considerable pressure made severe demands on Robert Runcie's stamina, and while we did our best to keep to the official programme, it was impossible to prevent it from running out of control at times.

On one of our first tours of the United States, a bishop asked if he could entertain the Archbishop at a private lunch. The Archbishop agreed, providing that the lunch really was private, and that there was an opportunity to rest before proceeding to a long afternoon and evening of engagements. I checked the arrangements. The Bishop assured me that the lunch was private, and that he had reserved a quiet room in an hotel.

We arrived to be greeted by a barrage of photographers and television cameras. We were ushered upstairs into a 'private' room, where at least two hundred 'privately invited' guests stood to welcome their visitor. The Bishop escorted the Archbishop to his place and assured him that he would be required to speak for only a few moments. This 'private' lunch meant that the Archbishop got no rest at all that day, and precious little during the two weeks of the visit.

He astonished me then, as he continued to astonish me, by his energy, courtesy and good humour. Somehow, the latter quality was rarely communicated through the media, leaving the general public, I suspect, with an inaccurate picture of the man. Now, as I think back to the Lambeth days, I remember him for his compassion and humour. He had a genuine concern for individuals who had got themselves into difficulties, and, to my mind, it was here that he demonstrated the true depth of his faith. He has been criticised by some for not being able to make up his mind on questions vital to the Church. If there is any validity in this criticism, it is because his mind is large enough to see all the arguments surrounding a question, and he realises that few matters lend themselves to absolute black-and-white decisions.

During my time at Lambeth, the Archbishop was assisted by two Chaplains, Richard Chartres and later John Witheridge. Both men were intellectually outstanding and superb travelling companions. I was incredulous when I learnt that John Witheridge had never been further than France before joining the staff at Lambeth Palace. He soon made up for this.

One of the most memorable journeys John and I made with the Archbishop was to Uganda in 1984 for the enthronement of Yona Okoth, the clergyman I had visited in prison during the first days of the Amin regime. Now, ten years later, Amin had gone into exile, and Milton Obote had returned to power. Silvanus Wani (the successor to Janani Luwum) had retired as archbishop, and the House of Bishops had elected Yona as its new leader.

Uganda was in a sorry state. Years of inter-tribal feuding had wrecked the infrastructure of the country. The university, once one of the finest in Africa, was barely functioning. The same could be said for most of Uganda's national institutions. I briefed the Archbishop and John as best I could. I had made a preparatory visit some months earlier and spoken with many of their leaders, including President Obote and Cardinal Nsubuga, the leader of the Roman Catholic Church. While all of them were depressed at the constant violence and bitterness, they had hopes that Uganda might rise above the dreadful events of the recent past and experience a new beginning.

As we were about to leave London for Kampala, news came through that four Europeans had been murdered in Uganda, and it was suggested that the murders were deliberately perpetrated to make the Archbishop cancel his visit. Obote continued to have many enemies in Uganda, and some Ugandans interpreted the Archbishop's visit as tacit approval of his government. Robert Runcie, although shaken by the brutality of the killings, would not be deterred. He was determined to lend his active support to a new archbishop and a Church which was attempting to reconsolidate after years of difficulty. This was the context for what was almost John Witheridge's first journey outside the British Isles. We departed wondering what to expect.

The supply of Westerns seems to be exhausted, and once again I am getting books more in tune with my taste. A few days ago I was given *Joseph Andrews* by Fielding. It's years since I read this novel, and the wit and stubborn good nature of Parson Andrews makes me laugh out loud. Next was a long, well-written novel by Susan Howatch. This is a book I would have passed by if I had seen it on a station bookstall, but the characters are so well presented that for a day or so I lose myself in the midst of a fictional family living between London and Ireland. It's odd how my mind works in this place. I feel a rapport with the author simply because the blurb states that she was born in 1940, one year after I was. I tend to feel, when I get into a book, that it was written especially for me, and the writer is speaking to me alone. In one sense this is true, but I make more of it here than most authors could possibly imagine.

I have abandoned further attempts to communicate with John McCarthy. The situation is too dangerous. I can only communicate during the exercise period and it's impossible for me to know if a guard is in their room while I am tapping. If John was chained to the dividing wall I would be able to talk with him during the night, but he is not. It is terribly frustrating to know that a fellow Englishman is next door and we cannot make contact. Once again, the only way I can cope with the frustration is to suppress it and think about other things. Dwelling on disappointment simply leads me down the road to despair.

I can only hope that John has registered my name; I must let someone know that I am alive and being held by this group. My breathing is getting more difficult. I am afraid the fumes may have damaged the lining of my lungs, because I wheeze and wheeze like an old asthmatic. I have no energy and can barely manage to walk around the room during my hour of freedom. The effect of this reduction in physical activity is to increase my interior life. Day in and day out I read, and when I am not reading, I am writing my own book. I continue to wonder if I will ever be able to endure human company again for any length of time. I want company, of course, but I don't know if I can cope with it. Perhaps they will move me in with the other two. Somehow I doubt it. They seem quite determined to keep me locked away, lost to the world. But not yet lost to myself.

Today I was given an unexpected laugh. With some reluctance, I returned Susan Howatch to the guard and received another volume in return. When I removed my blindfold I nearly dropped the book out of sheer surprise. *Great Escape Stories* by Eric Williams! The guards have no idea at all of what they are giving me. In this book, Williams, who became famous for his escape from a German prisoner-of-war camp, described in *The Wooden Horse*, chronicles a series of famous escapes from impossible situations. I wonder if he will be able to tell me how to escape from a welded chain, through a locked door, past ever-vigilant guards, through another locked door, down several floors, out of a guarded building, and through the southern suburbs of Beirut . . .

The Uganda I knew in the sixties had gone for ever. I walked past the Provincial Office and down the pathway to our former house. Ghosts from the past stared at me. They were not hostile. Some wept, some smiled, some remained mute as they walked with me to the small hospital where Mark was born. The tree where the suspected thief had died was green and flourishing. Bougainvillaea bloomed in a spread of royal purple, cloaking the sorrow of days past and lightening the misery of the present. Robert Runcie approached me.

'Is this where you lived?' I nodded. 'It's very beautiful.'

It was. A part of me belonged here.

'That was my office years ago.'

The Archbishop smiled.

'Quite different from Lambeth.'

The earthly shadows of John Wasikye and Janani Luwum stood by my former house, in which both had lived. Behind them were hundreds of African men, women and children. The first son of George Lubega looked curiously at me. He was murdered in his home village.

'There are many memories,' I said as we walked together to Yona's house. Upstairs John Witheridge was typing sermon notes, a portable typewriter balanced on his knee. Dusk had fallen. In an open space behind the house a huge fire had been lit. A black iron cauldron, which might have come directly from ancient Greece, hung over the flames. A steady procession of animals was led past our window.

'It's medieval,' murmured John. 'They slaughter them and drop them straight into the pot.' Even at a time of celebration Africa would not cloak the immediacy of experience.

Archbishop Runcie and I visited President Obote. He spoke of refugees, violence and a massive collapse of moral standards.

'I look to the new Archbishop and the Cardinal as my spiritual leaders,' he added.

The next day troops surrounded the cathedral when Yona was enthroned. There was no trouble then, but the threat of violence was in the air. An old African I had known years before greeted me, his body bent, his face wizened. He had walked for four days to attend the service.

'I shall never see the like of this again,' he said. He looked up at the cathedral. I remembered my father's words at the Coronation in 1953. Life was slowly ebbing away. Obote soon returned to exile. Yona, ever-smiling Yona, stayed the course.

> *Oh Time! who know'st a lenient hand to lay*
> *Softest on sorrow's wound, and slowly thence . . .*
> *The faint pang stealest unperceiv'd away.*

Before we left Uganda, Robert Runcie visited the Cardinal at his residence on Rubaga Hill. The Roman Catholic cathedral was packed with Ugandans anxious to welcome the Archbishop of Canterbury. As we left, the Cardinal indicated that he wished to make a presentation to his visitor. A young man stepped forward and unveiled a portrait of the Archbishop.

'But that's amazing,' said Runcie. 'How did he do it so quickly?'

The Cardinal laughed. 'When the Holy Father visited, two pictures were painted of him. One was given to the Pope, and this is the second one. Yesterday, the artist painted out the Pope's head and put your head on his body.'

The electricity has failed again, and I only have a tiny stub of candle which flickers and makes strange fizzing noises as it burns towards its end. It is too difficult to read, so I place the candle on my upturned plastic cup and make shadow pictures on the wall with my hands: a dog, a duck, Popeye. They amuse me for a moment, but I tire of the game quickly. I read a great deal about the psychological concept of the shadow once. The shadow or negative side of the self can be either projected away on to some other person or circumstance, or accepted as being an essential aspect of the self. In trying to confront the forces within, I am attempting to face up to my inner conflict with, I hope, the realistic recognition that I will always have to work hard for any semblance of inner harmony. Someone, I forget who, wrote, 'The worst enemy is in your own heart.' The doctrine of original sin has been given a bad name, but I think it's pretty near the mark.

My mind strays from these fragmented thoughts back to my narrative. Will I ever be in a position to commit my thoughts to paper, to be read by others? They might be of some small comfort to others struggling to find meaning in life. I have no answers. All I can do is share as best I can what has been helpful for me during these dark days.

I draw myself away from gloomy thoughts by leaping across the world to stand on the vantage point in Hong Kong, overlooking Communist China. The date? Some time in the seventies. An old man in traditional dress poses for the tourists' cameras; young men hire out binoculars that enable the curious to sweep across the flat countryside of Canton. I see a solitary peasant wearing a broad-brimmed straw hat, struggling with a plough pulled by oxen. I am curious about the China beyond Hong Kong. I cast my mind back to the forties and remember the picture on the front page of the *Daily Mail* of HMS *Amethyst* blazing its way down the Yangtze, an event that caught my young imagination. Back in Hong Kong I take a ferry to the island of Lan Tao. Young backpackers laugh and chatter as they climb through the woods past the Trappist monastery. I go in and meet the ancient Chinese guestmaster. He was born on the mainland and forced to retreat to this secluded outpost when the Communists took power. Many of his brothers remained behind. Some died, some were imprisoned, others went underground. Few people were clear about the situation of Christians, or indeed of any religious group in China, but occasionally news came out, carried by Chinese who crossed between Hong Kong and the mainland.

On my frequent visits to the Far East, I always tried to stop off in Hong Kong. Peter Kwong, the first Chinese Anglican Bishop in the Crown Colony, was a good friend, and Frances and I acted as guardians for his two children when they went to school in England. Peter often looked forward to 1997 when Hong Kong was due to revert to the mainland. In Hong Kong, the traditional Christian denominations – Anglican, Roman Catholic, Baptist, Methodist – continued to exist. On the mainland, non-Roman Catholics grouped together in what was translated as the 'Three Self' movement, although some Protestants would have nothing to do with it, considering it merely an arm of the State. The Roman Catholics were divided between an officially recognised Church, many of whose Bishops had been appointed without the approval of the Holy See, and an 'underground' Church maintaining an unswerving allegiance to the Pope. It was a complex picture. Peter felt that the time was approaching when the Archbishop of Canterbury might consider visiting the mainland, which no previous archbishop had done. We discussed it, and I presented the proposal to Robert Runcie, who was immediately enthusiastic. In 1981 I arrived in Communist China to explore the possibility.

I went to Beijing and other principal cities in the country and had discussions with government officials and with the British Foreign Office. Bishop K. H. Ting was my main Church contact in China; I visited him at his home in Nanjing. Although he was an Anglican, he had committed himself to the 'Three Self' movement and did not envisage the restoration of the Anglican Church, or indeed any of the non-Roman Catholic denominations. Rather, he anticipated a new era when a united Church would preserve the best of the various traditions which had been introduced into the country by missionaries; a Church that would be rooted in China and in sympathy with the hopes and aspirations of the Chinese people. He also wanted the Church in China to have international links and to make a contribution to Christianity throughout the world. During my preliminary visits I also made contact with the Catholics in the country and repeatedly sought permission to visit the bishops who were being held in prison. My requests were never refused – neither were they granted.

There appeared to be two main reasons for the State's anger against the Vatican: it claimed that the imprisoned bishops had been breaking the law and undermining the country by their unswerving opposition to the Communist government, and that the Holy See was secretly supporting an 'underground' Catholic Church. Because of his meeting with the Pope, I was politely asked on a number of occasions about Archbishop Runcie's relationship with him, and indeed during the Archbishop's tour a Chinese official told me there was a press report circulating that named Robert Runcie as a Vatican agent. I never saw such a report, and heard no more about it.

After several exploratory trips it was clear to me that the Chinese would welcome a visit from the Archbishop. They were anxious to hasten the process of 'opening up' to the West, and the presence of the Archbishop of Canterbury in his capacity as a world religious leader and a figure of significance within British society would advance this aim. For his part, the Archbishop wanted to give encouragement to the Christians in China and to foster the development of freedom of expression for all religions, a development which was still in its infancy but growing.

Councils of Churches from around the world were being invited to China to re-establish contact and, it was hoped, to carry back favourable impressions of the country. A minor difficulty arose when the British Council of Churches asked Archbishop Runcie to lead a delegation to China when he had already accepted the invitation to visit the country in 1983 as an official guest of the Chinese government. The issue was resolved when the Archbishop decided both to lead the British delegation and to make time to follow the state programme arranged for him.

On my earlier visits to China I had met Professor Zhou Fu San, an academic and an ordained Anglican priest. One of his many activities was to compile the entries on Religion and Philosophy for a new Chinese encyclopedia, and I scoured London for obscure books to assist him in his work. During the official tour Richard Chartres and I were able to slip away for an hour or so to visit this remarkable man in his home on the outskirts of Beijing. He and his wife lived on the upper floor of a featureless concrete block in the capital, an area that compared unfavourably with the dullest housing estate in the British Isles, with one notable exception: there was no vandalism, and the crime rate was exceptionally low. Both Zhou and his wife spoke flawless English and were a delight to know. He and many of his colleagues had suffered during the ravages of the Cultural Revolution, and he was forced to abandon his scholarly work for some years.

I met many groups of Christians when visiting China and heard of their experiences in the late sixties at first hand. Large numbers had been sent away from their homes into forced labour or to be 're-educated'. The majority had maintained their faith and continued to meet secretly during these years. They divided the pages of a

Bible between themselves, exchanging them from time to time. Now, as a slow thaw spread across the country, they had emerged and retrieved their appropriated church buildings. Not all were given back. On one occasion I tried to find the Anglican Cathedral in Shanghai. Eventually I discovered it; it was being used as a government office.

The Archbishop's tour was a whirlwind of activities: a luncheon in the Great Hall of the People; a meeting with the President of China; a service of Holy Communion in a hotel bedroom. The Mayor of Nanjing gave a tea party for the Archbishop in a room not dissimilar to a church hall, with men and women dressed in Mao uniforms sitting around small tables as if at a whist drive. The Mayor took his guest from table to table. As the Archbishop approached one group, a benevolent-looking Chinese lifted his cap and addressed him in flawless English.

'Tell me, Archbishop, where is Brasenose on the river these days?'

In their private meetings with the Archbishop, leaders of the country were anxious to state their policy towards religion. They explained that citizens had freedom to express their religious beliefs. There had been mistakes in the past, they admitted, but these had been corrected. Although it was forbidden to use religion to disrupt the Constitution of the country, this now stated that there must be no persecution of practising Christians.

The tour included the usual tourist sights – the Great Wall, the terracotta figures at Xi'an, the Ming tombs. A year or so later I went back to China with Frances and Mark. We sailed through the Yangtze gorges and visited the Great Wall. I told Mark the Chinese saying: 'You're not a man until you have been to the Great Wall.' Little did I realise then that Mark would have to become a man years before his time, and take on an extraordinary responsibility for his mother.

I AM SINKING LOW. My body aches from repeated coughing which I am quite unable to control. My lungs are congested, and for hours on end I fight for breath. To inhale and expel air requires tremendous energy, and much of the time I am exhausted. There are long periods when it is impossible for me to lie down, and so I remain sitting, cross-legged, attempting to control the spasms which attack me with great frequency. The guards express their concern at times but do little to help. A few days ago they brought me a bottle of cough mixture, which made me vomit.

In my mind I continue writing, and at a deeper level I struggle with my inner contradictions. Somehow I have to do two things. I must, if I am going to make any psychological progress whatsoever, continue my interior dialogue. At the same time I have to bolster myself to an almost ridiculous degree. If I let my inner confidence collapse, I will die. If I don't face my doubts and conflicts I will never progress. I must somehow cultivate a defiant arrogance and yet not believe it. How I long for the love and company of my family. How I yearn with a childish, selfish longing to be understood and cared for. I am frightened. Frightened that, in growing up, my identity may slip away. These are hard days, but I must hold fast to my resolutions: no regrets, no sentimentality, no self-pity. Ridiculous, pompous statements, yet they have some meaning for me.

'You have problem?' the voice of the old man addresses me. I remember him from early in my captivity. He beat the soles of my feet until they were so swollen I couldn't walk unaided.

Yes, my friend, yes. I have a problem, and you have a problem, a massive problem. You are a blind stupid coward. My head swims, I have no breath, I can hardly speak, but I force a response.

'I cannot breathe properly.'

'Why?'

I do my best to explain about the fumes and the necessity for fresh air. He speaks to the guard in Arabic. The door closes. I have a problem, you have a problem, we have a problem, they have a problem. Problem, problem, problem, problem. My head sinks with exhaustion. Death would surely be preferable to this non-life. There is no escape, even sleep is denied me now. Yes, I have a problem, old man, but I'm not finished yet, not yet.

I can breathe more easily today and even manage to lie down. There are no further books at the moment, and I miss them desperately. I continue with my own narrative, but I quickly tire of it and decide to write a totally different book. I set it in Wilmslow, Cheshire. My main character is a young man who gets his first job on a local newspaper, the *Wilmslow Advertiser*. I invent the story all day and become absorbed in what is turning into a comic novel. At least I find it comic. As night falls, I find that I can't stop creating the narrative. My mind rushes on and on as the characters take shape in my imagination. I continue throughout the night and all the following day. After thirty-six hours it is finished, and I am worn out. For two days I have been living in a world I knew forty years ago. Now I sleep and wake to another long day without books.

I haul myself back to my autobiography, trying to remember where I left off when I started on the novel. I believe I know now why I made a change. I had been thinking about my son, Mark, and that made me hurt inside. I try hard not to dwell on my family or friends. I hardly dare think about my mother, as I fear she may have died in the last years. There doesn't seem to be a great deal of faith in me. At least not the faith that gives a deep security. Any faith I have has been hard-won, and what little I have I value.

I make myself return to Lambeth in the eighties. My secretary, Rosemary, left to start a legal training, and Stella Taylor took her place. We made plans for the Archbishop's future visits: Nigeria, Canada, Cuba, the Caribbean, South Africa, Australia, New Zealand, Japan; each journey a book in itself.

In 1983 we travelled to New Zealand. Coincidentally, the Prince and Princess of Wales and the Prime Minister and Foreign Minister of China were there at the same time. A private dinner was arranged for the Archbishop's party and the royal couple, and later the Archbishop saw the Chinese Ministers at their hotel in Wellington.

My memory of the official programme in New Zealand is blurred, but I clearly remember my visit because of an event that puzzled me. One day I was driving with Paul Reeves, the Anglican Archbishop who later resigned to occupy the position of Governor-

General. He chatted about the history of the country, pointing out the places where Bishop Selwyn, the famous missionary bishop, lodged on his travels. At one point we drove off the new road down a side track and he stopped the car.

'There's something here that might interest you.'

To the left was a row of old cottages; to the right a small cemetery where British casualties of the Maori wars were buried. The whole place looked vaguely familiar. As we walked back to the car, I was startled to realise that the lane and the cottages were the subject of a recurring dream I had had all my life. The only rational explanation I could think of was that perhaps as a child I had seen a picture of this place, and it had lodged in my subconscious. The dream was never repeated after this.

I knew many of the Caribbean islands from my work in Rome. One summer I took my family to Montserrat while I was working in the region. Good days. Several years later, the Archbishop of Canterbury visited Anglicans throughout the Caribbean. In Guyana, the Bishop, a local man, was locked in a fierce dispute with Forbes Burnham, the President. The two had known each other since childhood and had both achieved positions of considerable prominence in the country. The Bishop was fierce in his condemnation of corruption and not slow in making his voice heard. At first there was uncertainty as to whether or not the Archbishop should pay a courtesy call on the President. The Bishop felt that Robert Runcie should do so, but he himself would not attend. The President held back for a day or two but finally issued an invitation to the Archbishop.

Burnham was living behind barbed wire, security gates, floodlights and every warning device known to man. We were taken through the barriers into an office building, its corridor lined with security cameras. The President was sitting behind his desk. He looked strained, but he managed to smile.

'Sit down, Archbishop.'

The Archbishop sat on a soft leather settee, and I sat next to him.

'Have a drink, both of you.'

He produced two enormous tumblers which he half-filled with neat gin, and topped up his own drink, which I suspected was not the first of the day.

'Do you think I might have something with this?' The Archbishop gave a nervous glance at his tumbler.

The President looked mildly surprised, rummaged under his desk, and produced a bottle of tonic water. There was not a great deal of room for tonic, but we filled our glasses to the brim. Burnham raised his.

'Welcome, Your Grace. Welcome to Guyana.'

The Archbishop sipped, coughed and quickly returned his glass to the table. The President became more relaxed. He told us about his childhood, his Methodist father, and the problems the country faced. Earlier in the week we had been to the cathedral, which was the largest wooden cathedral in the world. Termites had done their worst, and considerable sums were required to put it in order. International help was on offer, but the appeal required the signature of the President. The Bishop wanted the financial assistance, but would not under any circumstances ask the President himself. He had no objection to us raising the subject, however, so we did. The President promised his signature.

'You like cigars, Mr Waite?' Burnham smiled, pressed a button on his desk and boomed into a microphone:

'Gift-wrap a box of cigars for Mr Waite. What about you, Archbishop? Gift-wrap two boxes of cigars.'

A disembodied voice assented and was promptly cut off.

'Fidel sends me dozens of boxes every month.'

He beamed and offered us more gin. We declined. The TV set in the corner showed a young woman walking down the corridor. Burnham pressed another button and the door opened. The cigars were handed to us. We stood and said goodbye.

'Give my regards to the Bishop,' he said. 'Come for dinner next time.'

We never saw him again.

We travelled to Grenada soon after the American forces had landed on the island to restore civil order following the murder of the then Prime Minister, Maurice Bishop, for which the deputy Prime Minister, Bernard Coard, his wife, General Hudson Austin and a number of others had been arrested and were awaiting trial. We stayed with the Governor who on request arranged for the Archbishop to visit the prisoners in the local jail. We duly arrived at the prison to find a scene of great activity. Carpenters, masons and labourers swarmed into the tiny prison yard.

'We've never been so busy,' explained the prison governor who met us. 'This place is far too small for all the prisoners. We are expanding.'

We were led to a small building with six or so cells positioned next to each other. As we stepped into the corridor, the prisoners began to protest. An arm appeared through the bars and a clenched fist shook in our direction.

'Quiet,' bellowed the officer. 'The Archbishop of Canterbury has come to see you.'

The Archbishop stopped and spoke to each prisoner. I was taken to another room and met with Mrs Coard, who was pregnant and very distressed. I tried to comfort her as best I could.

The journey through the Caribbean would have been very difficult had it not been for the generosity of John Shearer, an old army friend of the Archbishop. He provided a small private plane for several legs of the tour, and we had a day of rest at his house on one of the Turks and Caicos islands. In Belize, an open-air service was arranged. Just as it began, the heavens opened. George Price, the Prime Minister, stood under his umbrella throughout and afterwards took us to his house, a modest bungalow, for a meal.

We flew over the country in an army spotter plane ordinarily used to detect marijuana crops. John Witheridge and I sweated to keep the Archbishop fully briefed on the people he would meet and on the social, political and religious factors in each country we visited. Then it was over, and we were on our way back to London. Hardly a conventional Caribbean holiday.

The comings and goings in the next room totally baffle me. I thought I heard someone being taken away, but this morning I counted two pairs of feet passing my door. It's a mystery.

I have been given another volume of the American encyclopedia and enjoy reading it, although general books would be preferable. While I have it, I suspend my own writing for a day or so and concentrate on reading entries from Burma to Cathay. I am reminded of a visit made to Burma with Robert Runcie and Richard Chartres. The Archbishop was forbidden to speak in public, but he decided to accept this humiliation in order to spend time with the local Church people. Visiting Rangoon was like stepping back in time: there were few indications that we were living in the twentieth century.

There is a map of Canada in the encyclopedia, which pleases me, and I trace the route of the railway from coast to coast with the vague hope that one day I might make that journey. I laugh to myself when I remember a ludicrous incident which happened on a tour of the country. The Archbishop, John Witheridge and I were in a remote rural town. The Archbishop was due to speak in a small parish church, and it had been suggested that he be driven down the main street standing in the rural equivalent of a 'pope-mobile' – namely, a pick-up truck. None of us was keen on the idea, but as we were assured that it would give the locals great pleasure the Archbishop agreed.

On the morning of the great day we drove a hundred miles or so into the countryside and stopped on the outskirts of the town. The organisers, expecting rain, had erected a wooden structure on the back of the truck and covered it with transparent plastic. The forecasters were wrong. There was a blazing sun and a bright blue sky. Robert Runcie in his purple cassock and John, also in ecclesiastical garb, reluctantly stepped up into this contraption. I travelled in the car behind. As the extraordinary vehicle cruised down the main street at little more than three miles an hour, I could see both occupants mopping their brows and looking increasingly desperate. Suddenly, John produced a penknife and began to slash at the polythene awning. We stopped outside the church, and I jumped out of my car. Both John and the Archbishop were soaked in perspiration and looked quite ill with the heat. The Archbishop disappeared into the vestry for a complete change of clothes. John, who didn't have any other garments with him, had to manage as best he could.

'Move here.' The voice of the guard breaks into my thoughts. I do as he says and from under my blindfold see that he is taking my mattress out of the room. He returns and collects my water jug, towel and toothbrush. My heartbeat increases, and I fight for breath. Someone crouches down and unfastens the chain around my ankle.

'Stand.' I struggle to my feet. A guard stands on my left, another on my right. They move me forward, and we go out of the door, down the corridor and into another room.

'Sit.' A chain is fastened around my ankle again.

'No look. Understand?'

'I don't know what you mean.'

'No look outside.'

I am not clear what he means, but I agree not to look outside. The door is locked, and I remove my blindfold. I am in a much smaller room, but to my delight there is no metal sheeting in front of the French windows. Instead, a large wardrobe has been placed directly in front of them to prevent me from seeing out, and when I peer beneath it I can see that the windows are covered with full-length lace curtains. The door to the balcony has been left ajar, and a gentle breeze fills the room with cool air. It's been so long since I breathed fresh air and experienced natural·light. The room is almost blindingly light. I can hear a bird singing and people chattering in the street below. This is sheer luxury. I look at my white withered skin. I am ageing quickly – too quickly. The air is sweet. Oh, so sweet. I draw as much as I can into my lungs. I hear children laughing and shouting outside. The breeze is lovely.

The old man must have ordered the move because of my bronchial problems. I like it here, I like it very much. I am sitting next to the door and directly beneath the light switch, which means that when there is electricity, I will be able to control it. Through the keyhole I can see straight down the corridor. To the right there is at least one other room, but I don't know if it is occupied. If it is, I might be able to get a glimpse of the inhabitants as they are led to the bathroom in the mornings. My line of vision doesn't allow me to see faces, but I can see the bodies of the guards as they pass at the end of the corridor. One is quite fat, the other is slight. The first must be 'the Frog', as I have nicknamed him. He is the one who is so unpleasant. I sit down, my back resting against the wall. Fresh air and sunlight. Could I ask for more?

The days pass, and the light and air make me feel one hundred per cent better. My lungs continue to trouble me, but now that I am away from the generator and have better living conditions, I can manage. There was a small setback this morning when the Frog and his companion came into the room to conduct a spot search.

'Stand up. Put hands against wall.'

I face the wall and rest my palms against it. Although I am wearing only shorts and a vest, they run their hands over the whole of my body. My mattress and blankets are thrown about. I hear someone flicking through my Bible and Prayer Book.

'What are you doing?'

'Not your business. No noise.'

They finish their search and leave the room. I begin to make my bed and fold the blankets. I find this disturbance quite upsetting; it seems so unnecessary and emphasises the fact that I have no rights whatever. I pick up my Bible and look through it. The Bunyan card has gone. It's not in the Prayer Book, nor is it on the floor. Joy

Brodier or Bradier – I must remember her name, and if I am ever able to track her down I will ask whether she sent it to the Red Cross, to Hezbollah, or where. I feel a deep sadness that this simple link with my own country has been taken from me, probably by the spiteful Frog. It is he who brings me a meal.

'Have you taken my card?'

'I don't know.'

'It was in my Bible.' I pick up the Bible and show it to him.

'I don't know.'

He is not interested and does not want to talk. The card has gone for ever, and I might as well accept the fact and forget it. At least life is much better with fresh air and natural light, and I am thankful for that.

Soon afterwards I experience another acute disappointment. My door is opened and I am told to fasten my blindfold and keep it on. Several people come into the room and begin to dismantle the wardrobe. Then I hear the ominous sound of an electric drill, followed by hammering. My heart sinks deeper and deeper. When the work is finished and the door locked, I remove the covering from my eyes. Metal sheets cover the French windows. A light bulb gives off a weak yellow glow, flickers and goes out. My fresh air and light have gone and I am once again living in a tomb. How could you? How, in God's name, could you?

DESPAIR GRIPS ME when I wake from a fitful sleep and it is dark. Yesterday I could lie on my mattress and see the light gradually grow stronger until the room was warmed by the sun. Now the metal sheets allow virtually no light to enter. One small beam reminds me of what I have enjoyed for the last few days. It is hard to fight despair, particularly as I feel physically weak. Months without exercise have brought me low, and the problem with my lungs is a constant trial. I continue to cough, but the combination of fresh air and psychological well-being acquired from living with natural light did wonders for me. I can only hope and pray that I won't sink again into the agony of not being able to breathe properly.

I turn on my mattress and face the wall, pulling the blanket around my shoulders and huddling into a foetal position. A battle rages within me and affects every part of me – mind, body, and soul. It's the classic conflict between light and darkness, life and death. I continue to pray each day, but I know that I'm not going to be given a palliative. This battle, which threatens me with total physical and psychological collapse, has to be fought by me as I am. There will be no favours, no special benefits, no allowances made. If I can draw any strength from outside myself, it will be from contemplating the crucifixion of Jesus. But I am wary of that. I don't want to make ridiculous false comparisons which would give me an over-inflated opinion of myself and my limited suffering. I find I cannot stop thinking of myself and my own survival. If this continues, I will be quite impossible to live with, should I ever have human company again.

There is a sound in the corridor; the guard is stirring. Soon he will bring breakfast. I will be taken to the bathroom, brought back to my room, and then face another long day with nothing to do but sit and think and continue writing in my head.

The detention of several UK citizens in Libya in 1984 brought me into a minor disagreement with Robert Runcie. Previously, Douglas Ledingham, an official of British Caledonian Airlines, and another expatriate worker, had been arrested. The latter was ordered out of Libya, and Ledingham was released after his company threatened to close down airline services to and from the country. Now four other Englishmen were being held on vague charges: Robin Plummer, an electronics engineer; Malcolm Anderson, an engineer with an oil company; Alan Russell, an English teacher; and Michael Berdinner, a university lecturer.

Alan Russell's wife Carol contacted me on behalf of her husband and the other men, and when we met, she told me that she had approached Lambeth Palace out of desperation and because she knew of the work I had done for the hostages in Iran. She was struggling bravely to maintain herself and her children. I promised to look into the case but could not, at that stage, give any assurance that we would be able to help. I checked with the Foreign Office as to whether any of the men were facing legitimate charges. They told me they believed not, but if there were any, the men should be formally charged and brought to a court of justice.

I discussed the matter with the Archbishop, who was not enthusiastic about my involvement. He reminded me that the hostage negotiations in Iran had taken a great deal of my time and stretched me to the limit to fulfil my normal responsibilities at Lambeth. He also pointed out that there was less justification for my involvement in Libya, since none of the men detained was working for the Church or had Church connections. I strongly maintained that the Church of England was the Church for all people of the country, whether they attended it or not. If citizens turned to the Church for help, then, if at all possible, help should be given. Robert Runcie finally agreed that I should see if anything could be done. As with Iran, I collected as much information as I could about Libya and the men who had been detained there. My findings indicated that Alan Russell was the only one of the four who had committed a minor breach of Libyan regulations, in passing information to a BBC World Service reporter during a twenty-four-hour news blackout. It seemed to me that this hardly warranted prolonged detention without charges being brought or a trial scheduled.

The background against which the hostage affair was played out was both unpleasant and dangerous. In April 1984, a month before the British hostages were taken, Yvonne Fletcher, a young policewoman, was shot while on duty outside the Libyan Embassy in London. The weapon was said to have been fired from a window of the Embassy. Around that time, several Libyan nationals had been arrested in the UK and charged with a variety of terrorist offences. Given the emotion these events had aroused in both Britain and Libya, the prospect of easing the situation did not seem hopeful.

It was Julius Nyerere, then President of Tanzania, who got the process going. In 1984 he was coming to the end of his term as president of the Organisation of African Unity and I wondered if he might be willing to approach Colonel Gaddafi to ask him if he would see me. I mentioned this possibility to the Archbishop, and one Friday afternoon Robert Runcie telephoned him. Nyerere immediately suggested a meeting at his home the following Monday afternoon. I flew out of London on Sunday, checked in at a hotel in Dar es Salaam, and the following day a car drove me to the President's modest house overlooking the Indian Ocean. His private secretary, who was European, took me through to the back of the house where the President greeted me warmly but confessed that he was puzzled as to what the Archbishop might require of him. I explained. He responded by saying that Colonel Gaddafi was an unusual man, with a mind of his own. He doubted that he would have much influence with him, but he would certainly do what he could when he saw Gaddafi at the next meeting of the Organisation of African Unity, due to take place in Addis Ababa.

A soft drink was served, and we talked about Uganda and the problems of development in Africa. I liked Nyerere very much. He seemed a warm and compassionate man with a genuine humility. After an hour or so, I left, encouraged by his obvious willingness to help. The next time we met was at his retirement from office in October 1985 when Margaret Thatcher gave a farewell dinner in his honour at 10 Downing Street. By then the hostages had been released, and I was able to thank him personally for his assistance.

I flew to Libya in October 1984 on what was to be the first of several visits. As in Iran some years earlier, the political situation in Libya was highly complex. Iran had taught me that a multitude of factors operate in bringing about the release of hostages, and I hoped that I might help by creating a situation in which Colonel Gaddafi could release the men without loss of face on his side and without breaking the rules of justice on the British side. The fact that I was received courteously by the Libyan authorities and given every opportunity to discuss the problem was a good omen, but no guarantee of a successful outcome. My first task was to try to understand the situation. I had learnt from past experience that a number of games would be played out, both within the country and between Libya and the United Kingdom. Some I would know about, some I might guess at; others would remain hidden from me. I knew I would have to step gently.

My primary concern was for the welfare of the four men, and I asked if I might see them as soon as possible. After a delay of a day or two, I was taken to an upstairs room in a house in Tripoli where several officials sat behind desks. After coffee, the four hostages were brought in. I was then able to speak with each man separately in the company of a Libyan official. It was not easy for them to talk openly, but they were able to tell me that the conditions under which they were being kept were not good. Although they were not chained, they were held in a locked room with no natural light. Understandably, they were all highly anxious, and two of the group appeared to be exceptionally stressed. All I could do at this stage was to assure them that everything possible was being done for their release, and that as a first step I would attempt to get them moved to more satisfactory accommodation.

I immediately raised this matter with the Libyans, who promised to look into it. Diplomatic relations with the United Kingdom had been severed earlier, but there were still two British diplomats living in the residence. Outside the main gate a group of young men, the Libyan equivalent of Iran's Revolutionary Guards, were on duty day and night, noting every arrival and departure. I made no secret of the fact that I kept in touch with the representatives of my country and was grateful for the extra briefings on the situation they were able to provide. I did not expect to make a lot of progress on this first visit to Libya, which, indeed, proved to be the case. I returned to the UK, met the hostages' relatives, and awaited developments.

There is a great deal of movement in the corridor. Quietly, I kneel by the door and look through the keyhole. I must be very cautious; the guards have a habit of flinging the door open without warning to check on me. On one occasion I was terrified when, just as I was putting my eye to the keyhole, I saw a guard preparing to do exactly the same from the other side. I withdrew instantly. Mercifully, he hadn't seen me.

Now the door of the room next to mine is open, and I can see bedding being dragged in. I can't see the guards' faces, but I recognise the Frog's body. It could be that the guards are taking over this room for their own use, or that it is being prepared for other hostages. If it is the latter, I might stand a chance of communicating with someone if he is chained to the dividing wall against which I sit.

At the far end of the corridor where the guards are, several weapons are lying around – a couple of machine guns and a pistol like the one I found in the bathroom years ago. Now, on reflection, I don't believe that pistol was left to trap me. It must have been an oversight on the part of the guard, and my chance of escaping would have been very small. I would have had to hurt him, and I'm glad I didn't. Someone walks towards my door. I leap away and fasten my blindfold.

'You OK?'

'Yes, thank you.'

'You want anything?'

'I would like some books,' I say, as always.

'Tomorrow.'

The door closes. Tomorrow – will it ever come?

I returned to Tripoli at Christmas-time and was introduced to an experienced Libyan diplomat. Mr Zlitni had spent a lifetime in the service of his country and was a survivor, of small to medium height and well rounded. He said that he had been brought out of semi-retirement especially to deal with the question of British prisoners. He was polished and professional. He told me he had a nephew, also in the Diplomatic Service, who would always be on hand to translate for me and give me any assistance I might require. The nephew spent a great deal of time with me and was a very pleasant person to deal with. During my visits to Libya, I got to know a number of nationals, and I liked many of the people I met. There is a courtesy and genuine friendliness among the Arab people which I am glad to have experienced.

By now I was beginning to understand one aspect of the story behind the capture of the British hostages. The young men who camped day and night outside the British residence were necessary if Colonel Gaddafi was to keep the Libyan 'revolution' moving forward. While it is doubtful that the Colonel shared their particular brand of Islamic fundamentalism, he needed their zeal and enthusiasm on his side. It looked as though the young revolutionaries had seized the hostages in order to trade them for the Libyans held in British prisons. This was clearly out of the question. The hostages were being held illegally, and the problem facing Gaddafi was how he could release them without undermining his position and without alienating the young radicals. In the inevitable gamesmanship that would follow, I realised that all parties, including myself, would need to play to the gallery from time to time.

By now, the media had taken up the story in a big way. Kate Adie from the BBC and Brent Sadler from ITN had arrived in Libya, together with numerous newspaper correspondents. Clearly, the Libyans wanted the story to be played up in front of the cameras, and I had little option but to follow that course. The situation gave me my first real insight into the difficulties faced by journalists eager for a news story but conscious that their reporting might hinder a resolution. I respected the way in which the majority handled this thorny problem.

I don't think that I am depressed in the way that term is defined clinically, but I am deeply disappointed and upset. It is horrible to return to artificial light and stale air, but deep within me a glimmer of hope remains. The words of the writer in the Epistle to the Hebrews comes to mind: '. . . faith is being sure of what we hope for and certain of what we do not see.' What is it that I hope for? Utopia, I suppose. An impossible dream, but probably a goal worth working for as an ideal. Scriptural texts taken out of context are virtually useless, but somehow my mind latches on to them in order to keep hope alive. At times I clutch at straws even though they give little nourishment. I can know in a small way the utter desolation Christ faced, and his steadfast courage inspires me. If this experience is teaching me anything, it is teaching me that I, the child who longs for the approval of the father, who is terrified of rejection, must grow into myself. There is no necessity to prove anything. I am a long way from the heart of the religion I profess. I hardly know the real meaning of love, which must surely be the very pivot of Christianity, but I long to make it strong and central in my life. I realise that throughout my life I have been driven by a desire for acceptance and approval. A small boy peering from behind the glass window where a man waves and a woman cries. Come on, Waite, it's time you grew up.

A cockroach edges across the floor. It runs and stops dead in its tracks. Now it moves towards my mattress. Its antennae wave back and forth as though it senses my presence. I hate cockroaches. They bite my feet when I sleep and threaten me with disease. I fasten all my anger and frustration on this solitary insect and kill it with an enormous blow from my plastic slipper. Then I lie there, staring like a madman at the lifeless body. A small party of ants emerges from a crack in the tiles. Even as I stare with a deadly fascination, they dismember the body. A lone ant struggles with a wing, a small party haul away a leg. In an hour the remains have disappeared.

> *There is no solace on earth for us – for such as we –*
> *Who search for a hidden city that we shall never see . . .*
>
> *We seek the City of God, and the haunt where beauty dwells,*
> *And we find the noisy mart and the sound of burial bells.*

The day drags on. I try to recapture days long since gone. Did I really travel to Libya, meet hostages and attempt to comfort them? How could I have hoped to do so? How could I possibly have known then the agony of living with constant threat and uncertainty? The authorities allowed me to conduct a Christmas service for the four men, and we were swamped by TV cameras. I agreed to their presence because it provided an opportunity for the families back in England to catch at least a glimpse of the hostages. I asked Mr Zlitni when the men would be moved to a better location.

'Don't worry, Mr Waite. We shall give them a villa. They will have fresh air and everything they need.'

'A villa?'

'Yes, just outside the town.'

'When do you intend to release them?'

'Ah, that is a problem. We must have patience, Mr Waite. These matters cannot be rushed. You are too impatient, Mr Waite, if you will forgive me for saying so.'

Malcolm Anderson was brought before a local court; to this day I don't know on what charge. Hugh Donachie, one of the two remaining British diplomats, suggested that I attend the proceedings and apply for bail with a request that Malcolm be released into my care. The small courtroom was packed to the doors on the appointed day. Television cameramen jostled for position. A large cage-like construction housed Malcolm and an assorted group of local suspects. When Malcolm's case came up, I stood and was permitted to address the court. I identified myself and offered to stand bail for him. The magistrate conferred and I was informed that bail would not be granted. On leaving the court I made a further request.

'Mr Zlitni, I would like two things. First, I want to visit the men in their "villa". Second, I would like to stay with them until they are released.'

'Ah, Mr Waite. Yes, you can certainly visit them, but stay, that would be difficult, Mr Waite. You are our guest; we can't allow you to stay there.'

'I am sure I would be quite comfortable in a villa, Mr Zlitni.'

One morning a driver took me out of the town and down a track to what appeared to be a disused camp. We came to a wire fence and a locked gate. Inside were several small huts crowded together. I turned to my companion, Fuad.

'Is this the villa?'

He smiled weakly. We stepped out of the car while several semi-military figures eyed us. Fuad addressed them and they shuffled their feet.

'What is it, Fuad?'

'May be a small problem. I don't know.'

'They don't want us to enter – right?'

'Well, perhaps, but only a small problem.'

'Tell them this, Fuad. Tell them we have permission to see the men. Permission from the very top. Tell them to open the gates right now.'

Fuad spoke in Arabic. A key was produced, and we entered the camp.

The four men were living in a small hut in surroundings remarkably similar to prisoner-of-war camps I had seen in films. They had a good degree of freedom and during the day could sit outside in the sunshine.

'You can stay all day,' Fuad told me.

'I would like to stay until they leave for home.'

'I will collect you this evening.'

Fuad walked across the dusty compound to his car. One of the men, Robin Plummer, turned to me.

'Quickly, take this.'

He had something in his hand he wanted to pass on to me. I was extremely apprehensive for many reasons. The room might be bugged, and I did not under any circumstances want to compromise my position. Also I hardly knew the men and had no idea of their mental stability. I virtually ignored Robin and continued talking to the others.

'Listen, for God's sake, listen,' he pressed. 'Take this.'

'Robin, be careful.'

'I know. Take this quickly.' He put a small package into my hand, and I slipped it into my pocket.

'Give it to British Caledonian. They will understand.'

'OK.'

I hadn't a clue what I had been given, and I hated the idea of breaking the trust the Libyans had put in me. Everything could well have been overheard, but there was nothing I could do other than accept the package.

I didn't learn the full story until much later. Before the airline official, Doug Ledingham, was released, his suitcase had been left in the room where Robin and the others were kept. They searched it to see if it contained anything incriminating and discovered three hundred Libyan dinars – about nine hundred pounds sterling, which they decided to keep in case they had an opportunity to escape. In return they hid an IOU in the lining of Doug's case. The package I had was the money. Eventually I returned it to British Caledonian.

I spent the whole day with the group. Michael Berdinner was depressed.

'Why? Tell me why they have taken me. I've done nothing wrong, nothing at all. Why? I can't understand it.'

Alan Russell was hyperactive. Robin and Malcolm Anderson were anxious.

Now, as I think back over that time, I understand. Don't ever feel guilty about your fear, Michael. It's real. It grips your soul and drags you into a pit of despair. Don't brood, Alan. You were fortunate, you had a marvellous wife and children to be proud of. Robin and Malcolm, now I know what you went through. Now I know what captivity does to a man. I tried to bring you comfort, but I didn't know the depth of what you all had to suffer. Now I do know.

'We will have Christmas dinner tonight, Mr Waite.' Mr Zlitni beamed. 'I shall meet you in the evening. We will dine in the hotel.'

Mr Zlitni was a true trencherman. We dined on lobster and drank non-alcoholic fruit cordial.

'I wish you a very happy Christmas, Mr Waite. May this small problem soon be over.'

He tucked into the lobster. I had little appetite.

'You must eat well. You worry too much, Mr Waite – if I may say so.'

You may say so, Mr Zlitni. You may say so. You know how to survive. You know politics. You measure the tides. You know when to step into the water and when to take to the hills. Beside you, Mr Zlitni, I am a babe in arms. I wouldn't survive for ten minutes in your world, nor would I wish to. Good luck, Mr Zlitni, good luck. Just let me have these men and go home. Let's ring the curtain down now.

'It would be good if you would care to speak to one of the People's Congresses, Mr Waite.'

'Would it?'

'The people debate every issue in the country. They decide policy.'

'Do they?'

'If you could speak to the People's Congress in Tripoli that would be most helpful to the case.'

A day or so later I was taken to a tent in the town where the Congress was in progress. It was packed. At the top table sat the party officials. I had no idea what to say. I looked around and depended upon intuition, one of my few gifts. I spoke of justice and respect for God's law. To protect the hostages, I deliberately said what in fact was the truth: that I had seen them and that they were not being tortured. People rose and began to leave. What had I said to drive them away? An official came towards me.

'Don't worry. They are only leaving for early-evening prayers. Keep speaking.'

I continued for another five minutes as the tent emptied of people and then I, too, left. Later I found that the hostages had been listening to my speech on the radio. They were on tenterhooks that I might put a foot wrong. Somehow I managed not to.

Hugh Donachie from the British Foreign Office drove me back across town in the Embassy armour-plated Jaguar.

'We send it to Cyprus for servicing. It's like driving a tank.'

We went past the British Embassy building. It was dusk, and lights burned on every floor.

'No one has turned the lights out since we vacated the place. Young men have been searching it for weeks.'

We saw the silhouette of a man framed in a lighted window. Outside, the same group of bearded guards stood round an open fire. They peered through the car windows as we passed. Hugh gave a cheery wave. A powerful police motorcycle roared past us and flagged us down. Hugh, as cool as ever, got out while documents were checked, then returned me to my hotel. I braced myself for the next act.

'You should relax, Mr Waite. Libya is a beautiful country, and you should see something of it.'

'Thank you, Mr Zlitni. I should like that.'

'We will arrange for you to visit Sabratah and Leptis Magna. They are magnificent, Mr Waite, quite magnificent.'

Mr Zlitni was correct. These Roman sites on the Mediterranean are two of the most beautiful and peaceful places I have ever visited. I travelled with a few journalists who were staying in the hotel, and we were the only visitors. We walked along streets rutted with tracks made hundreds of years ago. A huge basilica reminded me that St Augustine and the Church flourished in North Africa long before the coming of Islam. The two cities were superbly positioned. How clever the Romans were in choosing sites.

'Thank you, Mr Zlitni, that was a really good day.'

He beamed.

'We have beautiful places in our country, Mr Waite, but we have many problems. The desert is still littered with bombs and mines left over from World War Two. Europe has used us, Mr Waite. America has used us. Who gives us credit for the developments we have made? They abuse us if we don't jump to their tune. We have our dignity, Mr Waite. We have our dignity.'

The Libyan Foreign Office was a bleak-looking building in Tripoli. Mr Said Hafiana received me in his comfortable office on an upper floor. Unlike Mr Zlitni, Mr Hafiana had not retired and was actively dealing with a multitude of foreign policy questions. He was clever and, as were most of the Libyans I met, courteous.

'We are happy for your visit, Mr Waite. The role of the Church and the Mosque must not be underestimated. The case against the men? These are political cases. We have done nothing to hurt their dignity. Libyan people in Britain are subject to different treatment. We want better treatment for our detainees in Britain. Libyan people are always ready to have relationships with the UK. Do you know, Mr Waite, there are thirteen thousand British subjects in this country? Not one of these people has suffered any loss of dignity. Your students are not ill-treated. Every Libyan student in London has been worried. Don't let your country be a theatre for action against the Libyan government, Mr Waite. We want a better relationship.'

A meeting with Colonel Gaddafi was arranged. I did not go with a prepared brief, so I would have to respond spontaneously to any point he raised. There were the usual delays. Mr Hafiana accompanied me to a palatial building in town, and we waited. We were told successively that the Colonel would be along shortly; the Colonel would be late; there would be a delay of three hours; the meeting had been called off; the meeting was on again; we must move to a different location.

Finally, at night, I was escorted to the famous tent pitched in the midst of a compound in Tripoli. I entered. The ceiling of multi-coloured cloth was so low that I was forced to stoop, putting me in a permanently deferential relationship to the Colonel and his aides. Wooden bookcases lined the walls. There were a television and a video recorder behind the large modern desk. After a brief disruption while photographers and TV cameramen took pictures, we were left alone. The Colonel sat on a raised dais. I sat cross-legged on the floor in front of him.

We began with an exchange of traditional courtesies. I conveyed the greetings of the Archbishop of Canterbury. He responded by saying that he gave reverence to Canterbury and was looking for a sign of goodwill from the British government so that the two countries could find a solution to what was, after all, a diplomatic problem. What was required, the Colonel continued, was a meeting between senior members of the Foreign Office and Libyan officials. If Mrs Thatcher would not move from her position, why should the Libyans be expected to move from theirs?

I raised the question of the British hostages and was told that they were detained and charged according to the law. The charges were connected with state security. Gaddafi, too, expressed his concern about the treatment of Libyans in London. I said that I could not, and did not, speak for the British government, but I would certainly pass his views on to them. I suggested that, to help those who were frightened or claimed that they were being harassed, the Churches should be able to set up a telephone line which any Libyan in the United Kingdom could use for advice and information. I also said that while I could not interfere in any way with the due process of law I would certainly visit the Libyan prisoners, and that the Church should be able to give their families assistance when visiting them in the UK. The Colonel concluded the interview by saying that he appreciated the initiative taken by the Church in this matter and repeating that he was eager to have a good relationship with Britain.

Before I left, he presented me with a copy of the Koran. I gave him a book I had originally bought for Zhou Fu San in China. It was in my office when I left for Libya, and I took it with me as it seemed to me to be an appropriate gift. It was a history of Arab philosophy, and it pleased Colonel Gaddafi.

After the meeting I tried to decide how best to convey to the British government the Libyans' desire for a meeting with officials. It seemed to me that two demands were being made: at the foreign-policy level, the Libyans wanted diplomatic relations with the United Kingdom restored. At the same time the young radicals wanted to exchange the British hostages for Libyans held in Britain on terrorist charges. The latter was clearly an impossibility, and I felt it was unlikely that the former could be met quickly, but a high-level meeting between officials of both governments might well be feasible. I went to Tunis and communicated with the Foreign Office via the British Embassy. The response was that nothing at all could happen until all four British subjects were released. I returned to Libya for the next round.

The main battle now took place between the radicals on the ground and the diplomats in the Libyan Foreign Office. The radicals had no wish to alter their demands and, to my knowledge, never did. The diplomats recognised a possible opening if they could get secret talks moving and thus felt that this was an option worth pursuing. Colonel Gaddafi was faced with the delicate task of keeping both groups on his side while realistically he could give his full support only to the second option. I was informed that the British hostages were to be released into my care. And that, on the Colonel's orders, the release would take place in front of TV cameras.

I went on the appointed day to the grand building, which had been decked out for a joyful occasion. There were to be speeches, a public handing-over of the men, and a tea party. The radicals were far from happy. I met with their leaders, who were most polite but still insistent that the Libyans must be released from British prisons. I made it clear that I could not under any circumstances promise that, nor could I argue the case in England. All I could say was that I was sure the prisoners would be given a fair trial. That was not enough to satisfy them. The hostages' release was called off, and I went to my hotel with a heavy heart. I do not know what happened during the next twenty-four hours. Some say Colonel Gaddafi threatened the radicals with a big stick. He may well have done.

The following day the release was on again. Speeches were made. The radicals continued pressing their demands and made it look as though they were getting their way. I repeated in public and before the cameras that there was no way I could, or would, interfere with the course of British justice, but that the Church would do what it could for Libyans in London and for their visiting relatives. Robin, Michael, Alan and Malcolm were then handed over to me.

As in Iran, there was nearly a last-minute disaster. The Russell family was far from affluent, and Alan had all his savings in a bank on the far side of town. For this final visit, Andrew Acland, a young man then on the staff at Lambeth Palace, had flown out to Libya with me to aid in the release. I suggested that he go with Alan to the bank to collect his savings. We all knew that once Alan had left Libya, the chances of his seeing any of his money again were slim. Hugh Donachie and I took care of the other three men. No special provision had been made for their return home. As in Iran, I was supposed to bring them back on a regular scheduled flight. Understandably, we were anxious that something might go wrong at the last moment. Hugh was under exceptional pressure; he had received a message from 10 Downing Street, urging him to get the men home as quickly as possible. We drove to the airport. No sign of Alan. The hands of the clock moved inexorably forward. Still no Alan. Hugh was perspiring furiously.

'Get them on the plane. Alan can come later.'

I couldn't go without him. I thought of all that his wife and family had been through and how acute their disappointment would be if he did not return with the others. Fuad was by my side.

'Fuad, do me a small favour. Ring the control tower and ask them to refuse permission for the plane to leave. Andrew will surely get Alan here soon.'

Fuad disappeared and returned after a few moments.

'It's OK, the plane can't leave.'

We waited. Well after departure-time, Andrew arrived with Alan in tow. They had been delayed by traffic and endless red tape at the bank. We swept them forward on to the plane. It wasn't until we were out of Libyan airspace that I realised how exhausted I was.

Our arrival at Gatwick Airport was chaotic. We were totally engulfed by the media. I knew little or nothing about the effects of long-term stress on individuals and had made no arrangements for post-release support for the men. Andrew Acland and I did our best to see them safely into the hands of their families, and then we went home.

As soon as I could, I set up a telephone line for Libyan residents in the United Kingdom, and this was used for several months. I met with a large group of Libyan residents in London and took up a number of individual cases with the appropriate authorities. I had visited foreign prisoners held in British jails for many years, but now I made a special point of visiting Libyans, and on a number of occasions I saw to the welfare of their families when they came to the UK. The detained Libyans I met were kept in high-security establishments and were usually model prisoners. Some admitted outright that they had acted for political reasons, arguing that as they had not killed or injured British subjects, they should not be detained in a British prison. They also argued, more reasonably, that while UK citizens serving a life sentence for murder could be released on licence after twelve or so years, they had no such opportunity. They contended that it was politics, not justice, which dictated their continued detention.

Occasionally I met a truly pathetic case. There was a young man from a conservative Islamic background who came to Britain from Libya to study. He was introduced to fast living by some of his Libyan associates and then threatened with exposure to his parents unless he deposited a package containing an explosive device outside the house of another Libyan. Obviously no country can allow such battles to be fought on its soil, but in many instances of terrorism the real instigators are not brought to justice.

After the release of the hostages, the Libyan authorities kept in touch with me, and a secret meeting was indeed arranged between Foreign Office officials and representatives of the Libyan government. The meeting took place in Rome, and I travelled there to see some of the participants but declined an invitation to attend because of the political rather than humanitarian focus.

In 1986 the United States launched an air strike on Tripoli in retaliation for bomb attacks at Vienna and Rome airports which were believed to have been carried out by terrorist groups supported by Gaddafi, and which killed or injured a number of innocent civilians. I strongly and publicly opposed this action, and I continue to believe that in our legitimate fight against hostage-taking and terrorism we should tackle the root problems of injustice and long-standing grievances rather than retaliating with further violence. Violence should be used only as a last resort. In the case of the bombing of Libya, I doubted whether avenues had been properly explored, or even explored at all.

Some time after the event I met Oliver North.

'President Reagan was talking about you the other day,' he said.

'Oh.'

'He said he was surprised you had spoken out against the bombing. He thought you were on our side.'

'What did you say?'

'I told him you were a churchman and were opposed to violence.'

This morning I wake early. Everything is silent. Gently I raise myself to my knees and peer through the keyhole. A light is burning in the corridor. In the distance I see a bundle of blankets in which the body of a sleeping guard is wrapped. A machine gun lies by his side. What a curious life he leads. What does he think about hostages? He has guarded us for years, in my case for almost four years. When he leaves home for days on end, does he ever let slip to his wife or his parents the real nature of his work? A lot of people must know about the hostages, or at least have their suspicions. I have shared this and earlier locations with other unknown hostages. It's remarkable that we can remain hidden for so long in the middle of a busy suburb. How much longer will this go on? Four years – four years alone. I can hardly believe it. I have not had a proper conversation with anyone for over fourteen hundred days. The Jesuits are said to do a seventy-day retreat as they prepare for their ministry. Well, boys, I have just done twenty such retreats, one after the other! Have I got that right? Wasn't it seventy days' detention for suspects in South Africa? It hardly matters. I've been in chains for four long years – that I know.

I look back over the years of my captivity. I have had no great thoughts, no illuminating inspirations. Better men than myself would have been able to dig deeper into their inner experience. All I seem to have done is keep afloat and withstand the storms. I remember my student days when there would be furious arguments about doctrinal points. We debated as though our very lives depended upon correct formulations of dogma. Now, all my thinking seems to centre around basic points: love, hate, light, dark, fear, joy, life, death.

Each day I have walked through the Psalmist's valley. The shadow of death has been around me. Then, for a space, I have caught a glimpse of the warmth of light, and the shadow has receded. Christ in his teaching spoke so simply and yet so profoundly about the essential fundamentals of life. Who is this mysterious figure who speaks through the pages of the New Testament? My knowledge of him is culturally conditioned. I know that he has taught me to face life as it is and not to be afraid of death. I may die in captivity. I may not see my family and friends again. Whatever happens, I have not been destroyed. My prayers have been puny, but once or twice I have touched the awesome mystery which lies at the heart of the universe, and which I call God. Awesome is the only word I can find to describe what I mean. In Christ I see the light side of God, which gives me strength and hope. His death graphically illustrates the polarity I know in my inner being. By allowing my unconscious to work, I will find healing and strength.

The guard is stirring at the end of the corridor so breakfast should arrive soon. A break before I am taken to the toilet. As my skin trouble keeps recurring, I continue to be allowed to take a quick shower every day. I stand under the lukewarm water and look through a space in the metal shutter. It's a glorious morning outside. Back in my room, I kneel at the keyhole again. Two guards are out there. One holds a pistol, the other enters the room next to mine. He leads out a blindfolded man who wears a pair of striped pyjamas. I watch, fascinated. I am reminded of the photographs of pyjama-clad, gaunt figures herded together in concentration camps when I was a small boy. I can't see the guards' faces, and the hostage is blindfolded. He is led to the bathroom while the other guard covers them with the pistol. The same thing happens twice more with different men. Then the door is locked, and the guards move away. There are now three hostages next door to me. I *must* find out who they are.

22

EVERY DAY MY DESK in Lambeth Palace was covered with mail relating to overseas issues. Groups and individuals constantly lobbied the Archbishop on a multitude of problems, and every communication had to be answered and in many instances researched. The British Council of Churches and numerous anti-apartheid organisations were continually urging the Archbishop to lend his name and support to their activities, despite the fact that he had made very clear where he stood and maintained a close relationship with Church leaders in southern Africa. Many times he declined to sign anti-apartheid protest letters, not because he was out of sympathy with the cause but because he did not want to dilute his influence by actively supporting every endeavour. Desmond Tutu, who, as an Anglican bishop, was the General Secretary of the South African Council of Churches, maintained regular contact with Lambeth Palace, and the Archbishop listened carefully to his advice and supported him whenever possible.

In 1982, Robert Runcie asked me to represent him at the Eloff Commission, which had been set up to investigate the activities and administration of the South African Council of Churches (SACC). It was presided over by Justice C. F. Eloff and many South Africans believed that it was designed primarily to bring discredit on the SACC and Bishop Tutu. I travelled with two other Anglicans, a clergyman from the US and an Anglican lawyer from the Church in Canada. The lawyer, far from being radical, was somewhat conservative. We arrived at Jan Smuts Airport early in the morning. I had only hand luggage and waited for my companions to collect their cases. There was a long delay. Finally the bags appeared on the moving belt. The lawyer removed his.

'This has been searched,' he declared.

'How do you know?'

'I always tie this knot in a certain way.'

He pointed out a strap holding the items in his case. 'Look, it's been unfastened and refastened differently.' He was angry. 'I don't mind my baggage being searched in my presence by Customs officials,' he said. 'But to search it before it ever gets to me is quite out of order.'

The incident reminds me of a meeting I once had with Desmond Tutu. He met me off a plane and went to carry my suitcases.

'Come on, Bishop,' I said. 'I can manage them myself.'

He looked at me and smiled mischievously.

'But it's the black man's burden, Terry.'

We both laughed and took a case each.

While attending the Commission, all of us were conscious of being kept under constant surveillance. One of our party returned to his hotel room to discover that the papers in his locked briefcase had been rearranged during his absence. As both incidents were amateurish, we questioned whether the authorities were merely warning us that we were being watched. We began to appreciate the pressures under which opponents of the government's policy lived.

The Commission had been dragging on for weeks. We sat facing Mr Justice Eloff and two other Commissioners. When counsel appeared for the SACC, the opposing counsel behaved for all the world as if he were a prosecutor. Early one afternoon I was called as the first witness from the international team to give evidence. I found myself in the odd position of being a character witness for Bishop Tutu. I took the stand and did my best. Then I sat down. Mr Justice Eloff addressed the counsel.

'Have you any questions for the witness?'

The counsel looked at his notes.

'Not for the moment. I would like an adjournment until tomorrow morning, if it please Your Honour.'

An adjournment was granted; we left the court.

'What is happening, Desmond?'

The Bishop grinned.

'They will run further checks on you. Be prepared for them to fire any kind of question at you tomorrow. Anything at all.'

We reassembled the following morning.

Mr Justice Eloff spoke: 'Any questions for the witness?'

'No questions, Your Honour.'

I stood down and never subsequently discovered why further questions were not put. Representatives of the Anglican Communion remained in South Africa for the duration of the hearings. The SACC was given a ruthless examination. Certain administrative problems came to light and were dealt with, but the attempt to discredit Bishop

Tutu and the Council failed totally. To convene what would in England be a Royal Commission to investigate the SACC was in itself an indication of how seriously that organisation was taken by the supporters of apartheid.

Archbishop Runcie was convinced that the Church in South Africa ought to have a leadership representative of the people, and he tried diplomatically to further Desmond Tutu's appointment to the See of Johannesburg. Very shortly after the appointment, Bishop Tutu was elected Archbishop of Cape Town by his brother bishops, and I accompanied Robert Runcie to South Africa for his enthronement. Relations between Church and State were icy. No representatives of the government attended the ceremony or met with the Archbishop of Canterbury during his visit.

South Africa was an issue never far from my mind. An English member of the Community of the Resurrection had been arrested and imprisoned for refusing to divulge what was said to him in the confessional. When I went to visit him in a complex of new prison buildings, the officer on duty denied all knowledge of him and directed me to a smaller building. I rang the bell.

'He's not here,' said another officer. 'At least I don't think he is. They are all awaiting the death sentence here.'

I returned to the first location and tracked him down. We talked through a glass screen while an officer recorded everything that was said. The priest served his sentence of six months and was released.

I was not so fortunate with one of our black bishops who was imprisoned for conducting what was described as an illegal open-air meeting. In fact, it was a funeral service. I went to his house in one of the black townships and met his wife and their teenage son.

'They won't let me see him,' she said. 'They promise and give me a time to go to the prison. When I arrive, they tell me I've come at the wrong time.'

'Come on,' I said. 'Get ready. We'll have a try at seeing him together.'

We drove to the prison. The guard at the gate telephoned Administration. Administration contacted someone else. A man in plain clothes came to see us, and the lady was told to return next week. She left in tears.

By listening to people like Desmond Tutu, and the clergy who knew the life in the townships, one could appreciate the constant harassment black and coloured South Africans faced. There were also tremendous problems within the black community. I went to the squatters' camp, Crossroads, in Cape Town and watched while Desmond attempted to deal with intergroup rivalries, crime and corruption. Every day this man had to face and cope with pressures that would overwhelm a lesser individual, but his strength lay in the depth of his love and faith.

I represented the Archbishop of Canterbury in Oslo when Bishop Tutu received the Nobel Peace Prize in 1984, but even this joyous event was not without its peril. On the morning of the presentation, Desmond and his family, his guests and numerous dignitaries assembled in a great hall. An orchestra played, gentlemen in tails swept to and fro. The King of Norway arrived and sat in front of me to the left. A man I assumed was a bodyguard sat directly behind the King. The ceremony began. Someone entered the building and tapped my neighbour on the shoulder. He looked concerned, leant forward and spoke to the King. The King waved him away. The messenger quickly left the hall, and within a moment the proceedings were interrupted from the stage.

'There has been a bomb threat. Will everyone please leave the hall immediately.'

I have never seen an orchestra leave a building with such alacrity. They picked up their instruments and were gone. The King left under protest. Eventually only Desmond, his wife Leah and I remained.

'Come on,' I said. 'We'll make for the car.' We left by a back door and found the Bishop's official limousine.

'Let's drive round the town a bit,' I suggested.

We were alone. All the security men seemed to have left with the King. We drove for half an hour or so and then returned to the square outside the hall. The building had been searched, and nothing was found. I asked an official what was happening.

'Some want the ceremony to take place in the square, but the King wants it done properly inside.'

We went back into the hall. The orchestra had gone for good, but the King returned. Desmond, innovative as ever, called his African guests on to the stage.

'We have brought our own music with us,' he laughed.

The guests applauded, and the choir sang, as only a black South

African choir can sing. The day was transformed, and Desmond and his people were honoured.

The night is quiet. Outside the sound of small arms has ceased. The guards in the corridor have settled down. Beneath my door a candle flickers, sending flashes of pale yellow light which for a second illuminate a solitary cockroach. I turn towards the wall and flatten my ear against it, listening for a sound, any sound. I can smell damp plaster and the sour odour of decaying limewash. I hear a bump, which could have come from the flat below. Now there is total silence again. I am entombed, chained and entombed. The damp walls rot around me, and my body slowly, ever so slowly, decays. Gently I place my hand on the wall and with my forefinger begin to tap. One – two – three. Silence. Again, one – two – three. Silence. Once more, one – two – three. I wait. My breathing is laboured, my body aches. One – two – three. One – two – three. A response. Can I be hearing things? There it is again: one – two – three. There is someone in the next room who is able to reach the dividing wall and respond to my signal. At long last, someone to talk to. WHO ARE YOU? I tap out in answer. I stop and wait for a reply. TERRY ANDERSON TOM SUTHERLAND JOHN MCCARTHY.

'At last,' I reply, like a line from a bad movie. 'At last I've found you.'

It appears as though Terry is chained to the dividing wall, and if that is the case, we will be able to speak regularly. He understood my code immediately. Now that we can talk, it should be possible to devise a less laborious one, but I think it might be difficult to operate. I have no writing materials, and a code such as Koestler used would require making brief notes. Also, being alone, I constantly have to listen for the guards, so the simpler the code, the better. When I had the very brief exchange with John, I missed the name of the other hostage. It could have been Brian Keenan. Perhaps Brian has been released? If that is so, he will have let my family know that I am alive; thank God for that. I must ask Terry about Brian. What else must I ask him? My list is endless. How is Frances? Have my twin daughters graduated? Is my mother alive? What are Gillian and Mark doing? Has the Archbishop of Canterbury retired? What is happening in the world? How many hostages are there? I could go on and on and on. So it appears that the same group of kidnappers have been holding John and Brian as well as the Americans. Years ago when I met them, they declared knowledge of the four Americans only. They told me they knew nothing about John or Brian or Alec Collett or any of the others.

They have a radio next door and a TV. Not only do they have a radio, they can listen to the news! Now Terry will be able to brief me every day. But we must be careful. It would be terrible if our line of contact were discovered, and I was plunged back into total ignorance. Hundreds of thoughts rush through my mind. The questions fly out as though a mechanism had been released. I must calm down. There will be plenty of time to talk. Or there may not be. Terry might be moved tomorrow before I can get an answer to desperately important questions. But I can't disturb him again. He will want to sleep, and it would be unwise to push my luck too far. Tomorrow, tomorrow.

We have had another conversation. I am surprised at how quickly we manage to exchange information. My cousin and brother have been heard on the World Service. As far as Terry knows, my family is well. There is no news about my mother. As I hoped, Brian Keenan has been released and let it be known that I am alive. The Archbishop has been heard on the radio, but there is no news of his retirement. How fortunate I am to be next to a journalist who knows how to get essential information across succinctly.

I have a message for Terry which I don't know how to deliver. Before my capture, his father died. I try to break the news gently, tapping out that his father was very sick. He responds: 'I know – he died.' My mind goes back across the years to the night my own father died. I remember how important it was for us to learn how to understand each other during his last days. Terry Anderson has been denied that, and my heart goes out to him.

I lie on my mattress and rest for a while. I could spend hours talking to Terry; he is an excellent communicator. We speak late at night and early in the morning. I feel guilty at times as I seek information from him with the urgency of a thirsty man looking for water. He is very patient. He tells me that they listen to the BBC World Service, The Voice of America, local radio, and Radio Monte Carlo. The men next door must be better informed about world events than most free people! Terry now remembers something about the Archbishop of Canterbury. He has announced his retirement, and Terry thinks the Archbishop-designate is the Bishop of Wells.

Wells? What Terry must mean is Bath and Wells, a diocese in the west of England, next to Bristol where we used to live. I don't think that can be right at all. 'What's his name?' I tap. 'Don't know,' he replies. The Bishop of Bath and Wells was on the point of retirement when I was captured, and it would be impossible for him to be elected Archbishop of Canterbury. The whole business is a total mystery. Terry tells me what he knows about the Iran–Contra affair. Oliver North continues to be a figure of controversy. Robert McFarlane has attempted suicide. George Bush has become President. Mrs Thatcher is still in power ... I am flooded with information.

We have speeded up our technique. If Terry is spelling out a word and I guess what it is before he taps out all the letters, I give two quick taps. He then moves on to the next word. If I get lost by miscounting, I tap repeatedly, and he starts the message again. If I ask a question to which the answer is in the affirmative, he will start to tap quickly, which indicates to me that he is racing towards Y, the first letter of 'yes'. I can then stop him with two taps, and we save more time. I learn that Terry, Tom and John are well and actually get books *and* news magazines. I tell Terry I am in poor physical shape because of my bronchial condition. He says they can hear me coughing and will ask the guards to get me medicine. I am eternally grateful to this man. He has provided a lifeline when I most needed it.

The excitement of the last days has made me lose track of my inner narrative. Before I established contact through the wall, I was thinking about Desmond Tutu. Now, new thoughts are continually passing through my mind, and I am distracted. I ask Terry a question, get an answer, which of necessity must be brief, and start to think of dozens more I want to ask. I am starved for information and human company. Perhaps next door they have too much of both. It would be good discipline to return to my story. I don't want to become scatterbrained if I can possibly help it.

What was Desmond's secret? Surely his love, his compassion and his deep faith. Somehow he was able to absorb the attacks made on him and understand that many of his enemies were fearful men and women. We went together one day to a courtroom in South Africa where seven or eight black Africans were on trial. We sat in the well of the court. The proceedings were adjourned in the early afternoon.

One of the accused was decked out in his best suit. The door opened, and his fiancée appeared. Desmond conducted their marriage service in the courtroom, after which there was singing and a small reception. Then the accused was led back to his cell. We walked out of the courtroom and over to the car. Neither of us spoke.

In 1983 the Archbishop of Canterbury sent me to join an international team of Anglicans who were to visit Namibia. The Archbishops of Japan and New Zealand, Charles Cesaretti from America, Jim Thompson, then Bishop of Stepney in east London, and myself, the one lay member, made up the group. Although we were asked to report to the Archbishop of Canterbury on the situation facing the Church, our main purpose was to offer encouragement and support.

South-west Africa has a unique beauty. The rolling desert stretches across the land until it loses itself in the depths of the Atlantic. We saw men literally push the sea back behind gigantic dunes as they scrabbled for diamonds in the bedrock. We stood by the ruins of a theological college and viewed the one stone which stood firm. On it was recorded the fact that it was laid by a one-time Bishop of Stepney, Joost de Blank, later Archbishop of Cape Town. Jim Thompson stood looking at the stone for a long time. The college was on the Angolan border, and we spoke with the clergy and teachers who lived in this remote outpost.

'We know what happens,' they said. 'South African troops disguise themselves as terrorists and cause havoc.'

'Do you have proof of that?'

'We know.'

Later, in an unguarded moment, a South African intelligence officer admitted to me that such tactics had indeed been used.

Namibia is a lovely country. Southern Africa has wonderful people of all races caught in a negative myth and trapped by self-destructive political theories. God save Africa, and God protect you, Desmond.

More about the new Archbishop of Canterbury has come through the wall. Terry is certain that it's the Bishop of Bath and Wells, and that his name is George Carey. I find this difficult to puzzle out. I met a George Carey years ago in Rome and later in Durham, but he was not a bishop then, and certainly not the Bishop of Bath and Wells when I was captured. If it's the George Carey I remember, then he has made surprising progress. There are instances in Church history of popes attaining office by acclamation, but the Church of England is hardly given to such gestures. Eventually the news will come through no doubt.

So Robert Runcie is to retire. There will be a major change of staff at Lambeth Palace as the new man, whoever he is, will want to bring in his own people. It's only when Runcie has gone that people will realise what a good archbishop he was. We had our differences, and in the year before my capture I was often ready to accuse him of what I thought was lukewarm support for the hostages. Looking back, I can see that the Archbishop wanted to protect me by advising me to withdraw from the situation. But I had gone too far down the road by then. I was also too proud to do so, and that was both a failing and a strength.

Robert, I wish you well in your retirement. Few people will ever know the burdens you've had to bear during your years in office, but, as they used to say in Ghana, you've done well.

My health is failing. For hour after hour I struggle to breathe. An asthma attack continues for two or three days, after which I get a brief respite. I collapse and sleep while I can breathe when I lie down. I have been reading a novel by James Jones and seem to remember that while he was writing his last book, he sat at a type-writer in his caravan, struggling with emphysema. He died before the book was completed. I don't want to die yet, but it would be a relief and a release. I could continue alone for a long time if I was physically well, or even if I had reasonable medical attention, but the life I have lived during the past weeks has been a living death. Only Terry has brightened the days. He reports regularly with a news bulletin and is patient with my questions.

I am doing my best to rise above my illness, but I can't master it. When I feel an attack approaching, I sit calmly and attempt to breathe regularly. It has no effect. I can literally feel my bronchial tubes constricting, and in no time at all I am locked in battle. There are no fumes in the room now, but neither is there any fresh air. There must be some medicine that would bring relief. I have little personal knowledge of asthmatics, but surely I have read that they can be helped to lead a normal life. It must be so, as no individual could survive for years with the strain that is put on my body. If I don't get some help, something is bound to give. My heart probably.

All these thoughts are terribly self-centred: me, my identity, my illness. But what else can I think about? The room is virtually bare.

I have an occasional book. Terry communicates two or three times a day, and I battle to keep *me* alive. Shouldn't I just give up? Bow to death? It's going to come sooner or later. Why hold on? I've made a fool of myself before the world, caused enormous problems for my family and friends. What is there to live for? My life has been full. There have been moments of deep happiness but also of great pain. 'You worry too much, Mr Waite.' Thank you, Mr Zlitni. My father worried, I worry. Who can live in this crazy world and not worry, Mr Zlitni? Tell me that. 'You must be patient, Mr Waite.' Yes, Mr Zlitni. I must be patient. I must sit here day in and day out and fathom for myself what the whole crazy process we call life is about. And now, Mr Zlitni, if you don't mind, I am going to sleep while I have the breath. I can worry tomorrow.

I wake before dawn. I have an urge to talk to Terry, but it's too early, and I don't want to disturb him. He spends hours tapping information to me, and that must deprive him of sleep. Communicating with Terry has reminded me of 1986 and the year before my captivity. It's years since I've thought in any detail about my endeavours on behalf of the Beirut hostages, but speaking with Terry has brought back memories: memories of phone calls from Peggy Say, Terry's sister; visits from Jean Sutherland, Tom's wife; appeals from relatives of French hostages; a journey to Italy on behalf of the hostage Alberto Molinari. Hostages and their relatives dominated my life totally.

In 1985 a TV producer approached me to ask if I would make a series of programmes speaking with individuals from different walks of life. These were to take the form of conversations rather than interviews, during the course of which the guest and I would talk about experiences that had made a deep impression on our lives. I agreed, thinking it might be a diversion that would provide me with a total change from the hostage pressures. However, the series was not well received by the critics, some of whom played with the fact that my initials were the same as Terry Wogan and suggested that I was trying to become a chat-show host. A number of people were confused at my apparent change of role, and this also led to negative criticism. Just as one of the programmes was about to be filmed, the shattering news came through that the two British teachers, Philip Padfield and Leigh Douglas, and Peter Kilburn, a librarian at the American University of Beirut, had been murdered. I finished the programme and left immediately to get more information about this latest tragedy.

Not long afterwards a video tape was released, purporting to show Alec Collett being hanged. The information I received through my own channels was that Alec had died in captivity as the result of an illness, and that the hanging was a cynical and horrible way of putting pressure on the West. I was invited by Philip's and Leigh's families and friends to give the address at their memorial service at St Martin-in-the-Fields. What I remember best is that during the service a young man sang the hauntingly beautiful melody 'Sleep' to a setting by Ivor Gurney. It moved me to tears then, and it continues to do so.

The murder of these men took place after the US had bombed Libya, using the UK as a refuelling base. Although I had no proof that the deaths of the three hostages were directly related to the American action, it seemed to many people that this was the case. Alec's family suffered the terrible dilemma of not knowing what had happened to him. Some believed he was dead, others refused to accept this. A private memorial service took place in Lambeth Palace, and I realised once again the agony which families of hostages have to endure.

As in previous hostage cases, it was impossible for me to know the full picture. I had little idea what diplomatic initiatives were being taken behind the scenes by the United States, Britain or France. According to Colonel North, my point of contact with the highest level of the US government, the Americans were considering a variety of options. He mentioned one of these, which was to seek the release of Shiite prisoners held in southern Lebanon by the retired Major General Antoine Lahad of the so-called 'South Lebanon Army'. It was said that if the prisoners were released, this might ease the situation throughout the region and increase the chances of freeing the Western hostages. This whole business was far too complicated for me to handle alone, so, when North asked me if I would be willing to explore the possibility, I agreed to do so. I thought it would be of considerable help if those who were detained outside the law could be released.

One night I left Lambeth quietly and caught the last plane to Paris where I was met at the airport by an American who identified himself as my driver. We walked outside to his car.

'Are you armed?' he asked.

His question surprised me.

'Of course not.'

'I will drop you just beyond your destination. If you are not out after three hours, we will come and collect you.'

It was raining. We drove across the city and into a side street in one of the suburbs. I recognised the address I had been given. We stopped at the end of the street.

I walked back through the drizzle to the apartment block and pressed the bell beside the entry phone marked with the name I had noted down. A female voice answered. I identified myself, the door clicked open, and I entered. An ancient elevator took me to the top floor. I looked at my watch – it was almost midnight. I was received by a lady who I assumed was Lebanese. She took me through the living room in which there were several Lebanese men and women who glanced at me in passing. We went into a small office at the back of the apartment and sat down.

'So,' said the lady, 'you would like to meet General Lahad?'

I had expressed no such desire. I said I would be interested to hear what she had to say. She spoke for some time about the problems of Lebanon and the southern Lebanese forces. If I ever wished to meet the General, it could be arranged, she assured me. No mention was made of releasing Shiite prisoners. I thanked her and left. The next morning I returned to London.

Early in 1986 I received another message from Oliver North. He suggested that I go with him to East Beirut (not West Beirut, the Hezbollah-dominated area of the city) where he hoped I would be able to meet people who would be influential in securing the release of the prisoners held in southern Lebanon. While I was continuing to concentrate my efforts on the Da'wa prisoners in Kuwait, it seemed to me important to follow as many leads as possible.

Colonel North met me at Heathrow Airport early one morning. He had spent the previous night in a hotel near by. I was sure that our movements were being observed by British security, for the simple reason that it would be a matter of routine for them to record the activities of an official of the National Security Council. We cleared passport control and went to the correct departure gate where our tickets were taken by a representative of a charter company; then we were directed to an executive jet bound for Cyprus. We were the only passengers.

We spoke very little during the journey. North was engrossed in paperwork and I was reading. Throughout all my meetings with him, he gave very little away. He was not the sort of person who talked about his work and he rarely mentioned his private life.

In Cyprus a US military helicopter was waiting. We boarded it and within moments were airborne. A crew member handed us a set of headphones so that we could speak to each other.

'Don't be alarmed,' he said. 'When we approach our destination we make certain manoeuvres to minimise the danger of a missile attack.'

A soldier sat by the doorway, a machine gun at the ready. Below, the Mediterranean sparkled in the sunlight. We approached Beirut. Suddenly the helicopter swooped downwards like a sparrowhawk diving towards its prey. The pilot levelled it off, and within a few moments we had put down on a landing pad close to the American Embassy.

I was driven away in a car while Colonel North disappeared in another direction. The American officials who collected me looked startled when they recognised my face. They had not been told whom to expect. All they had been asked to do was pick up a visitor and arrange for him to keep out of sight for a day or so for his own security's sake. As we journeyed through the town, they seemed embarrassed and apologetic.

'I'm sorry,' said the older man. 'We didn't know it was you coming. If we had, we would have arranged more adequate accommodation.'

I told them not to worry. We stopped outside a modern apartment building, and I was shown into a minute flat.

'It belongs to an officer in the Lebanese Army.' The American looked sheepish.

There was a tiny kitchen, an even smaller bathroom, and a bedroom dominated by a huge double bed and a bar which equalled the variety of drinks on display at Harry's Bar in Rome. The flat was clearly used by the unnamed officer for his assignations.

'How long will you be here?' asked the younger man.

'I don't know. I hope not long.'

'Please don't go outside. We'll call every evening, but don't answer the door to anyone other than ourselves. You will see us through the security glass in the door. There's food in the fridge and plenty to drink.'

Fortunately I always travelled with books in my briefcase and had several with me. I waited alone in the flat for five days. The Americans brought food every evening and stayed briefly for a drink. At the end of the week they brought a message for me from Oliver North, saying there was no point in my waiting any longer. I never discovered what he did during those days, and he never explained why my meeting did not take place. All he said was that he had met some very unpleasant men and that his hopes had come to nothing.

I imagine one of the reasons why the novels of John le Carré are so popular is that, apart from being very well written, they capture the bizarre world of the intelligence operative: the apparently meaningless meetings, the petty criminals, the moral deceptions and at the end – what? Often disillusion and disappointment. As I sit here in the semi-darkness, I remember le Carré's books: how, when one started to read them, it seemed impossible for there to be any coherent conclusion. And yet, behind the complexity, there was a pattern – often a distasteful one.

Now, as I think back over 1986, I struggle to find coherence in what was happening. Visits to Paris or Beirut might have held the promise of a breakthrough, but as far as I could see they were sterile. I continued to feel that Kuwait was the most promising line to follow, and yet I was making little or no headway in that direction either. However, Kamal Khoury, a Lebanese contact in London, remained hopeful that I would eventually gain entry, and he kept in close touch with influential friends and contacts there. For my part, I was confused and increasingly feeling the pressures of a situation which dragged on and on with no apparent end in sight, and which, I now realise, was putting a great strain on my relations with my family. Fortunately my friends, both inside and outside the Church, came to my aid and helped preserve my sanity during the darkest days.

23

AT THE MEETING of Anglican Primates held in Canada in July 1986, the Archbishop in Jerusalem requested that the Archbishop of Canterbury give his support to a medical project which was being developed in Jordan. A young Jordanian surgeon, currently practising neurosurgery in Canada, wished to return home to make his skills available in his own country. Apparently, resources for such surgery were limited in Jordan, and there was a need for skilled practitioners. The Archbishop in Jerusalem had suggested that charitable support groups might be formed throughout the world to aid this development, and such a group, the Society for Care of Neurological Patients in Amman, Jordan, was established in the United Kingdom.

I visited Jordan later in the year for the launch of the project. I had known the surgeon's father, also a doctor, for some time. Samir Habiby was there at the same time and was optimistic about the hostages. He had heard that a release was imminent, and that it would probably be Father Jenco, a Roman Catholic priest of the Servite Order who had been captured in January 1985. Lawrence Jenco, known to his friends as Marty, was active in the Lebanon, working for refugees and other victims.

While I was in Jordan I had a private meeting with King Hussein and discussed the hostage question with him. I doubted whether there was anything he could do directly, but I was anxious to pursue every possible avenue. The news we were half-expecting came through on a Saturday morning. Father Jenco had been released and was on his way to Damascus.

I was at the house of Jordanian friends when the information was passed to me. I wanted to see him immediately as almost certainly he would have brought out a message from the kidnappers, together with news of the other hostages. The Polaroid picture of him taken during my visit to the kidnappers flashed across my mind. The white beard, the gentle eyes looking intently into the camera. I was excited that Father Jenco had been freed, not only because of another release but because the captors had decided it should be the other clergyman. When Ben Weir was freed in 1985, I had taken this as being an encouraging sign to me personally. In fact, my subsequent contact with the kidnappers had indicated that this was so. Now I interpreted Father Jenco's release as being another such sign, to encourage me to continue my efforts on behalf of the Da'wa prisoners.

As it was the weekend and I had no visa to enter Syria, I decided to request help at the highest level. I telephoned the White House and asked to speak to Colonel North. Understandably, he was not in his office and my call was put through to his home. I told him of Father Jenco's release and, to my surprise, he said he had not heard about it. I said that I would value the help of the US Embassy in Amman to enable me to get into Syria and meet with Father Jenco as soon as possible. He promised to do what he could. I then telephoned the British Embassy and explained the situation. The Syrian Embassy in Jordan was closed but one of the British Embassy staff tracked down an official who gave me a visa at once. The Americans organised transport: a car to the Syrian border and one on the other side to take me to Damascus. It was evening when I reached the city and went into the American Embassy residence to meet Father Jenco for the first time.

My breakfast has arrived. I can eat with only a part of my mouth owing to cracked and broken teeth, but I manage. I will wait until evening before speaking with Terry. Now it is too dangerous: I might start to tap when there is a guard in the room, and that would be disastrous. We have partly anticipated this problem by agreeing on a warning signal that either of us could send which means 'Danger – do not communicate anything'. As yet we have not had to use it, but we may.

I am finding it very difficult to recount the experiences leading up to my capture, and I need to understand why this is so. In Iran, Libya and, finally, Beirut, again I knew only a part of the picture. It's hardly possible to determine which single action led to Father Jenco's release. The truth is probably that it was due to a combination of factors. As to any part that I may have played in it, I want to justify my actions to myself, reassure myself that what I did was worth the personal cost involved. If my faith had been deeper, if I had had the humility which is such an essential part of Christianity, would I be here now? I remember examining myself long ago and doubting whether I, or any human being, was capable of taking a purely altruistic action. Well, let me face up to myself. I did, and do, care about others, but I also care about myself, my reputation, my pride, my desire to succeed. Back we go, back across the years, back to my father and his warnings and hopes for his eldest son.

Waite, you don't know the first thing about humility, or love, or compassion. Inwardly you are a small, frightened child, anxious to impress people. I suppose it's at this point in my experience that the faith I profess so inadequately comes into its own. Human nature is flawed and divided. There is no healing without suffering. The kingdom, which I say I want, does not belong to this world, but this world must be lived in, and, in part, the kingdom must come, on earth as it is in heaven.

Something disturbingly odd is happening. Outside the apartment there is a great commotion. People are shouting in the streets, and there is the rattle of gunfire. A tank rumbles by, followed by several heavy lorries. There is the sound of shelling. The noise is deafening. For the past weeks it has been peaceful, now all hell seems to have broken loose. The guards shout to each other in the corridor. There is activity in the room next to mine. My door is flung open and the Frog leaps in. He is excited and shouts incomprehensibly. It sounds as though he is repeating 'a room, a room'. Perhaps he wants me to move to another room. He is much too excited to talk, and after a few more incomprehensible sentences he leaves. They seem to be moving Terry, Tom and John. A quick glance through the keyhole reveals one of them being led down the corridor. Someone approaches my room, and I fling myself back against the wall.

'Come, quick.' The chain is removed from my ankle and from the wall. 'Go, go!' I am pushed forward along the corridor into the dark bathroom. 'Get in douche.'

I stumble into the bath. A blanket has been placed there.

'Lie down.' I do so. Chains are fastened around my feet and secured around the taps. 'No speak, sleep.'

The door is closed, leaving me in darkness. Outside the battle rages. Trucks and tanks rumble along the road. Shells explode, and small arms clatter. I can't imagine what is happening. Has Lebanon been invaded – is it factional warfare? There is a tremendous explosion. Flecks of paint fall from the ceiling, plaster lands in the bath. The chilling sound of screaming is followed by the noise of an ambulance. The screaming continues. Men shout, a child's voice calls out, something collapses. I lie in the bath, half-expecting a shell to land on the building and put an abrupt end to this whole miserable saga. Hours pass, and the noise subsides. Emotional exhaustion catches up with me, and I fall asleep.

Later in the evening, when all is quiet and I am back in my room, Terry tells me that General Michel Aoun, a Maronite Christian, former Chief of Staff to President Amin Gemayel and leader of a caretaker government, has been overthrown. At last I understand what the Frog was attempting to tell me: 'Aoun', not 'a room'! We have all survived to live another day. God only knows how many of our neighbours have been killed.

I met Father Lawrence Jenco in the garden of the American residence in Damascus. It was evening, and he had recently finished one of his first meals as a free man. He was bearded and looked well, although there was a haunting sadness in his eyes. We embraced each other but spoke little, as he was exhausted. My first impression was that he was a good man, and the more I got to know him the more that impression was confirmed. He told me that Terry Anderson, Tom Sutherland and David Jacobsen were also in reasonable health. American officials informed me he would be leaving for Wiesbaden on a military plane the following day. That night I stayed at the British residence and the next day returned to the American residence where Father Jenco celebrated Mass before we left together for Germany. The American Ambassador with his family and members of the Embassy staff knelt quietly while the priest prayed for his fellow hostages and for his captors.

As I sit here remembering that service, my heart warms to the faith I have known since childhood. In the last years I have been locked in inner battle and conflict, but now, for a moment, I rest in the peace of God. The memory of that simple service, of the prayers for understanding and forgiveness, convinces me again of the essential 'rightness' of Christ's teachings.

'Forgive us our sins as we forgive those who sin against us' – words from the Lord's Prayer which have such depth and resonance. I see Father Jenco with his white beard distribute the Sacrament, and in my heart I thank God for this good priest.

As well as being anxious for news of the other hostages, British,

American and French, I was most concerned to learn what message the captors had asked Father Jenco to convey to the Pope and to President Reagan. A group of his relatives were flying to Wiesbaden from the United States and it was arranged with the officials who were responsible for Father Lawrence that the whole party would stop in Rome for an audience with the Pope, and in London for a meeting with the Archbishop of Canterbury, before travelling on to Washington. Father Lawrence had a large and affectionate family. They arrived in Germany and were taken on sightseeing tours of the area during his period of debriefing.

The message from the kidnappers turned out to be both vague and unsatisfactory. They simply requested that the priest tell the Pope and the President to be vigilant against falling moral standards. Father Jenco was convinced that the captors were serious about this and I suggested that we give it a high profile, without publicly revealing the contents, so that they knew that Father Jenco was keeping his promise to them.

In conversations with his family, Father Jenco described his experiences in captivity. He needed to talk about them, and his family was anxious to hear what he had to say. Reporters had, of course, descended on Wiesbaden, determined to get every scrap of information they could. I was acutely aware that the family, in speaking with the press, might inadvertently repeat something that would anger the captors and thus jeopardise the position of the remaining hostages. I constantly warned the family of this danger, which did not make me too popular with them at the time.

Terry has told me more about the fall of Aoun. The battle was short and sharp. It lasted hardly a day. The sounds of collapsing masonry I heard were the result of a shell landing on the next-door apartment block. There were casualties. During the coup Terry, Tom and John had been kept in a room next to the bathroom.

I am amazed at how quickly we can communicate. I now understand how it is that Morse code operatives can distinguish the individual characteristics of the sender. Terry has a distinctive style: precise, careful, patient – I can't thank him enough for his company, and the fact that I say this reveals to me how starved I have been over the past four years. Terry suggests I ask for a radio. He thinks there is a good chance the guards might give me one now. I will take it only if they give me unrestricted access to news.

Having gone for so long without TV or radio, I can continue to, although it would be wonderful to hear music again. There hasn't been much music in my soul during these years. I would like to hear Elgar or Bach.

'Can I have a radio, please?'

The guard has entered my room with lunch.

'I ask Chef. You can have TV.'

'Can I watch news on TV?'

'I don't know. I ask Chef.'

'When will you see Chef?'

'I don't know. Perhaps soon.'

The door is closed and locked. I eat my meal with a ridiculous plastic teaspoon. Some time ago my metal spoon and fork were taken away and replaced with flimsy white plastic utensils. Food is now served on a plastic airline tray. Today it is cooked green beans, boiled rice and a few pieces of meat. I also get a banana – not bad.

In some respects, security has been tightened. Years ago I was allowed nail clippers; now, when I need to cut my nails, I have to ask for them and hand them back immediately. I wonder if someone has attempted suicide or tried to attack a guard. Paper tissues seem in short supply. I get a handful from time to time. Formerly I was given a boxful.

'Chef says you can have TV.'

'Can I watch news?'

'Chef says you watch news.'

'What about radio?'

'Chef says I buy radio for you tomorrow. OK?'

'I can watch news?'

'No problem.'

The door closes. I can hardly believe my good fortune. At long last I can hear news directly over the radio.

I am sitting with my back against the wall. In my hand is a small pocket radio marked 'Sanyo. Made in Japan'. It is probably one of the cheapest radios one can buy, but to me it is priceless. There are two bands. A VHF frequency and Medium Wave. Terry has told me that the BBC World Service broadcasts on the Medium Wave for virtually twenty-four hours each day. I switch it on and attempt to find a station – Arabic music, popular music, there it is, a British voice. I mentally leap with excitement. The announcer is giving details of programmes to be broadcast during the next few hours. Thank goodness they continue to do that and don't assume that everyone has access to *London Calling*. In a few moments *Words of Faith* will be broadcast. My mind goes back to Bush House in central London. Back to the days when I sat in a small studio and read my script for this very same programme. I long to hear what will be said. The speaker is announced. I don't know him, but he is identified as an Anglican clergyman from the west of England. At long last, after years alone, some words of spiritual comfort. He starts to speak. At first I am puzzled, then disappointed, and finally I burst into laughter. He is speaking about the spiritual lessons to be learnt from reading *Winnie the Pooh*! I can hardly believe it. All I can say to myself is that the dear old Church of England doesn't seem to have changed much while I've been away – not much at all.

In Wiesbaden, an upper wing of the military hospital was reserved for returning hostages. Each ex-hostage had a private bedroom, a sitting room, and free access to a telephone. Normally, relatives were accommodated in a hotel at the military base. After a thorough medical examination, several days were spent on a security debriefing, after which the individual and his family were flown back to the United States.

In early November 1986 I flew from Beirut to Germany with David Jacobsen, an American hospital administrator who had been captured in May 1985. Rumours about a release had been circulating for some time. I continued to explore all possible openings, but very little seemed promising. The Vatican continued to do what it could through its own channels, and Samir Habiby was active throughout the Arab world. Experience had taught me never to give up. If one kept on working at a problem, eventually there would be a breakthrough of some kind. Some days earlier I had received a message from the Americans, alerting me to the fact that another hostage release was imminent. No reasons were given as to why a hostage should be freed at this particular time. I reasoned that since there was a plentiful supply of hostages in Beirut, the captors could afford to release one from time to time to keep the whole process alive.

I met David in the American residence in Beirut with the US Ambassador and Oliver North. David and I chatted together while North and the Ambassador made arrangements for David to go to

Wiesbaden. He was cheerful and looked well in spite of his ordeal. Jacobsen, North and I then flew back to Europe via Cyprus. David was able to give up-to-date information about other hostages but had no idea why he had been released at this point. Before leaving for Washington, Oliver North assured us that President Reagan was greatly concerned about the hostages and doing everything possible to obtain their release. That was the most he was prepared to tell us.

I was in the military hospital at Wiesbaden when I got the first indication that something might be seriously wrong. David had been telling me what he could about his captors and the conditions under which he was kept. I left him and went to another room to sit quietly for a while. The door opened, and one of the security men entered. He looked puzzled.

'Have you heard the news?'

'No.'

'It's being reported that McFarlane and Ollie North were arrested in Iran in May. There's some talk about arms dealing.'

'*What?*'

'That's what's being reported.'

'Arms – arrested?'

The American looked bemused. I leapt to my feet. 'I must contact North immediately.'

I felt a sickness rising in my stomach. This was a total shock to me. Up to this point Oliver North had always seemed to confirm what Fred Wilson and I had observed months earlier – that, despite his secretiveness, he was utterly dedicated to the cause of the hostages. But if arms had been traded, then that could be nothing short of disastrous for the whole situation.

I hurried along the corridor to the temporary communications centre which had been established in the hospital. Two technicians were sitting in the corner.

'I need to speak to the White House immediately.'

'Sure – use that.' They pointed to the satellite telephone.

'We'll leave you while you call.'

'That's not necessary.'

Within a moment I was connected to the White House switchboard, and after a few seconds I was speaking to Colonel North.

'What is going on? We're getting very strange reports here about a visit you made to Iran.'

He attempted to reassure me. He didn't want to say much now, but everything would be OK. I replaced the phone with a deep sense of foreboding. Every intuitive instinct I had told me that it would not be OK. It was bad news – very bad indeed. I slowly began to realise how serious the consequences would be.

A portable black-and-white television has been put in my room. As the guard promised, I can watch all programmes, including the news. I prefer the radio; it stimulates my imagination in a way that television fails to do. Tonight the TV news made me weep. Gunmen had broken into the home of a Lebanese politician and murdered the whole family. A picture was shown of a small boy of about six or seven with a bullet hole through his head. No imagination is required to feel the impact of the brutality and suffering these people experience. It doesn't matter whether they are Christian, Muslim or Druze. All weep as they are touched by subhuman brutality. I switch off the set and say a prayer for peace in this land.

I returned to London from Wiesbaden. The atmosphere was thick with rumour and speculation: arms had been traded with Iran; Waite had been seen with North in Cyprus. There was little or no ground left to support me. All that I could do was stand firm and refuse to be intimidated by anyone. I said nothing to Frances about the very real danger I was in, but she was certainly aware of the strain I was under. I spoke with Samir Habiby and told him I wanted to return to Beirut to try to pick up the pieces, if that was at all possible. I was completely ignorant of any deals which, it was claimed, had taken place between the USA and Iran, but what I had heard filled me with despair.

Samir shared the view that it would be worth my returning to the Lebanon to see if there was any way to ease the situation. I especially wanted another meeting with the kidnappers to demonstrate my own good faith and to indicate that I was willing to continue working until a resolution was found. I was also determined to convince them that I had had no dealings at all with arms for hostages. I summoned up all the strength I could muster and started to plan for a return visit. Robert Runcie was not happy with my decision, but he knew that, had he stopped me, I would have resigned and returned to Beirut without his support. In the days between November 1986 and January 1987 I began to understand in quite a new way what it meant to stand alone in the face of hostility and criticism. I remembered that Terry Anderson, Tom Sutherland, Lawrence Jenco and David Jacobsen had signed a letter asking the Archbishop to help them. There was no possible way that the Church – and I as a representative of the Church – could desert those who remained in captivity, when everything appeared to be crashing in flames.

Some friends told me that if I went back to Beirut I was returning to certain death. My only response was that I had done nothing to be ashamed of and would stand on the only ground left to me, the moral and spiritual ground. I probably replied somewhat arrogantly, but arrogant defiance helped me to keep going in the face of all the attacks. Walid Jumblatt, leader of the Druze community, generously agreed to provide protection for me in Beirut. I decided to visit as many leaders there as I could, in an attempt to get the process moving again.

I got up early on the morning of 13 January. Frances and the children were sleeping, and I decided not to disturb them. I thought for a moment about how much the events of the past year had cost us as a family, then, putting such feelings to the back of my mind, I went out through the front door. Heavy snow lay on the ground. My taxi was delayed, and I almost missed my flight at Heathrow. Kamal Khoury, who had given me so much help in the past, said goodbye to me at the airport. He had good news for me. At long last he believed that I would be able to visit the Da'wa prisoners in Kuwait. I would have to wait several days until an international Islamic Conference was over, but by the time I returned from Beirut I would almost certainly be able to go there.

As I looked down from the aircraft window at the carpet of snow covering the drabness of London in winter, I closed my eyes and whispered a brief prayer. I never got to Kuwait, and I was not to see my family again for five long years.

In his daily despatches through the wall, Terry brought me up to date on main news events, but now with the radio I get the details. As the programme is relayed on Medium Wave, the reception is excellent, and it's quite possible to listen to and enjoy music. I develop the same relationship with the radio I had when I was a child. The broadcasters become welcome friends. Some I know personally. Indeed, today I heard my cousin John broadcasting on the *Outlook* programme. He made no mention of hostages, but to hear his voice again gave me a direct link with home.

The last article I wrote for publication was for the Christmas 1986 edition of *The Listener*. I reminisced about the World Service and urged that it be supported. Now, I am one of its most grateful listeners. I am terrified that when the batteries in my radio run out, the guards will not replace them. I cling to this little set obsessively. To lose it now would be a terrible torture. Now that I am in touch with the outside world, Terry is relieved of the chore of communicating with me so often. We continue to talk daily, but he need not pass on world news unless he gets an item from Radio Monte Carlo, which I can't receive on my set. He also tunes in to The Voice of Israel, which gives local news, and he taps out information from this source from time to time.

Life would be reasonable if it weren't for my worsening physical health. The bronchial attacks strike with alarming frequency, and I am getting weaker and weaker. Today I couldn't find enough energy to fold my blanket, and when I was escorted to the toilet I almost collapsed. I returned to my room and sat with my back against the wall, struggling to control the spasms that so exhaust me. I can't, I simply can't, control my breathing. Terry tells me that they have asked the guards to move me in with them, but the guards either say that I am an Arab and speak no English, or that I am a very bad man and would cause them too much trouble. I have mixed feelings about moving. I long for human company, but I don't want to inflict my illness on others, and I seriously wonder if I will be able to communicate properly. The vision of the forgotten prisoner gibbering incoherently after years in solitary flashes through my mind. I think I am still reasonably balanced, but I am self-centred. I have had to be to keep alive.

Now that I have broken through the barrier, memories return of my final days of freedom in Beirut. I visited the Syrian leaders, the Prime Minister, Sheikh Fadlallah, the spiritual head of Hezbollah, leading figures in the Druze and many other influential people.

One evening the telephone rang. It was Dr Mroueh.

'Your friend would like to see you.'

'When?'

'Tonight.'

'Where?'

'At my place.'

'I will be there.'

I took the familiar route and left my Druze bodyguards at the end of the street. Dr Mroueh greeted me in his apartment, and we chatted for a while. Then the doorbell rang and my contact, the man in the suit, entered.

'Good to see you again,' I said. 'You have put on some weight.'

He gave a half-smile. We went back into the doctor's study and sat down. I opened the conversation.

'Much has happened since we last met, but I must tell you directly that I know nothing about arms dealing. I could have nothing to do with that, nor could the Church.'

He remained silent.

'The Church will continue to work until this problem is solved. I do believe that I shall now get into Kuwait very soon.'

He nodded and then said, 'You remember the last time we met?'

'Yes.'

'You asked to visit the hostages.'

'I did.'

'Then, we said no. Now we have changed our minds. Tom Sutherland and Terry Anderson are ill. They are very depressed about what the American government has been doing. They may die. We will now let you visit them because you are from the Church.'

I thought of Alec Collett and the others who had died in captivity. 'Are they very ill?'

'Yes.'

'If I come with you, you will keep me.'

'No.'

'Will you give me your word as a Muslim that you won't?'

I stretched out my hand. He clasped it.

'We will not keep you.'

'When can we go?'

'Now.' It was almost midnight.

'I can't come now. It's much too late and I must think about this.'

'OK.'

'If I decide to come, I will return here tomorrow night at eight.'

'That is OK.'

He stood and left the apartment. I sat facing the doctor.

'Will they keep me?'

Dr Mroueh lit his pipe. 'If he has given you his word as a Muslim, he should not keep you. That would be wrong.'

I returned to the Riviera Hotel. The next day, for security reasons, I hardly dared discuss the prospect of a visit with anyone. I wrestled with my conscience. If the man in the suit was telling me the truth and I turned down an opportunity to visit critically ill hostages, then I could not live with myself in the future. My faith, such as it was, would have been a sham.

The book I am writing in my head is almost completed. If I ever commit it to paper, what more might I want to say? Will I want to sum up, dot i's, cross t's, make the story totally watertight? I don't need to justify myself or apologise for anything. I did my best for those who appealed to me, and for those who didn't.

It wasn't good enough, so be it. Now the tables are turned. The would-be rescuer needs help, companionship, healing. I have been brought very low, but I have not given in.

I switch on my radio. The announcer is introducing the Sunday morning service. I put the radio on the iron bar to which my chain is secured and close my eyes. The service comes from a small church in Belfast, Northern Ireland. For a moment I allow myself to think of Frances, of the May morning when we walked together down the aisle, out of the church and into an unknown future. The new wave of violence had not yet started in Ireland. I pray for her and for my children, wherever they may be. The service continues. An elderly man says: 'We pray for all captives, and here in Belfast we especially remember Terry Waite and his family.' Thank you, old man, who-ever you are – I pray for you also. There are invisible bonds which link us together, and nothing will break them.

24

I AM SITTING at a plain wooden desk in a small room. The windows are barred but not shuttered. I am free to come and go as I please. Outside there is a narrow street which leads to Clare College and beyond that to King's College Chapel. Each day a steady stream of visitors passes by. Occasionally one will glance in my direction as I sit writing. Here in my room in Trinity Hall, a Cambridge refill pad is before me as I transcribe the story I wrote in my head during the long years of captivity in Beirut.

I came to Cambridge a year ago. Each weekend I return home to London, but for the main part of the week I continue to have a solitary existence. This has been necessary for many reasons, not least because it's only when I am totally alone that I can begin to write down what has been stored in my mind for so long. I also need to come out of isolation slowly.

The book I wrote in captivity is finished, but my story is not quite over.

One day, earlier than usual, the guards enter the room and, my eyes tightly covered by my blindfold, I hear the chilling sound of masking tape.

'What are you doing?'

'No speak.'

I hear my belongings being collected together. I am about to be moved. Panic grips me. I have been in this place for years. Where am I going? Will I lose my radio? My Prayer Book? What about the other hostages?

'Get in.'

I am pushed into a canvas sack, which must be my mattress cover, and hauled out of the room, bound, gagged and totally helpless. Thank God I am breathing easily at the moment or I would suffocate. We bump our way down in the lift, the guards manhandle me out of the building, and I am tipped into a car boot.

'No speak.'

The lid is slammed. Immediately I set to work to free my hands and remove the gag from my mouth. I have to be able to breathe freely, and there may be a possibility of opening the boot from the inside. Someone else is in here with me. We exchange whispers, and I discover it is John McCarthy.

'I don't think we had better talk, TW, they might hear us.'

I agree, but my need to communicate with another human being is so great that I push my hand through a hole in the sack, find John's hand and begin to tap out a message. The car sways and lurches on its long journey. I find the catch of the boot but it is impossible to open it. I hear boards rattle as we cross a bridge. Then we turn off the road on to what sounds like a rough track. The car stops, and we wait. The boot is opened, and we are taken up a slight incline and into a building. I am alone in one room, and I think the other three are next door. It was so hot in the boot that my clothes are wet through with perspiration. Now I am shivering. I remove my pyjama jacket and wrap a blanket around my shoulders. I feel seriously ill.

Our new house is on a hill in the countryside. I am given some dry clothes and the remainder of my bedding.

'Where is my radio?' It is put in my hand. 'My Prayer Book?'

No response.

My Prayer Book has gone, and I know I will never see it again. Well, it had a short but useful life, and I still have a Bible.

The room I am in reminds me of a country cottage. There are rough wooden shutters and the sun streams through the gaps where they fit badly. I can hear birds singing, and the wind blows through the shutters. It is cool and sweet and healing. Winter is approaching, and this room, which is little more than a stable, will be cold. But now it gives me a touch of the sun, a breath of the wind, and the song of an unknown bird. All these promise me a better future.

The guards are perfectly well aware that my identity is known to the other hostages, but as they have not received authorisation from the Chef they can't move me in with them. This morning I managed to snatch a conversation with Tom while the door between our rooms was left open. Later the guard closed it, and I returned to solitary. I can hear the others chatting in the next room, and I wonder what their lives have been like during the past years. Have they been able to give each other support, or have they fought? Did I once read that rats kept together for long periods of time destroy each other? Do human beings behave in the same way, or do they unite against a common enemy? I hear someone laugh. Probably Terry Anderson. I envy the companionship the other hostages seem to have. Tom has told me that they are continually asking the guards to move me in with them and the guards say they will ask the Chef.

Today there was a great upheaval next door. I think Terry, Tom and John are being moved. In recent days the guards have been suggesting that I would be put with the other hostages, but over the years I have learnt never to believe anything until it actually happens. Now that I am on the brink of moving in with them, my feelings are mixed. I need their support as I constantly feel so ill. Also, I am curious for news. What has happened to them over the years? How have they survived?

The guard comes into my room and collects my few belongings.

'Stand – no speak – quick.'

He stands behind me and grasps both my arms firmly. Under my blindfold I can see that there is a guard in front of me. We move forward into the cool night air, and it is very quiet. There is no traffic noise – no noise at all except the hurried breathing of the guards and the shuffle of feet as we make our way round the building.

'Up.'

We are walking up a gradual slope. Now we are indoors. My feet sink into a deep carpet and I can smell its newness. This must be the country house of someone of moderate wealth. I am directed along a short corridor and turned right. We enter a room.

'Sit.'

A chain is fastened around my ankle. When the door is locked and I remove my blindfold, Terry, Tom and John are in the room. They sit on their mattresses on the bare floor, each man chained by the feet to an iron staple driven into a concrete wall. My days of solitary confinement are over.

I am so disturbed and confused, I have difficulty in knowing what to say. Suddenly to be in the company of three other men after spending so long in solitary brings me both relief and apprehension. The move was disturbing. I had become accustomed to the room in which I was kept. Now I am in a new place with men who must have worked very hard to adapt their behaviour to each other. My experience has been very different: year in, year out I have had to live totally from my own inner resources. There was even a time when I wondered if I was in danger of losing the power of speech. Now, I am going to have to learn to relate once again with people other than myself. I will even have to learn how to communicate with them.

My eyes wander round the room, and I see how badly it needs decorating. One wall is disfigured by a huge damp patch which stands out like a map of China. Metal sheets cover the windows, so once again there is no natural light. Our mattresses are unreasonably close together; there is only about nine inches between mine and Tom's. I look again at my comrades. In a curious way they are strangers and brothers at the same time. Over the last years we must have shared many experiences in common, and even before my captivity we were inextricably linked. Their lives dominated my life, filled my dreams and drove me to exhaustion. I remember the words of my friend, Christine; she said that in seeking their liberation, I was seeking my own liberation. True, Christine, inevitably all motives are complex.

I look across at John McCarthy: he is pale, clean-shaven, slightly built. His mattress is at the far end of the room. I recall how his mother, his father and his girlfriend, Jill Morrell, were all known to me in the months before I became a hostage.

When I first saw Terry Anderson in the Polaroid, he was heavily bearded; now he has a moustache only. Again, I knew his sister Peggy and many of his colleagues and friends.

I last met Tom's wife at Heathrow Airport. She was passing through London on one of her many journeys in search of information about her husband. I promised her, as I promised all the families, to do what I could for the hostages. Now that I am with other human beings again, it is very strange to be with these three of all people.

Tom has latched on to me and pours out his life story. Once he begins, he continues to speak for hour after hour. To follow Tom's history and at the same time keep control over my breathing demands an effort of will which drains me. I note that Terry and John keep out of the exchange such as it is. They must have heard these stories time and time again. As I half listen, I wonder if Tom is doing the very same thing that I have done: drawing on his memories in an attempt to hold on to his identity and convince himself that he had a life and was and is a person of worth. My feelings towards him are mixed. I have an enormous sympathy for this clever, humiliated individual but a growing weariness with his story.

I would have expected John, as a fellow countryman, to be a little more forthcoming, but for reasons I don't understand he holds back. He has probably learnt to be cautious, and he needs to protect himself. Very wise when we have all lived daily on the brink of death. As Tom totally dominates me at our end of the room it has the effect of throwing Terry and John together. Terry is clearly the leader of the group. He takes the initiative in speaking with the guards and is warm, generous and funny. All I can say after two days in the constant company of three other people is that it's difficult, demanding and exhausting. I can't imagine how they have survived together for so long.

Weeks pass. We have a chess board, and to my surprise I discover that I have forgotten how to play. Terry reminds me of the rules. He is an excellent player, and, try as I may, I cannot beat him. Tom is not so advanced. I notice that while we insist that chess is only a game, we play it with deadly seriousness. Recently I beat Tom two or three times. After the final game he sent the pieces flying with one mighty sweep of his arm, turned round and refused to speak for forty-eight hours. How difficult it is to know how to proceed in this strange place. Our most powerful emotions are barely covered and so easily triggered. My illness is putting an enormous extra strain on the group. Night after night I sit struggling for breath while my companions try to sleep. The guards bring me Ventolin tablets, but they have little or no effect. Terry, the most compassionate of men, asked them to give me an inhaler.

'You must get him to a doctor. He is very sick.'
'We tell Chef.'
During the night Terry sits up with me. Both he and John have given up smoking for my sake. They must be cursing the day they invited me to join them.
'Breathe evenly, TW. Control your breathing. You can do it.'
'I can't, Terry. It's outside my control.'
'Breathe slowly. Be calm.'
Tonight I felt so ill I asked Terry to read aloud from the Bible. He did so, quietly choosing words of hope and comfort. I shall never forget his care and understanding.

'Stand.'
I stagger to my feet. I can hardly hold myself upright.

'Where am I going?'

'We take you to doctor.'

I don't know if they are telling me the truth; perhaps they won't bring me back to this room. I say goodbye to Terry, Tom and John and am led out wrapped in a blanket, half expecting never to see them again. The night air is cold and I feel my skin tingle.

'Sleep.'

I lie down in the back of a van, blindfolded but not bound. I couldn't walk twenty-five yards, let alone escape.

'When doctor see you – no speak.'

'No speak?' I am incredulous.

'No speak. We speak with doctor.'

The driver puts the van into gear, and we bump along a rough track, down an incline, and turn left on to a paved road. After driving for several minutes, to my relief, we stop.

'No speak – wait.'

Everything is silent. Then I hear voices. Someone bends over me, and I recognise the smell of antiseptic. He seems to be having a disagreement with the guards.

'Come.'

I am guided out of the van into a house. I lie full length on the floor of the entrance lobby while the doctor attaches electrodes to my body. I assume he is testing my heart. He listens to my breathing and talks with the guards. Then we are off again, and within half an hour I am back in chains with the others.

But now I have a Ventolin inhaler, and the difference it makes is unbelievable. If only I had been given this months ago, life would have been so much easier for everyone. The attacks continue with dreadful regularity, but at least now I have some relief.

Both Terry and John have cautioned me to be careful with Tom. They have told me he is capable of dramatic mood swings and may easily get offended if I tease him. When he was narrating his stories, I had tried to lighten things up by making what I thought were humorous remarks. Tom took them the wrong way. Now I realise I made a serious blunder and want to kick myself for my insensitive stupidity.

The interchanges Terry, Tom and John have with the guards are totally different from those I had as a solitary hostage. They can banter and support one another in their communications with our captors. A one-to-one relationship does not allow for such freedom.

Tom irritates me considerably in his exchanges with the guards. He seems to be praising them, then, when they leave the room, he curses and threatens to break their necks if he ever comes across them in Beirut. One day I couldn't stand it any longer.

'Tom, don't be such a bloody hypocrite. Either say nothing or be consistent.'

As the words left my mouth, I realised I should not have said them. I should have had enough insight to see that each man in the room had to find his own way of surviving. That was what Tom was doing – surviving.

After four years without news it now floods in on me. We have two radios, a television, and, most weeks, *Time*, *Newsweek* and *The Economist*. Terry and John tend to watch the television while Tom and I listen to the radio. All of us are alert to every scrap of information which will give us a clue to our situation. Ridiculously, I tend to interpret every world event as having a bearing on this. When I have favourable news, my spirits soar, then come crashing down when I hear the opposite. My three companions exercise daily, but I don't have the strength to walk even the few paces my chain would allow. Now and again I have had to ask Tom to fold my bedding because the exertion exhausts me.

I still find it difficult to enter into the group. Over the years the other three have discovered ways of living together in captivity, and I am conscious that my presence has disturbed their routine. My illness continues to be disrupting, and I told them one day that it would be better for everyone if I went back to a room of my own. They wouldn't hear of it, but I know it would relieve the situation. I'm not sure the guards would allow it, but if I don't improve, I intend to ask them to move me. Last evening I lost consciousness. I had been sitting attempting to breathe when I collapsed. The guards have fitted an alarm in the room so that they can be called in an emergency. Today I was told that I was to get some fresh air. I was blindfolded and bundled out of the room on to a balcony. A gentle breeze was blowing. It was silent and peaceful.

'Sleep.'

I lay down, and immediately a blanket was thrown over my head. All benefit I might have gained from the fresh air was lost. I lay still for twenty minutes or so and was then returned to the room.

The radio is a wonderful companion. Normally reception is excellent, but tonight it was not at all clear. As I was straining to listen to the BBC development programme, I heard the announcer mention Y Care International. Y Care, a development organisation of the YMCA, was an agency I helped to found in the 1980s. Dr Judith Ennew was introduced as the new director. I didn't know her. She said that she had recently been in the Lebanon where Y Care had been funding projects for many years, and spoke of travelling around Beirut and being told by her driver that he could not take her down a certain street as that was where Terry Waite was being held. He may have been telling her a tall story, but it fascinated me. I remember the project being started. We wanted to give young people from all the different communities in the Lebanon vocational training, and Dr Ennew spoke of the many hundreds who were still being helped. I felt proud of Y Care, and my spirits were lifted.

At long last news of my family came through on the World Service. At the end of the *Outlook* programme John Tidmarsh, the presenter, said that next day there would be a message for Terry Waite. Throughout the night, announcers repeated this. They clearly didn't want me to miss it. The following day my cousin John introduced the programme. I got news that Frances and my children were well, and a piece of organ music, Bach's Toccata and Fugue in B Minor, was played. I felt numb and could only hope and pray that the days of captivity were finally running out.

Christmas Day 1990. Terry's made a Scrabble set from a cardboard box. John, Terry and I play a few games. The Queen's Christmas message contains a reference to us. These constant messages of support are so very encouraging.

All of us follow the progress of the war with Iraq, wondering what effect it will have on us. We hear that the Da'wa prisoners held in Kuwait have disappeared from their prison. Surely that means we will go home soon. We wait, we pray, we hope.

George Carey is enthroned in Canterbury Cathedral. There was some criticism of the service in the press. We listened to it on the World Service and enjoyed it. It was a great boost to us all that hostages were remembered in the sermon.

The days drag, emotions are suppressed. We chat, sleep, play chess, quarrel, and hope to God we won't be here much longer.

« 25 »

IT IS EVENING in Cambridge. Today graduates and undergraduates have been streaming back into college after the vacation. Now Trinity Hall is quiet, and the street outside my window is empty. I look up and stare at the wall of the Old Schools opposite. Several months ago some wit scrawled on it in chalk, 'Now is the winter of our discontent.' It is now summertime, and no one has seen fit to remove it. In a moment I will put my pen down for the day and meet my friends and colleagues for an evening meal. I look forward to their company and for the first time in my life feel as though I am finding a balance between solitude, friendship and my family.

There is much more to say about the last months with Terry, Tom and John. Our shared hopes, fears, raw emotions. They may write about them, and I may return to them myself one day, but they are not part of this book.

John went home first, and we heard him on the radio.

'Well done, John,' we said. 'Why is he spending so long with a psychiatrist? He wasn't crazy.'

Tom and I were released together. A car, a change of car.

'No look.'

'No speak.'

Syrian Intelligence headquarters.

'Would you like anything, Mr Waite?'

I remembered Lance-Sergeant Swire and the lessons he had drilled into me thirty years before.

'A haircut, please.'

A young man entered with a small leather case. He cut my hair and trimmed my beard.

To the British Embassy: a doctor, a psychiatrist, my brother David.

'How are Frances, the children, Mother?'

'Fine, fine, you will see them in England tomorrow.'

To the Royal Air Force jet. Richard Chartres, my friend and former colleague from Lambeth.

'Richard, how very good of you to meet me.'

We were airborne. He turned to me.

'You may want to say a word or two to the press before you meet your family. It would be better to get that over with first.'

'Will there be many press people there?'

'One or two.'

He gave me a pen, and I jotted down headings on the back of an envelope.

'Right, that's it.'

We approached England. It was raining and there was a high wind. We landed at RAF Lyneham. Robert Runcie came on board. We laughed together, as we had done so often in the past. I hobbled across the tarmac, into a car, and we drove to a hangar. I made my speech, hobbled out and climbed into another car. We drove to the far side of the airport. My companions melted away. I stumbled through a glass doorway and stared. Ruth, Clare and Gillian ran towards me. Frances and a young man I assumed was Mark stood quietly in the background. They moved forward. We wept and embraced each other. Gillian, my youngest daughter, looked at me.

'Daddy,' she said, 'take all the help they will offer you here.'

I nodded my head.

One week later I remembered the dream dreamt in the first weeks of captivity: the beach, the sea, my family.

This evening, in the quiet of my room in Cambridge, I recall the words that were discovered written on the wall of a cellar in which a victim of Hitler's persecution hid and died:

> *I believe in the sun even when it is not shining.*
> *I believe in love where feeling is not.*
> *I believe in God even if he is silent.*

EPILOGUE

The extempore speech made on arrival at RAF Lyneham,
19 November 1991

LADIES AND GENTLEMEN, *I think you can imagine that after
1,763 days in chains it's an overwhelming experience to come back and
receive your greetings. From the bottom of my heart thank you for turning
out on such an awful day, but a typically English day, and thank you so
much for your welcome. This is an emotional day for me, it is a day when
thanks are due to many people. First of all, of course, to the Secretary-
General of the United Nations and his envoy for their hard and persistent
work to seek a resolution to the problem of all hostages who are detained
in the Middle East. Also to my old boss, Lord Runcie, whom it has been a
particular pleasure for me to meet again and who I'm glad to say is looking
as fit and as well as ever. I know he has kept all of us close to his heart
and his prayers and has worked so hard on our behalf in the last years. It's
been a great pleasure, too, to meet the new Archbishop of Canterbury,
someone whom I have met previously on a couple of occasions and who
I know has worked equally hard, and will continue to do so until this
problem is resolved. My thanks go as well to all the Lambeth staff; they
are small in number but they are keen, good people and I must pay
a personal tribute to the late John Lyttle who worked tirelessly for
our release and unfortunately died before he could see this and other
happy days.*

    *It was also my privilege and pleasure a moment or two ago to meet the
Foreign Secretary who has had in these last years the unenviable job of
trying to walk on eggshells over a territory that is indeed difficult and
dangerous, and to meet members of his staff, both in Damascus and again
on the plane. I extend to them my gratitude and thanks. And, of course,
what would a homecoming of this kind be without the RAF? I can tell you
one thing, when I left Hezbollah yesterday afternoon they did their best to
kit me out with a sweater and a pair of trousers but they couldn't find a
pair of shoes my size. When I got to Cyprus late at night all I had to say
to the RAF was, 'Can you find a pair of size 14s?' and within half an*

hour they had contacted the Navy and provided me with two barges. Thanks to the RAF.

I must also thank the many many people both here and around the world who have kept the name and the cause of hostages alive; they have kept us alive in their prayers, in their thoughts and in their actions, and the presence here today of so many people is indicative not only of your concern for Western hostages but your concern for justice, for peace and for truth throughout the world. I'll tell you a little story which I told in Damascus. I was kept in total and complete isolation for four years. I saw no one and spoke to no one apart from a cursory word with my guards when they brought me food. And one day, out of the blue, a guard came into my room with a postcard; it was a postcard of the stained-glass window from Bedford showing John Bunyan in jail, and I looked at that card and I thought, My word, Bunyan, you're a lucky fellow, you've got a window out of which you can look and see the sky and here am I in a dark room; you've got pen and ink and you can write and I've got nothing; and you've got your own clothes and a table and a chair; and I turned the card over and there was a message from someone whom I didn't know simply saying, We remember, we shall not forget, we shall continue to pray for you and to work for all people who are detained around the world. I can tell you, that thought sent me back to the marvellous work of agencies like Amnesty International and their letter-writing campaigns. I would say to you all, never despise those simple actions. Something, somewhere, will get through to the people you are concerned about, as it got through to me and to my fellow hostages eventually.

The occasion today would not be complete without a word of special thanks and affection to the World Service of the BBC. For four years, again, one had nothing and then out of the blue a small radio appeared, just a cheap set, and I said thank God I'm in the Middle East where the World Service can be received on the Medium Wave for virtually twenty-four hours a day. In the last twelve months the World Service helped keep us alive both spiritually through the work of the religious department and mentally through the variety of cultural and news programmes that are broadcast with such excellence. Thank you, World Service, thank you very much.

My family, of course, who have had the unenviable task of having to face so many difficulties, I'm proud of them, and I'm proud of all those I love and care for and look forward to seeing soon. Today, also, Terry Anderson is very much in my thoughts. When Tom Sutherland and I left our prison yesterday afternoon, we had to leave Terry behind; fortunately yesterday, for the first time, after we had made a special plea to our guards, his chain was released and he was at least able to walk around the room in which we were confined. My captors assured me yesterday that in a few days' time Joseph Cicippio and Alann Steen, the other two American hostages, will be released. They also assured me that Terry Anderson, a journalist of whom the profession can be justly proud, will be released by the end of this month. I trust that Hezbollah and those who hold these men will honour the commitment that they made to us; we also asked about the German hostages but we were not able to get as definite a response concerning them. We were told that it was hoped they would be freed by the end of the year, so we trust that will be the case.

And, finally, it would not be right for me to leave this podium without remembering all those, and in particular all those in the Middle East, who are held captive. It is wrong to hold people in such a way, it is self-defeating and those who do it fall well below civilised standards of behaviour no matter who they are, no matter what nationality or what organisation they belong to. We have lived in these last years through the appalling sufferings of the people of Lebanon, we have been in the midst of shelling, we have seen people die and killed in most brutal ways, and those from whom I have just come can be assured that we in the Church for our part will not rest until all are freed and there is justice and peace brought to people who deserve a better deal.

Ladies and gentlemen, enough for the moment. Once again, my gratitude to you, my thanks to you, and I hope that I shall have the opportunity at a later date of speaking in greater detail and perhaps a little more personally. Thank you very much.

INDEX